Modernism as Memory

Also by Kathleen James-Chakraborty
Published by the University of Minnesota Press

Bauhaus Culture: From Weimar to the Cold War

Architecture since 1400

Modernism as Memory

Building Identity in the Federal Republic of Germany

Kathleen James-Chakraborty

University of Minnesota Press
Minneapolis   London

Copyright 2018 by the Regents of the University of Minnesota

All rights reserved. No part of this publication may be reproduced, stored in a retrieval system, or transmitted, in any form or by any means, electronic, mechanical, photocopying, recording, or otherwise, without the prior written permission of the publisher.

Published by the University of Minnesota Press
111 Third Avenue South, Suite 290
Minneapolis, MN 55401-2520
http://www.upress.umn.edu

Printed in the United States of America on acid-free paper

The University of Minnesota is an equal-opportunity educator and employer.

22 21 20 19 18   10 9 8 7 6 5 4 3 2 1

Library of Congress Cataloging-in-Publication Data
Names: James-Chakraborty, Kathleen, author.
Title: Modernism as memory : building identity in the Federal Republic of Germany /
    Kathleen James-Chakraborty.
Description: Minneapolis, MN : University of Minnesota Press, 2018. | Includes bibliographical references
    and index.
Identifiers: LCCN 2017042182 | ISBN 978-1-5179-0291-9 (pb) | ISBN 978-1-5179-0290-2 (hc)
Subjects: LCSH: Architecture–Germany (West)–History–20th century. | Architecture and society–Germany
    (West)–History–20th century. | Collective memory–Germany (West). | BISAC: ARCHITECTURE /
    History / Contemporary (1945–). | ARCHITECTURE / Criticism.
Classification: LCC NA1068 .J36 2018 | DDC 720.943–dc23
LC record available at https://lccn.loc.gov/2017042182

For Oliver Radford and Friedegund Holzmann

Contents

Introduction: Making Memory Modern 1

1. Making German Architecture Modern 13

2. Inserting Memory into Modern Architecture 33
   West German Churches

3. An Architecture of Fragmentation and Absence 81
   West German Museums

4. Critical Reconstruction or Neomodernist Shards? 137
   Postunification Berlin

5. Manufacturing Memory in the Ruhr Region 185

6. Assimilating Modern Memory 213

Conclusion: The Kolumba Museum in Cologne 237

Acknowledgments 245

Notes 247

Index 299

Introduction

Making Memory Modern

Just under a decade after the fall of the Wall, the longest queues in Berlin were no longer in front of shops in the eastern sector of the city but instead wrapped around the Reichstag as Berliners and tourists alike lined up to view the recently renovated building and, above all, to use the walkway that spiraled up its new cupola (Figure I.1). The building reopened in May 1999 after the British architect Norman Foster readied it for the shift of the government of the Federal Republic to Berlin from Bonn, where it had been located for a half century. Foster's cupola, which replaced one that had been damaged beyond repair in World War II and pulled down in 1954, quickly became one of Berlin's most prominent landmarks as well as the symbol of the Berlin Republic, as the government of a unified Germany was now often termed. A transparent structure that at night transforms into a glowing beacon, it allows the people to stand above their elected legislators. This powerful symbolism was intended to reassure those who remained nervous about the stability of German democracy. Particularly notable was the juxtaposition between Foster's glazed bubble and the stolid nineteenth-century parliament building on which it sat. Designed in 1884 by Paul Wallot and completed a decade later, it was set aflame in the early months of the Third Reich. It also bore the scars of the 1945 battle for Berlin, wounds Foster left exposed in ways that suggested a retreat from conventional nationalism's heroic narratives.[1]

Foster did not focus on history. Instead, he wrote, "I believed that if we were to introduce a symbolically resonant structure that would signal the changed use of the building then that structure should also be an integral part of the building's ecology."[2] He explained the design in terms of sustainability: "The building remains a model for the future by burning vegetable oil to produce electricity. In its vision of a public architecture that redresses ecological balance, providing energy rather than consuming it, lies one of its most intrinsic expressions of optimism."[3] And yet even he acknowledged, "The reconstruction takes cues from the old building, as we

Figure I.1. Paul Wallot, Reichstag, Berlin, 1894, with cupola by Norman Foster, 1999. Source: Matthew Field/Wikipedia Commons.

peeled away the layers of the past—mason's marks and Soviet graffiti—scars that have been preserved as a 'living museum.'"[4]

The pairing of old and new and the frank acknowledgment of the Reichstag's checkered past were immediately hailed not only as uniquely appropriate to the task of reinvesting this structure with the task of housing German democracy but also as epitomizing a distinctively postmodern strategy. In 2003, for instance, Andreas Huyssen, one of the most insightful observers of twentieth-century German culture, wrote:

> One of the most interesting cultural phenomena of our day is the way in which memory and temporality have invaded spaces and media that seemed among the most stable and fixed: cities, monuments, architecture, and sculpture. After the waning of modernist fantasies about *creatio ex nihilo* and of the desire for the purity of new beginnings, we have come to read cities and buildings as palimpsests of space, monuments as transformable and transitory, and sculpture as subject to the vicissitudes of time.

He continued:

> The analysis of how memory and forgetting pervade real public space, the world of objects, and the urban world we live in becomes crucial. The reconstruction of Berlin as the German capital after unification provides a perhaps unique case in which this latter dimension has produced a paradigmatic public memory space.[5]

Huyssen here makes two assumptions that permeate the literature on memory and on postunification Berlin.[6] The first is that there is something new and specifically postmodern about the palimpsest and the memory discourse in which it plays such a prominent role.[7] In fact, this strategy predates even the founding of the Federal Republic in 1949. With the exception of one even earlier key precedent, it emerged immediately following the war, initially in the reconstruction of churches, and continued to be popular in West Germany, although only in 1989 did it begin to carry the burden of acknowledging the suffering the Germans had caused during the Third Reich rather than representing what they had endured and lost. This shift happened when Daniel Libeskind won the competition to design the extension to West Berlin's city museum that became the Jewish Museum. Originally the use of the palimpsest alluded above all to the destruction and displacement that accompanied defeat in 1945. This morphed after the construction of the Berlin Wall in 1961 to encompass a focus on the country's continued division. In the first postwar decades the incorporation of ruins as well as the use of fragments and the attempt to represent absence featured prominently in a series of churches and museums that were de facto symbols of a new democratic, capitalist Germany.

Huyssen and the many others who have written about Berlin since the fall of the Wall generally assume that this city is the paradigmatic place where public memory spaces have been created. Postunification Berlin has indeed been central to the discussion of memory that has been a prominent aspect of scholarship in the humanities on both sides of the Atlantic since the 1980s.[8] Its buildings have helped transform architecture globally, while offering compelling evidence of the capacity of Germans to confront very directly the most difficult chapter in their long history. The representation of memory had been an important facet of West German architectural culture since the 1940s, however, and it was hardly absent in other countries in the aftermath of the war and the deindustrialization that followed several decades later.[9] In the Federal Republic it was made manifest before and after 1989 in buildings in Pforzheim, Stuttgart, and Munich as well as Cologne, Düren, and Essen, to name only a few examples.

That memory was a prominent feature of some of the most celebrated buildings erected in the Federal Republic in its early years has been overlooked by those who presume that memories of the war, because not often present in texts, were absent in this period. Admittedly its manifestation in architecture originally operated independently of much open public discussion or a clear theoretical base. The first emerged in the late 1950s in debates over Kaiser Wilhelm Memorial Church in Berlin; Aldo Rossi provided the second in his influential book *L'architettura della città*, published in Italian in 1966 and in German seven years later, well before the beginning of the memory boom.[10] In the interim, however, during the immediate postwar years, ruins were nonetheless an omnipresent feature of daily life in most German urban neighborhoods, as was new construction. In some cases these two experiences remained in equilibrium, as architects consciously juxtaposed them in order to mourn the shattering of what was remembered as Wilhelmine stability at the same time that they recalled the utopian promise of the experimental architecture that replaced it. The enduring impact of this architecture of fragmentation and absence is a story that has been hiding in plain sight precisely because it was articulated in stone and concrete, steel and glass rather than through the spoken or written word. The ephemeral meanings associated with it nonetheless float free of the intentions of architects and patrons alike, and remain subject to continual change.

Serving as a de facto representation of the state long before it was adopted for the Reichstag, this architecture helped knit the new state together. Its defining feature is the pairing of obviously historic fabric—or the representation of it—with abstract form constructed out of modern materials. The pairing suggests an awareness of past trauma as well as the possibility of a better—and, in the case of the Reichstag, quite clearly a more democratic—future while providing Germans with a compelling and influential expression of an almost antinationalist identity.[11] What often appears to be the collage of old and new is in fact a restaged clash between two different revivals. Like the Reichstag, almost all of the historic fabric preserved or quoted in these situations was designed to look older than it was by nineteenth-century architects proud of their command of architectural history. And like Foster's cupola, most of the new insertions into such fabric, while often heralded as being of their time, depend greatly upon precedents established in the 1910s and 1920s, above all the designs that sit slightly outside the mainstream of the New Building or International Style as delineated by such defenders of modernism as Walter Gropius, Nikolaus Pevsner, and Sigfried Giedion.[12]

Uncovering how remembering modernism built identity in the Federal Republic takes us outside an architectural history that is primarily about either architects or style. It also is a story that has only a tangential relationship to architectural theory. Instead, this is a tale of how architecture operates within society and how it contributes to the construction of new social and political realities. Participating in the process of determining what should be built and where quite literally helped construct democracy, first in West Germany and West Berlin, and after 1990 in a Federal Republic that now encompassed the former German Democratic Republic (East Germany), even when—as often happened—those finding their voice through such debates did not get their way. Complex negotiations between multiple constituencies, including architects, civil servants, intellectuals, politicians, religious leaders, and an often outspoken general public, produced places that matter partly for their formal and experiential qualities but also because of what they communicate about how a variety of Germans wanted to present themselves and their societies.

This began as a local story, although from the beginning those engaged in it were trying to reintegrate Germany into a variety of international communities. In part because of the quality of the architecture it generated but also because beginning in the 1970s German clients so often turned to architects from the countries that had defeated it in two world wars, it eventually became an international one. Especially for those outsiders like Foster charged with creating national symbols, it transformed a tradition into which they could integrate themselves while working in what was for them a foreign architectural culture.[13] More recently, who within Germany has access to this heritage has itself become a matter of dispute, including when Muslims want to build mosques that allude to distinctively German ways of making sacred architecture.

The specific character of this story relies on a diverse array of sources. Tracing the design process of particular buildings through the drawings produced by an architect's office mattered less here than trawling through the newspapers as well as the architecture magazines that record the often agonized and very public discussions of what should be built and why, not to mention the websites and other literature that then market the results to tourists, an increasingly important audience for this architecture and for the stories of national and regional identity it tells. These provide clues regarding the changing contexts in which these buildings have been experienced in ways that could not have been anticipated by either their designers or the original clients. The buildings themselves are also important primary sources, in that how they are constructed and the spaces they create are as crucial to their impact as the contrasting styles out of which they are assembled.

Although this book is about national identity, my examples cluster in particular corners of the country. In part this reflects my personal experience as someone who has visited Berlin regularly since 1985 and whose husband has taught in Bochum since 1999. The phenomenon I chronicle, however, is also more easily discernible in Berlin and the state of Baden-Württemberg, as well as the Rhineland and the Ruhr region than in Bavaria, the part of the Federal Republic with the strongest sense of regional autonomy and identity, or Hamburg and Bremen, which are outward-looking port cities.[14] My focus in *Modernism as Memory* is on places that understood themselves to be specifically German rather than local or international.

History and historicism, memory and modernism are not equivalents here but partners, dancing in complex and shifting patterns around one another. The way historicist architecture references the past was relatively easy for its original designers and their clients to identify and remains within the reach of scholars to discern. When represented by abstract form, however, memory is often much more elusive. Yet modern architecture has its own history stretching back over a century, and those who draw upon it are seldom ignorant of the web of associations connected to it. Indeed, architects are often acutely aware of such precedents, even when their patrons and publics are not. In the late 1940s modernism, very much against the grain of its own rhetoric, became a historical style. Furthermore, its pairing with an earlier historicism placed it in a dialectical relationship with exactly the architecture it had supposedly overthrown and cast the character of that victory into question.

With a nod to the American cultural and literary historian Paul Fussell, I originally wanted to refer to the approach that is the subject of this book as the architecture of modern memory.[15] The term is too trite, however, to capture the tension between how history and memory operate here.[16] If history consists of scholarly accounts of the past such as this one, memory, whether collective, communicative, or cultural, to use terms employed by the French sociologist Maurice Halbwachs, and German scholars Jan Assmann and Aleida Assmann, is clearly operative, assisting individuals and societies alike in addressing the past in ways that ideally contribute productively to the formation of stable identities.[17] The architecture discussed in these pages performed exactly that role, and drew upon the architecture of the past to do so. Importantly the architects, clients, and audiences knew that past, however, not so much by reading written accounts of it but through their own memories and experiences, as well as what had been passed down to them orally. Architects' visits to buildings that served as precedents have been particularly crucial in this regard. Moreover, the divergent views of the recent past that sparked debates over what buildings should occupy particular sites were exacerbated by what kind of memory was being privileged. Clashes were particularly common between what individuals and grassroots communities remembered and how those with cultural authority acted to support the perceived interests of institutions, including the state, but also the church, cultural organizations (especially museums), and city and regional bodies. In the first decades after the war the architectural aspects of such efforts were seldom articulated in words; more recently they have often been carefully stage-managed by publicists.

Discussions of the way in which this more official kind of memory is embedded in architecture typically focus on commemorative structures, but this account bursts beyond those narrow limits. Memoryscapes in the Federal Republic of Germany have often engaged everyday life. Visitors to the Topography of Terror documentation center in Berlin are usually tourists intent on seeing how Germany officially addresses the Holocaust. Those who pop into the Galeries Lafayette in Berlin to buy a blouse, stroll through the New State Gallery in Stuttgart on their way to work, worship at St. Anna in Düren on Sundays, or go rock climbing in the Landscape Park in Duisburg on a holiday weekend may not pause, however, to think about how these places relate to multiple pasts, but their unusually high quality arises directly out of the effort to do so.

Indeed, the presence of the past within modern German architecture can be traced back not to a monument but to an office building. Most of those who waited in 1999 to enter the Reichstag believed they were seeing something new and fresh. Few realized that a half-hour stroll away an earlier era of political violence had long been marked through very similar means. Between 1900 and 1903 the firm of Cremer and Wolffenstein erected the headquarters of the Rudolf Mosse publishing company (Figure I.2).[18] One of the most modern Berlin office blocks of its day,

Introduction

Figure I.2. Cremer and Wolffenstein, Mossehaus, Berlin, 1903, with addition by Erich Mendelsohn, Richard Neutra, and Paul Rudolf Henning, 1923. Source: Landesdenkmalamt, Berlin.

its design demonstrates at least a passing acquaintance with Dankmar Adler and Louis Sullivan's much larger Auditorium Building in Chicago, completed in 1889.[19] Mossehaus's architects and their client were upwardly mobile Jews, born in the middle of the nineteenth century, who became key participants in Berlin's explosive growth in the final decades of the nineteenth century and the first years of the twentieth. In January 1919 the corner of the building was badly damaged during the brutal suppression of the Spartacists, which fatally split the German left. Between 1921 and 1923 Erich Mendelsohn, ably assisted by Richard Neutra and Paul Rudolf Henning, replaced the burned-out corner and added three stories. The Jerusalem Street facade was destroyed in World War II, after which it was rebuilt in simplified form; the building was restored again in 1992–93, when the postwar facade was largely replaced by Peter Kolb, Bernd Kemper, and Dieter Schneider.[20]

Designed shortly after Hannah Hoch crafted her pioneering Dada photomontage,

Cut with the Kitchen Knife through the Beer Belly of the Weimar Republic, Mendelsohn, Neutra, and Henning's intervention boldly rejected the paradigm of the office building as Renaissance palace that remained common on both sides of the Atlantic in favor of a dramatic juxtaposition, whose violent cause they did not entirely obscure.[21] Instead, their new tile- and stucco-clad stories embedded in, as well as floating above, Cremer and Wolffenstein's masonry mass announced a dynamic alternative to historicism. They exploited the possibility an underlying skeletal frame allowed for expansive glazing, while capturing a sense of the excitement and novelty of the new speeds at which automobiles rushed by. At the same time their refusal simply to mask what had occurred here, unusual in the immediate aftermath of a war that had wrought relatively little physical damage on German soil, foreshadowed the destruction that was to come.[22]

Mossehaus and the many buildings that followed in its wake challenge myths about modern architecture that must be put aside if we want to understand fully how a select group of German buildings of the last hundred years has shaped the world around them and, more particularly, how cannibalizing modernism's own history, and contrasting it to historicist alternatives, has been fundamental to the way the Federal Republic has presented itself to citizens, residents, and tourists alike. Recovering the ways in which prewar modern German architecture served as a useful precedent after 1945 requires accepting the limitations of modern architecture's own theory in order to understand how it actually worked in practice and indeed why it could be so effective. Five such preconceptions must be dismissed. The first is that new technology necessarily generated modern architecture's forms. The second is that modern architecture was objective rather than symbolic. Third, that modern architecture was necessarily the work of heroic geniuses is another persistent misperception. Fourth, that modern architecture was inherently socialist, or at least politically progressive and thus democratic, is an equally stubborn, if factually incorrect, assumption.[23] A final myth is that modern architecture was both masculine and specifically Western.

This book's six chapters demonstrate a continuum, one that stretches across the whole trajectory of modernism's history, at the same time that they destabilize our understanding of that past. The opening chapter addresses buildings erected for the Werkbund Exhibition held in Cologne in 1914 and completed in Stuttgart in the late 1920s.[24] This discussion demonstrates the original range of the modernism available to later architects. The industrial aesthetic manifested in the Model Factory in Cologne and the Weissenhofsiedlung in Stuttgart was never the entire story. The Glashaus and the Werkbund Theater in Cologne and the train station and the Schocken store in Stuttgart introduced themes of spiritualism, plasticity, monumentality, and commercialism that reappeared again and again. Although most of these buildings were erected out of modern materials, more important in this context is the nearly complete rejection of history as a source of form, as well as an equally relentless commitment to abstraction. Most of what was modern in the remembered modernism of the postwar decades was overtly technological in its use of glass, steel, concrete, and even wood, but there are important exceptions. Too often these are understood as diverging from the mainstream of the modern movement rather than being a part of it, because that movement has itself been defined so narrowly. Wolfgang Pehnt's inclusive approach provides a key precedent for my account.[25]

The relationship between technology and an emphasis on tactility is clear in two of the examples addressed in chapter 2, which focuses on churches completed between 1947 and 1968. Otto Bartning's Church of the Resurrection in Pforzheim and Rudolf Schwarz's St. Anna in Düren are monumental buildings with solid stone walls, even as Bartning employed laminated plywood trusses and Schwarz structural concrete to support their roofs. Considering them in the context of Egon Eiermann's Kaiser Wilhelm Memorial Church in Berlin and Gottfried Böhm's Pilgrimage Church of Mary in Neviges emphasizes that, although abstract, built form conveyed and continues to convey meaning. William Jordy explored the symbolic essence of Le Corbusier's Villa Savoye as early as 1963, but this dimension of modern architecture remains underexplored by those who assume it is exclusively postmodern.[26] Eiermann may not have appreciated the contribution the bombed-out steeple made to the design of the Memorial Church, but it remained because so many others did. Meanwhile both Eiermann and Böhm drew quite explicitly upon expressionism in order to create modern sacred spaces whose spiritual qualities were derived from the manipulation of space and light, rather than being dependent on representational art.

Bartning, Schwarz, Eiermann, and Böhm were major German architects, but they are not the stars who stand at the center of most international histories of modern architecture. At the beginning of his survey of modern architecture, Alan Colquhoun, one of the most astute historians of the subject, declared, "If [this book] is still largely a history of the masters, that is because that was the nature of modernism itself, despite its many claims to anonymity."[27] The middle ground between giants like Le Corbusier and Ludwig Mies van der Rohe on the one hand and anonymous engineers on the other merits more attention, not least because without it one cannot understand that the giants were not always such geniuses but rather were talented men and women well aware of the work of their contemporaries and their predecessors. Huyssen conceives of Foster's use of the palimpsest as new because he has overlooked Mossehaus and the Kaiser Wilhelm Memorial Church.[28]

The connecting thread that ties these buildings together has been ignored because what was being remembered changed, even as the architectural means for invoking memory remained relatively constant. Developed to acknowledge specifically German suffering, and to comfort survivors by preserving the traces of a more stable past as well as hinting at the possibility of rebirth, this architecture encompassed a dual haunting, in which the previously antithetical polarities of militarist

Wilhelmine historicism finally came to terms with the revolutionary art and politics that had challenged but not completely toppled it during the 1910s and 1920s. The wounds of the battle between them, and of the fissures within the society that had prompted such catastrophic violence, remained on display, almost as a warning. Although this was a profoundly historicist architecture, anchored in a dueling past, the modernist half of it was typically presented as new.

Acting as a bridge between these postwar churches and the canonical architectural examples of postmodern German memory that dominate the literature on the subject are the museums that are the subject of chapter 3. From Hans Döllgast's reconstruction of the Alte Pinakothek in Munich to Daniel Libeskind's successful entry in the competition to design the addition to West Berlin's city museum that became the Jewish Museum, West German and West Berlin museum architecture became a place where experimentation in referencing the past from within modernism flourished, even as postmodern alternatives also emerged. Not all of these buildings explicitly paired ruins with new construction, but they were part of a conversation influenced by this possibility. In the New National Gallery in Berlin and the New State Gallery in Stuttgart, Mies and James Stirling, respectively, allude to Schinkel's Altes Museum, located in what was then East Berlin. Representing absence mattered in a variety of contexts, whether that of the destruction that accompanied Germany's defeat in World War II, the division of Berlin by the Wall, or the elimination of Berlin's Jewish community in the Holocaust. Sometimes, as with Frank Gehry's Vitra Design Museum, drawing upon modernism's past in a way that emphasized instability and displacement was probably, paradoxically, partly just a way to fit in.

Chapter 4 pairs four memoryscapes erected in Berlin in the first two decades following reunification with examples of critical reconstruction, as Berlin city authorities termed their preferred approach to rebuilding East Berlin. My discussion highlights the degree to which the Galeries Lafayette by Jean Nouvel, the renovation of the New Museum by David Chipperfield, and the Topography of Terror by Ursula Wilms and Heinz Hallmann, as well as the Reichstag, emerge out of the architecture addressed in earlier chapters, while the reconstruction of the Hotel Adlon and the Hohenzollern Palace, as well as Oswald Mathias Ungers's Friedrichstadt Passagen and Peter Eisenman's Memorial to the Murdered Jews of Europe are more conventional examples of a postmodernism that drew instead upon neoclassical precedent. Often forgotten in the highly politicized debates over which histories to preserve and reference was the long association that Christian Democrats had with the palimpsest and with transparency, whereas Hans Stimmann, the Berlin civil servant whose regulations often chafed both architects and preservationists, came from the left wing of the local Social Democratic Party.

The emphasis on Berlin has hampered recognition of the variety of purposes memories of modernism served in these same years.[29] In Berlin the palimpsest was almost always understood, pace Huyssens, as a particularly honest way of addressing the Third Reich. In the Ruhr region, close to the Belgian and Dutch borders, the remnants of the coal mining and steel foundries that had propelled Germany's industrial and economic modernization were transformed into the cultural infrastructure the region had always lacked in a bold effort to attract economic development. Here, however, as chapter 5 makes clear, the Third Reich was glossed over, as the degree to which heavy industry was implicated in its crimes distracted from this goal. The redevelopment of a blast furnace into a park, and a colliery into museums and a design school, was, as in Berlin, accompanied by narratives aimed at tourists. These often ignored lived memories of visits paid by Nazi dignitaries, the use of slave labor during the war, left-wing unions, and industrial pollution, which, as the local Social Democrats leading the effort rightly realized, were unlikely to attract investors.

Finally, until very recently the story of German modernity, and with it of modern German architecture, has usually been told as one led by men on behalf of ethnic Germans. It was always more complicated, not least as modern architecture has long been one of Germany's most successful exports with an impact in Turkey and other Middle Eastern countries that rivaled the one it has had in the United States. Chapter 6 addresses the efforts of devout Muslims in Cologne, almost all of Turkish heritage, to mark their place in the city and in German society by building one of Europe's largest and most modern mosques. That their effort to work within modern German sacred architecture was misread as a demonstration of Muslim hegemony defines the limits of integration in the Federal Republic less than a decade ago. At the same time Zaha Hadid's ability to generate enormously favorable publicity for the futuristic ambitions of design-oriented German manufacturers is a potent example of the way this heritage of diffusion has fed back into recent German architecture and identity.

Rather than making the definitive break with the past that modernism was supposed to accomplish, the architecture addressed in this book bridged old and new. It created a new antimonumentality that stood in powerful distinction to the bombast of the Second Empire and also the Brutalism of the immediate postwar decades. Refusing to paper over the damage done by war and division, it provided a template for eventually addressing the full range of the horror unleashed by the Third Reich. And it provided a model for a renascent modern architecture, tempered by postmodernism's respect for context and attention to scale but independent of its often shallow focus on surface and its superficial trust in being able to restore an ideal order that never existed. Whereas Aleida Assmann astutely writes, "Reconstruction makes place not for a new future but for another past," this architecture created a dialogue on the basis of which one could continue to move forward.[30]

The architecture that juxtaposed ruined historic structures with the re-creation of modernist idealism has provided the Federal Republic of Germany with its most potent postwar symbols, onto which new meanings have and will continue to be attached; future generations may end up seeing these buildings as representations of when they were built rather than of the historical events they originally evoked. Moreover they were always exceptional. Exposing the wounds of war is never going to be the dominant approach for a successful city or country. Nonetheless, in a few extraordinary cases this creative use of modernism's own history has created impressively meaningful places, whose full impact is best conveyed through personal experience rather than mediated images. It has also made contemporary Germany one of the rare countries in which civic spaces are regularly more compelling than their commercial counterparts. Finally, this is an architecture that has challenged and will certainly continue to challenge residents and visitors alike both to confront and to overcome a tangled and terrible past.

One

Making German Architecture Modern

On 1 October 2010 the international online version of *Der Spiegel*, Germany's leading weekly newsmagazine, reported on the suppression of a demonstration in the southwestern city of Stuttgart, the capital of the state of Baden-Württemberg and the home of the internationally renowned automotive firms Daimler-Benz and Porsche:

> A hardline police operation against demonstrators protesting against a new railway station project in Stuttgart has shocked Germany, after more than 100 people were injured by tear gas and water cannon. . . . Around 600 police used water cannon, tear gas, pepper spray and batons in an operation against over 1,000 demonstrators. . . . The activists had tried to use a sit-down protest to prevent the city's Schlossgarten park from being cleared so that work could begin on felling trees in the park as part of construction work on the new station. Thursday's protests were attended by a broad cross-section of society, including pensioners and children.[1]

Cem Özdemir, the coleader of the Green Party, commented that the state interior minister was "confusing Germany with Putin's Russia" and complained that "pepper gas was sprayed in the eyes of grandmothers and children at close range. We are in Germany. Such methods do not exist here."[2] A wide array of German newspapers from across the political spectrum seconded this view, while Roland Nelles, a *Spiegel* columnist, associated the unsubtle tactics with "the young democracy that was the Federal Republic 30 years ago," rather than what he implied was the mature state of 2010.[3] Popular revulsion against the strong-arm police tactics propelled the Greens on 27 March 2011 into their first chief ministry of a German state, although eight months later the majority of Baden-Württemberg voters who turned out for a referendum cast their ballots in favor of the project, whose slow pace of completion continues to raise eyebrows in Germany and abroad.[4]

Figure 1.1. Paul Bonatz and Friedrich Eugen Scholer, main train station, Stuttgart, 1928. Source: Harke/Wikipedia Commons.

The controversy over the replacement of large sections of Stuttgart's main train station, and the mammoth rail project to which they were attached, was hardly the first time the Federal Republic had seen debates over architecture serve as expressions of German democracy as well as of its limits. The two have been intertwined since at least the late 1950s, when the citizenry of West Berlin rallied, as will be described in chapter 2, in support of the preservation of what had long been seen as an example of relatively conservative architecture. The debate over the fate of Stuttgart's main train station, which had been designed in 1911 by the firm of Paul Bonatz and Friedrich Eugen Scholer, and finally completed in 1928, doubled as one over the definition of modern architecture and the degree to which what had not so long again been new should now be preserved as historic (Figure 1.1).

Any understanding of the way in which the modern architecture of the late Wilhelmine period and of the Weimar Republic has been used since in the architecture of the Federal Republic must begin with a discussion of what modern German architecture originally was. Recognizing the use of an earlier modern architecture in the buildings erected in postwar West Germany and the postunification Berlin Republic, as well as in a reunited Germany since 1989, requires an acceptance of a broader definition of modern architecture than has been widely used by architectural historians, especially those writing from the 1940s through the 1980s.[5] Modern German architecture was never limited to the Weissenhof Housing Estate, erected in Stuttgart in 1927, or the Bauhaus building that opened in Dessau the previous year, nor even to the New Building, that is, the office buildings, department stores, cinemas, and housing constructed of new materials in a spare, lean but also often exciting style during the short economic boom of 1924–29 and slightly after it, and the expressionist ferment out of which its more rational and functional approach emerged.[6]

A trio of buildings erected on the grounds of the exhibition staged by the German Werkbund in Cologne in the summer of 1914 and a second triplet completed in Stuttgart by the end of the following decade provide a useful point of departure for a more nuanced understanding of modern German architecture's original range of style and purpose. Their diversity challenges the notions that modern architecture was objective rather than symbolic, that new technology necessarily generated its unfamiliar forms, that it was inherently socialist or at least politically progressive, that it was always the work of heroic geniuses, that its mediated image was as important as the physical facts of the building, and that it was both masculine and specifically Western. This account also restores to a central position within the architecture of the period the precedents employed most often by those postwar architects who used modernism as a historical source. The Cologne buildings and the first two Stuttgart examples give a sense of modern German architecture's original breadth; the final Stuttgart case, that of the Weissenhof Estate, marks the point when stylistic definitions began to narrow in ways that would influence the subsequent writing of the history of modern German architecture much more than they have the practice of modern architecture in the Federal Republic.

Objective or Expressionist: The Werkbund Exhibition in Cologne

The German Werkbund, a group composed of architects, designers, critics, and industrialists, was formed in 1907. It aimed to integrate modern industrial production with high art by paying unprecedented attention to the design of factories and shops, as well as of the goods made and sold in them and the way in which they were advertised. The group was remarkably successful in persuading its peers that the quality and character of design mattered enormously. Good design, they argued, could advance the German economy, above all by increasing exports, but they were also interested in the impact it had upon maintaining what many saw to be the unique characteristics of German culture.[7] Although many of the figures associated with the movement espoused both innovative new designs and relatively progressive political positions, there was an overall emphasis on using design to transcend the challenges that industrialization posed to traditional German social organization (community rather than society, in the words of the pioneering German sociologist Ferdinand Tönnies).[8] This inherent respect for an underlying status quo helps explain the appeal that Werkbund positions would eventually have for established institutions like the Catholic Church.[9]

Seven years after the Werkbund was established it sponsored an exhibition in the Rhineland city of Cologne, just across the river from the cathedral, which had finally been completed in 1880.[10] Midcareer architects, such as Peter Behrens, Theodor Fischer, Hermann Muthesius, and Bruno Paul, stuck to convention. The somewhat ponderous neoclassicism of their contributions disappointed those who had hoped for a reprise of the collective boldness these men had earlier displayed. The three exceptions were the Model Factory by Walter Gropius and Adolf Meyer, the Werkbund Theater by Henry van de Velde, and the Glashaus by Bruno Taut. The first two faced each other; the third stood on the exhibition's periphery. Together they proposed a series of new directions for modern architecture.

Ever since Nikolaus Pevsner, then a young German émigré, published *Pioneers of the Modern Movement* (later retitled *Pioneers of Modern Design from William Morris to Walter Gropius*) in London in 1936, the Model Factory (Figure 1.2) has been seen as the building that anticipated Gropius's Dessau Bauhaus, and therefore as the last key step toward the establishment of what would come to be known as the International Style. Pevsner, who was only twelve in the summer of 1914, probably knew the building only from photographs. Clearly thinking of it more in terms of the context of the cathedral than of the other exhibition buildings, he wrote of the glazed corner stair towers of its administration block:

> There is something sublime in this effortless mastery of material and weight. Never since the Sainte-Chapelle and the choir of Beauvais had the human art of building been so triumphant over matter. Yet the character of the building is entirely un-Gothic, anti-Gothic. While in the thirteenth century all lines, functional though they were, served the one artistic purpose of pointing heavenwards in a goal beyond this world, and walls were made translucent to carry the transcendental magic of saintly figures rendered in colored glass, the glass walls are now clear and without mystery, the steel frame is hard, and its expression discourages all other-worldly speculation. It is the creative energy of this world in which we live and work and which we want to master, a world of science and technology, of speed and danger, of hard struggles and no personal security, that is glorified in Gropius's architecture, and as long as this is the world and these are its ambitions and problems, the style of Gropius and the other pioneers will be valid.[11]

Making German Architecture Modern

Figure 1.2. Walter Gropius and Adolf Meyer, Model Factory, Werkbund Exhibition, Cologne, 1914. Copyright Bildarchiv Foto Marburg.

In the Model Factory Gropius and Meyer drew upon their acquaintance with American concrete-framed factories, such as those in which Henry Ford was manufacturing Model T cars, and with Frank Lloyd Wright's Wasmuth Portfolio, which they fused with the artistic ambitions embodied in recent German factories by

Figure 1.3. Rear facade, Model Factory. Copyright Bildarchiv Foto Marburg.

architects such as Behrens, for whom Gropius had worked, and Hans Poelzig.[12] The result combined a matter-of-fact assembly hall with the much more original administration building. The middle story of the facade facing the assembly hall was almost completely glazed and, in part because it projected out farther on both sides, appeared to float almost free between the more conventional piers of the ground story and the hovering planes of the cantilevered roof slabs of the corner pavilions and of the roof terrace set between them (Figure 1.3). It was almost certainly based on Wright's City National Bank and Hotel, completed two years earlier in Mason City, Iowa, and published in Germany in the Wasmuth Portfolio. The facade facing van de Velde's theater was scarcely more conventional. Terminated at both ends by the projecting stair towers, it consisted otherwise mostly of a brick screen wall divided by a row of vertical recessions and pinned to the ground by squat pavilion-like insertions on either side of the door. Here Gropius invoked the solidity of an ancient Egyptian mastaba or pylon, against which he contrasted the transparent glazing of the stair towers.

Only in the angled side view published by Pevsner does this building appear to be a precursor of the building Gropius completed a dozen years later for the Bauhaus, the twentieth century's most influential school of art and design, which he had founded in Weimar in 1919. In other respects the lingering interest in monumentality, albeit expressed in terms of ancient Egypt and modern America, especially as realized in the largely opaque entrance facade, appears characteristically

Making German Architecture Modern 19

Figure 1.4. Henry van de Velde, Werkbund Theater, Werkbund Exhibition, Cologne, 1914. Copyright Bildarchiv Foto Marburg.

Wilhelmine, even as the form it took was obviously novel. The collage-like quality of the administration building's paradoxical juxtaposition of glazed volumes and nearly transparently thin walls, with its self-consciously archaic main mass was more prescient of the postwar German architecture that is the chief subject of this book than of the far more dynamically composed Bauhaus.

Visitors to the exhibition, such as the young critic Adolf Behne, found the theater and the Glashaus at least as intriguing.[13] The theater, designed by a leading proponent of art nouveau old enough to be Gropius's and Taut's father, proved that sculptural forms devised largely independently of the structural properties of materials could create an equally compelling path to abstraction (Figure 1.4).[14] Its strongly sculpted volumes emerged out of reforms in theater and set design associated with the emergence of a mass audience rather than from the development of new building materials or construction techniques. Trained as an artist rather than an architect, van de Velde was always more interested in form for its own sake than in following his fellow Belgian Victor Horta's lead in exploiting the simultaneously structural and ornamental properties of iron and steel. Nonetheless, published photographs of the building's facade inspired the young Erich Mendelsohn's experiments with reinforced concrete in ways that would be remembered in postwar Germany even before Le Corbusier's church at Ronchamp reawakened interest in such plasticity.[15]

Although they were probably made largely out of plaster, the apparent solidity of van de Velde's tiered masses, which stepped from a low vestibule up to the roof over the auditorium and the fly tower at the back of the stage and splayed out at the rear to encompass backstage facilities, starkly contrasted with the weightless volumes of Gropius's stair towers. For contemporaries, however, the difference between the two buildings was not so much a question of form as of the approach the two architects took toward social issues. In a lecture delivered at the Folkwang Museum in Hagen in 1911, Gropius argued that industrialists should build modern factories in order to promote better relations with their workforces. In remarks that anticipate Le Corbusier's slogan "architecture instead of revolution," Gropius wrote, "The uneducated worker not only cares about light, air and cleanliness, but also possesses an unappreciated respect for the form of the building in which he works and the pristine feeling of beauty in its spaces."[16] Although van de Velde's commitment to political reform has been exaggerated, there is no doubt that he designed the theater in keeping with a degree of social engagement that Gropius did not yet share.[17] The theater's unusual lack of tiered and box seating flattened out distinctions in status among audience members, while innovations in the shape of the stage and in atmospheric lighting were part of larger efforts in the contemporary theater world to generate a sense of community through the creation of shared empathetic reactions to the spectacle they were witnessing. Van de Velde, whose network of friends and collaborators included the producer Gordon Craig, and who had already proposed theaters for Weimar and Paris (control of the latter had been wrested from him by the contractor Auguste Perret), had long been interested in such reforms.[18] Indeed, he had originally intended to design a cinema rather than a conventional theater for the exhibition.[19]

For van de Velde, being modern depended not on how or where an object was made, but on what it looked like and how it was used. Should one seek to impose formal order in order to dignify industrial processes and their products, thus raising them to the status of culture? Or did the dynamic energy of modernity better merit artistic expression in designs that literally broke the bounds of convention? In his architecture for the Glashaus, Taut synthesized many aspects of these competing positions in a building whose marginal position at the edge of the original exhibition can be contrasted with the enduring impact that it, and expressionism more generally, have had on subsequent German architecture.[20]

Built ostensibly as an advertising pavilion for the glass industry, the Glashaus doubled as a demonstration of how the spiritual ambitions of German expressionist literature and painting might be conveyed architecturally (Figure 1.5). Designed to look like a crystal, the apparently circular building, which glowed from within with colored light, in fact had a substantial rear appendage. This housed a cascade

Figure 1.5. Bruno Taut, Glashaus, Werkbund Exhibition, Cologne, 1914. Copyright Bildarchiv Foto Marburg.

of water, illuminated from below, and flanked on both sides by stairs (Figure 1.6). The walls of this chamber were covered with colored mosaics; Taut set stained glass by leading expressionist painters into the windows (Gropius and van de Velde had also collaborated with important contemporary artists). The room under the faceted dome housed a display of glass products and exhibited some of the novel ways in which glass could be used as building material. The dramatic lighting effects, now detached from the production of a particular play, were intended to evoke the experience of medieval worship in a Gothic cathedral or chapel, with the crystal form intended as a mystical replacement for the steeples of medieval churches. Taut commissioned a series of aphorisms from the writer Paul Scheerbart, several of which he inscribed on the concrete lintel supporting the faceted roof structure. The most

Figure 1.6.   Interior, Glashaus. Copyright Bildarchiv Foto Marburg.

famous of these—"Colored glass destroys hate"—captured his aspirations for what glass architecture could achieve.

It was not to be. Even before the outbreak of the First World War brought an early end to the exhibition, the Werkbund was nearly sundered by internal divisions about the appropriate relationship between art and industry. When Muthesius recommended increasing standardization, van de Velde, who led the counterattack, championed the importance of individual artistry. He garnered the active support not only of August Endell and Hans Obrist, prominent Germans who had been early advocates of art nouveau (or *Jugendstil* as it was known in German), but also of Taut and Gropius, who did not want to have their own chance to make a mark precluded by the adoption of neoclassical norms.[21]

The debate, which was also between those who saw design reform principally in terms of the contribution it could make to the German economy, and particularly the export market, and those who took a more internationalist position, had important ramifications for Gropius. The following year van de Velde included his name, with those of Endell and Obrist (whose sculpture ornamented the Werkbund Theater), in the list of his possible successors he sent to the authorities in Weimar, where he had been forced to resign from the directorship of the Grand Ducal School of Arts and Crafts, which he had founded in 1908. This would lead to Gropius's assuming the directorship of the Bauhaus. Meanwhile, following the revolution of November 1918, Gropius joined Taut and Behne in founding the Arbeitsrat für Kunst. A workers' council, established in November 1918 along the lines adopted by many trade unions but intended for artists, it unsuccessfully lobbied the new Social Democratic president Friedrich Ebert, who was preoccupied with establishing political control in the face of often violent opposition from both the far left and the far right. In declaring that "art and people must form a unity," its founding manifesto set the tone Gropius would take less than six months later in the Bauhaus Manifesto, when he concluded with a vision of "the new structure of the future, which will embrace architecture and sculpture and painting in one unity and which will one day rise towards heaven from the hands of a million workers like the crystal symbol of a new faith."[22] In late 1919 and throughout 1920, Gropius and Taut were also active in the Crystal Chain, a group of architects who corresponded about their aspirations for a utopian architecture along lines largely inspired by Taut's visions of crystalline city crowns, expanded versions of the Glashaus that were intended to foster democracy.[23]

The positions represented by the three standout buildings at the Werkbund Exhibition would thus be closely bound together in the years that immediately followed, although this would not be consistently reflected in the literature on modern architecture over the course of the subsequent century, which would long favor objectivity over expressionism. This was due in part to Gropius's refusal to share credit with contemporaries and to the hawk's eye he kept, especially during his years in the United States, on what historians had to say. As early as 1923, he objected vehemently to Mies's proposal to include van de Velde's theater in an enlarged version of the exhibition of contemporary architecture Gropius had organized at the Bauhaus.[24] Others were more generous, however. After the Second World War the Academy of the Arts in West Berlin, as the successor to the Prussian Academy, made Gropius, Mies, and van de Velde honorary members.[25] Gropius was more gracious about Taut, describing him to an American scholar in 1962 as "a close friend of mine.... Though we were quite different characters, we got along very well, complementing each other, so to speak."[26] Some sense of the continuing complexity of the subject can be gained from a consideration of three buildings completed in Stuttgart in the late 1920s and their subsequent fate.

Stuttgart: Multiple Modernisms and Their Fates

Most of those who arrived in Stuttgart in the 1920s to view its new buildings would have traveled by train. They would have alighted in the first major German train station to break with nineteenth-century historicism. The final touches were put on the building in 1928, seventeen years after Bonatz and Scholer (the building has always been credited to Bonatz) had won the competition for its design.[27] From the station they could have walked downtown to see one of Europe's most stunning new department stores, the Schocken store designed by Mendelsohn and also completed in 1928, or traveled to the suburbs to the Weissenhof Housing Estate, where housing for civil servants designed by architects from across Western Europe had opened for public exhibition in the summer of 1927.

Here, too, a variety of modern architectures was on display. Their purposes, as the traveler would quickly have realized, ranged from civic to commercial to domestic. Although used by people of all classes, these buildings were clearly designed to address a middle-class observer, who would have been more likely than his or her working-class contemporaries to grasp the allusions they made to sources as diverse as ancient Mesopotamia, the subject of some of the latest German archaeological discoveries, and recent American factories. It was also this middle class that could afford the modern conveniences on display in the model dwellings of the Weissenhof.

As important as reconstructing the original diversity of what was considered modern in Stuttgart at the end of the 1920s is understanding the way in which later, narrower definitions of modern architecture governed the fate of these buildings. Mendelsohn's store was demolished in 1960, and parts of the train station were pulled down in 2011 and 2012. Although much more badly damaged in World War II, what survived of the Weissenhof now appears in relatively pristine condition, following extensive renovations in the 1980s. Public discussions over the preservation of the Schocken store and the Weissenhof never prompted the intervention of riot police, but they remain illustrative of the importance of architecture to local—and national—definitions of cultural identity.

The monumental station, whose surviving crisp rectangular volumes are clad in a homogeneous facing of boldly rusticated stone, was regarded as a major example of modern architecture in the 1920s and well beyond.[28] As such it stood for the creation of fresh and viable alternatives to the surfeit of ornament, as well as the historical sources of that ornament, that had enveloped most civic buildings in Germany, Europe, and indeed much of the rest of the world, in the decades before it was begun. In Germany, this break with the immediate past was strongly associated with the reforms espoused by the Werkbund, but also with the proud nationalism that, as in the case of Muthesius and many other Werkbund leaders, often fueled reform efforts.[29] The massiveness and palpable weight of the station walls, as well as the impressive scale of its major interiors and the neo-Assyrian style of the carving of the few sculptures that ornamented them, all indicated that this was a building designed not to conform to the whims of fashion but to outlast them. At the same time the simple rectangular design of the glass-and-steel structures over the tracks suggested a matter-of-fact acceptance of the technology they were built to serve. Just as Gropius borrowed from ancient Egyptian architecture as well as what he understood to be the equally primitive forms of American industrial architecture, Bonatz turned for inspiration to reconstructions of Babylon as well as his own travel sketches of Cairo.[30]

The terminal was modern because both its forms and the technology used to build at least the tracks were obviously new. By the time it was completed, however, its very weight and apparent permanence distinguished it from more up-to-the-minute trends in architecture, collectively known at the time in Germany as the New Building. For this reason, although its status as one of Stuttgart's most imposing twentieth-century buildings was never in doubt, the importance of preserving the entire structure could be called into question in the 1990s, when ambitious efforts to transform both the city and the regional rail line were developed. These entailed converting the terminal to a through station, and involved the demolition of much of Bonatz's building as well as the creation of a new, largely underground station designed by Ingenhoven Architects and still under construction in 2018.[31] These changes will free land behind Bonatz's station for development, and create a faster train connection between Stuttgart and Ulm, and thus also between Paris and Bratislava and Budapest. They come, however, at the cost of parts of the earlier station and also the trees in a neighboring park.

Yet precisely because the station was not an avant-garde building, opposition to the scheme, although led by the Green Party, was clearly never exclusive to the left. Many in the historically relatively politically conservative city of Stuttgart simply opposed change and found the existing train station more to their taste than Ingenhoven's futuristic design. Others opposed the development of a new quarter behind it. Farther afield, however, where the building was not a familiar friend, it could appear almost menacing. The American architecture critic Nicolai Ouroussoff weighed in, writing in 2009:

> Completed several years before Hitler took power, the Stuttgart terminal may be Bonatz's most masterly architectural balancing act. Its imposing front facade, marked by a shallow arcade and towering stone pillars, is as haunting as an early de Chirico painting. Framed by stone entry halls at either end, it has a severe, stripped-down Classicism that also suggests why Bonatz was able to continue building well into the Nazi era.[32]

Debates over how to define modern architecture and what about it might be worth preserving were scarcely new in Stuttgart. The Schocken Department Store stood between 1928 and 1960 less than a kilometer to the south of the train station (Figure 1.7).[33] Unlike the latter structure, it was completed quite quickly, having been designed only in 1926. Occupying an entire city block, the store, which was dedicated to the sale of inexpensive, mass-produced goods, was dramatic by day and even more so by night, when apparently weightless shop windows and the corner stair tower glowed from within as did the giant lettering spelling out the Schocken name.[34]

Like Gropius, Mendelsohn had been inspired by American factories and department stores, which he had seen for himself during a 1924 tour of New York City,

Figure 1.7.   Erich Mendelsohn, Schocken Department Store, Stuttgart, 1968. Copyright Bildarchiv Foto Marburg.

Buffalo, Detroit, Pittsburgh, and Chicago.[35] Forsaking the escapism that resulted in many such stores resembling palaces, he instead jazzed up the relatively straightforward engineering of the concrete-framed factories in which Model T Fords were produced and took obvious inspiration as well from the glazed stair towers of Gropius's Model Factory. The result was emblematic of the New Building. Mendelsohn's attentiveness to shape, and particularly the plastic approach to concrete he thought he saw in the Werkbund Theater, which had infused his breakthrough building, the Einstein Tower in Potsdam, helped him slot a new scale of structure sympathetically into the existing cityscape. He wrapped four different facade treatments, each calibrated to the scale of the streets they faced, around the store. Moreover, although he had been critical of Taut's mysticism, Mendelsohn's careful attention to lighting clearly reflected the lessons he had learned from the adherents of the Crystal Chain.[36]

The commercial architecture of the New Building flourished not only because it was inexpensive, but because it conveyed an appealing image of Germany as being, despite its recent disastrous defeat and the lingering weakness of its economy, entirely up to date. Architecture has always been in part about articulating aspirations and desires through concrete physical form and spaces. Mendelsohn's Schocken store was an unusually pragmatic building, but it also intentionally sizzled with seductive allure; the sleek packaging of the tautly wrought surfaces of many of the Weissenhof dwellings were even less informative about how they were actually constructed and intended to be used.

Mendelsohn's ability to fuse objectivity and expressionism in a building that was commercially successful and yet obviously avant-garde made him one of the most renowned and influential architects of the interwar years. Gropius tacitly acknowledged his influence in 1923, when, in an early attempt to exclude expressionism (defined as Häring, Hermann Finsterlin, and Scharoun) as well as van de Velde from definitions of modern architecture, he instead organized his exhibition of contemporary architecture at the Bauhaus "from a very specific standpoint, namely that of the dynamic-functional side of the development of modern architecture, away from ornament and profile." *Dynamic functionalism* was a term Mendelsohn had already employed, as Gropius must have known, for the title of a lecture.[37]

None of this was enough to save the Schocken store. Mendelsohn died in exile in San Francisco in 1953; his patron Salman Schocken in Switzerland in 1959.[38] Both men were Zionist Jews who had fled Germany for first Jerusalem and then the United States. The campaign to preserve the building was led by students and young staff from the Technische Hochschule in Stuttgart, including Jürgen Joedicke, who was to become a prominent historian and critic of modern architecture. Their position in many ways presaged that of the so-called sixty-eighters who would attempt to distance themselves from their parents' generation, which they saw as compromised by their collaboration with, or at the least passivity toward, the Third Reich. Joedicke and his friends received support from prominent elders, however. Gropius sent a telegram stating, "The Mendelsohn building must remain."[39] The star-studded list of those who rallied behind its preservation included Alvar Aalto, Reyner Banham, Max Bill, Richard Döcker, Sigfried Giedion, Ludwig Hilberseimer, Ludwig Mies van der Rohe, Richard Neutra, J. J. P. Oud, and Eero Saarinen, a veritable who's who of the founders of the modern movement and the next generation of their supporters.[40]

The Schocken store, however, was vulnerable on several grounds. First, there is little reason to believe that the Stuttgart authorities were impressed by the appeals from figures they had never particularly respected. Most had trained during the interwar years at the local architecture school, which under the leadership of Bonatz and Paul Schmitthenner had remained conservative stylistically throughout both the Weimar Republic and the Third Reich.[41] Second, modernism's own rhetoric, which was functionalist rather than respectful of history, meant that the building could be and was labeled obsolete by both planners and its owners. The first wanted to widen Eberhardtstrasse; the second preferred an interior with clear spans, rather than one interrupted by a grid of pillars. Older architects, including one who had

Figure 1.8. Weissenhof Estate, Stuttgart, 1927. Copyright Bildarchiv Foto Marburg.

known Mendelsohn personally, argued that according to the tenets of modernism it should be replaced, without preserving even the facade, the solution that Egon Eiermann, who designed its successor, professed to prefer.[42]

The chief reason, however, the Schocken store was demolished was that by 1959 modern German architecture had been redefined. Two stories, the Bauhaus and an exhibition held in Stuttgart in 1927 under the leadership of an architect who in 1930 would become the influential school's third director, dominated the new narrative. The Weissenhof Estate, organized by Mies van der Rohe under the auspices of the Werkbund, was a collection of dwellings for the city's civil servants designed by avant-garde architects from Austria, Belgium, France, and the Netherlands, as well as two generations of Germans, including both Gropius and Taut (Figure 1.8). The estate was located on a hilltop site less than two kilometers north of the train station (the Schocken store was south of the station), and there the utopian ambitions of Taut's city crown were reconfigured relatively pragmatically in terms of a new style of upper middle-class domesticity, brimming with the latest conveniences and comfortable enough in the case of Oud's row houses to include rooms for live-in servants.[43] There was enormous interest in what became the defining moment in its crystallization. Half a million visitors came to view the exhibition held in the buildings before they were turned over to their inhabitants.[44]

The interior of the largest single contribution, Mies's apartment block, gave an inkling of the way in which the same skeletal frames (here in steel rather than concrete) that enabled Gropius and Mendelsohn to glaze the exteriors of their buildings could be used as well to reconfigure interior space now that walls did not necessarily have to be load bearing. Mies wrote:

> I intend to try out the most varied plans in the apartment house. For the time being, I am building only the outside and the common walls, and inside each apartment only the two piers that support the ceiling. All the rest is to be as free as it possibly can be. If I could contrive to get some cheap plywood partitions made, I would treat only the kitchen and the bathroom as fixed spaces, and make the rest of the apartment variable, so that the spaces could be divided according to the needs of the individual tenant. This would have the advantage that it would make it possible to rearrange the apartment whenever family circumstances changes, without spending a lot of money on a conversion. Any carpenter, or any practically minded layman, would be able to shift the walls.[45]

In order to demonstrate this flexibility, the layouts of the twenty-four different apartments in the building varied as much as possible, and different designers were charged with furnishing them. One was the work of Mies's personal and professional partner, Lilly Reich (Figure 1.9). Although none of the "heroes" of the modern movement were female, a cluster of independently minded women eagerly adopted modern architecture and design in the 1920s as a means of both creative expression and professional achievement. Perhaps because few of the group led conventional personal lives, they, too, were written out of the story in the postwar period, when modernism's message of social empowerment was recast to consist of the betterment of the working classes rather than the emancipation of women, with which it had arguably originally had just as much to do. The group, which also included Sonia Delaunay, Eileen Gray, and Charlotte Perriand in Paris, and the staff and students of the Bauhaus's weaving workshop, of whom Gunta Stölzl and Anni Albers are the most renowned, played a crucial role in establishing austere but flexible alternatives to established bourgeois furnishing conventions and thus pioneered new forms of domesticity.[46] Reich, already an experienced interior and exhibition designer when she designed this interior, wrote that "the vital thing, here as elsewhere, is to give expression to the mentality of the kind of woman who wants to be what she is, rather than to seem what she is not."[47]

Unsurprisingly Reich's apartment featured one of the most open of all the layouts. Besides the kitchen and bathroom, whose locations were fixed, there were only two distinct spaces, a living room with a large desk and a small dining alcove, and a bedroom, which was separated from a dressing area by a curtain. The latter featured a large mirror and small stool executed in tubular metal, which was the latest fashion,

Figure 1.9.   Lilly Reich, interior, Weissenhof Estate. Copyright Bildarchiv Foto Marburg.

while Reich set a more conventionally upholstered armchair and a large low cabinet against the far wall of the living room. The elegant understatement was typical of Reich, although the responsibility for the design of the individual pieces remains a matter of dispute, with attribution shared between her and Mies.[48]

Little was especially remarkable about many of the quite frankly generic components of the Weissenhof, several of which were designed by architects such as Victor Bourgeois, Josef Frank, Adolf Rading, and Adolf Gustav Schneck, who are now largely forgotten outside the lands in which they practiced. Yet this showcase for a relatively unified approach to architectural modernism covered a far narrower stylistic band than the New Building, much less the move toward an often archaic simplicity represented by Bonatz's station. Instead of resembling a factory, as the Schocken store did, the sharp-edged volumes of the Weissenhof dwellings looked machine made. Many of their components were indeed mass produced, as the exhibition doubled as a display of new construction systems. Mies had originally intended that a broader stylistic array of positions be represented, but Mendelsohn and Häring dropped out after a misunderstanding over whether he had planned to include them.[49] One of the ramifications of their exclusion was an angry response from Bonatz, who as the city's leading architect and the professor of its architecture school, correctly saw his position being challenged, something Mendelsohn, who had eagerly sought and received his approval for the Schocken store, had assiduously avoided doing.[50] The caricature of the Weissenhof as an Arab village can be traced to this disaffection, while the founding of the Congrès Internationaux d'Architecture Moderne the following year, which Häring and five of the seventeen Weissenhof architects (but not Mendelsohn) attended, helped crystallize the sense of an international avant-garde focused on housing and planning issues, rather than a German group whose commercial commissions were often slotted with some sympathy into existing downtowns.[51]

The redefinition of modern architecture as the International Style, a term that would be popularized by the exhibition held at the Museum of Modern Art in 1932, helped preserve the parts of the Weissenhof that survived World War II. The tide began to shift relatively early. In 1958, only thirty-one years after the units had been built and well in advance of comprehensive protection being extended to other modernist icons, the estate was designated a historic monument. Since that time it has been widely recognized in the scholarly literature and has become a significant local tourist attraction. In the 1980s it was comprehensively renovated.[52]

As Bonatz's and Gropius's support for Mendelsohn and Mies's intention to include him in the Weissenhof demonstrate, the multiple modernisms present in Stuttgart by 1928 were not seen at the time as mutually exclusive. Indeed, Bonatz's Graf Zeppelin Hotel, which was completed in 1931 and still stands across from the train station, closed much of the gap between him and the architects of the Weissenhof Estate as well as Mendelsohn. The fabric of a unitary interpretation has gradually unraveled, but while it held sway it limited the recognition of the way in which the postwar architecture in the Federal Republic was often grounded in the memory of the full range of modern architecture of the 1910s and 1920s. So, too, did the building type in which this memory would originally be most widely manifested.

That so little physically remains of the buildings that are the subject of this chapter would suggest the appropriateness of the increasing focus on the history of modern architecture as seen through the lens of photography and of exhibitions.[53] Certainly the understanding postwar architects had of the Werkbund Exhibition in Cologne was derived almost entirely from photographs, which is why Mendelsohn could so easily mistake van de Velde's plaster building for concrete construction. Outstanding as the recent scholarship on the subject with specific relation to Mendelsohn's Schocken store and the Weissenhof has been, it was not mediated images, however, but the experience of actual places that prompted students in Stuttgart in 1959 to mount a campaign to save the Schocken store, while an even more visceral attachment to place undoubtedly motivated the thousands who just over half a century later were teargassed by the same city's riot police. Creating specific places in which people could remember the past at the same time that they used specific aspects of it to imagine a better future was integral to many of postwar Germany's finest churches.

Two

Inserting Memory into Modern Architecture
West German Churches

On 17 December 1961, Otto Dibelius, the bishop of Berlin, consecrated the reconstructed Kaiser Wilhelm Memorial Church (Figure 2.1).[1] More than a thousand people witnessed the proceedings. The chapel was not yet finished, nor was the sacristy, but enough had been achieved for the coupling of the new building by Egon Eiermann, one of the Federal Republic's leading architects, and the ruins of the church that had been completed less than six decades earlier, to serve immediately as the symbol of West Berlin. The response of two very differently positioned voices gives a measure of the importance quickly accorded the structure. Within weeks the German architecture critic Ulrich Conrads gave a radio broadcast that was later republished first in the newspaper *Die Zeit* and then in *Bauwelt,* the weekly journal for the architecture profession and constructions trade that he edited. Conrads declared, "This is the first and only new church building in postwar Germany that—in the entirely literal sense—is a sign for the lost center [*Mitte*]: for the center of the old German capital." Playing with the double meaning of *Mitte* (the word for "middle" was also the name of Berlin's central district, which includes both the medieval core and its eighteenth-century extensions, and which was at the time located on the other side of the Wall in Communist East Berlin), Conrads went on to say that it needed to serve as a substitute for and a memorial to this district. "This church building must itself be the Mitte, the economic and cultural focal point of the free Berlin."[2] Three years later the American photographer and architectural critic G. E. Kidder Smith commented:

> As stern sentries flanking and guarding the bomb-shattered—but to Berliners still precious—ruins of the old church, this new nave and tower by Eiermann

Figure 2.1. Franz Schwechten, Kaiser Wilhelm Memorial Church, Berlin, 1895, with addition by Egon Eiermann, 1963. Source: SAAI Karlsruhe.

are among the most unflinching statements in today's religious architecture. Unrelentingly hard, taut as piano wires, they function magnificently as aesthetic and psychological statements—and as counterpoints to the old tower. They might, indeed, be said to reflect the brave congregation they serve.[3]

Dedicated just over four months after the erection of the Berlin Wall cut West Berlin off from the rest of the city and the surrounding countryside, all of which were controlled by the Communist German Democratic Republic, and less than two months

Inserting Memory into Modern Architecture

Figure 2.2.   Night view, Kaiser Wilhelm Memorial Church. Source: Dr. Kralle/Wikipedia Commons.

after a dangerous standoff between American and Soviet tanks occurred at one of the new wall's few crossing points, the Memorial Church served for the next three decades as the most prominent architectural emblem of the supposedly capitalist—but in fact heavily subsidized—western half of the city.[4] Emblazoned on stamps, and prominently featured in almost every guide to West Berlin, it also appears in the opening scene of *Wings of Desire*, Wim Wenders's classic 1987 film.[5] It stands at the beginning of the Kurfürstendamm, the boulevard that was West Berlin's main commercial artery, where despite being a sacred building it doubled as a symbol of plenty. This was especially the case at night when its stained glass windows, illuminated from within, rhymed with the neon lighting of its commercial surroundings as well as with the head and tail lights of automobile traffic (Figure 2.2).[6] Last but by no means least, the church made clear the contrast between the officially atheist German Democratic Republic and the overtly Christian Federal Republic and, by extension, West Berlin (West Berlin was officially governed by France, the United Kingdom, and the United States). In a letter to Pastor Günter Pohl, the head of the church's building committee, Eiermann noted "the meaning and importance this church has for the whole Christian world."[7]

The story of how the two halves of this building came to be the most prominent

Cold War symbol of West Berlin and, by extension, of the free market and religious freedom of the Federal Republic is inseparable from the way in which two pasts were juxtaposed in a much larger series of postwar churches. Between 1946 and 1968 a distinctively West German sacred architecture emerged that paired memories of the modernism on display in Cologne in 1914 and (albeit to a lesser degree) in Stuttgart in the late 1920s with the forms, and often the literal stones, of earlier medieval and neomedievalist churches.[8] Other examples of a much larger phenomenon include the Church of the Resurrection by Otto Bartning in Pforzheim (1946–48), St. Anna in Düren by Rudolf Schwarz (1954–56), and the Pilgrimage Church of Mary in Neviges by Gottfried Böhm (1963–68). These buildings, and postwar German churches more generally, served as impressive architectural ambassadors for the Federal Republic, especially in the religious networks that assisted the country's reintegration into the international community. Because they represented one of the most acceptable faces of the new country, they were also often showcased abroad in books and exhibitions targeted at architects as well as a more general public.[9] The collage of the Kaiser Wilhelm Memorial Church's original neo-Romanesque building and its emphatically modernist—but simultaneously firmly historicist—successor proved particularly important. In addition to being West Berlin's most widely recognized edifice, it provided a key precedent for much of the most effective architecture erected in the reunified city during the 1990s and the first decade of the new millennium.

Between 1940 and 1945 aerial bombardment and the Allied ground invasion reduced huge swaths of many German cities to rubble.[10] As late as 1948 Bruno Taut's brother, Max, also an architect, wrote Mies van der Rohe, after thanking him for a care packet of food:

> Rather than "intelligent" futuristic fantasies, I am interested above all in the present. I concentrate on how we can best and most quickly create a roof over our heads. The smallest and most modest task seems to me at the moment the most important, so that I cannot believe that we soon will be able to build as we used to. We are limited to the simplest construction. . . . Provisional buildings can naturally also be decent and seen from a civilized standpoint, and to a pleasing standard. I am really not against projecting and build also gladly "castles in the sky," but one is not permitted to forget and neglect reality.[11]

The task of reconstructing West Germany's war-torn cities, which nominally included West Berlin, was an immense challenge.[12] Much of the effort focused, as Taut predicted, simply on making habitable buildings.[13] Deciding how much to adapt city plans that often dated back to the Middle Ages to the requirements of modern automobile traffic proved another major issue. In the wake of the bombastic state architecture of the Third Reich, it was not at all clear that the new Federal Republic established in 1949 needed to be represented architecturally; that year Hans Schwippert converted a teacher training academy in Bonn into modest quarters for the new parliament.[14] By the late 1950s the International Style, itself much transformed over the course of the previous three decades, was increasingly used for prestigious commissions, where it conveyed an antifascist and also an anticommunist message. This occurred, for instance, in the Interbau exhibition staged in West Berlin in 1957 and in the pavilion that Eiermann designed in collaboration with Sep Ruf for Expo 58, the world's fair held in Brussels the following year.[15] Walter Gropius, who had left Germany during the Third Reich for first London and then the United States, played an important role in these developments. He kept a close eye on the architectural scene in the Federal Republic and was acutely aware of the style's utility both for Cold War propaganda and his own reputation.[16]

In the immediate aftermath of the war, however, this was decidedly a minority position. Like all those engaged in reconstruction, the bishops, priests, pastors, and congregations involved in the project of rebuilding and expanding the Federal Republic and West Berlin's infrastructure of Catholic and Protestant houses of worship first had to decide when to build anew. Along with the rest of historic city centers, badly damaged centrally located historic churches were frequently rebuilt, albeit often in simplified form, particularly when it came to interior fittings. Those churches that had been erected in the late nineteenth and early twentieth century in newer districts were not generally considered worthy of such respectful and expensive treatment.[17] Although there had been a consensus in Werkbund circles by the outbreak of the First World War that most of this typically neo-Gothic and neo-Romanesque architecture was outmoded, intact steeples from damaged churches were frequently retained. Parishes proved loath to sweep away what survived of these buildings, unpopular as they were with architects and most intellectuals to the left of center, which at the time churchgoers typically were not.

In addition to replacing less historic churches, architects were also charged with the creation of thousands of new buildings. Some of these served congregations in new suburban districts, but others accommodated the influx of refugees from the east, as formerly Catholic regions suddenly absorbed large numbers of Protestants, and vice versa.[18] In 1958 Jürgen Joedicke, the young architectural historian who would soon battle unsuccessfully to save the Schocken store in Stuttgart, wrote that more churches were built in Germany in the first years after the war than in the centuries since the Reformation.[19] He summarized the character and the appeal of these mostly modest buildings:

> The church type of our time is no longer the cathedral but the small house of God. This change indicates a symptom of the churchly life: in place of an anonymous mass congregation, a small but active community meets, not only on Sundays for services, as is their conventional duty, but also as an expression of

an approach to living. This idea developed in Germany above all in the time of the church's resistance during the thirties.[20]

In fact, neither Catholics nor Protestants had systematically opposed Nazism and this emphasis on community had deeper roots, but there was no denying the postwar effectiveness of this understanding of active community in fostering a healthier civic society.[21]

Churches, and particularly Catholic churches, served in Germany after both world wars as alternatives to discredited or destroyed national institutions.[22] In the first years after World War II, Christian ideology provided a reassuring contrast in the Federal Republic to Nazi dictatorship as well as socialism and communism at a time when liberal democracy had not yet established deep roots. Church attendance soared in West Germany and West Berlin, as it did more generally in Western Europe. As Jörg Arnold describes, during the war as well as after, "The places of worship may have been destroyed in the air raid, but as a social network, the Church had survived, ready to assemble the dispersed parishioners around the word of God."[23] Its contribution encompassed both physical sustenance and emotional comfort.

The church provided community and continuity with traditions that extended far further back in time than the Nazi regime, or indeed the memory of any single worshipper. Equally importantly it offered a sympathetic frame for coping with the suffering parishioners endured during both the war and its immediate aftermath. Describing the role of the Protestant church in postwar Nuremberg, the historian Neil Gregor writes, "Neither did the church confine itself to offering consolation, to endowing death with meaning or to giving expression to anguished hope. It also played a key role in the mobilization and articulation of public opinion, for which return of the prisoners of war was a central demand."[24] Furthermore, it "argued consistently for mercy" toward former Nazis and for the end of the war crimes trials.[25] Josef Cardinal Frings, the archbishop of Cologne from 1942 to 1969, was particularly active in this regard. In 1951, for instance, he advocated a Christmas amnesty.

For the Catholic leadership, who were nearly as suspicious of liberal capitalism as of Marxist alternatives to it, the problem with Nazism was above all that it was a manifestation of modern materialism. In its place, they emphasized an integration of family, church, and state that they believed to be unique to the Christian West (the usual term for which was *Abendland*) in buildings the character of which space was more important than the richness or detailing of their material surfaces. This provided a viable if profoundly conservative social structure for a postfascist society, while allowing those who adopted it to evade any meaningful discussion of the degree to which those who were not devout German Christians had suffered far more at the hands of the Third Reich.[26]

In the first postwar decades the West German Catholic Church in particular enjoyed a more prestigious position than it had been able to claim since the unification of Germany in 1871, or—in the case of the Rhineland—since the French invasion of 1794. Although until 1932 the Catholic Center Party participated in all of the governments of the Weimar Republic, its role compensated only partially for the marginalized position of Catholics in Second Empire Prussia, especially during the *Kulturkampf* of the 1870s, when Bismarck temporarily imposed restrictive legislation that resulted in many bishops and priests being imprisoned or exiled.[27] The establishment of the Federal Republic in 1949 saw a shift in the political and religious leadership of the truncated country away from Prussia's Protestant heartland and toward the Catholic Rhineland.

The churches in which memory was integrated into modern architecture featured in this chapter were to some degree the architectural equivalent of the political party that commanded the loyalty of most of those involved in commissioning and designing them, even as those churches also involved the displacement to built form of issues not often openly addressed by politicians. From the founding of the state in 1949 until the election of a Social Democratic government led by Willy Brandt twenty years later, the Christian Democrats held the chancellorship and dominated the government of the Federal Republic. Under the leadership of Konrad Adenauer, who served as chancellor until 1963, they and their Bavarian allies, the Christian Social Union, adopted a pragmatic stance, adopting democracy without confronting any more than was absolutely necessary the compromised past of many of their members, government employees, and the larger society (the diplomatic corps, judiciary, and medical profession were particularly tainted).[28]

Despite the sympathy former Nazis could expect from him Cardinal Frings was similarly engaged in establishing the foundations of a profoundly conservative but by no means fascist regime. Like Adenauer, Frings, who was one of the ten men who served on the presidium for the Second Vatican Council, sought to embed the new republic in international institutions that provided a compelling alternative to generations of German nationalism. After the war, despite the Catholic prohibition on the clergy's participation in political activity, Frings indicated his support by briefly joining the new party. He retreated from secular politics only once he had ensured that the state would generously fund the two established churches, one Catholic and one Protestant.[29]

This money was key to the prominent role church construction played in the architecture of the Federal Republic in the 1950s and 1960s.[30] With most West Germans paying church tax, during the years of the so-called economic miracle both denominations were amply equipped to build. Although most new churches were not designed in an emphatically modern style, those that were garnered the lion's share of publicity. West Germany's most striking new churches were modern, but they were not examples of the International Style, which Schwarz specifically attacked as a template for postwar building in the so-called Bauhaus Debate of 1953. Although almost all of modern architecture's most vocal supporters assumed that it was uniquely appropriate for functions associated specifically with modernity, it instead proved particularly effective in serving an institution oriented toward eternity.

Catholic architects like Schwarz and Böhm, whose work was increasingly published in Germany in equal measure alongside that of their Protestant counterparts such as Bartning and Eiermann, were acknowledged to have taken the lead in developing a more consistently impressive balance between the new forms apparently mandated by new building materials and—although it was seldom mentioned—low budgets at a time of rising wages for construction labor on the one hand, and the emphasis on the creation of community through the organization of space that had long been Bartning's and Schwarz's forte on the other.[31]

Within modernism, the most important precedent for the new churches was Bruno Taut's experiments, including the Glashaus, with city crowns. Even more architects drew upon the solidity of Stuttgart's main train station, although by the late 1950s, the popularity of this model was challenged by enthusiasm for the plasticity of the Werkbund Theater. The overtly industrial aesthetic of the Model Factory, the Stuttgart Schocken store, and the Weissenhof Housing Estate—different as they were from one another—played almost no role. Instead these churches paired expressionist utopianism, now channeled away from political revolution and toward the creation of communally expressed spirituality, as well as stripped of the starkly functional form the New Building had taken during the brief economic boom of 1924–29, with the respectfully exhibited residue of the nationalism of the Second Empire and of more recent German suffering. This architecture served, as the grassroots movement to force Eiermann to preserve the ruined stump of the original Memorial Church steeple demonstrates, as much to honor the Second as neutralize the Third Reich. After all, many of those involved in building these churches remembered the years 1871 to 1914 fondly; it had been a time of bourgeois prosperity, if not of strictly democratic government (there was universal manhood suffrage, but the power of the Reichstag was carefully circumscribed with the chancellor being appointed by the emperor). This approach to fusing two architectures of the past was not in the beginning implicitly progressive or even necessarily democratic. It acquired these associations only gradually, as the Economic Miracle helped the new government acquire legitimacy and stability.

This period is often characterized as one devoid of memory, and yet when one turns to architecture that is emphatically not the case.[32] Instead one finds embedded in the overtly modernist designs of Catholic as well as Protestant churches of this period references to the Middle Ages, to the neo-medievalism of the Second Empire, to the multiple modernisms of the early twentieth century, and to the damage wrought by the Second World War. What is almost entirely absent, however, is any acknowledgment of precisely that which made many later examples of the modernist evocation of the past so powerful: the articulation of the consequences of the Third Reich for anyone other than German gentile civilians. That would take time.

The Church of the Resurrection in Pforzheim

The Church of the Resurrection in Pforzheim was aptly named as it was the first Protestant church completed in postwar Germany (Figure 2.3). The prototype for forty-three more emergency churches Bartning erected according to similar principles in both the Federal Republic and the German Democratic Republic, it descended directly from the experiments the architect had made during the Weimar Republic with a reformed church architecture but took less radical form. In particular, Bartning's decision to clad the building with stones taken from the ruins of what was one of Germany's most badly bombed cities established a sense of both literal and metaphoric continuity with a more stable past, while acknowledging the violence that had taken place.[33] A contemporary account declared, "The first new church building in Germany has grown directly out of the desertification and emergency of the borderland in Baden in the last months of the war."[34]

Although Bartning designed the Church of the Resurrection from the inside out, the facade also mattered. Here we find the same sense of understated monumentality that characterizes Stuttgart's main train station, which then as now links Pforzheim, less than fifty kilometers to the west, with Zurich and Munich to the south and east, respectively. Anchored by a squat tower added in 1954, the church sits on a slightly elevated position close to the corner of a block-long residential street just beyond the city center. This area was relatively protected from the bombing raid that on 22 February 1945 leveled 80 percent of the city's buildings and killed a third of its population.[35] The stone exterior walls, which incorporate decorative fragments from an assortment of mostly unidentified prewar buildings, including Gothic churches, provide a comforting sense of vaguely medieval stability even as they reference the city's destruction. They thus double as a memorial for the physical fabric of the city, if not necessarily for those who lost their lives. The reuse of the stones, whose random character is clearer on the sides than the front of the building, was hardly surprising considering that the church was built in extremely difficult economic and social conditions.[36] Indeed, the congregation began to assemble this building material even before Bartning arrived on the scene. Subsequently, he constructed the exteriors of his emergency churches entirely of brick, also typically salvaged. Here he reserved that material for the interior walls.

The defining feature of these buildings was not the use of rubble but a standardized system of prefabricated wooden trusses. These were employed with only relatively minor variations, often with little or even no on-site input from Bartning himself.[37] Although factory made, their angled forms and variegated surfaces shared little with the industrial aesthetic on display at the Weissenhof (in this they are much like Alvar Aalto's bent plywood furniture). In Pforzheim Bartning arranged them to provide a slightly raised polygonal rather than flat altar end; a band of windows separates the brick interior walls from the timber roof (Figure 2.4). The effect of the space, which is divided only by the arrangement of pews on both sides of a

Figure 2.3. Otto Bartning, Church of the Resurrection, Pforzheim, 1948. Source: Livia Hurley.

Inserting Memory into Modern Architecture 43

Figure 2.4.   Interior, Church of the Resurrection. Source: Foto Marburg.

central aisle and the very slight elevation of choir and altar above the nave, is warm and intimate.

For Bartning and for his Protestant clients, such spaces in which worshippers were not divided from one another, and only slightly from their pastors, were the template for a vision of community that was originally conceived as an alternative to democratic government, but would come to serve as a template for it. German Protestants had codified the belief that spatial unity fostered social cohesion in the Wiesbaden Program of 1891, which declared:

> The unity of the community and the principle of universal priesthood should be expressed in the unity of the space. There must be no division of the latter into several aisles, nor a distinction between nave, aisle, and choir. . . . Communion should not occur in a separate, cordoned off space, but in the midst of the congregation. Hence the altar, which should be designed with an ambulatory, must therefore be positioned accordingly, at least symbolically. All sightlines should lead towards the self-same.[38]

Almost all postwar German churches shared this spatial strategy, as well as relatively inexpensive construction techniques that downplayed any but the most abstract recall of history on the part of even the most conservative architect, clergyman, or parish.

Bartning was undoubtedly selected as the architect of the Church of the Resurrection because during the Weimar Republic he had been Germany's most prominent advocate of the reform of the design of Protestant churches. This must have impressed the American and Swiss donors who funded the construction of the emergency churches in what was an important early step in welcoming what became the Federal Republic into a larger community.[39] While the emergency churches reprised many aspects of Bartning's Weimar-era theory and practice, the substitution of masonry and wood for steel and concrete did much to make them more acceptable to middle-class parishioners. At the same time, the explosion in new church construction across Western Europe and North America in the first two postwar decades focused increased international attention on Bartning's prewar achievements, which in tandem with the emergency church project helped him become one of the leaders of the architectural profession in the Federal Republic. More than any other Protestant architect who had remained in Germany during the Third Reich, Bartning thus represented a welcome continuity with architectural reforms that were now being posited, not always correctly, as the antithesis of Nazi architecture.[40]

As a glance at the pages of any German architectural journal published during the fifties shows, most postwar buildings were anything but radical. Manfred Sack, an architectural historian, has written of the buildings of these years:

> The architects of the Nazi era (very few had needed to emigrate) were now the architects of reconstruction. The principle of the times was to build sparingly, simply, modestly. It was not an aesthetic principle but a realistic one of which aesthetic advantage was taken, especially in architecture. What was built was not inclusive or innovative, as high modernism with its expressionistic cascades of fantasy had been; after WWII and its devastation, no one could afford that luxury. There were no visionaries, only pragmatists.[41]

The practical approach Bartning took in his churches, where he emphasized ease of construction over his earlier embrace of first expressionism and then the New Building, squared with the spirit of the age, which was fed up with extreme experimentation of any kind.

In his youth Bartning had not been so timid. It was this combination of earlier radicalism and contemporary caution that ensured his postwar success. In 1919, at the age of thirty-six, he published *Vom neuen Kirchenbau*.[42] The book established his reputation as an expressionist-inspired reformer. Here he focused above all on the use of space to draw congregations together in an empathetic experience of shared worship and on the provision of facilities to sustain a sense of community. All this was intended to enable the church to provide the social bulwark that the weak new

Inserting Memory into Modern Architecture 45

Figure 2.5. Otto Bartning, Steel Church, Cologne, 1928. Source: Paul Girkon, *Die Stahlkirche* (Berlin: Furche-Kunstverlag, 1928).

republican government could not provide. Three years later his "star church" project for a building whose eccentric roof structure crowned a floor that sloped theater-style down toward a raised altar consolidated his reputation for experimentation. Three churches—the steel-framed Presse church built for an exhibition in Cologne in 1928, which was demounted and reerected in Essen, where it was destroyed in the war (Figure 2.5); the circular concrete-framed Church of the Resurrection, consecrated in Essen in 1930; and the more conservative but larger concrete-and-brick Gustav Adolf Church, completed in Berlin in 1934—consolidated his reputation.[43] Much more than the emergency churches, they were widely published internationally into the 1960s in collections of modern church architecture targeted at congregations as well as their architects.[44] Bartning's credentials were further burnished by his leadership of the institution that replaced the Bauhaus in Weimar after the experimental art school was forced to move to Dessau.[45] Like his use of modern industrial materials and his eschewal of any ornament except large areas of stained glass, this role confirmed his association with the New Building at the same time that it established his distance from what those suspicious of it saw as its unnecessary stridency.

The Resurrection Church was consecrated on 24 October 1948, seven months before the Federal Republic was established. It is unlikely that its neighbors compared it to a factory, as did those of the Gustav Adolf Church, who nicknamed it "the Jesus Christ Power Plant," but its completion did confirm Bartning's status.[46] From 1950 until his death in 1959 he was the president of the Bund Deutscher Architekten (BDA), the country's foremost professional organization for architects.[47] The Swiss journal *Werk* described him as having been selected because of "his artistic worth and the spiritual and human integrity of his personality."[48] In addition to his official duties he continued to publish on the subject of church architecture and played a key role in the early "Darmstädter Gespräche."[49] This series of symposia, inaugurated in 1950, brought philosophers and other intellectuals, very much including architects, together in an attempt to establish the underpinnings of a reformed society. Bartning moderated the second Darmstadter Gespräch. Held in 1951, it famously featured Martin Heidegger's presentation titled "On Dwelling." Although Bartning gave a platform to a philosopher who notoriously never apologized for his early enthusiasm for the Third Reich and who remained critical of the New Building and also extended a hand to Bonatz, by inviting Eiermann, Schwarz, Schwippert, and Scharoun, he also provided a forum for those who would be instrumental in developing the postfascist face of West German architecture.[50]

The Resurrection Church is a small and relatively staid building, but its simultaneous ties to Pforzheim's prewar architecture, out of whose ruins it was literally built, and to some of the most innovative interwar thinking about sacred architecture established the slightly contradictory approach upon which Bartning's successors would continue to build the sacred infrastructure of the Federal Republic.

St. Anna in Düren

The Catholic Church of St. Anna in Düren was, like the Church of the Resurrection in Pforzheim, constructed out of rubble and designed by an architect who had established his reputation for innovative church design during the Weimar Republic (Figure 2.6). Rather than being a prototype for a building that could be erected in the immediate aftermath of the war with relatively little outside assistance and at a rock-bottom cost, however, St. Anna was an imposing structure that immediately attracted international attention as one of Europe's best new churches. The memories evoked here were also more specific, as the stone came from the Gothic church on the site that had been destroyed during the war and because the plan of the church quoted Schwarz's Corpus Christi Church. Designed in collaboration with Schwippert and completed in nearby Aachen in 1930, it was widely regarded as one of the most important Catholic churches erected during the Weimar Republic (Figure 2.7).[51]

The political context in Düren was very different from that addressed by Bartning. Although the design of St. Anna was largely the response of a pious pilgrim to a site he venerated, it came to stand, especially abroad, for a progressive,

Inserting Memory into Modern Architecture

Figure 2.6.   Rudolf Schwarz, St. Anna Church, Düren, 1956. Source: Livia Hurley.

internationally oriented Federal Republic. Bartning erected emergency churches in eastern cities like Rostock and Stralsund, but the German Democratic Republic was historically Protestant and no important Catholic churches were constructed there. Furthermore, although many new Catholic churches were built in southern

Figure 2.7. Rudolf Schwarz and Hans Schwippert, Corpus Christi Church, Aachen, 1930. Source: Livia Hurley.

Germany, the most celebrated Catholic architects, including Schwarz, were active above all in the Rhineland and the neighboring Ruhr region, where they enjoyed the support of Cardinal Frings. Cologne, whose postwar planning Schwarz directed, was also the political stronghold of another conservative reformer. Adenauer, who placed the capital of the Federal Republic just to the south in Bonn, had been its mayor from 1917 to 1933.

Unlike the Church of the Resurrection, whose site is suburban, St. Anna stands at the center of a plaza in the middle of the small city of Düren. Located near the German border with Belgium and the Netherlands, roughly halfway between Aachen and Cologne, Düren was badly bombed on 16 November 1944, when its most important church was completely destroyed. The L-shaped replacement, erected after the revival of the Marshall Plan–fueled German economy was well under way, is far larger and more obviously modern than Bartning's modest building. Schwarz claimed that it was in its day the largest stone building under construction in Europe; the imposing masonry is broken only by the perforations over the altar, symbolic of the Tree of Life, and the large areas of clerestory glazing tucked inside the angle of the L (Figure 2.8).[52] The adjacent bell tower, designed by Schwarz's widow Maria and Erwin Drese, was added between 1963 and 1965.

Since 1501, the parish of St. Anna has owned a reliquary containing the skull of

Inserting Memory into Modern Architecture 49

Figure 2.8. Interior, St. Anna Church. Source: Livia Hurley.

its patron saint. The city's leading parish church thus doubles as a place of pilgrimage. Following the plan of Corpus Christi Church in Aachen, Schwarz designed a low aisle to the right of the main nave to accommodate the relic and its pilgrims. As it reaches the altar end of this building, this aisle flares out slightly to meet the single transept, an element not present in Aachen. Schwarz carefully conceived the church to give maximum visual access to the altar, which sits on a stepped podium and can be approached from all four sides.

Since the 1920s, Schwarz had worked closely with the liturgical reformer and theologian Romano Guardini. Guardini's book *The Spirit of the Liturgy,* first published in 1918, emphasized the shared experience of the celebration of the Mass over personal devotion and drew particular attention to the community it created.[53] For Schwarz this meant an undivided space in which no choir separated the nave from the freestanding altar. At Corpus Christi he and Schwippert paired the execution of this spatial strategy with a radical simplification of form that clearly tied them to the New Building and the International Style. The church's spare white stucco surfaces would not have been out of place at the Weissenhof; its bell tower could almost have been a factory smokestack. Only the black stone flooring, out of which the altar was also crafted, communicates the sense of permanence conveyed by the Stuttgart train station's more obviously primeval stonework.

Like Bartning, in his postwar architecture Schwarz moved away from the extremes of his earlier work. Words he wrote his friend Mies in 1948 regarding his plan for Cologne could stand as well for the approach he would take in Düren:

> In principal I am, as I ever more observe, a very conservative man, who finds it ever more difficult to believe in the visions of some of our modernist friends. It is terrible how much growth has been destroyed; this applies to each memory of the past's expensive stones, as well as to the coherence of the body politic.[54]

St. Anna was much darker than the glowing box of Corpus Christi. More than Bartning and much like Bonatz, Schwarz now emphasized the integrity of materials; he left the structural stone walls of the church exposed on both interior and exterior. He did not forsake technology, however. The clerestory windows have an industrial character; the flat roof and the braces that support it are both bare concrete. Finally, as in Aachen, the lighting fixtures consist of chains to which he attached naked bulbs.

Schwarz characteristically emphasized the theological dimension of his plan over its stylistic execution. He described the form of the building as being like the open coat of St. Anna. Standing for maternal love and eternal goodness, this coat, "brightest at the altar where the light comes from two sides," was "to wrap people in its embrace and take them to heart."[55] Note that Schwarz crafted it out of immaterial light rather than the solid stone that defined the outer edges of the building. Nonetheless, for parishioners the fact that the walls of the new church shared the same color and texture as those of its predecessor, even as they were reconfigured into new forms that paradoxically appeared more archaic and thus more permanent, was quite likely to have been immensely reassuring. Because the relic, too, had miraculously endured, one could now add personal as well as communal, rather unspecific, prayers for forgiveness and redemption to the pleas for intercession that had long been made to the saint.

Schwarz was the most consistently lauded abroad of all his German church-building contemporaries, with St. Anna almost certainly the most widely publicized and highly praised example of their work. It was included in books that appeared in Great Britain and the United States, the countries most responsible for the destruction of its predecessor, and in collections of new church buildings targeted specifically at Protestant congregations and their designers.[56] Kidder Smith was especially enthusiastic. He called it "one of the most magnificent statements yet achieved by today's religious architecture." "Schwarz," he wrote, "in a remarkable spatial sequence, takes us into St Anna under a low pilgrimage wing then hurls us with stunning force against the sheer high wall of the nave. This progression from the low and dim to the lofty and bright almost shatters by its intensity."[57]

None of this praise outweighed the utility of associating the de-Nazification of architecture in the Federal Republic with the supposed ascendancy of the International Style. And few expressed more outright opposition to this equation than

Schwarz himself. In 1953 he triggered an uproar over the issue in the pages of the journal *Baukunst und Werkform*.[58] Instead of blaming the Nazis alone for what he perceived to be the faults in contemporary architecture, he also attacked the architecture of the Weimar Republic, including the Bauhaus. He claimed that the best in German architecture was predicated upon the less strident reforms embodied in van de Velde's, Taut's, and Gropius's contributions to the Werkbund Exhibition in 1914. Tradition, if not historicism, mattered to Schwarz, who praised the lingering influence of the Gothic upon Bartning and the antique upon Mies. Schwarz admitted Gropius's talents as an architect, and that he had nothing against the Bauhaus's painters, but he doubted that the school's rhetoric, and in particular the stress it placed upon functionalism, was matched by the properties of the objects designed there.[59]

This explicit retreat from the affiliation with the International Style he had courted during the last years of the Weimar Republic indisputably compromised Schwarz's standing with younger architects. By picking a feud with Gropius, he ensured that, no matter how greatly he would be respected by architects and architectural critics within the Federal Republic, his work would stand slightly to the side of that being championed by the founder of the Bauhaus as the appropriate face of a democratic Germany.[60] Yet although no longer an adherent of the International Style, Schwarz remained firmly committed to modern architecture, which he defined far more inclusively than Gropius. His modernist credentials were burnished by the fact that there remained a less modern alternative. For example, his churches were not published and seldom referred to in the pages of *Baumeister*, the house organ of the BDA, the group led by Bartning. Its editors preferred—when they published Catholic churches at all—the work of Schwarz's former assistant Emil Steffann, which drastically simplified medieval precedent.[61]

Schwarz's reputation was also sustained by the loyalty of Mies, whose reputation in the postwar years quickly eclipsed that of Gropius as the most celebrated of all German-born architects. In 1947 a startled but pleased Schwarz wrote Mies to thank him for the care package that had arrived out of the blue on his fiftieth birthday:

> It was a great joy and surprise for me. We aren't doing particularly well; we hardly have the most important things and also sometimes not even these, and the winter was difficult.[62]

He wrote of a second, received more than a year later, "Your package, which recently arrived here, was a great joy to me, as it showed that you still remember me."[63] The continued support of Mies, who had immigrated to Chicago in 1938, from where he wrote the introduction to the American edition of Schwarz's book, *The Church Incarnate: The Sacred Function of Christian Architecture,* ensured that the impact of the Bauhaus debate on his German reputation did not extend to the English-speaking world.[64] First published in Germany in 1938, *The Church Incarnate* solidified Schwarz's importance for Guardini's many American disciples in particular.

The parallels between the paths taken during the first years of the Federal Republic in the Rhineland by Adenauer and Schwarz, charged respectively with the economic and political reconstruction of western Germany and the literal rebuilding of Cologne, as well as the design of many of its archdiocese's churches, are striking.[65] Having neither embraced the Third Reich nor engaged in active resistance to it, both men provided a less threatening way forward than did Socialist politicians like Brandt, who had consistently opposed Hitler, or émigré architects like Gropius, who was closely allied with the American occupation.[66] And both men stepped slightly back from more overtly radical positions they had taken during the Weimar Republic in order to engage broader public support for fundamental change. Schwarz himself was nearly as alert to Cold War politics as Adenauer. In 1947, two years before the establishment of the Federal Republic, Schwarz wrote Mies:

> We stand on the Rhine, exactly as said in Cologne and Frankfurt, on the last line of retreat of the Occident [*Abendland*]; behind us is nothing more, and the Occident hears us from a distance of a hundred kilometers. One feels like a solider who holds the final post that can still be defended, and no longer asks if he can maintain it.... We must in a short while muster what still is able to be snatched; again a last shimmer of the old sinking light over the world (our world, which becomes so small) allows us to illuminate, so that the old people still once see how base they are and take in that remembrance of what awaits them.[67]

While Adenauer is often accused of sponsoring amnesia, however, Schwarz encouraged remembering, if not of the Third Reich, then certainly of two very different alternatives to it. The first of these was a nearly timeless but overtly Christian past that stretched back to before the time of Charlemagne, whose Palatine Chapel stood less than forty kilometers west of Düren, the second that of the move toward liturgical reform with which he had already been affiliated during the Weimar Republic. Stripped of its most radical stylistic trappings, the core of Schwarz's approach, which was always primarily spatial, made the eternal modern and the modern eternal.

The Kaiser Wilhelm Memorial Church in Berlin

St. Anna served as a symbol of the Federal Republic, but this was only a by-product of Schwarz's intention to design a church that promoted a sense of shelter and community and thus functioned as a sanctuary where the psychological as well as physical damage wrought by the war, and also by the Third Reich, could begin to be healed. In both its pre- and postwar incarnations, however, the Kaiser Wilhelm

Inserting Memory into Modern Architecture 53

Figure 2.9.   Kaiser Wilhelm Memorial Church. Source: Livia Hurley.

Memorial Church was as much an emblem of the state than simply a house of worship. The specifics of what was being both remembered through the reuse of an older architecture and recalled through the quotation of expressionist and other modernist precedents were also far more politically significant than the generic evocation of a timeless past and the dependence upon the architects' earlier work found in the Church of the Resurrection and St. Anna. The Memorial Church was one of many West German churches in which ruins were paired with new construction, but the degree to which its ruins were emphatically nationalist and their reconstruction became a symbol of capitalism remained unique, as does the attention paid by so many over such a sustained period of time to what should be done with the site. Bartning and Schwarz had enjoyed relatively free hands in Pforzheim and Düren; Eiermann, in contrast, operated in a field restricted in part by Berlin city planners and church authorities but above all by a popular outcry against his intention to demolish the ruined steeple of the original structure.

Few buildings so emphatically embodied the close relationship between the church and state in Germany during the Second Empire and the first decades of the Federal Republic as the Memorial Church (Figure 2.9). Erected with the help of private donations that symbolized loyalty to the relatively new imperial order, and rebuilt with the help of a generous grant from the government of West Berlin, the site morphed in the wake of the severe damage it sustained during World War II from being a symbol of German unification to representing capitalist West Berlin; only slowly did it acquire its current status as evidence of the futility of war.[68] Following a competition held in 1890, construction of the Kaiser Wilhelm Memorial Church began in 1891 and was largely completed four years later, although the entrance hall was not consecrated until 1906. Its postwar reconstruction was completed in 1963, two full decades after the bombing of the original building.

The original church's neo-Romanesque style corresponded quite closely to the taste of its patron, the German emperor Wilhelm II, who built it to honor his grandfather Wilhelm I, the first emperor of a united Germany. He was so pleased with the result that he commissioned Franz Schwechten, its architect, to design the Imperial Castle in Posen (now Poznan, Poland) for him. Wilhelm II favored a style that recalled the imperial architecture of the Holy Roman Empire in the tenth and eleventh centuries. Although this Romanesque Revivalism overlapped with and was influenced by both the American architect Henry Hobson Richardson and the National Romanticism popular across Scandinavia, the Memorial Church was more literally historicist than those contemporary sources.[69] The choice of Romanesque celebrated the achievements of the Ottonian, Salian, and Staufer dynasties of Holy Roman emperors, who reigned before control of the empire was ceded in 1452 to the Hapsburgs in Vienna.

Few societies have taken memorial culture as seriously as Second Empire Germany (one of its few rivals in this respect is the Federal Republic since the reunification of Germany in 1990). The Memorial Church was one of the many large and often bombastic structures, mostly designed in a vaguely Romanesque style that often also implied that they had somehow emerged through geological processes out of the surrounding landscape, that were erected by supporters both of the kaiser and of his rival Otto von Bismarck.[70] Many celebrated German unity (for which credit was split between Wilhelm I, in the kaiser's view, and Bismarck, in that of many of his subjects), medieval heroes, and allegorical figures. Located on prominent hillside sites as well as in the centers of cities and public parks, they provided the backdrop to middle-class leisure and were focal points for the burgeoning tourist industry.[71] The ceremonies involved in their groundbreaking and dedications created occasions attended by a wide array of people, from royal and local dignitaries to ordinary citizens, to participate in the civic rituals that created a sense of being German, rather than Prussian, Bavarian, or Hessian. Kaiser Wilhelm II laid the foundation stone of the Memorial Church on what would have been his grandfather's ninety-sixth birthday. Its originally martial as well as imperial status was confirmed when it was dedicated in the presence of dignitaries including the kaiser, his wife, the grand duke and duchess of Baden, and the king of Saxony, on the twenty-fifth anniversary of Sedan, the key German victory in the Franco-Prussian War.[72]

The church was vulnerable to criticism from the beginning. A conservative contemporary said of its subordination of religion to the state, "One builds churches in order to destroy the church."[73] The memorial culture it embodied would quickly seem outmoded, even pompous, to those like Bonatz, who in the early years of the new century began to advocate a new simplicity in German architecture. Although these reformers were often ardent patriots, none were close to the kaiser or his court. Indeed, the kaiser was an outspoken opponent of the new architecture.[74] By the end of the 1920s there were already calls to demolish the building, ostensibly because it was an obstacle to the speed of automobile traffic, but almost certainly as well because the café and cabaret culture that flourished along the Kurfürstendamm, which had already in Wilhelmine times excelled at poking fun at imperial taste, was, following the demise of the Second Empire, taking aim at its most prominent local relic.[75]

One indication of the gap between the slightly older Memorial Church and the new direction in art and design was the degree to which the interior of the former was encrusted with mosaics by Hermann Schaper celebrating the Hohenzollern dynasty. Although technically a Byzantine art form that was seldom employed in medieval Germany, mosaics with gold backgrounds were a prominent aspect of neomedieval religious architecture in the Second Empire. Their imperial associations were highlighted following the restoration in the early 1880s of the mosaics in the Palatine Chapel in Aachen, originally built by Charlemagne.[76] The mosaics in the vestibule of the Memorial Church glorified the Hohenzollerns. Their mixture of neorealist portrait detail and lavish historicist ornament was an example of exactly the eclecticism reformers deplored, while the focus on the dynasty's political and military greatness, was already called into question by Socialists before Germany's defeat in World War I.[77] When bombs shattered the nave on 23 November 1943, the vestibule mosaics were left largely intact, ensuring that the original political context of the church remained clear to all who took a close look at its ruins.

Although it would seldom be mentioned in the postwar debates about whether or not to demolish the church's ruined steeple (there was little dissent regarding the apse), the appointment in 1930 of Gerhard Jacobi as the church's pastor probably had a bearing on its fate. Jacobi, who was partly of Jewish ancestry, became one of the leaders of the Protestant clergy opposed to the Third Reich. He was subjected to beating, house arrest, and court cases, all of which were reported in the international press, and, although his stance was probably not as widely known within the country as a whole, it would certainly have been familiar to his former parishioners. After the war he became bishop of Oldenburg; in 1959 he was encouraged to become a candidate for the presidency of the Federal Republic, an honor he declined in favor of remaining active within the church.[78]

Thus by the time it was bombed, the Memorial Church no longer conveyed a univalent message. A symbol of German unification, closely allied with the militarism through which it had been achieved, the church had first been dismissed as outmoded and then become a site of principled resistance to a far more dangerous version of the nationalism that had produced it. Whether the destruction of much of the building by bombs cleansed it of its original associations and converted the remains into a symbol of wartime destruction and victimhood was the key question surrounding the discussion of its being rebuilt on the same site and, if it were, whether the ruins should be preserved.[79]

Three different constituencies participated in what was perhaps postwar Germany's most vociferous debate over architecture and planning. First was the church. Because this was the largest and most prominently sited church in West Berlin, the deliberation included the local Protestant leadership, as well as the parish authorities and secular luminaries, such as Prince Louis Ferdinand, Wilhelm II's grandson. Although insistent that it be rebuilt on the original site, church officials wavered about the importance of retaining the traces of the original structure.[80] Second was the architectural community. Here there was near unanimity that the ruins be demolished and a nearly equally strong sense that the church be rebuilt on a different site. Finally there was the public, as featured in local newspapers; residents of West Berlin apparently overwhelmingly supported the retention of the ruins. Each group found in the site, the ruins, and the possibility of a new building a container for its own cherished memories, but there was little consensus regarding what should be remembered and why. Democracy brought with it the ability to voice dissenting opinions; the outcry over the Memorial Church was one of the first in a long line of controversies about architecture that would mark the maturation of the Federal Republic, of which West Berlin was not strictly a part, but whose political culture it largely shared.[81] Eiermann himself commented sardonically, "Unfortunately, our so-called democracy excels at allowing many people to think that they can discuss things that they do not understand."[82]

The discussions over the site's fate took place between 1947 and 1958.[83] Neil Gregor, who insists that "the past was always present in post-war West Germany," notes that "a critical, confrontational memory politics was not compatible with the reconstitution of a functioning civil society; conversely, only once this civil society had been re-established, as it had been by the 1950s, could the possibility of a more critical discussion be entertained."[84] The debate was inseparable from the building's particular position in Berlin and the division of the city following the Second World War. The Memorial Church stands near the beginning of the Kurfürstendamm, the new boulevard that became the premier commercial artery of the west end of the city in the final years of the nineteenth century. Its original position was on a traffic island surrounded by apartments; the scale and spectacle of its neighbors were ratcheted up first during the building boom of the late 1920s and again by reconstruction after the Second World War as what had been an expensive residential district became almost entirely commercialized.[85] Although the bifurcation of West and East Berlin by the Berlin Wall occurred only in August 1961, the division of the city into four sectors, and the joint administration of the American, British, and French sectors as West Berlin, resulted in the area around the church becoming the focus of a new downtown. By the 1950s office buildings as well as entertainment clustered around it, while hotels, luxury shops, and restaurants lined much of the adjacent boulevard.

The fate of the damaged church began to be addressed even before the establishment of the Federal Republic and its Communist counterpart, the German Democratic Republic of which East Berlin became the capital, when an inconclusive competition for the area was held in 1947. Seven years later a design commissioned by the church leadership from Werner March, who suggested a simplified reconstruction of the original building, satisfied few (Figure 2.10).[86] The Cultural Circle of the Federal Union of German Industry was so disturbed that it wrote, in protest, "The March design offers no apparent evidence of the artistic forcefulness exemplary of the modern German desire to build. It lacks the spirit of modern artistic will."[87] Two more years elapsed before the parish sponsored a competition with the hope of finally arriving at a definitive solution for rebuilding on the original site. This emerged only slowly. Expressing dissatisfaction with the original entries, the jury, which included Bartning, invited three of the teams to compete in a second stage. Eiermann, who like Schwarz had studied in Berlin with Hans Poelzig in the 1920s, won by submitting a lightly revised version of his highly regarded St. Matthew's Church in Pforzheim, whose concrete incorporated chunks of rubble.[88]

The publication of Eiermann's winning design for the Memorial Church in 1957, which entailed the demolition of the entire remains of the original building, triggered torrents of commentary, most of it negative, in the Berlin press (Figure 2.11).[89] Although it was accepted by the parish and praised by Eiermann's many supporters in the architectural community, opinion polls revealed that the vast majority of Berliners opposed it. After the *Tageszeitung,* a local newspaper, sponsored a poll that recorded more than forty-five thousand votes for retaining a tower to less than a thousand against, even Willy Brandt, West Berlin's newly elected mayor, said that he would regret its demolition.[90] In the teeth of this opposition, the already somewhat ambivalent client quickly caved in, and Eiermann was forced, much against his will, to rework his site plan to preserve the ruined vestibule and steeple of the original building.

The limitations placed on Eiermann are particularly noteworthy considering his stature at the time. He was the foremost exponent in the early years of the Federal Republic of building upon foundations laid by the New Building and brought up to date by Mies's recent American work (in a letter written in 1953, Eiermann described Mies as "the most famous architect in the world").[91] Writing in 1964 on the occasion of Eiermann's sixtieth birthday, the German architectural critic Hans Eckstein noted that during the Third Reich Eiermann had refrained from both sentimental regionalism and megalomaniac neoclassicism, focusing instead on industrial

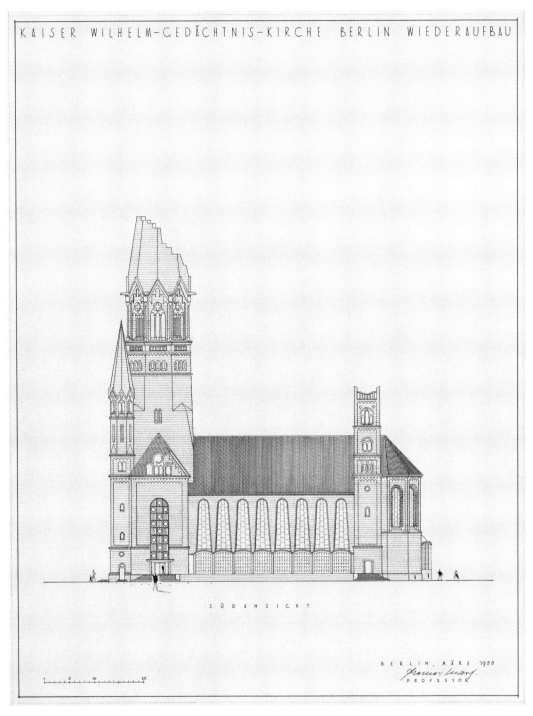

Figure 2.10. Werner March, proposed design for reconstruction of Kaiser Wilhelm Memorial Church, 1954. Source: Architectural Archive, TU Berlin.

Inserting Memory into Modern Architecture

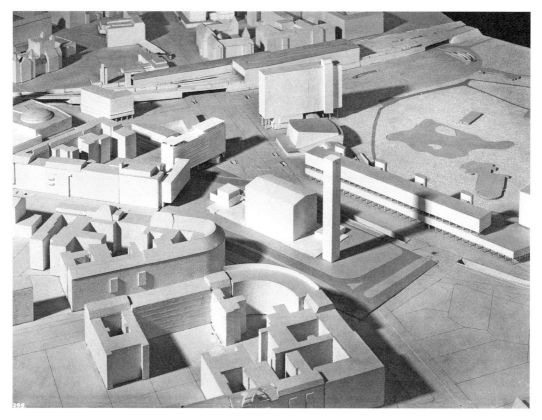

Figure 2.11. Egon Eiermann, competition design for reconstruction of Kaiser Wilhelm Memorial Church, 1957. Source: SAAI Karlsruhe.

architecture.[92] In the aftermath of the war, such loyalty to the tenets of the New Building was understood as having signaled political resistance. Although this formulation was disingenuous, to say the least, considering the role industry had played in the Nazi war effort and in Eiermann's own oeuvre, it was extremely common for decades afterward.[93] Eiermann himself noted in 1958 in relation to the German pavilion he codesigned for Brussels, "This country is burdened with so much guilt that it is very difficult to find the right tone."[94] He was not, however, above appealing to the example of the high quality of Nazi-era construction when battling for more expensive detailing in his own work.[95]

Dedicated in 1953, Eiermann's St. Matthew's Church, which he designed to be a paradigm for new Protestant churches, was one of his first postwar buildings to attract favorable attention (his earlier work had been regularly published during the Third Reich) (Figure 2.12).[96] And although derived from a factory he had designed during the Second World War for the Luftwaffe, the German pavilion at the World's Fair in Brussels in 1958 was widely heralded for offering a radical alternative to Nazi state architecture, such as Albert Speer's contributions to the World's Fair in Paris in

Figure 2.12. Egon Eiermann, St. Matthew's Church, Pforzheim, 1953. Source: Livia Hurley.

1937 and to the party parade grounds in Nuremberg, which had been constructed in part out of stone quarried by slave labor from the regime's network of concentration camps.[97] In the wake of the success of the Brussels pavilion, Eiermann became the closest thing the Federal Republic had to a state architect. In 1958 he was charged, for instance, with designing the country's embassy in Washington, D.C. Another heavily glazed structure, it was completed six years later.[98]

The Protestant church was committed above all to retaining a prominent presence in the West Berlin cityscape, but the particular form it took mattered considerably less to its leaders than it did to their architect. Nonetheless, in 1956 the pastor Günter Pohl expressed a preference for the use of modern materials: "The architects would like to serve the means given by our time; they should not be controlled by to the up-to-date materials, however, but allow themselves to make the materials useful."[99] The Protestant church had remained closely tied to the Prussian monarchy, and Protestant parishioners, despite Jacobi's principled dissent, proved more sympathetic to the National Socialists than their Catholic counterparts.[100] At parish, city, and national levels, many involved in the church were now anxious to separate themselves from its long association with German nationalism, embodied by the Memorial Church's originally largely secular decoration. Thus, although there was considerable sentimental attention to the jagged remains of the ruined steeple, which Eiermann compared to a rotten tooth, church authorities were willing to consider something very different.[101]

Although in a position to call the shots, the church authorities were clearly interested as well, however, in having public support for their decisions. They quickly backed away from March's tepid design when it was widely criticized. Indeed, engaging with public opinion was key to their new participation in the democratic process, about which Otto Dibelius, bishop of Berlin-Brandenburg and chairman of the Council of the Evangelical Church, the umbrella organization for German Protestants, had historically been skeptical.[102] Dibelius was in many ways the Protestant equivalent of Frings in the degree to which he simultaneously exerted moral leadership of his denomination at the national level and at the highest international levels, while all too often looking out for those accused, frequently with justification, of being war criminals.[103] Between 1954 and 1961, he was the president of the World Council of Churches. In the dozen years between the establishment of the German Democratic Republic and the erection of the Berlin Wall, which resulted in his being banned from traveling to the parts of his diocese that lay in the Communist east, Dibelius campaigned aggressively for the country's reunification. Unlike Adenauer, he was ready to espouse neutrality in order to achieve unity.[104]

Church officials were adamant on one point: they insisted that a church—whether or not it incorporated the ruins of the original—remain on the original site.[105] That for years, until the traffic pattern was reorganized, it was all but marooned in a sea of automobiles mattered little to them, not least because it remained relatively accessible to worshippers on Sunday mornings, when the surrounding businesses and shops were closed.[106] Above all they cherished the symbolism of being present in what was now more than ever before the heart of the city.[107] This was particularly important to them as their cathedral was in East Berlin.[108]

Architects, city planners, and those who made their living writing about the two professions were far less ambivalent. Almost all who weighed in on the matter, particularly in the pages of *Bauwelt,* which was published in West Berlin, favored the demolition of the ruins. For the architects and city planners who took this position, the Memorial Church and its imperial patron, if not necessarily his grandfather, were objects of ridicule. Only a modern building, preferably on another site, could embody Christianity rather than the poor taste and failed policies of Wilhelm II.[109] The architectural historian Gustav Adolf Platz declared in 1947 that "we architects will shed no tears over [its proposed demolition]."[110] Three years later Hans Josef Zechlin described it as "more of an exhibition of the glorification of the Hohenzollerns than arising from the glorification of God."[111] In 1957 another architectural critic, Hans Eckstein, while admitting that the ruin was more imposing than the original, declared that "today no one regards this church building as worthy of preservation because of its artistic worth. However, since [its destruction] it has become the object of love for the native place, which like love overall is so often blind to ugliness."[112] The professional and the international press were both careful to point out, when critiquing his design, that March was the architect of the Berlin Olympic Stadium, thus drawing attention to his ties to the National Socialists (he had designed the stadium before the Nazis came to power but joined the party quickly afterward).[113] This was an unusual strategy at a time when the German architectural community was generally silent about the degree to which it had collaborated with a building-obsessed dictator, but March was equally unusual in proposing a simplified and still historicist version of the original church rather than a more overtly modernist design.

Although the debate over the ruins of the Memorial Church was framed in terms of popular sentiment versus modernist architectural and city planning orthodoxy, those who supported demolition were certainly aware of the building's original nationalist context, and it can be assumed that their opponents were as well. At a time when the adoption of modernism was often considered crucial to purging the professions to which they belonged of associations with the Third Reich, the German middle class was far more hesitant to express contrition through embracing forms that seemed—quite rightly—to be partly an expression of their current poverty.[114] Despite the leading role architects from the Federal Republic continued to play in the creation of modern sacred architecture, congregations were often less than enthusiastic about the results. While more radical designs played well in international publications of recent church design, some German architectural publications, such as *Baumeister,* mocked precisely the buildings most often showcased abroad.[115] Even *Bauwelt,* which supported more adventurous designs, occasionally reported on the misgivings the general public often had about modernist churches.[116] The specific situation of the Memorial Church made it easier to voice such reservations, particularly when they could be couched in terms of creating a monument to the destruction wrought by war.

The reasons, said and unsaid, for supporting the retention of the ruins were diverse. Demographic change probably played an unspoken role. During the Third Reich many of those who would have been unsympathetic to both the church's style and iconography had been either forced into exile or murdered. What had been before 1933 partially an alternative scene, in which bourgeois tenants and avant-garde intellectuals, often in both cases Jewish, coexisted in rather amicable distinction to the stuffier center of aristocratic, bureaucratic, and military authority running from the imperial palace and Museum Island along Unter den Linden to the Reichstag and Tiergarten, became after 1945 a great deal more conventional, and almost entirely Christian.[117] Although few of those who opposed Eiermann's design expressed overt admiration for the builders of the original church, the surrounding neighborhood was far more conservative than it had been thirty years earlier. It certainly contained more than a few who viewed the Second—and probably also the Third—Reich with considerable nostalgia. Many of its now staunchly anticommunist inhabitants had recently left East Berlin, the German Democratic Republic, and formerly German territory farther to the east.

The preservation of the mute and shattered stones of the original Memorial Church almost certainly indicated a respect for rather than a challenge to the nationalism that had produced the original church, even as new, more acceptable, and thus more openly voiced meanings were layered onto it. The debate not only allowed West Berliners to challenge a prominent modern architect and a Protestant church that had moved uncomfortably far to the left, but also gave them a platform to articulate a nostalgia for a discredited nationalism that would otherwise have been almost impossible to articulate.[118] That the building was no longer intact helped. Many concurred with Eckstein, who wrote in 1957, "The ruin is unquestionably more imposing than the intact church building was. Only this makes it understandable that one has come upon the idea to at least preserve the steeple as a kind of memorial to Berlin's destruction."[119]

Newspaper accounts from 1957 echoed these sentiments and often stressed the benign way in which the building was regarded. The *Spandauer Volksblatt* set the tone:

> The old Memorial Church was no work of art; it was not "beautiful" (the "beauty" of the new church also will be much debated!). The ruin of the old church, however, which was treated terribly and is yet steadfast, began to symbolize the rough will of the Berliners, who, in looking upon it, took it to heart. At the beginning a ruin among ruins. And then witness to the "better life," first made visible exactly in the Zoo neighborhood, a memorial of Berlin's most difficult houses in the middle of the glamorous reconstruction, in short the landmark of the city.[120]

Der Tag concurred, describing the steeple as "a reminder of our disastrous past," which had become "a world-famous landmark" of the city. The *Morgenpost* and *Telegraf* (which also termed it a "monument") noted the scarcity of such steeples.[121] Moreover, as the reporter for *Der Kurier* noted, the tower of the Memorial Church was a symbol not of Berlin but of "free Berlin."[122] Echoing the sentiment that the church's meaning had shifted with the emergence of the new prosperity surrounding it, a second article in the *Telegraf* lauded it as "a piece of shredded building that stands as the war left it. A remaining memorial against the horror of the nights of bombings, against the arbitrary, against the violence, absolutely against Germany's darkest history," which is here, characteristically for the period, understood as military defeat and the sufferings of civilians rather than an acknowledgment of the murderous violence perpetrated by the Third Reich.[123]

Eiermann noted that "most of us associate the Memorial Church with friendly memories of our youth in a lighthearted time and as symbolic of the bitter times of the war."[124] He struggled, however, with the degree to which he and the church leadership should be responsive to public opinion, terming it "close to the grotesque."[125] And he believed that "this stump really can stand for only a few years, and that the new generation will have no understanding of the current clinginess."[126]

There were clearly contemporary political reasons for supporting retaining the ruins, as well. Memories of the church's original function increasingly gave way to new considerations as West Berliners worked to distinguish themselves from their East German neighbors. This change of heart took place in the context of Berlin's centrality to the Cold War. Following the 17 June 1953 uprising against the Soviets in East Berlin, culture—and particularly architecture—became an important battleground in the conflict between East and West Berlin and between East and West Germany.[127] While the attention of most historians has remained focused on housing and city planning, that is the difference between the Stalin (now Karl Marx) Allee in the east and the new Hansaviertel (Interbau) in the West, the campaign to retain Schwechten's tower was another skirmish in the same conflict.[128]

Two of the most obvious policy differences between the two Germanys, and between the two halves of Berlin, were the approaches they took to religion and to historic preservation. While the Christian Democratic (CDU) party dominated the government of the Federal Republic in its initial two decades, the East German Communists were avowedly secular. In the Federal Republic and in West Berlin, war-damaged churches were quickly repaired or rebuilt as part of the respect for religion that characterized most of the society. In the east meanwhile, reconstruction proceeded slowly at best and entirely new church buildings were extremely rare.[129] Furthermore, while the East Germans scorned the relics of the Hohenzollerns, demolishing the Royal Palace in 1950 and its Potsdam counterpart in 1959–60, West Berliners rallied to preserve a church dominated by associations with the dynasty.[130] The British, French, and American sectors had few historic buildings from earlier periods; there was no landmark along the Kurfürstendamm older than the Memorial Church.

Conservative political undertones were clear in many of the published comments, and retaining the steeple mattered more to the old than the young.[131] A husband and wife from Wilmersdorf wrote to *Der Tag,* insisting that "it would be an outrage of the worst sort, if the landmark of Berlin was destroyed the same way as the Palace. . . . A modern new building can never compensate for the old historic one. One asks oneself if we are living in a 'dictatorship of the new.'"[132] A retired teacher wrote to the same paper that "strangers who visit Berlin will never muster love for the planned 'exclamation mark' to be built of concrete. The old church was loved. . . . Quiet tears for a lost piece of my adored father-city Berlin."[133] A refugee wrote that he "loved Berlin with its Kurfürstendamm and the ruins of the Memorial Church as much as his former homeland."[134] And yet there were always dissenters. One

Inserting Memory into Modern Architecture 65

Figure 2.13. Dieter Oesterlen, Christ Church, Bochum, 1959. Source: Hans-Jürgen Wiese/Wikipedia Commons.

commentator concluded, "One who witnessed the construction of the Schwechten church hit the nail on the head when he pronounced that this church was always only symbolic and never a spiritual center. That is objective and exactly the truth that every old Berliner will confirm."[135]

As a result of the outcry, Eiermann was forced to reconfigure his design, which he did with Bartning's active encouragement and support.[136] The pairing of surviving neomedieval steeples with modern architecture was relatively common in the Federal Republic, especially in the Rhineland and Ruhr region. Prominent examples include the Protestant Christ Church in Bochum (Dieter Oesterlen, 1959) and the Catholic St. Rochus in Düsseldorf (Paul Schneider-Esleben, 1954) (Figure 2.13). Two of the most widely published postwar churches, both were specifically mentioned in commentary about how to rebuild the Memorial Church.[137] Dominikus Böhm and Emil Steffann, two leading architects of Catholic churches, adopted this strategy as well, for instance in St. Anne in Cologne-Ehrenfeld (1954–56), which Böhm designed in collaboration with his son Gottfried, and St. Bonifatius (1951) in Dortmund, where the top story of the tower is Steffann's.[138] In Hamburg, the steeple of St. Nikolai, designed by the English architect George Gilbert Scott and completed in 1874, was left in ruins as a memorial, with a new church erected on a different site.

At first glance, such pairings not only symbolize resurrection but also mark the church as an institution with a reverent attitude toward its own past and particularly toward the medieval period. Almost all the steeples collaged with patently new construction were medieval, and usually Romanesque rather than Gothic, in style. Like the Memorial Church, however, the bell towers preserved in this way were relatively recent constructions and many were tinged with the same nationalism. Where medieval, Renaissance, baroque, and even neoclassical structures were rebuilt whenever possible, it was only relics from the relatively recent Second Empire that were likely to be collaged with dramatically new construction.[139] Bochum's Christ Church was completed in 1879, St. Rochus in Düsseldorf in 1897, St. Anne in Cologne-Ehrenfeld in 1908, and St. Bonifatius in Dortmund only in 1910. And these steeples either survived intact or were repaired; they lacked the jagged outline of the ruined Memorial Church.[140]

Nor was the preservation of bombed-out churches uncommon in the larger European context. It was a particularly popular means in England of commemorating the Blitz. The most celebrated is undoubtedly Coventry Cathedral. Here the shell of the late Gothic St. Michael's, an immense parish church elevated to cathedral status only in 1918, stands next to a postwar cathedral designed by Basil Spence, itself inspired in part by the work of Gottfried Böhm's father, Dominikus.[141] St. Thomas's in Birmingham, St. Luke's in Liverpool, and St. Dunstan-in-the-East in London are additional examples. Like the Kaiser Wilhelm Memorial Church, many of these sites developed strong associations with peace and reconciliation. In 1987 Coventry donated a cross of nails to the Berlin church.

Berliners, however, would have been aware of another important collage of a patently ruined sacred building with new construction that sat only two blocks to the west of the Memorial Church and could be seen from the front of it.[142] The Fasanen Street synagogue, the largest in Berlin, was designed in 1909 by the architect Ehrenfried Hessel and dedicated in 1912. Fully cognizant of the nearby Memorial Church, Hessel employed a Romanesque Revival style, albeit studded with reminiscences of the exotic Islamic architecture in which many synagogues, including the one on Oranienburg Street in Berlin, had been built in the second half of the nineteenth century. The emperor evidently approved; he visited the building. This synagogue was damaged during the Kristallnacht pogrom in November 1938 and bombed in 1943. With the encouragement of its leadership, Dieter Knoblauch and Heinz Heise, the architects of the new synagogue and community center, incorporated fragments of the original structure, including the entrance portal and three

Inserting Memory into Modern Architecture 67

Figure 2.14. Dieter Knoblauch and Heinz Heise, Jewish Community Center, Fasanen Street, Berlin, 1959. Source: Livia Hurley.

tiers of paired columns, into their building (Figure 2.14). The commemorative brochure for the community center made the intention clear: "Everyone who passes by this house should gaze upon the memorial column. . . . Non-Jews should remain . . . constantly aware of the guilt of the past, since what has happened cannot be completely undone through reparations."[143] Knoblauch and Heise's synagogue, for which the design competition was held in 1957, was completed two years later. Here for the first time, the architecture of memory in West Berlin explicitly addressed the terrorism unleashed by the Third Reich.

The reworked design for the Memorial Church that Eiermann published in 1958 met with nearly universal approval. Commentary focused almost exclusively on the preservation of the ruins rather than on the details of the design.[144] Unlike Bartning and Schwarz, Eiermann, who was not primarily an architect of churches, focused on style, as developed through structure, more than on the organization of space; his approach to the project was not altered by the need to reorganize its plan around the retention of the tower stump.

What had once been an island containing only the church was now enlarged; a pedestrianized plaza tied the platform on which it sat to two neighboring clusters of commercial buildings, greatly facilitating access to the complex. Eiermann originally proposed a circular church and cylindrical steeple with other circular appendages; in his second design, which he developed in more detail for the second phase of the competition, he reverted to rectangular forms that more exactly recalled St. Matthew's Church. Here a larger building fronted a smaller plaza. As built, the truncated ruin stood between a rectangular foyer and octagonal church on the one hand and a hexagonal bell tower and rectangular chapel on the other.[145]

At no point in the design process did Eiermann seize definitive control of the organization of the interior; his client rejected all three of his projected arrangements of the seating for the built version. While most postwar churches in the Federal Republic and West Berlin were at least nominally designed from the inside out around increasingly antitraditional plans driven by liturgical and theological reforms, the common denominator in all of Eiermann's attempts to respond to the constraints of the site was the structural system. In an arrangement prefigured in Pforzheim, this consisted of a steel frame into which he inserted a concrete grid infilled with stained glass. Although the exterior of the building shared the same treatment as the interior, there was actually a space between the two walls; this provided crucial soundproofing against the noise of the surrounding traffic. Artificial lighting tucked into the space between the two layers of glass ensures that, regardless of the time of day or year or the weather, visitors enter a glowing box.

The effectiveness of the Memorial Church's exterior comes from the juxtaposition of the ruined steeple and vestibule of the original church with the pieces of its successor; although easily reduced to a caricature, this works best when experienced firsthand, as the size of the ruin and its blackened details are key to the impact it makes. There is little aesthetically compelling about the new volumes, whose scale now seems relatively crude in comparison to the fine-grained detailing of both the New Building of the 1920s and more recent neomodernism. The interior, however, impresses almost everyone (Figure 2.15). The overwhelmingly blue glass, studded with gold notes, but also some red and green, as well as the relatively intimate scale of the octagonal form, invariably causes the casual tourists who constitute the largest group of visitors to the building, not to mention more reverent visitors and parishioners, to recognize that they have entered a special place. The space is now dominated by a gold-colored sculpture of Christ, his arms outstretched in the form of a cross, that is suspended above the altar. The work of Karl Hemmeter, this over life-size figure donated by Dibelius was not part of Eiermann's original design—indeed, he strongly objected to it.[146]

This is probably the closest the contemporary visitor can get to the admittedly far more overtly spectacular experience of being inside Taut's Glashaus. Even after the church's completion, when Eiermann's choice of precedents became more obvious, his careful citation of German expressionism and of the work of the French architect Auguste Perret was almost entirely ignored, however, although they are central to the effect it produces.[147] Midcentury modern architects and their critics seldom articulated the way in which contemporary buildings drew upon the rela-

Inserting Memory into Modern Architecture 69

Figure 2.15. Interior, Kaiser Wilhelm Memorial Church. Source: Johann H. Addicks/Wikipedia Commons.

tively recent past, even as almost everyone within the professional community certainly recognized the connections and the specific way in which they critiqued the nationalism of the original building. Eiermann's explicit references to the Glashaus and Taut's later schemes for crystalline city crowns made respectful nods toward one of the most socially engaged and politically radical strands in the recent history of German architecture. Meanwhile, his equally obvious quotation of Perret's Notre Dame du Raincy, built in a suburb of Paris in 1922–23 to commemorate French victories in the First World War, reached outside German utopian socialism to embrace the architecture of one of the countries that still officially governed West Berlin (Figure 2.16). This rapprochement was consolidated by the decision to hire a Frenchman, Gabriel Loire, from Chartres to create the stained glass. The key to the building's aesthetic impact was that it was executed in the same color palette used in the famous windows of that city's Gothic cathedral.

The reconstruction of the Memorial Church provided West Berlin with its key symbol for reasons that had relatively little, however, to do with the design intention

Figure 2.16. Auguste Perret, Notre Dame du Raincy, 1923. Source: Livia Hurley.

of either its architects or their clients. No one in 1958 could have anticipated the importance the Memorial Church would soon assume. In November of that year, Nikita Khrushchev, the Soviet premier, warned that the East Germans would soon deny access to the city, as the Soviets had already done a decade before.[148] Although this did not occur, the reception of the finished building would be shaped almost entirely by a single event that took place on 13 August 1961 as the church was nearing completion: the imposition of the Berlin Wall.

The Wall did not change everything, but it changed a great deal. West Berlin suddenly superseded Hungary, invaded by Soviet troops in 1956, as communism's most prominent victim. The sense of an enclave under American protection fostered during the blockade of 1948–49 quickly returned as journalists as well as spies poured back into town to assess the new situation. West Berliners had always at least had access to the Communist east; these links were now largely severed and would remain so until Willy Brandt's *Ostpolitik* resulted, beginning in 1972, in a somewhat improved situation. It was in this context that the dedication of the Kaiser Wilhelm Memorial Church in December 1961, long before the building was actually completed, became a major international news story.

Berlin's political importance grew across the final months of 1961. Just weeks before the Wall went up, John F. Kennedy had declared:

> For West Berlin, lying exposed 110 miles inside East Germany, surrounded by Soviet troops and close to Soviet supply lines, has many roles. It is more than a showcase of liberty, a symbol, an island of freedom in a communist sea. It is even more than a link with the Free World, a beacon of hope behind the Iron Curtain, an escape hatch for refugees. West Berlin is all of that. But above all it has now become—as never before—the great testing place of Western courage and will, a focal point where our solemn commitments stretching back over the years since 1945, and Soviet ambitions now meet in basic confrontation.[149]

Although the debate over the Memorial Church's preservation had long been framed in relation to the East German demolition of Hohenzollern palaces and of the refusal by that government to rebuild the steeples of other damaged Berlin churches, only now did the building come to serve as the symbolic replacement for the Protestant cathedral (another bombastic Wilhelmine edifice), to which the West Berlin church no longer had access as it was located behind the Wall across from the site of the demolished royal palace. Only now could the relatively banal character of Eiermann's church when seen by daytime from the exterior and the political antecedents of the original building be resolutely overlooked in the interest of creating an appropriately poignant monument for a divided city. Only now did postwar West German Protestantism finally possess a new building that, without being entirely purged of the physical traces of its earlier militant nationalism, rivaled the aesthetic achievements of contemporary German Catholicism while surpassing those accomplishments in symbolic effectiveness.[150] And only now could a church come to represent capitalism, not least through the rhyming of its colorful stained glass, when illuminated from within at night, with the frantic illuminated advertising of the commercial buildings that surrounded it.[151] As Eiermann proudly noted, so many flocked to worship here that services were initially held at five different times on Sundays.[152]

The debate over the Memorial Church helped revive the public sphere in West Berlin and the Federal Republic following the censorship of the Third Reich. The very fact that meaning and memory were communicated through images rather than texts—and quite often through a relationship with the surrounding cityscape—provided a welcome elasticity. The vagueness that seemed to envelop iconography was offset, however, by the specificity with which buildings display their wounds. While much of the physical and emotional damage endured by survivors, like that to older monuments that were completely restored, was eventually rendered invisible, the incompleteness of the Memorial Church's steeple provided an acceptable way of expressing the destruction and suffering that had indeed taken place.[153] Memory here certainly encompassed the very recent past, if only from the perspective of German suffering from Allied aerial bombardment and during the subsequent invasion, rather than empathy with the victims of the Third Reich. That, with the important exception of the Fasanen Street synagogue, would find expression only a generation later. Monument building had been central to the establishment of the nation-state in the nineteenth century; the Nazi manipulation of this tradition had rendered the Federal Republic initially almost incapable of constructing new symbols. This task instead fell to the church, which in turn, as a mark of Protestantism's growing commitment to democracy in particular, shared its authority with both professionals and the public. The resulting strategies, which seemed at the time to be piecemeal compromises, provided a key precedent for the postmodern fascination with palimpsests and for the commemorative strategies of absence as well as presence that have accompanied the memorial boom of the last thirty years.[154]

Pilgrimage Church of Mary

The Church of the Resurrection, St. Anna, and the Kaiser Wilhelm Memorial Church all collaged the remains of earlier buildings with modern architecture that drew upon precedents established during the Weimar Republic. The simultaneous recollection of Weimar expressionism and the Gothic precedents upon which it had drawn within a postwar modern church did not require the presence of neomedieval or actual medieval remains, however, as the example of the only postwar German church built on the scale of a medieval cathedral (it remains the second-largest church in the archdiocese of Cologne) clearly demonstrated.[155] The Catholic pilgrimage church of Mary, known in German as the Mariendom, in the largely Protestant village of Neviges in Velbert, represents the apex of the sponsorship of modern architecture by the postwar German church (Figure 2.17).[156] It was designed by Gottfried Böhm in 1963 and dedicated five years later. Although Cold War mythology suggested that only in the democratic capitalist conditions of the United States could the aspiration of Weimar-era modernism reach fulfillment, Böhm was able to fuse Taut's visions of faceted civic crowns with the way in which Catholics transformed church interiors in the wake of Vatican II.[157]

Cardinal Frings initiated the project.[158] He greatly admired Böhm's father, Dominikus, arguably the most important designer of twentieth-century Catholic churches. Frings wrote in his introduction to a survey of the father's work that Dominikus had been "a pioneering master, who freed church architecture from the bonds of historicism and built according to the demands of new materials and in accordance with new liturgical insights."[159] Frings would certainly have recognized the relationship between the son's scheme and his father's Church of St. Engelbert of 1932 in the Cologne suburb of Riehl (Figure 2.18). It was here on the final day of 1946 that Frings delivered a famous sermon in which he permanently endeared himself to his parishioners by condoning the taking of small amounts of badly needed coal. The verb *fringsen* became slang for such petty theft in the face of enormous hardship.[160]

After inheriting his father's office upon Dominikus's death in 1955, Gottfried

Inserting Memory into Modern Architecture

Figure 2.17. Gottfried Böhm, Mariendom, Velbert-Neviges, 1968. Source: Arved von der Ropp.

Böhm eventually, alongside Hans Scharoun, became the most important postwar keeper of the expressionist flame. For Böhm, unlike Scharoun, the abstract recollection of a medieval past was often as important as the creation of apparently eccentric forms that were in fact carefully conceived to promote social gathering. No doubt inspired as well by Le Corbusier, whom he noted was "more impulsive, fizzy, and more uncontrollable but also because of that perhaps . . . had a more human feeling," when compared to Mies or Gropius, Böhm began in the early 1960s to extend in two different directions the way in which postwar West German churches drew upon the past.[161] Having already, at times in collaboration with his father, designed churches that combined medieval and neomedieval fragments with new construction, he moved this respect for medieval precedent into the civic sphere when he placed the town hall in Bensberg, now a part of the municipality of Bergisch Gladbach, within the ruins of a medieval castle. Meanwhile, in a nearby orphanage in Refrath as well as in the Mariendom he created places that respectfully recalled medieval urbanism, not least in the way in which the church continued to tower over the entire village.[162]

The Mariendom represented the culmination of the reforms in Catholic architecture instigated at the beginning of the Weimar Republic and enshrined following

Figure 2.18. Dominikus Böhm, St. Engelbert, Cologne-Riehl, 1932. Photograph by Hugo Schmölz. Source: Wikipedia Commons.

the Second Vatican Council. For Schwarz, the focus on creating an appropriate space for the communal celebration of the Mass resulted in an otherwise reductive architecture in which the material intruded as little as possible upon the domain of the spiritual. Others, including Dominikus Böhm, the Catholic theologian Johannes van Acken, and especially Gottfried Böhm, believed that modern sacred architecture should appeal more overtly to the emotions.[163] For Gottfried, this encompassed in the Mariendom the recall of Taut's city crowns, which he resanctified, not least by alluding abstractly to the same medieval precedents that had inspired his expressionist precursor (Figure 2.19). The result was one of the most imposing and memorable

Figure 2.19. Interior, Mariendom. Source: Arved von der Ropp.

buildings ever erected in the Federal Republic. Its relatively remote location in a village on the edge of the border between the Rhineland and the Ruhr region, as well as on what were then the expressionist margins of modern architecture meant that the scope of his achievement received relatively little attention beyond the rapidly narrowing circle of those interested in the problem of a modern sacred architecture, even as it indicated the commitment to the same participatory public that was also fundamental to the consolidation of German democracy.[164]

Unlike Eiermann, Böhm's purpose was strictly religious; the Mariendom has not at any point in its history been understood to stand in any way for the increasingly secular Federal Republic. And yet this church, far more successful from an aesthetic point of view than its Protestant counterpart in Berlin, embodied many of the achievements of the young country. Its architect, who described its interior as a "sacred marketplace," created an unusually antihierarchical public space in which even the altar, which stands atop a relatively low three-tiered platform, is set amidst rather than beyond the congregation (Figure 2.20). Moreover, in keeping with the trend at the time to conceive of the church as a multifunctional community space, Böhm envisioned it as a place that in addition to the Mass, would house, in his own words, "communal prayer and song, as well as musical festivals, also dance performances or plays, lectures and discussions, films and slide shows."[165]

The Mariendom was built to rehouse a seventeenth-century print of the Immaculate Conception. Credited with the ability to work miracles, it routinely from the 1910s through the 1950s drew crowds of more than one hundred thousand pilgrims annually. At Neviges, Böhm was charged with the creation of an ensemble that extended well beyond the church itself, whose roof flamed over the approach to the building, to encompass a convent, a kindergarten, an old age home, and a hostel for pilgrims. The urbanistic character of Böhm's design, which threatens to overwhelm the modest scale of its environment, draws freely upon Taut's visions of city crowns set into mountain landscapes. Instead of being constructed out of glass, the church's multifaceted peak is a forceful concrete presence looming over the road and rail approaches and the pilgrimage path. The monumentality of so many institutional buildings of the 1960s is here reconfigured with an unusually subtle sense of scale, precisely what is lacking in the exterior of Eiermann's Memorial Church in Berlin, as well as attentiveness to the way space is bounded. This begins with the processional route to the doorway. Framed on one side by a wall and on the other by the gentle undulations of buildings housing offices below and a convent above, a series of stacked terraces evokes the favorite urban precedent of the period, Italian hill towns, far more effectively than most schemes of the day. It maintains precisely the same scale, even while transposing the original brick and stone into concrete.

No precedent prepares one for the experience of the interior, which is one of the most entirely original of any twentieth-century church. The freestanding altar, now designed to allow the celebrant to face the congregation, is not quite on axis with

Inserting Memory into Modern Architecture 77

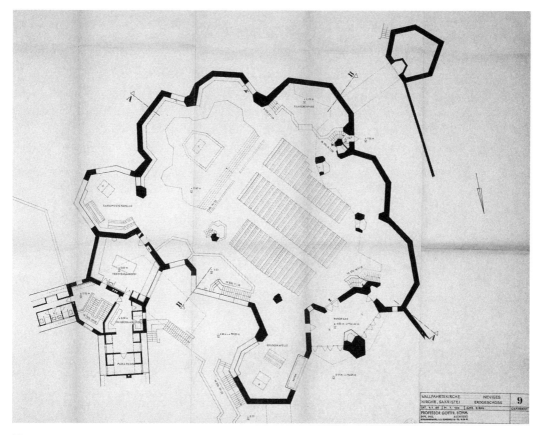

Figure 2.20. Plan, Mariendom. Courtesy of Böhm Studio.

the entrance. To the left of the large, relatively dark sanctuary cluster the chapels of pilgrimage where the image and the Blessed Sacrament are housed. To the right and above the entrance rise three tiers of balconies, ensuring that none of the thousands of pilgrims is too far from the altar or has a poor view of it. The faceted forms of the roof, into which small windows are set, tower dimly above. Böhm pragmatically used streetlamps to illuminate its cave-like dimness. The entirely irregular and not always clearly perceivable boundaries of the interior make it one of the most mystical churches in a tradition more often associated with a rational approach to both space and construction.

Svetlozar Raèv, who edited a book on Böhm, wrote of the Mariendom:

> The sheer size of the building's volume and the heaviness of the building material anchor it visually to the ground as if it were the offspring of the earth. The crystalline tips in the upper section that tower upwards in all directions are held together by an invisible vertical axis. The ambivalence between a worldly and heavenly attitude towards life is repeated in the interior of the church. Here

the outer form of the concrete shell appears again but this time in negative form, whose solid, sculptural composition in the upper sections calls to mind a dramatically turbulent sky.[166]

Many of the ways in which Böhm organized this space would have been inconceivable before the reforms that followed the Second Vatican Council, where his patron had played such a key role.[167] First was the sense of spatial unity between the congregation and the now freestanding and only slightly elevated altar. These were no longer separated by an altar rail; the fact that the celebrant now faced the congregation also eroded the previous sense of hierarchy. Furthermore, the creation of a separate chapel for the Blessed Sacrament, which had earlier been displayed upon the high altar, emphasized the importance of communal worship over private devotion. And finally, as Wolfgang Pehnt points out, the roof reaches its "peak above the congregation and not above the high altar."[168]

Stained glass and sculpture contribute to the success of the interior, providing welcome detail and warmth. The windows, which feature the Marian theme of the rose, are Böhm's own design. The most striking, with rich reds that dapple the walls, are in the two main chapels. There is a hint of the art nouveau work of Margaret Macdonald Mackintosh about these stylized flowers. These relatively representational designs humanize what threatens to be a cold if mannered building; when the sun shines through them they cast a warm glow on the concrete interior. The issue of popular attachment to older sculptural traditions is tactfully addressed through the placement of older works transferred from the earlier pilgrimage church in the crypt near the confessionals. Upstairs three monolithic sculptures in wood, designed and carved by Elmar Hillebrand specifically for the Mariendom, house the image and the Blessed Sacrament, and serve as the altar.

By 1968 the construction of the postwar infrastructure of the two German churches was basically complete; in the decades that followed, the role of both Christian denominations in the politics of the Federal Republic would gradually wane. The Mariendom received little of the international publicity that had surrounded earlier landmarks of postwar German sacred architecture.[169] By this time, the sophisticated integration within modern Germany of multiple architectural pasts was already shifting away from churches and toward museums, institutions that better represented both the Federal Republic's increasingly secular orientation and the degree to which architecture was becoming the purview of a cultural elite, rather than the working- and middle-class congregations who had filled churches in the first decades after the war.

It is one of the great paradoxes of the history of modern German architecture that new building materials and abstract forms were espoused more quickly by the church, especially in the Weimar and the Federal Republic, than by many of the industries and institutions whose modernization sparked demands for an architecture reflecting the spirit of the times. Although the modern was more often defined in terms of mass production than spiritual renewal, it was particularly useful for communicating that the churches were reforming themselves, not least by promoting a sense of community that transcended class divisions even as the church remained located outside expressly socialist or even democratic politics. Through the construction of inexpensive but impressive structures, many located in new working-class suburbs, the German churches portrayed themselves as both reassuringly permanent and impressively up-to-date. Although many architects of sacred buildings continued to quote medieval traditions obliquely, hardly a church was erected in the Weimar or the Federal Republic that did not feature abstraction of surfaces, expression of structure, and undivided interior spaces, all humanized through the careful control of natural light. Reforms in German church architecture anticipated Vatican II and encouraged the adoption worldwide of a moderate modernism, shorn of its associations with industrialization and socialism but not of modernity or social progress.

The architecture pioneered in the churches of the Federal Republic and West Berlin fused memories of the modern architecture of the Weimar Republic with recollections of an at times indeterminate, if vaguely medieval, past. The latter offered reassurance and continuity. It tempered once radical forms, purging them of any uncomfortable associations with political revolution. This architecture was forged within the church, the Federal Republic's first stable social institution. Whether Catholic or Protestant, Christian leaders sought to establish viable communities that, although not originally inherently democratic, were at least reconceived as participatory. Indeed, the experience church leaders had of this new democracy eventually encouraged them to embrace a new openness and spirit of reform, in the architecture as well as the governance of their own institutions.[170]

If not avant-garde, these churches were also in no way old-fashioned, much less historicist. Their architecture was predicated upon modernism's ability to stretch to include references to both the recent and the more distant past within buildings that remained relentlessly abstract and in many cases proudly built out of patently new materials, as well as predicated upon modern assumptions about the decisiveness of space in shaping experience and behavior. Flying in the face of the rhetoric that by the 1960s dominated architecture schools and the professional press, they nonetheless served key social functions.

These churches were enormously reassuring in multiple ways. Even as they documented the destruction of the war, they also provided places for repentance, forgiveness, and renewal. Only the contribution of the Memorial Church, Cold War West Berlin's most iconic architectural symbol, was widely acknowledged. Nonetheless all the churches discussed in this chapter—and many more besides—contributed in important ways to creating the conviction that stable communities could be re-created and form the basis of a viable society. The churches accomplished this in many cases long before the outlines of the economic miracle and the success of the Federal Republic's integration into the European Economic Community, the forerunner of today's European Union, became clear. This was why the approach to architecture they embodied would endure.

Three

An Architecture of Fragmentation and Absence
West German Museums

On the evening of 9 March 1984, a huge party took place in Stuttgart, directly across a busy road from the park that twenty-six years later would be filled with protestors demonstrating against the partial demolition of the main train station.[1] A spirit of slightly raucous celebration, rather than the tear gas that filled the air in 2010, was discernible as the city's dignitaries joined art world figures from across Western Europe to mark the opening of the continent's boldest new museum building. There was a great deal for the guests to enjoy. Designed by the British architect James Stirling, the New State Gallery represented the apex of postmodernism's imaginative integration of architectural and urban precedent into late twentieth-century design (Figure 3.1). Imbued with a strong sense of irony, the building, which rapidly became the Federal Republic's most visited art museum, was in no way conventionally historicist.[2] Instead, it paired fragments recalling nineteenth-century architecture with overtly modernist elements in a way that would have been familiar to any astute observer of the country's postwar churches. In the central atrium, whose upper edges would soon be rimmed with the same kind of greenery romantic painters often showed growing out of classical and medieval ruins, Stirling invoked the spirit of Karl Friedrich Schinkel's celebrated Altes Museum in Berlin, showing it as if it had been bombed and left to decay at a time when whole trees were indeed sprouting on Communist-controlled Museum Island out of the New Museum. He juxtaposed this against quotations from Le Corbusier's contribution to the Weissenhofsiedlung, and Renzo Piano and Richard Roger's Centre Pompidou in Paris, which had opened just as he was completing his competition design. The effect of producing a community-oriented progressive face for the Federal Republic was the same as it had been in churches such as St. Anna and the Mariendom. The community was now secular,

81

Figure 3.1. Stirling and Wilford, New State Gallery, Stuttgart, 1984. Photograph by Waltraud Krase. Copyright Bildarchiv Foto Marburg.

however, and, more controversially in the West German context, the effort to stay abreast of international architectural trends now entailed addressing neoclassical civic architecture as a possible source for a specifically democratic architecture.

By 1968 the importance of new church buildings as symbols of the Federal Republic was on the wane. The Christian Democrats began in 1966 to share power with the Social Democrats in a grand coalition, which unraveled in 1969, allowing Willy Brandt to become West Germany's first socialist chancellor. After the building boom of the previous two decades there was, moreover, very little demand for new church buildings; those damaged or destroyed in the war had been repaired or replaced, and the needs of most new neighborhoods had been addressed as well. In the introduction to a bilingual survey of new German museum buildings published in 1985 and clearly targeted at an international audience, the German architectural critic Heinrich Klotz wrote:

> In the decades following the last war, the rebuilding of public institutions in the Federal Republic was subject to phases of differing priority.... Work began on

building new churches immediately after the end of the war—Bartning's prefabricated wooden churches were just one aspect of this—in the worst years of poverty and hunger. The 1950s were the years in which church building dominated as the most evident task of public reconstruction. . . . Museum construction, which also began in the 1950s, increased in importance, only reaching its zenith now, in the early 1980s.[3]

In this context the art museum came to symbolize the Federal Republic, albeit still by proxy rather than in buildings that housed key governmental institutions, as culture gradually replaced religion as the glue that bound West Germans (and above all West Berliners) to their democratic neighbors.[4] The increase in the number of new West German museum buildings, as well as the architectural ambition with which they were executed, was part of the explosion that began in the 1960s in the construction of civic buildings, as the state began to play an increasingly active role in the shaping of both society and the cityscape. This new infrastructure included many large facilities, such as universities and hospitals. These, however, as the new universities in Bochum, as well as Bielefeld, Dortmund, and Siegen clearly demonstrate, were typically located well outside historic city centers. Museums were not only prominently sited in or close to the historic core, but they had been almost since the inception of the type, clearly associated with the national ambitions of the multiple German kingdoms during the crucial half century before German unification in 1871. At the same time, and paradoxically for the same reason, they served the diffuse political structure of the Federal Republic particularly well because, at least until the 1990s, Bonn's museums were easily outclassed by those in larger cities. Museums thus represented an older, highly cultured if still intensely patriotic Germany worthy of revival, supported by a federal structure that encouraged competition between different cities even as they sponsored risky new art. By the 1980s the Federal Republic hosted a vibrant and polycentric museum culture, highly attuned to the ways in which innovative architecture drew favorable attention.

The effort to create an architectural identity for the Federal Republic now migrated not only to a different building type but also to a different class of citizens. By the 1970s museums were explicitly engaged in becoming more popular, but they continued to reinforce the status of the well educated. Museums moreover participated in what was increasingly seen as the necessity to develop marketable urban identities that would appeal to both investors and tourists in addition to providing the stage sets on which local elites could demonstrate their cultural superiority.[5] Stuttgart politicians were very clear about their goals for the New State Gallery. In 1976, when the competition to design the replacement for the Crown Prince's Palace destroyed in the war was announced, the local newspaper wrote that what was wanted was "a strong cultural and political emphasis that would also serve to enhance the city of Stuttgart from an architectural and urban planning perspective," before quoting the minister-president of the state of Baden-Württemberg, Hans Filbinger, as saying, "Stuttgart should take another leap forward."[6] The next day a follow-up article stressed that even at a time of economic difficulties such a project was key to the city's image and "cultural prestige," and that its completion would allow masterpieces "to rise up like a phoenix out of storage into the light."[7]

The art museum as an institution and a building type coalesced in what became Germany in the years between the signing of the Treaty of Vienna in 1815 and the revolutions that broke out in 1848. Klotz noted that "all over the country, wherever a petty principality or an independent Free City strove for recognition, theatres and museums sprang up. No country can vie with Germany for the sheer number of such institutions."[8] The erection of early and influential examples such as the Fridericianum in Kassel (1779, Simon Louis du Ry), the Glyptothek in Munich (1816, Leo von Klenze), the Altes Museum in Berlin (1830, Karl Friedrich Schinkel), the Staatsgalerie in Stuttgart (1838, Gottlob Georg von Barth), and the Gemäldegalerie in Dresden (1847, Gottfried Semper) were closely associated with the rise of the *Bildungsbürgertum,* the educated upper middle class, which included professionals such as pastors, lawyers, doctors, professors, and architects, as well as the civil servants charged with many aspects of governing the different German states, several of which aspired to lead a united Germany.[9] After the middle of the century, the creation of Berlin's Museum Island became key to forging a pan-German identity for this class.[10]

Strongly tied to nationalism and the professional strata of the bourgeoisie, the art museum was nonetheless implicitly adopted by the Social Democrats as the enlightened face of the Federal Republic. New changes in cultural policy instituted in 1968 helped ensure that the construction of new art museums made a prominent contribution to culture, replacing Christianity as the key component of the effort to integrate the Federal Republic into an increasingly secular Western European as well as a broader international community.[11] In addition to an emphasis on the achievements of "good" Germans, such as Bach and Beethoven, which helped prompt generous subsidies accorded to "high" art, there was also a shift in the 1970s toward sponsoring often highly experimental cultural events at home and abroad. Nor did the Christian Democrats object. At the dedication of the New State Gallery, Lothar Späth, Filbinger's successor as minister-president, and like him a member of that party, noted that more Germans visited art museums than attended first division football matches. Späth then made clear the conception of democracy that underpinned the museum boom:

> The measure of freedom that exists in a state, can be assessed by the measure of the public for art and artists. The denial of such a public is always a denial of the freedom of the citizenry. In this respect all art is also political. . . . The construction of the new State Gallery is thus also an extension of freedom.[12]

Before museums could serve this role, however, a new approach to their architecture needed to be developed. The uncritical revival of the monumental classicism of the nineteenth-century originals would not suffice. Four German museum buildings conceived between 1962 and 1989, as well as two key precedents for them, demonstrate the way in which the new museum buildings came to encompass a far broader array of memories than those contained within postwar churches. Taking a leaf from the architecture of those churches nonetheless allowed the architects of these new buildings to reframe the imposing precedents offered by Germany's original museum infrastructure as either transparent or fragmentary in ways that emphasized contrasts with a respected but now distant past. Early examples, such as the reconstruction between 1952 and 1957 of the Alte Pinakothek in Munich by Hans Döllgast and the new Historical Museum in Hanover, designed by Dieter Oesterlen and built between 1960 and 1966, juxtaposed old and new fabric, a strategy both men had first used in churches. By the 1960s, however, new means for invoking absence were being developed in museum buildings that evoked the past entirely within modernism. Foremost among these was Ludwig Mies van der Rohe's New National Gallery in West Berlin's Cultural Forum, which was commissioned in 1962 and completed in 1968.

The shift coincided as well with the emergence of new approaches to architecture, as postmodernism increasingly posed a challenge to the modern architecture that was widely, if almost certainly too glibly, accepted as evidence of the Federal Republic's rejection of Nazism. The New State Gallery was a key example of the new approach. Gerhard Feldmeyer wrote in 1993, as the popularity of postmodernism was already waning, in a volume on new German architecture directed at an English-speaking audience:

> This epoch, so characterized by an absence of theory and by a thoughtless, artless pragmatism, provoked polemic and exaggerated reaction in its wake, culminating, perhaps, in James Stirling's masterful Neue Staatsgalerie in Stuttgart, one of the clearest responses to the stylistic chaos that had preceded it. Buildings like this exemplify an architecture which relies not on the abstraction of purely stereometric forms but on the diversity of form inherent in pictures and images, decoration and ornament, symbols and signs. With wit, irony, and playful lightness, Stirling brought an impressive architectural vocabulary to bear without seeming superficial or banal and without forgetting the true essence of architecture: to create space, to define space.[13]

This was, for a German, a charitable assessment of a building that was initially viewed with considerable suspicion by those West German architects who had long been engaged in nurturing alternatives to fascist monumentality. Even the revival of neoclassicism in the 1970s and the arrival of deconstructivism in the 1980s did not preclude, however, continued references to modernism's own past, as the New State Gallery's allusions to the Centre Pompidou clearly demonstrate. The fragmentation displayed in the shorn-off steeple of the Kaiser Wilhelm Memorial Church now became the point of departure for entirely new structures, almost regardless of style. This was the case even as a growing consensus emerged, especially in the 1980s, that the urban fabric had to be rewoven to repair the damage that modernist urbanism, just as much as aerial bombardment, had wrought.

This introduced more explicit confrontations with the theme of memory into German architecture long before memory had coalesced as an important topic in other countries or in other disciplines. In *The Architecture of the City*, first published in Italian in 1966 and in German seven years later, Aldo Rossi phrased his opposition to modernist functionalism in terms of a vision of the city as the locus of collective memory, a term he borrowed from the French sociologist Maurice Halbwachs:

> "The soul of the city" becomes the city's history, the sign on the walls of the municipium, the city's distinctive and definitive character, its memory. As Halbwachs writes in *Le Mémoire Collective*, "When a group is introduced into a part of space, it transforms it to its image, but at the same time, it yields and adapts itself to certain material things which resist it. It encloses itself in the framework that it has constructed. The image of the exterior environment and the stable relationships that it maintains with it pass into the realm of the idea that the city has of itself."
>
> One can say that the city itself is the collective memory of its people, and like memory it is associated with objects and places. The city is the *locus* of the collective memory. This relationship between the *locus* and the citizenry then becomes the city's predominant image, both of architecture and of landscape, and as certain artifacts become part of its memory, new ones emerge. In this entirely positive sense great ideas flow through the history of the city and give shape to it.[14]

For Rossi, good buildings outlived their original purposes, and adaptive reuse made a crucial contribution to successful cities. His imaginative leap from the way the far more conservative Halbwachs had written about collective memory ensured the concept's utility, originally to architects, but eventually to their audiences as well.[15] Although often conceived in opposition to postmodernism, the new approach to commemoration, especially but not exclusively of the Holocaust, would help trigger the subsequent boom in public and scholarly interest in how individuals and societies remember the past.

Rossi's text was published in German in 1973, but it did not appear in English translation until 1984. As Rossi was one of Europe's most prominent architects, Stirling and the British and American critics who penned the first key reviews of the

New State Gallery were nonetheless certainly all aware of its basic precepts.[16] Thus nearly two decades before Pierre Nora began the publication of the three-volume *Les lieux de mémoires* in 1984, and even longer before Jan Assmann coined the term *cultural memory* in 1992, Rossi began the process of ensuring that architects were unusually well versed in the issues surrounding a discussion in which they would participate with alacrity and flair.[17] Not least because he provided a theoretical underpinning to an approach that had already been employed in Germany for nearly two decades, his work was particularly well received there, even by those not interested in his revival, however abstract, of classicism.

The reemergence, especially in Italy, the United Kingdom, and the United States, but also as far away as Japan, of historicism, and specifically of the monumental neoclassicism popularly associated with the Third Reich, posed enormous problems for tastemakers in the Federal Republic, however, which they dodged as often as possible by turning commissions for prominent new museum buildings over to foreigners. Jews, in particular, were free of any fascist taint.[18] In part because of this, these buildings have been understood more often in terms of Western, if not global, trends in contemporary architecture rather than as specific responses to a particular German situation in which they were also embedded.

Such is especially the case for Frank Gehry's Vitra Design Museum, which opened in a German suburb of Basel less than a week before the fall of the Wall. This building shifted the focus of this Canadian-born architect's creative reuse of modernism's past away from Southern California, where he had lived since 1947, and toward the work of the German architect Hans Scharoun, who had been one of the contributors to the Weissenhof, yet the results are all too often attributed simply to Gehry's personal genius. In June 1989, the Polish-born Daniel Libeskind won an open and anonymous competition to design an extension to the (West) Berlin Museum. Although the resulting building, which was completed a decade later, has always been understood to be embedded in the specifics of its Berlin site, it, too, has not been well integrated into a larger history of postwar German architecture. The example, in particular, of the postwar reconstruction of Berlin's Fasanen Street synagogue, demonstrates that the explicit recall of the absence of the city's once thriving Jewish community was not without precedent. Moreover, the means Libeskind employed, while widely broadcast as new and daring, were far from unfamiliar to perceptive observers of German architecture of the previous four decades.

Although designed in different styles, all of these buildings share fundamental characteristics. The effectiveness of the antimonumental stance taken by their architects depended, except in the case of the Vitra, in part on their discernible proximity to older structures. And although each building appeared resolutely new and unusual when it was completed, each architect relied heavily on Weimar-era precedent. The allusion to a classical past whose wholeness was eroded in part through the quotation of modernism, makes the New National Gallery, the New State Gallery, and the Jewish Museum worthy successors to churches like Egon Eiermann's Kaiser Wilhelm Memorial Church and effective representations of the Federal Republic's effort to appear (and indeed to be) cultured, while being mindful of the limits of culture as a path to the forgiveness of what were not yet really ancestral sins.

The Alte Pinakothek and Historisches Museum

As early as the 1950s there were glimmers of a relationship between the new churches that incorporated ruins and museum architecture, although at that time this certainly did not yet overtly incorporate a critical approach toward the firmly patriotic origins of nineteenth-century museums. The debate over the reconstruction of the Alte Pinakothek, as covered in the pages of *Baumeister,* the house organ of the professional organization for West German architects, gives an indication of the clearly expressed conservatism that governed much rebuilding in the Federal Republic and particularly in Bavaria. Hans Kiener, the author of several articles on the building, hailed the original structure as an example of the munificent patronage of King Ludwig I.[19] This aura of respect for an undemocratic, if hardly totalitarian past, strongly colored Döllgast's repair job. Indeed, in the context of Munich in the 1950s, what stands out about the Alte Pinakothek is that there was an ongoing discussion of replacing it with an entirely new building and that the scars of wartime damage were left so visible; the facades of most of Ludwig I's many contributions to the city, if not necessarily their interiors, were generally made whole again.[20]

The foundation stone for von Klenze's design was laid in 1826; the building was completed ten years later.[21] The original building was thus second only to Schinkel's celebrated Altes Museum among the wave of museums housing Old Master paintings that opened between the Treaty of Vienna in the capital cities of the independent kingdoms of what became in 1871 a united Germany. Already as crown prince, even before he ascended in 1825 to the throne of Bavaria (only elevated to the status of a kingdom in 1806), Ludwig I founded an important museum housing antique sculpture. The Glyptothek, begun in 1816, was, however, originally his private property, whereas later museums made royal collections accessible to the public.[22] The creation of this new cultural infrastructure, which included theaters and opera houses, provided the kings of Baden, Bavaria, Prussia, Saxony, and Württemberg with a means of acknowledging the aspirations of the educated middle class, without requiring reforms that transferred authority to them.

Badly damaged in 1943 and again the following year, the Pinakothek was rebuilt by Döllgast, who left the extent of the destruction clearly visible on both the facade* and the monumental interior staircase. He restored the brick walls of the middle eight bays of von Klenze's twenty-seven-bay facade without reapplying the classical window surrounds of the ground-story elevation or the engaged Ionic columns of the upper story and the entablature it originally supported (Figure 3.2). Simi-

An Architecture of Fragmentation and Absence 89

Figure 3.2. Leo von Klenze, Alte Pinakothek, Munich, 1836, as reconstructed by Hans Döllgast, 1957. Photograph by Waltraud Krase. Copyright Bildarchiv Foto Marburg.

larly, he failed to replace the details of the attic story. Döllgast, who had studied with Peter Behrens and first been named a professor in Munich in 1939, was active across the Weimar Republic, the Third Reich, and the Federal Republic. His reconstruction of the Alte Pinakothek drew upon his work on the Church of St. Bonifaz in Munich, which began in 1948. He rebuilt this church, another one of Ludwig I's donations, without its original ornament.[23] Döllgast's sensitive reconstruction of the Pinakothek's staircase demonstrated a high level of design skills married to an understatement understood by contemporaries as modern (Figure 3.3). At the same time, the literally stripped classicism of this monumental space was not as far from the aesthetics of Nazi state architecture as either the original building or an entirely new structure would have been.

The reverence that local architects still felt for Ludwig I, who was deposed in the revolution of 1848, in part because of his notorious affair with the dancer Lola Montez, was in keeping with Bavarian postwar politics, which were dominated by the Christian Social Union, a local and generally more conservative offshoot of the Christian Democrats.[24] While middle-class Germans in other parts of the Federal Republic often felt nostalgia for the Second Empire, their Bavarian counterparts focused instead upon the reign of a king who had sponsored much of the city's

Figure 3.3. Staircase, Alte Pinakothek. Photograph by Waltraud Krase. Copyright Bildarchiv Foto Marburg.

An Architecture of Fragmentation and Absence

Figure 3.4. Dieter Oesterlen, Historical Musuem, Hanover, 1966. Source: Rilke/Wikipedia Commons.

civic architecture. That he had done so because of political pressure from the city's *Bildungsbürgertum* as well as because of his aspirations to acquire the support of their counterparts across German-speaking Europe for the potential creation of a pan-German state under his leadership was less often voiced. Following the catastrophes of the Third Reich, his must have seemed a very benign imperialism.

Döllgast's restoration of one of Germany's most important art museums demonstrated the appropriateness of the transfer to museums of the approach to reconstruction taken in so many churches. The success of Oesterlen's Historisches Museum am Hohen Ufer in Hanover, which married part of the city's medieval wall and other historic fabric, some of it damaged in the war, with new construction gave a second indication of the effectiveness of this strategy in a building type that focused on the way in which the past operated in the present (Figure 3.4).[25] Like Döllgast, Oesterlen had first paired old and new construction in churches, in his case in the reconstruction of Hanover's St. Martin's and Bochum's Christ Church, before applying the same strategy to a museum.[26] Oesterlen, who was twenty years younger than Döllgast, had in many ways received more conservative training, but as an ambitious young architect working in the less conservative environment of Hanover, he quickly embraced modernism after the war, albeit not to the exclusion of understanding the potency of older architecture.[27] Not least because it was located in a smaller, more provincial city upon whose history its collections focused, the Historisches Museum received far less attention than the Alte Pinakothek. Nonetheless, it also indicated the benefits that could accrue by weaving new institutions sensitively into the existing urban fabric, rents in which could be restored through this process.

New National Gallery

The tone for the explosion in museum construction that took place in the Federal Republic between 1968 and 1989 initially appeared to have been set, however, by a far more ambitious structure, the New National Gallery in West Berlin's Cultural Forum (Figure 3.5).[28] Ostensibly a purely modernist building by Mies van der Rohe, the man who was simultaneously the Federal Republic's and the United States' most revered living architect, it was in fact carefully designed and sited in order to collage the revival of notions of transparency pioneered during the early years of the Weimar Republic with respect for an older historicist architecture. Both the architecture and the program—to house a space for changing exhibitions and the city's collection of late nineteenth- and twentieth-century painting—embodied the canonization of modernism as retaining the ability to stand for a progressive, if not necessarily utopian future. It was in that regard an enormously optimistic statement on land that had initially been cleared not by bombs but by Adolf Hitler and Albert Speer's plans for a monumental north–south boulevard through the city they planned to rechristen Germania and that sat only hundreds of meters from the Berlin Wall.

In 1938 Mies left Berlin, where he had lived for thirty-three years, for Chicago. Although he was willing to work for the Third Reich, his victory in the competition for the Reichsbank in 1933 had not translated into a commission, and he had also lost the job of designing the German pavilion for the 1935 World's Fair in Brussels.[29] With little work and no sympathy for the Nazi regime, he was relieved to get the position as director of the architecture school at the Armour Institute of Technology, soon renamed the Illinois Institute of Technology (IIT). Initially his new campus on Chicago's South Side drew little attention, but the situation changed dramatically in 1947 when an exhibition of his work, curated by Philip Johnson, went on display at the Museum of Modern Art in New York. The catalog, authored by Johnson, was the first monograph on the architect.[30]

The result was immediate. Key Mies works—the two projects for a skyscraper on Berlin's Friedrichstrasse (1921 and 1922) (Figure 3.6); the German pavilion for the World's Fair in Barcelona (1929); the Tugendhat House in Brno (1930); the new buildings for IIT (beginning in 1943); a pair of apartment towers on Chicago's

Figure 3.5. Ludwig Mies van der Rohe, New National Gallery, Berlin, 1968. Source: Livia Hurley.

Lake Shore Drive (1947–51); and a weekend house in the country for Dr. Edith Farnsworth (1945–51)—became some of the most celebrated and influential examples of twentieth-century architecture.[31] This although the first two were never built, the second stood for only a matter of months, the third was now located behind what Winston Churchill had recently termed the "iron curtain," and the last two were still under construction.[32] Consciously overlooked in the exhibition and catalog were almost all of the understated classical villas Mies had constructed in Berlin's suburbs between 1911 and 1926, when he finally committed himself completely to the New Building.[33]

Mies's American work appeared to its German supporters as an appealing antidote to the architecture of the Third Reich. In 1951 a young Frei Otto wrote, "Thus Mies van der Rohe is a healthy counterpoint in our culture . . . where we have hardly sensed freedom, as we try to forget that there are reins, reins that no dictatorial state holds in their hands, but that arise only from the neighborly relationship of people to one another and to their environments."[34] In 1959 the German consul in Chicago, when presenting him with a government decoration, reported that when the president of the Federal Republic, Theodor Heuss, who earlier had been the director of

Figure 3.6. Ludwig Mies van der Rohe, project for a skyscraper on Friedrichstrasse, 1921. Charcoal and graphite on brown paper, mounted on board, 68¼ × 48 inches. The Mies van der Rohe Archive, the Museum of Modern Art, New York. Gift of the architect. Source: Artists Rights Society (ARS), New York/VG Bild-Kunst, Bonn Digital Image. Digital image copyright The Museum of Modern Art. Licensed by SCALA/Art Resource, NY.

the Werkbund, had visited the United States the previous year, "He wanted to shake hands with those who, after the First World War, had worked closely with him at achieving—vainly alas—a new lasting German culture. Among those whose names ranked highest on the list of presidential visits was Professor Mies van der Rohe. Heuss wanted to tell him personally that he is still regarded as one of the outstanding personalities in the field of German architecture. He wanted his old friend to know that the seed Mies had planted in his mother country was growing steadily, not only in Germany but in Europe as well."[35] A similar tone marked the special issue of the German architectural periodical *Bauen + Wohnen* that marked the architect's seventieth birthday in 1956, to which the Swiss architectural historian Sigfried Giedion contributed an essay titled "The Moral Influence of the Architecture of Mies van der Rohe."[36]

Despite this high level of renown Mies was slow to build in the Federal Republic. In 1953 he won a competition to design a national theater in Mannheim, but it was never realized.[37] Two years later he wrote in English to Otto Bartning, "Basically I am willing to build something in Berlin if it will give me the opportunity to demonstrate my ideas about building without spending to [sic] great an amount of time on it. Please tell me which possibilities exist. I might possibly make a counter-suggestion."[38] His chance finally came in 1962 after the journal *Bauwelt,* edited by Ulrich Conrads, led a campaign to pressure the city government to find an appropriately prestigious commission for him. Over twelve hundred people, including many prominent cultural, political, and economic figures, signed the resulting petition.[39] The project was initially for a city-sponsored gallery of twentieth-century art; it morphed into New National Gallery, which became the home for the Prussian Cultural Heritage Foundation's collection of late nineteenth and twentieth century art, much of which had originally been exhibited on Museum Island and in the Crown Prince's Palace.

The awarding to Mies of one of the first two institutions, and the first museum, to be located in West Berlin's new Cultural Forum, was a major event, one with significant political overtones. The Interbau Exhibition organized by Bartning, with strong input from Gropius, had taken place in 1957. It resulted in the reconstruction of the Hansaviertel by an international array of architects, including Oscar Niemeyer and Alvar Aalto, and was the opening West Berlin salvo in the Cold War architectural skirmish between the two Berlins that had begun with the construction of the Stalinallee as the showpiece of the Communist east. However, the Hansaviertel was never deemed an unqualified aesthetic success.[40] The establishment of the Cultural Forum offered an opportunity to do better, as well as to set the stage for another act in the uneasy relationship between Gropius and Mies, which was based as much on rivalry as professional respect.[41] While Interbau demonstrated West Berlin's—and by implication the Federal Republic's—ability to provide higher living standards than the German Democratic Republic, and the Memorial Church a commitment to religious freedom as well as respect for the Hohenzollerns, the Cultural Forum focused more broadly upon freedom of expression and the preservation of patrimony.[42] Beginning in the eighteenth century, the city had gained an impressive array of civic buildings devoted to cultural functions. Moreover, its most celebrated institutions, which included the Opera, the State Library, Museum Island, and the theater on Gendarmenmarkt, were almost as famous for their architecture as for the activities and collections they housed.[43] All were located in the Soviet zone of the divided city.

Through the erection of the Cultural Forum, West Berlin proposed to create alternatives for some of these facilities.[44] The process of creating parallel institutions had begun in 1948, with the founding of the Free University in the American zone to counter Communist control of the University of Berlin.[45] The Free University was established in the leafy suburb of Dahlem; the Cultural Forum was instead placed close to the dividing line between the American and Soviet zones. This was intended to have the double result of neutralizing wasteland originally cleared for the Third Reich's north–south boulevard (the uprooting of the city's Jews had begun when their apartments were turned over to residents who were evacuated for this project) and making the new institutions easily accessible to East Berliners.[46] In fact, the Wall was erected between the time the first building in the ensemble, Scharoun's boldly sculptured Philharmonie, was commissioned and its completion in 1963.

When Mies was asked to house the city's collection of modern art in what became the New National Gallery, access from West Berlin to the museums established on Museum Island and in the Crown Prince's Palace on Unter den Linden between the 1820s and the 1920s, was difficult at best. Many of the celebrated works originally housed in these institutions had proved more portable than the buildings. After being moved during World War II for safekeeping, the vast majority, with the significant exception of the contents of the Pergamon Museum, ended up in the hands of the Allies rather than the Soviets. Beginning in 1957 those works belonged to the Prussian Cultural Heritage Foundation, based in West Berlin, which was charged with finding suitable homes for them in that part of the city.[47] The modern collection, however, had not fared so well, as the Nazis had denounced German expressionism and deaccessioned most of the celebrated works displayed in the Crown Prince's Palace during the Weimar Republic. Assembling an outstanding new collection and exhibiting it in a prominent building on a site originally cleared during the Third Reich made a compelling statement about the break West Berlin was making with its immediate past.

Mies is often described as having recycled for Berlin his design for a headquarters for Bacardi in Santiago de Cuba, but that scheme was to be built of concrete, whereas this one was executed in steel.[48] The Bacardi project, begun in 1957, was terminated following Fidel Castro's overthrow in 1959 of the dictatorship of Fulgencio Batista. In fact, Mies substantially reworked the Bacardi design in order to relate the New National Gallery both to an earlier Berlin museum and to its site in the Cultural Forum. The result balanced the classical decorum of his early work in Berlin and the neighboring suburb of Potsdam with the resolute commitment to the exposure of structure, whether actual or metaphoric, that characterized his American oeuvre.

Mies greatly admired Schinkel. He wrote in 1966: "Karl Friedrich Schinkel has remained for me even today a great role model."[49] Three years earlier he described his design for the New National Gallery as "a clear and strong building that in my opinion harmonizes with the Schinkel tradition in Berlin."[50] The comment signals his awareness that his work would be widely viewed as a substitute for the greatest of Berlin's nineteenth-century museum buildings, Schinkel's Altes Museum (Figure

An Architecture of Fragmentation and Absence

Figure 3.7. Karl Friedrich Schinkel, Altes Museum, Berlin, 1830. Source: Wikipedia Commons.

3.7).[51] The kernel of the Museum Island complex, which over a century expanded to include five separate institutions, this was the first art museum designed to offer a comprehensive introduction to the history of European painting, with royal donations forming only a small core of a collection acquired mostly by professional art historians.[52] Although the New National Gallery inherited collections originally housed in the Old National Gallery, which had opened on Museum Island in 1876, and the Crown Prince's Palace, it was Schinkel's museum that served as Mies's touchstone. The building, universally agreed to be Berlin's finest example of nineteenth-century architecture, was modeled on ancient Greek stoas, a building type Schinkel chose as particularly appropriate because it was secular rather than sacred. He intended the museum to double as a space in which the *Bildungsbürgertum* would gather for conversation and enlightenment.

Facing the royal palace across the Lustgarten, the stately procession of Ionic columns, backed by deep-red faux marble panels on the wall behind them, establishes the relatively austere tone of the building. A generous staircase, as well as a projecting attic, focuses attention upon the center of the composition. The visitor who ascends these stairs was confronted with two paths into the building. Flanking the recessed main doorway is an external double stair leading to an upstairs porch, from which one can also enter the building. The centerpiece of the interior is a large domed rotunda; two courtyards separate it from the outer range of galleries (Figure 3.8). Although the building did not function well for the exhibition of paintings, as the side lighting proved less than ideal, its cool logic ensured its central position

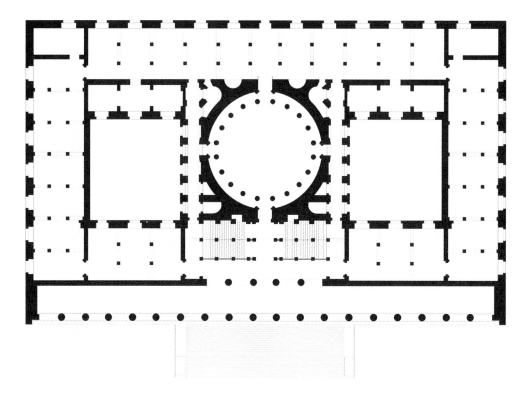

Figure 3.8.   Plan, Altes Museum. Source: Conor Rochford.

in the history of neoclassical architecture, and particularly in the fusion of Greek detailing with modern French planning (the plan was derived from a plate in a handbook by Jean-Nicolas-Louis Durand).[53]

Johnson illustrated the Altes Museum in his 1947 catalog on Mies in order to underline the neoclassical roots of the architect's elegant reduction of unnecessary detail (he made no mention of Lilly Reich's contribution to the practice; Reich died in Berlin at the end of 1947).[54] In the 1920s these had been supplemented, as his projects for a skyscraper on Friedrichstrasse and for a brick country house demonstrated, by an awareness of first expressionism and then De Stijl. In America, however, Mies often returned to classically infused compositions, which he brought up to date through the use of exposed steel framing or, in his high-rises, the appliqué of what looked like it. The rhythm of the Altes Museum is perhaps more deliberately recalled in Crown Hall, which Mies designed in 1950 to house IIT's School of Architecture, than in the New National Gallery, where the central entrance to a building conceived to be viewed in the round justly receives less emphasis.[55] Perhaps the aspect of the New National Gallery that most specifically reprises the Altes Museum is the degree to which parts of the building did not suit the display of the art it was originally intended to house. Although the basement galleries for the permanent collection have always worked well, the ground floor area for temporary exhibitions has proved awkward for the display of paintings. This space is now largely dedicated to installations of sculpture, architecture, and site-specific works.[56]

Nonetheless it is almost inconceivable that an informed visitor to the New National Gallery does not recall Schinkel's building, located only about two miles to the east. From Potsdamerstrasse, low stairs lead to the platform upon which sits the pavilion for temporary exhibitions. The location of the stairs, although not the details of their organization into two tiers or their breadth in relation to the facade, echoes that of the Altes Museum. Square in plan, where the Altes Museum is rectangular, the proportions of each of the nearly identical elevations of the pavilion also recall those of Schinkel's museum. Its roof slab corners, unlike Schinkel's, float free of any supports; they are instead carried by only two steel supports per side. The rhythm of the glazing bars suggests not only the verticality of Schinkel's colonnade but also the proportions of the faux marble panels on the wall behind it.

The raising of the roof on 5 April 1967 provided the most dramatic moment in the construction of the building. Mies, who was too frail the following year to attend the opening, traveled from Chicago to be present. It took twenty-four hydraulic presses to lift the coffered steel roof slab eight meters.[57] According to one account, "Mies watched the lifting of the 1250 ton roof for ten hours from his white Mercedes. The car was parked underneath the moving roof; it had moved in as soon as there was enough clearance. The architect trusted his engineers at the risk of being turned into a historical pancake."[58] While reviews of the building stressed the degree to which Mies adopted a consistent design position across more than four decades, they also acknowledged that the roof was a state-of-the-art engineering achievement, "unique in the history of architecture."[59] It adhered to the philosophy he expressed in a letter written in 1960 in which he declared, "I believe that in buildings you must deal with construction directly. You must, therefore, understand construction. When you refine this structure and when it becomes an expression of the essence of our time, it will then and only then become architecture."[60]

Phrased in terms of the proportions of the composition, the references to the Altes Museum are in the New National Gallery transposed into a resolutely twentieth-century material and the high-tech vocabulary that arose out of that decision. The unornamented pairing of steel structure and glass infill provides for a much more transparent, if only apparently flexible, architecture. The space of the pavilion, which one perceptive critic described as a "non-building," appears to be a sliver of air sandwiched between the deep stone podium and the thick black line of the coffered roof.[61] That the glass is set well back from the edge of the latter, and also of the supports, enhances the sense of this as a void. By the 1960s, the equation of such generous glazing in the Federal Republic with political transparency was well established, as was its utility as a powerfully symbolic alternative to the monumental architecture of the Third Reich. Traceable back to the industrial architecture of nineteenth-century exhibition halls and train station sheds, in the German context it was also associated with expressionist utopianism. Although the first curtain wall in Germany had been built for Margarete Steiff's stuffed toy factory in Giengen an der Brenz in 1901, the idea that such walls were appropriate for office towers was significantly advanced by Mies's glazed skyscrapers projects.[62]

The avant-garde architecture of the Weimar Republic served only intermittently as a source for buildings erected in the early years of the Federal Republic, but in few circumstances was it as eagerly adopted as for buildings that publically symbolized the new state. Hans Schwippert, who in 1949 renovated a university building in Bonn to house the new parliament, had worked first for Erich Mendelsohn and then Rudolf Schwarz, with whom he had collaborated on the design of the Corpus Christi Church in Aachen. He was also a great admirer, if not close friend, of Mies.[63] Schwippert's low-key design featured floor-to-ceiling glazing of two walls of the parliamentary chamber, which the architect intended to communicate the transparency of democratic government.[64] The effectiveness of this strategy was further demonstrated by the success of Egon Eiermann and Sep Ruf's German pavilion at the Brussels World's Fair in 1958.

Mies's pavilion, with its four nearly identical elevations, might appear an example of the placeless quality for which modern architecture is often criticized. The way he crafted the podium, which includes the permanent exhibition galleries as well as a sculpture garden, on which it sits, however, demonstrates a sophisticated understanding of the site, as well as considerable sympathy for the oldest building in the area to have survived the demolitions instigated by Hitler and Speer.[65] Many photographs of the New National Gallery highlight its relationship with Friedrich August Stüler's Matthew Church, designed in 1845 and completed the following year. Such a view reprised key features of the Memorial Church by pairing a nineteenth-century church, in this case one whose exterior had been faithfully reconstructed between 1956 and 1960, with an avowedly modern structure associated with the architectural achievements of the Weimar Republic. Writing in the *Architectural Review,* the British critic J. M. Richards commented, "The view across the platform, with the outline of the church truncated by the horizontal lone of its boundary edge and thus detached from its natural base, has an arresting dreamlike quality, which would be a lesson to all those architects who prefer a tabula rasa to a historically integrated townscape."[66]

Moreover, if the axial approach on Potsdamerstrasse recalled neoclassical precedent, the off-center location of the stairs running perpendicular to the Reichpietsch Ufer and Sigmundstrasse instead recalled Mies's abiding fascination with the contrapuntal geometries of Frank Lloyd Wright, De Stijl, and constructivism. These had been, along with expressionist-inspired expanses of glazing, the stimulus for the creative breakthrough in the early 1920s that propelled him from being a designer

Figure 3.9. Sculpture Court, New National Gallery. Photograph by Waltraud Krase. Copyright Bildarchiv Foto Marburg.

of safe suburban mansions into the first tier of the European avant-garde. The sense of the central space as a void, and the dialogue he established here between that void and the surviving church, as well as his willingness to depart from Schinkel's absolute symmetry, are all suggestive of the direction taken later by Stirling, Gehry, and Libeskind.

Conceived and completed before the Federal Republic's new cultural policy triggered a wave of museum construction across the length and breadth of the country, the New National Gallery demonstrated the degree to which outstanding museum architecture could produce, both for the country's own citizens and a still wary international community, the institutions as well as the image of a democratic society. Nowhere was this clearer than in the galleries tucked into the plinth (Figure 3.9). Because Mies glazed the entire wall facing the sculpture garden, which runs the length of the west facade, there is little of the sense of the black box spaces common in museums of this period. Instead, these rooms, in which art denounced by the Nazis as degenerate is usually displayed, are infused with light and with a sense of spaciousness.[67] Until the Wall fell and the Gemäldegalerie housing the city's collection of Old Masters moved in 1998 from its Cold War exile near the Free University in Dahlem to its new quarters in the Cultural Forum, the art of the first third of the twentieth century occupied the position of honor in West Berlin's museum landscape. The art exhibited in the New National Gallery deliberately upends conventions of beauty through allusions to so-called primitive sources and through a relentless depiction of unpleasant social realities, including prostitution and war wounds. The antihierarchical flexibility of the building's spatial planning further underlined West Berlin's openness to experimentation.

Once again Conrads authored some of the most perceptive remarks made at the time of the building's completion:

> In the opening exhibition in the large hall of the new Berlin National Gallery [the Dutch De Stijl painter Piet] Mondrian's search for the balance of the unbalanced confronts Mies van der Rohe's entirely clearer, entirely unquestioned, entirely undramatic creation of space.... I know of no building that is quieter, clearer, and more static than this. It is Mies van der Rohe's most decisive walk arm in arm with Schinkel.... Mies van der Rohe accepts all reductions, in order to allow the structural idea the absolute credit. That is a decision. His decision. It weighs heavily, it brings some drawbacks, it provokes, it wakes associations, it ensnares misunderstandings. It galvanizes the conversation over the role of the monumental in the second half of our century.[68]

Located in what continued until after the fall of the Wall to be a neighborhood of vacant lots, the New National Gallery was not as effective a tourist symbol for West Berlin as the Memorial Church, but it was the most widely admired of the city's postwar buildings. It communicated a respect for the Schinkel's Altes Museum and Stüler's Matthew Church but also continuity with the most radical proposals of the Weimar Republic, above all the entirely glazed skyscraper projects Mies had designed for a site on nearby Friedrichstrasse. Magisterial in its simplicity, Mies's pavilion perched lightly on its plinth in a way that implied that monumentality need not be oppressive and that the best face of a democratic Germany could be found not in the shop windows lining the Kurfürstendamm but in its commitment to the enduring value of what had once been a radically new and subversive art. As an antimonumental monument, it anticipated the role museum architecture, ostensibly in a very different style but in crucial ways quite similar in approach, would come to play in the Federal Republic in the 1980s.

The New State Gallery

With the possible exception of the museum district erected in Frankfurt during the same years, nothing spoke more eloquently of Germany's architectural, cultural, and political ambition during the 1970s and 1980s than the three designs the British firm of James Stirling and Michael Wilford entered in successive competitions for new art museums in Düsseldorf (1975), Cologne (1975), and Stuttgart (1977). Although the museums in Frankfurt were largely by the stars of the German-speaking architectural firmament, Stirling's triumph in Stuttgart, along with Richard Meier's Decorative Arts Museum in Frankfurt, signaled that the Federal Republic's cutting-edge buildings were no longer being designed by émigrés but by natives of the Western countries most responsible for the country's defeat less than four decades earlier. That Meier was Jewish only added to the sense that the Federal Republic was ceding control of the design of its civic sphere to its former victims, as well as enemies.

The tension between creating a new museum infrastructure, keeping at bay the nationalism, monumentality, and elitism associated with the building type, and remaining au courant with an international architectural culture that was shifting away from the modernist consensus of the postwar years, was embodied, if not always resolved, more specifically in Stuttgart than in Frankfurt.[69] Stirling himself defended the importance of having monumental buildings, which he claimed did not have to be either large or an expression of power. "Monumentality," he declared, "has a great deal to do with presence, and that means that a building vibrates, it sings."[70] Although Stirling (the building's design was consistently attributed to him, although of course many others made key contributions) repeatedly dismissed the term *postmodern* as journalistic and denied that he was a neoclassicist, his New State Gallery was certainly viewed at the time as one of the exemplars of an architecture that embraced both history and symbolism, in contrast to modernism's foregrounding of structure and abstraction.[71] This approach reached the apex of its popularity around the time the New State Gallery was completed; to many perceptive observers modernism could only now be spoken of using the past tense.[72]

Stirling in his own words struck a balance here between *abstract,* by which he meant "the style related to the Modern Movement of the 20s and 30s and the language derived from Cubism, Constructivism, de Stijl and the other isms of the new architecture," and *representational,* which he defined as "related to tradition, vernacular, history and recognition of the familiar."[73] In the German context, this dichotomy can also be understood as an example of the dialectic embedded within the architecture of many postwar churches and museums. Inspired in part by the rebuilt Alte Pinakothek, a building Stirling studied while designing the New State Gallery, as well as the Altes Museum, he evoked the neoclassical past as a ruin.[74] At the same time, he insisted, much to the frustration of many British contemporary critics, on a collage of old and new rather than straight historicism.[75] Although few of his references were specifically to the New Building, he paid particular attention to Stuttgart's own modernist heritage, quoting Bonatz as well as Le Corbusier's contribution to the Weissenhof Housing Estate. He also addressed the more recent high tech of the Centre Pompidou, in many ways the New State Gallery's chief contemporary rival.

Stirling won the limited competition to design the New State Gallery after losing

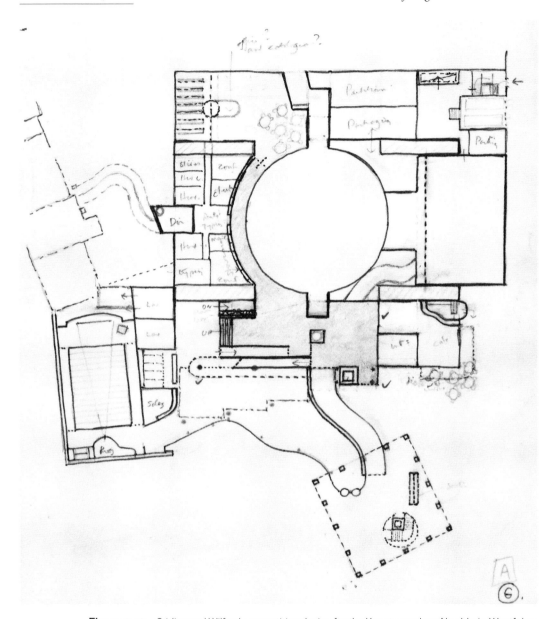

Figure 3.10. Stirling and Wilford, competition design for the Kunstsammlung Nordrhein-Westfalen, Düsseldorf, 1975. Source: Collection Centre Canadien d'Architecture/Canadian Centre for Architecture, Montreal.

a pair of earlier contests for the Kunstsammlung Nordrhein-Westfalen in Düsseldorf and the Wallraf-Richartz Museum in Cologne (Figure 3.10); Peter Beye, the director of the State Gallery, invited him to compete for the commission after being impressed by his Düsseldorf entry.[76] The Kunstsammlung was moving out of the building Rudolf Schwarz had designed for it after the war, into new quarters between the cathedral and the Rhine. As was widely recognized at the time, many details of the Stuttgart design, as well as the general approach of integrating it into the urban context, had their origins in the two unsuccessful entries.[77] In Düsseldorf, Stirling had organized the volumes on a tight urban site and planned to clad the structure, which was to be constructed, as in Stuttgart, out of reinforced concrete, in stone panels. As suggested by the brief he also retained the facades of an earlier library building. Invisible from the street, the core of the building was a circular courtyard, around which he wrapped a circulation route that passed through it. He ran a similar path, made more complex by a shift in grade, but also by its proximity to the city's enormous cathedral as well as the main train station, through the Cologne site.

Both the preservation of an existing facade and the creation of paths through the interiors of blocks responded to the contemporary nostalgia, which was particularly strong in Germany, for the small-scale urban fabric and the irregular juxtapositions of styles that had characterized cities like Stuttgart before the destruction wrought by the war followed by rebuilding on the scale of the automobile and of reinforced concrete. This nostalgia had been encouraged by Rossi, who had argued for a typological approach, in which new construction conformed to the height and footprint of neighboring buildings, and was also being adopted by this point by younger architects active in Germany. These included Eiermann's former student O. M. Ungers, who had been teaching at Cornell University with Stirling's former tutor Colin Rowe, as well as Rem Koolhaas, who assisted Ungers with the summer studio he ran in Berlin in 1977.[78] Rob Krier, who worked for Ungers in 1965–66, exhibited many of the drawings of his influential book on urban space in London in 1975, where Stirling was particularly likely to have seen them given that Rob's brother Leon had worked for him from 1969 to 1972. These schemes displayed Krier's propensity for the circular elements Stirling would shortly employ in his German competition entries; they also provided the British architects with a lens through which to understand Stuttgart, as the city figured prominently in Krier's argument.[79]

There were, however, important differences between Stirling's approach and that of the Kriers. Although they shared some of the same formal vocabulary, the Kriers insisted on restoring the blocks characteristic of eighteenth- and nineteenth-century Central European cities, while Stirling drove paths straight through the middle of them, compiling a cluster of disparate volumes. (Although in Britain Stirling's oeuvre was often understood as the antithesis of that of Alison Smithson and Peter Smithson, it is highly likely that their celebrated Economist Building, completed in London in 1964, was an inspiration as well.)[80] In Stuttgart Stirling also refused to create a strong street wall, instead recessing the mass of the building behind a terrace and a series of ramps.

High-profile British and American critics flocked to Stuttgart in the mid-1980s to write largely favorable reviews of the building. These did a great deal to contribute to its reputation as among the most important new European buildings of its day. These men largely defined its German context, as did Stirling in his published remarks about the building, in relation to the requirement that public paths not requiring entry to the museum run through the center of the site, and the obvious relationship between its plan and that of the Altes Museum.[81] With the exception of Peter Blundell Jones, the group, which also included Reyner Banham, Alan Colquhoun, Peter Cook, William Curtis, Martin Filler, and Charles Jencks, appeared unfamiliar with the city and its recent history. Cook described it as the capital of Westphalia rather than Württemberg; Filler termed the museum "the most significant building to rise in the Cleveland-sized city since Paul Bonatz's and E. F. Scholer's Hauptbahnhof of 1911–27," ignoring both the presence of the Weissenhof and the memory of the Schocken store.[82] Blundell Jones alone focused on the relatively negative reception of the building by Germans uncertain about precisely the aspect of the building that had garnered the most praise from British commentators: Stirling's revival of neoclassicism.

By the time the New State Gallery opened in 1984, it appeared to Rossi, Jencks, Ungers, Koolhaas, and the Kriers that modernism was over and that it was being replaced with an architecture whose roots were explicitly classical and might even encompass the revival of ornament. Many commentators in the Federal Republic took this line once the building was completed, but others did not. Falk Jaeger wrote in a local newspaper that Stirling had "thrown the twentieth century overboard and replaced functionalism with long outdated historicism."[83] Nonetheless, the initial controversy triggered by Stirling's competition victory was fought over slightly different issues, not least because in 1977 few were yet aware of the term *postmodern,* which only became widely used following the publication that year of Jencks's *The Language of Post-modern Architecture.*[84]

Part, but by no means all, of the problem was sour grapes. In 1974 the local firm of Behnisch, Kammerer and Belz had won an earlier competition for the same site, which also included an extension of the state parliament building. Three years later four additional firms, including Stirling's, were invited to compete with the original seven.[85] This time Behnisch, Kammerer and Belz placed only third, with the Danish firm of Jørgen Bo and Vilhelm Wohlert coming in second. Günter Behnisch, who had been appointed a professor at the Technical University in Stuttgart in 1967 and whose designs with Frei Otto for the Munich Olympics made him one of the Federal Republic's most celebrated architects, and his allies quickly lashed out. What was at stake, they agreed, was the future direction of architecture in the Federal Republic, as well as its relationship to democracy.[86] Less seldom mentioned, but clearly also a concern, were the inroads foreign architects were making in obtaining prestigious commissions.

The worries expressed by Behnisch and his allies were not entirely unjustified. For instance, Leon Krier notoriously upheld the architecture of Speer as a model for urban design, in a book that appeared a year after the gallery's completion.[87] In retrospect, by 1984 much of the opposition seemed "an anachronistic misunderstanding" to those who wrote favorable reviews in German of Stirling's building, but in the last four months of 1977, a time known as "The German Autumn," in which the very stability of the Federal Republic appeared endangered by the activities of the Red Army Faction (RAF; also known as the Baader Meinhof Gang), these were by no means trivial concerns.[88] In July and September the gang assassinated two leading businessmen; after a failed airplane hijacking by other members of the group, three incarcerated leaders were found dead in their cells in a Stuttgart prison. The government declared that they had committed suicide, but few on the left were willing to believe they would had been able to kill themselves in such a high-security prison, especially since two of them had been shot.[89] Moreover, the following year Filbinger would step down as minister-president after a controversy erupted over his role as a judge at the end of the war.[90]

Following the two assassinations but before the hijacking, Otto wrote to the leading Stuttgart newspaper:

> The architecture of the modern is dead. Monumentality is back. . . . Twenty years ago Stirling's entry—dismissed as fascist—would have been unthinkable.

He continued:

> The spirit of Mies van der Rohe, Le Corbusier and Scharoun, Häring and Finsterlin has faded. The Weissenhof is distant history, an object of historic preservation, nothing more.[91]

Although Otto and his allies dismissed Stirling's design as an example of Brutalism rather than postmodernism, they were clear about the political implications of such an approach.[92] Writing in December, after the deaths of the RAF leaders, Behnisch was even more explicit:

> The task falls to independent [Behnisch used the word *free* to describe architects who do not work for the state] architects, therefore to ensure that architecture remains tied to social conditions and goals, and it is here that they face their political responsibilities. A preeminent goal in our time is to see that conditions are produced in which the individual finds happiness . . . thus a free society. . . . Stirling misuses his power. He relinquishes architecture to the powers that be; he makes architecture manipulable.[93]

He went on to say that it was worse that Stirling did this in a civic building than in a commercial one, "built for capital." And although one critic dismissed Stirling's competition entry as "a throwback to expresssionism," a supporter of Behnisch's position concluded an attack on the apparent rationalism of Stirling's design by noting, "An example of the desired kind is Gottfried Böhm's pilgrimage church in Neviges, which is a work of art without 'snubbing the people.'"[94]

Although Stirling did not alter his design to address these concerns, the photographs of the model published at the time of the competition did not convey the high-tech details that give the completed building much of its character, nor was there yet any indication of the bold color scheme eventually employed. Drawings documenting Stirling's design process focus above all on the circulation through the core of the composition.[95] In 1984 he defended his approach:

> Architecture is for people, one builds for the public. . . . There cannot be anything but a democratic architecture. I don't believe that architecture in Germany is boring. The country has in this respect an enormous past. German architecture until the war was fantastic. . . . It is important that a city have monumental buildings. They serve as landmarks, as recognizable emblems of the city. A monumental building is not necessarily an expression of power. . . . Monumentality has a great deal to do with presence, and that means that a building vibrates, that it sings.[96]

While admitting its monumentality he also, however, "hope[d] that it is information and populist, hence the anti-monumentalism of the meandering footway and the voided centre and much else including the colouring."[97] Looking back, he all but welcomed the controversy, declaring in 1989, "The Germans are democratic regarding style, more open and modern in their approach to architecture, and better informed."[98]

Germans reviewing the completed building often seem relieved at the way in which these ironic touches, which they often described as pop rather than postmodern, leavened the monumentality they had feared at the time of the competition, although dissenting voices remained.[99] Manfred Sack, writing in the *Frankfurter Allgemeine Zeitung,* said that Stirling had, "in a building for the beautiful art of the twentieth century, [built] a fortress against democratic attitudes."[100] While they recognized the sources of Stirling's many citations, and despite the architect's comment that "a certain amount of monumentality is important for a city," many disputed that the building was overbearing. Nonetheless, no connection was made either to Mies's National Gallery or to more explicit examples of postwar German buildings that made creative use of the architecture of both the recent and distant past.[101] Ulrich Wanner, in a largely negative review, made the perceptive comment, however, that "this playful freedom, the courage, that occupies this postmodern field of ruins with individual fantasy, fills the mannerist emptiness with crafty humanity."[102] If one looks beyond the polemics that greeted the reception of the design, however, the connections to this earlier architecture remain clear.

Most visitors approach the New State Gallery from Konrad Adenauer Strasse, the multilane high-speed road that runs in front of it. Like the New National Gallery, Stirling's building sits on a plinth, which was a condition of the program drafted by the client. This contains parking, entered from a side street, as well as a black box space for temporary exhibitions, a lecture theater, and space for a music school (now housed next door in a separate structure), accessed from the same side street as the parking. An open pavilion constructed of red and blue steel beams and capped with a glazed gable marks the center of the main facade. Instead of allowing access directly onto the podium, it is where one may turn to the left to ascend a ramp or to the right to climb steps to reach the next level. Both paths are edged with oversize electric pink railings, whose size Stirling expanded to meet the German code for the gap between railing and wall.[103] Nor does reaching this point make clear where to go next in order to enter the building. This is, in other words, far from the standard axial entrance to a nineteenth-century neoclassical building like the Altes Museum or the Alte Pinakothek, or for that matter the postmodern successors to them. It is closer to the side approaches to the podium of the New National Gallery, of which Stirling was almost certainly thinking, as well as the many ramps designed by Le Corbusier. Stirling himself commented, "We did not make a conventional facade but a staggering of the depth.... Instead of a facade it is a series of events."[104]

In part because the entrance, tucked around to the left, is not easy to find, one is encouraged to linger on this complex podium. As at the New National Gallery, its character is determined in part by the borrowed view of mid-nineteenth-century architecture, in Berlin of the Matthew Church, in Stuttgart of the Old State Gallery (Figure 3.11). The degree to which Stirling followed a typological approach and echoed the Old State Gallery's U-shaped form is not clear from the podium, but becomes so when one enters his building and tours the similarly laid out permanent galleries (Figure 3.12). The connection between the buildings is established at the podium level by the way in which the far end of Stirling's building mimics the soft yellow stucco of the Old State Gallery, and by the way in which one of Stirling's choice of local stone (travertine from Cannstatt and sandstone from Sinsheim) for the cladding of his concrete structure echoes the trim of its predecessor.

Although critics lambasted postmodernism in general and postmodern museums in particular for their commercialization of public space, in Stuttgart Stirling created more rather than less public space than Mies had in Berlin.[105] While late modern museum designers like I. M. Pei and Cesar Pelli borrowed from shopping malls to create popular alternatives to the sense of privilege critics charged were embedded in neoclassicism, Stirling's podium, although it includes a café, is largely a venue for informal conversation in the context of a views out over the city and into the building (the shop inside was originally minuscule). Individuals rather than the museum itself staged most of the spectacles that occurred here. The podium and its ramps were also originally popular with skateboarders, some of whom may even

Figure 3.11. Georg von Barth, Old State Gallery, Stuttgart, 1838. Photograph by Helga Schmidt-Glassner. Copyright Bildarchiv Foto Marburg.

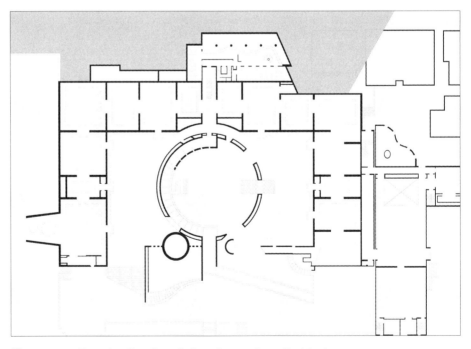

Figure 3.12. Floor plan, New State Gallery. Source: Conor Rochford.

An Architecture of Fragmentation and Absence 111

Figure 3.13. Rogers and Piano, Centre Pompidou, Paris, 1977. Source: Wikipedia Commons.

have recognized the references the garish railings made to the Centre Pompidou (Figure 3.13).[106] From here one has the choice of entering the museum or continuing up a second, entirely public, route through the building. Either brings one to a second major civic space, the circular void at the building's heart.

Clearly derived from the Pantheon-like structure at the center of Schinkel's Altes Museum, this space, which also included a half-buried reference to a design for a tomb by Schinkel's contemporary Friedrich Weinbrenner, whose design also provided the pattern of the cladding, was left open to the elements (Figure 3.14).[107] Planters around its upper edge added to the sense of a ruin, which was also enhanced by the way in which Stirling detailed the cladding. He exposed the nonstructural character of the alternating bands of two kinds of stone by leaving the joints between them, which would normally be filled with mortar, empty. It is easy to run one's finger between them and thus to sense the relative thickness of the veneer as well as

Figure 3.14. Courtyard, New State Gallery. Photograph by Waltraud Krase. Copyright Bildarchiv Foto Marburg.

locate the metal clips holding it in place. One of these stones is identical to that used by Bonatz on his nearby Graf Zeppelin Hotel. The banding and the organization of the building around an open courtyard echo the same architect's Art Museum in Basel of 1936 (Figure 3.15).[108] The quotations of modernism that stud the entire complex include the oversize vents at the back of the building, which refer to the Pompidou, and an echo, also at the rear, of one of Le Corbusier's contributions to the Weissenhof.

Stirling's rejection of functionalist planning and his acceptance of a strong street wall aligned him with Rossi, but the playfulness of the results went far beyond the pop iconography embraced by Robert Venturi and Denise Scott Brown. Whether

Figure 3.15. Paul Bonatz, Art Museum, Basel, 1936. Source: Livia Hurley.

the stones punched out of the parking lot and left anchored in the nearby grass or the "contextual choice" of cladding the lobby floor in the acid green flooring then found at Frankfurt Airport, these were overtly architectural jokes that had little to do with the signage that fascinated the American couple. Caricatures of classical pediments

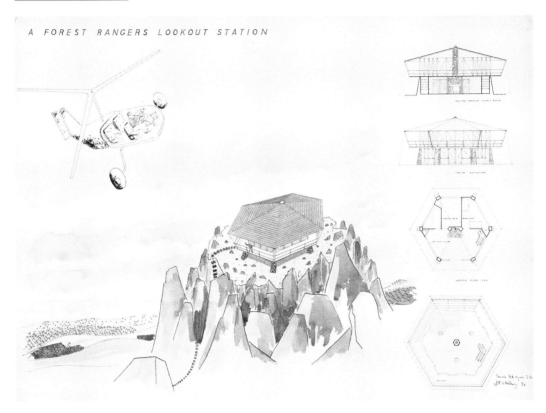

Figure 3.16. James Stirling, project for a forest ranger's lookout station, 1949. Source: Collection Centre Canadien d'Architecture/Canadian Centre for Architecture, Montreal.

capped the doorways between the galleries, but the overall strategy was to layer ornamental references to modernism upon a core built to resemble a neoclassical ruin. This inverted the reconstruction of ruined churches only to the degree that modernism was now reduced to the ornament the movement had supposedly spurned and the ruin was composed of entirely new construction.

Stirling was particularly well positioned, despite being British, to contribute to a specifically German invocation of memory of which he was clearly more aware and in which he was more interested than were most of the English-speaking critics who reviewed the results. As a student he had quoted Bruno Taut's *Alpine Architecture* in a sketch for, of all things, a forester's hut (Figure 3.16).[109] Although Le Corbusier clearly provided the touchstone for his early projects and built work, in his three seminal English university buildings of the 1960s—the Engineering Building at Leicester (1959–63), the History Faculty at Cambridge (1964–67) (Figure 3.17), and the Florey Building at Oxford (1966–71)—Stirling demonstrated his continued awareness of Taut's crystalline schemes, which reinforced his interest, widely recognized by British observers, in Victorian industrial architecture and its glaz-

An Architecture of Fragmentation and Absence

Figure 3.17. James Stirling, History Faculty, Cambridge University, Cambridge, England, 1967. Source: Seier + Seier/Wikipedia Commons.

ing.[110] Equally relevant was the way in which at Leicester he pioneered a historicist approach to modernism. In particular, his quotation of the cantilevered auditoria of Soviet constructivist architect Konstantin Melnikov's Rusakov Workers' Club in Moscow repeated a strategy that the architects of German churches of the 1950s and 60s frequently deployed when they quoted expressionism and the New Building.

Although Stirling's three major university commissions had garnered him a great deal of professional prestige, each had had its share of practical problems; the net result was that by the early 1970s it proved impossible for him to get commissions in Britain. Thus he must have been extremely anxious to figure out what the Germans wanted, and how he might provide them with it. Rather than designing the pure postmodern showpiece most of those who reviewed his building in English clearly sought, he appears to have been after something slightly different. Nor is it clear that this was simply the more overtly modernist building recent writers, anxious that his achievement weather the shift in fashion away from postmodernism, seek to uncover.[111] Instead, the New State Gallery should be seen as part of the continuum in German architecture that began with the Bartning's Church of the Resurrection in nearby Pforzheim and included as well the Alte Pinakothek and the New National Gallery. Stirling's awareness of these was not apparent to a generation of critics engaged in debating the merits of postmodernism. They had no cause to be attentive to the lingering impact of circular spaces for community on contemporary German architecture and were probably overwhelmed in any case by the number of sources he did choose to advertise. In retrospect, however, the New State Gallery informed a number of later buildings, including the Jewish Museum, the Reichstag, and the New Museum. All balance a sense of absence, whether conveyed through actual ruins, transparency, or void, with the strong presence of nineteenth-century architecture, which in turn encompassed actual historical fragments, the borrowed view of neighbors, and the more elusive way in which Stirling invokes this past as one of the many layers of the New State Gallery. But the revival of the classical past was not the only strand of postmodernism that would be imported into German museum architecture and be transformed there.

The Vitra Design Museum

The focus of most postmodern classicism, if not the New State Gallery, was the reconstruction of a sense of wholeness that appeared splintered by cubism and the artistic movements, including De Stijl and constructivism as well as the New Building, which descended at least in part from it. Moreover, functionalist planning made picturesque asymmetry, once the chief alternative to classicism, appear old-fashioned and sentimental. By the 1980s many postmodernist architects, including Ungers, focused on formal discipline as an alternative to what appeared to be flexibility run amok. And yet postmodernism quickly extended far beyond the return to history and to order, whether infused, in the case of Venturi and Stirling, with irony and wit, or not, in that of Rossi and Ungers.

Postmodernism, which began as an appellation for a particular strand of contemporary architecture, came to encompass a much broader critique of modernism across many forms of cultural production, from music and drama, to literary studies and even self-consciousness about the authorial voice of the historian. As it became more diverse, the span of architectural responses to the original critiques of modernist orthodoxy voiced by Rossi, Venturi, and Scott Brown extended out in new directions. One of the most original of these comprised the work created in and around Los Angeles between 1978 and 1986 by Frank Gehry.

Until 1978 Gehry had a conventionally successful career, producing unremarkable buildings, often on tight budgets, for a diverse array of clients, ranging from local artists to the Maryland-based developer James Rouse. Following his second marriage, Gehry and his new wife purchased a bungalow in Santa Monica, which he refurbished in a way he was able to describe with a comedian's skilled sense of timing. He claimed to have adhered to many of the precepts of postmodernist historicism but hilariously upended them by substituting ingredients of the Southern California modernist vernacular, including chain-link fencing and the particular shade of blue that swimming pools are usually painted, for classical convention (Figure 3.18). The result quickly made him a star. He consolidated his reputation as

An Architecture of Fragmentation and Absence   117

Figure 3.18. Frank Gehry, Gehry House, Santa Monica, California, 1978. Source: Gehry Partners LLP.

one of North America's most imaginative architects through a series of buildings in Los Angeles and its suburbs, each more startling than the next in its juxtaposition of what often appeared to be fragments of unfinished buildings. Several of his clients turned to him, not so much because they were champions of the avant-garde but because he could be trusted to come in under their tight budgets.[112]

In 1988 an exhibition at the Museum of Modern Art in New York curated by Philip Johnson and Mark Wigley lumped together various strands of contemporary architecture, including Gehry's recent work, under the label of deconstructivism, a word derived both from deconstruction, a postmodern literary theory, and Soviet constructivism, an art movement of the 1920s.[113] Gehry, who had gained courage for his subsequent experiments from designing the installation of a pioneering exhibition of constructivism, appears to have been almost entirely unaffected by literary theory.[114] He admitted to deriving considerable inspiration from the appearance of unfinished wood-framed structures found on small-scale construction sites across the United States. "Buildings under construction," he declared, "look nicer than buildings finished. How could a building be made to look like a process? Buildings that are just done by ordinary people—they look like hell when they're finished—but when they are under construction they look great."[115] Designing his buildings

Figure 3.19. Frank Gehry, Vitra Design Museum, Weil am Rhein, 1989. Source: Livia Hurley.

to make them look as if they had literally been deconstructed, that is, as if finished buildings had been partially disassembled or even exploded, was one of the hallmarks of this stage of his career.

Much of Gehry's original success derived from the degree to which his work was anchored in the specific history of the Los Angeles region, where it could be argued that modernism rather than classicism was the indigenous tradition, and where the Austrian émigré Rudolph Schindler's late houses featured a similarly eclectic collage of what appeared to be parts of separate structures. How Gehry would manage the transition to working on a national and even international scale was one of the great questions surrounding his career in the late 1980s.

The answer came above all through his first European building, the Vitra Design Museum on the grounds of the Vitra factory complex in Weil am Rhein, a German suburb of the Swiss city of Basel (Figure 3.19).[116] Gehry's client, Rolf Fehlbaum, was a furniture manufacturer. He built the museum, which now has an active exhibition program, to house the Vitra's collection of chairs. Fehlbaum had originally hoped to commission Gehry to design a chair, only later arriving at the idea of a museum. When Gehry pointed out how expensive his airfare and fee for such a small building would be, Fehlbaum threw in a factory,[117] which received considerably less attention.[118] Gehry encouraged Fehlbaum to make the Vitra campus (which already

An Architecture of Fragmentation and Absence

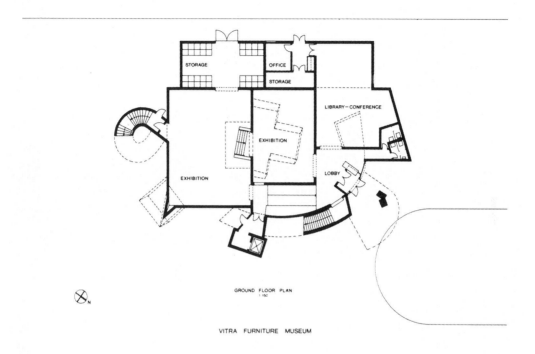

Figure 3.20. Plan, Vitra Design Museum. Source: Gehry Partners LLP.

included a factory by Nicholas Grimshaw) a showcase of contemporary architecture. The presence of buildings by some of the world's leading architects, including Tadao Ando, Zaha Hadid, and Jacques Herzog and Pierre de Meuron, burnishes the reputation of a company that holds a license of manufacture for the work of the Americans Charles Eames and George Nelson, two of the twentieth century's most celebrated modernist furniture designers.[119]

Gehry energized what in plan appeared largely to be a dumb box by extruding its volumes (Figure 3.20). Two of these house stairs connecting the building's two major levels; a third pokes through the roof to create a sky-lit gallery. Zinc cladding of the "roofs" of the protrusions, some of which are actually almost perpendicular to the ground, adds variety to the largely stuccoed surfaces. Critics invoked Le Corbusier's church at Ronchamp (1954) and Rudolf Steiner's Goetheanum (1923–28), just over the French and Swiss borders, respectively; the most perceptive also noted a stronger influence as Gehry tried to situate himself in a new environment—the work

Figure 3.21. Hans Scharoun, Philharmonie, Berlin, 1963. Source: Livia Hurley.

of Scharoun, including the Philharmonie as well as much earlier contributions to the Weissenhof Estate (Figure 3.21).[120] This is confirmed by the degree to which the Philharmonie served as the key precedent for Gehry's Disney Concert Hall in Los Angeles, designed and built between 1991 and 2003.[121]

There are no ruins in sight in the flat floodplain of the Rhine. Fragmentation inspired by the history of modernism nonetheless appeared the appropriate strategy for an architect who, while committed to abstract forms, insisted on the degree to which his startling architecture was rooted in a sensitivity to the local context. There is an innate sympathy here with the sculptural expression of Gottfried Böhm and the antimonumentality of Stirling, as well as an admiration for Scharoun. Missing in the work of the American transplant is the emphasis on creating a community-focused space that had fascinated all three of these predecessors, as well as his more local precedents.

In the Vitra, and in working within a specifically German reframing of his own already fragmented approach to modernism's own past, Gehry, who had seemed for a decade to be in the constant and exhilarating process of reinventing himself with almost every new commission, found the formal language to which he has largely adhered ever since. It was only, however, with his much larger and more expensive museum in Bilbao, Spain, completed in 1997, that he demonstrated the impact outstanding design could have on the local economy by drawing tourists from every corner of the globe.

Gehry, like Stirling before him, was widely viewed as having injected a foreign, and distinctively postmodernist, architectural strategy into the design of a German museum, which was also informed, in ways that were not often acknowledged at the time, by attentiveness to a German context. The next time a Jewish architect based in the United States accomplished a similar feat, the recollection of suffering finally extended to the annihilation Germans imposed on the Jews, and substituted for the communication of Germany's commitment to the latest in art and culture. It nonetheless embodied this, too, and the result was in consequence a far more powerful symbol than Gehry's bijou pavilion for the Vitra.

Jewish Museum

Rooted in an appreciation of ordinary construction sites and constructivist gymnastics, Gehry's approach to fragmentation and to modernism's own history was by no means the only one encompassed by the label of deconstructivism. Gehry, like Stirling, would continue to build in Germany, but the Vitra was quickly overshadowed by a museum by a much younger architect. Libeskind's Jewish Museum in Berlin, designed just months before the fall of the Wall and built in the context of German unification, rivaled the Bilbao Guggenheim as the most trumpeted museum building of the 1990s (Figure 3.22). Its defiant thunderbolt, set against the eighteenth-century courthouse that from 1969 to 1993 housed West Berlin's Berlin Museum (to which it was originally intended to be an addition) and against the postmodern urbanism that has characterized planning in the city since the 1980s, seared the importance of fragmentation and the communication of absence into the city's fabric. It established the importance of such architecture to the identity of the Berlin Republic, begun upon the transfer of the national capital to a reunited Berlin in 1999, the year the building was finally completed. The building opened only two years later, by which time it housed an independent institution supported by the national government.[122]

Libeskind's design emerged as well out of the mapping exercises that were being used in Berlin at the end of the 1980s by adherents of deconstructivist architecture to create a middle ground between the influence Rossi, Ungers, and their disciples were having upon the reconstruction of the Kreuzberg district of the city, in which the museum sits, on the one hand and the lingering interest both German and American architects had in abstract form on the other.[123] Nestled in the shadow of the Wall, Kreuzberg was the easternmost of West Berlin's neighborhoods. The Wall cut it off from the original center of the city, which in the interwar decades had been growing toward it. This left it marginal in the postwar period; by the 1970s it was dominated by recent immigrants from Turkey and by student activists, some of them squatters. Beginning in 1979, the International Building Exhibition (International Bauausstellung; IBA), organized by Josef Paul Kleihues, brought many of the world's

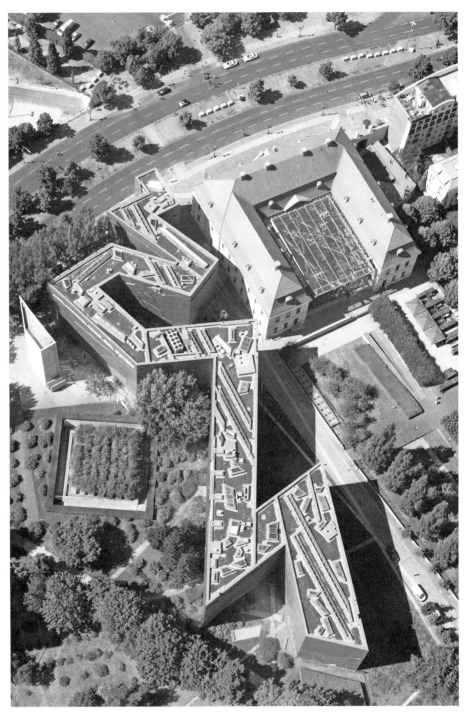

Figure 3.22. Daniel Libeskind, Jewish Museum, Berlin, 1999. Source: Gunther Schneider.

most ambitious architects into the district to build subsidized housing, much of it intended to attract better-off tenants.[124] Equally important to Libeskind's design was the reemerging international importance in the 1980s of memorials. The type had played a relatively minor role in modern art and architecture until a wave of Holocaust commemorations, assisted in the United States by the success of Maya Lin's Vietnam War Memorial in Washington, D.C., made memory a central concern of late twentieth-century art and architecture. Despite Libeskind's originally extremely obscure rhetoric, the Vietnam War Memorial and the Jewish Museum proved far more legible to a mass audience than postmodern classicist alternatives; their effectiveness contributed to the revival of modernist forms at the century's end.

The respect for the eighteenth- and nineteenth-century city that underlay Stirling's adherence to the street line in his New State Gallery, and his deference to its immediate neighbor began to play an important role in the reconstruction of Berlin in the 1970s. It was at this point that East German architects and planners began to rehabilitate late nineteenth-century apartment blocks rather than replace them with new constructions.[125] It is hardly surprising that Rossi's theory, which was inspired in part by his admiration for the Stalinallee, which he had seen when a guest of the East German Bauakademie in 1960, had an impact on this side of the city first.[126] Western architects did not lag far behind, however. Already in 1977 Ungers's summer school had been focused on the West Berlin district of Kreuzberg. Together with the work of Rob Krier in the same district, this helped set the tone for the IBA.[127]

The wariness many in the Federal Republic had of the revival of neoclassicism in civic architecture did not often extend by the 1980s to support for tower-in-the-park urbanism. Although the large housing complexes on both sides of the Wall had relatively few of the social problems associated with similar apartment blocks in France, the United Kingdom, and the United States, the West Berlin planning community had many allies in its conclusion that, whatever style architects chose, they should adhere to the street lines established a hundred years before and that new inserts into this established fabric should also maintain the old rooflines and about the same proportion of solid wall to window opening. (The insistence on this scale was greatly assisted by the fact that the population of West Berlin had declined substantially following the war.) Across the course of the 1980s, West Berlin became one of the centers of international architectural culture, as the IBA offered an array of avant-garde designers, many of whom had hitherto built very little, the opportunity to erect housing, provided they played by the ground rules.

Most of the new housing was located in Kreuzberg. Many residents were wary of the attempt to improve the city's attractiveness for "yuppies" (a new term at the time) by building fashionable new apartments, which in many cases almost abutted the Wall. Planners had to compromise and provide infrastructural upgrades, including day care centers located in back courtyards; in the end very little new housing was built in the heart of the neighborhood as opposed to near its least comfortable edge.

Figure 3.23. Aldo Rossi, Wilhelmstrasse IBA housing, Berlin, 1987. Source: Livia Hurley.

Commissions were decided in an unusual fashion that ensured the participation of a who's who of contemporary architects. Competitions were held to determine the guidelines for particular sites, to which the losers had to adhere. This meant that an invitation to compete entailed a commission. Among the talent the IBA lured were Arata Isozaki from Japan, Peter Eisenman and John Hejduk from the United States, Koolhaas's Office of Metropolitan Architecture from the Netherlands, and Rossi; elsewhere in the city a cluster of housing was designed by Charles Moore and other American postmodernists (Figure 3.23). The project put West Berlin back on the map after more than a decade in which little of international note had been built there.

In this context a competition was held in 1989 for an extension of West Berlin's Berlin Museum, which was housed in the Kollegienhaus, a baroque courthouse designed by Philipp Gerlach and erected in 1735; the museum's original building and much of its collections remained on the other side of the Wall. The most notable occupant of the extension was intended to be the museum's substantial Jewish collection. Only after the reunification of Berlin prompted returning the bulk of West Berlin's Berlin Museum's collections to their original home did the Jewish Museum emerge as an autonomous institution occupying this entire site. Indeed, this happened largely because retreating from constructing Libeskind's extremely expensive building would have sent the wrong signals about the newly expanded Federal Republic's ability to confront Germany's troubled past. The building was so powerful that a new museum dedicated specifically to the history of the city's Jewish community was founded to fill it. The Kollegienhaus, which had housed West Berlin's Berlin Museum, was thus reduced to an entrance and administrative appendage to Libeskind's building.

Although it was not part of the IBA, which was just wrapping up its activities, the extension project was in many ways an expansion of its aims. The site was in a part of Kreuzberg studded with IBA buildings, and Kleihues chaired the competition jury. Moreover, the museum benefited from the enormous attention the IBA had bestowed on West Berlin in general and this neighborhood in particular. Finally, the winning design, which Libeskind termed "Between the Lines," drew upon both the history of the immediate environs and the example of one of the most prominent IBA buildings, located a scant three blocks away, Eisenman's apartment block (1981–85) at the intersection of Kochstrasse and Friedrichstrasse, right next to Checkpoint Charlie, a crossing point for citizens of the four powers who officially still governed the city (Figures 3.24 and 3.25).

An American, Eisenman was one of a group of architects nicknamed "the Whites" who opposed the ironic, pop-oriented architecture espoused by Robert Venturi and Denise Scott Brown.[128] In its place Eisenman originally espoused a geometric formalism that owed a great deal to his admiration for Italian rationalism of the 1920s and 1930s, and more than a little to the influence of Rowe, with whom he had studied at Cornell.[129] His early buildings and projects consisted of a series of numbered houses. In 1982 he published a book about the way in which the design of the last of these, the unbuilt House X, was derived from the linguistic theory of Noam Chomsky.[130] Soon afterward, he became interested in deconstruction, which led him to engage in a sustained conversation with the French literary theorist Jacques Derrida (at the time he designed the building on Kochstrasse, however, that collaboration lay in the future).[131] Also in 1982 Eisenman stepped down from the directorship of the Institute for Architecture and Urban Studies in New York, which he had held for fifteen years and which had put him in the center of the American discussion of new directions in architecture and architectural theory.

For Eisenman, the Berlin commission was an enormous opportunity, as he had not yet built anything larger than a private house; only in 1983 did he win the competition for the Wexner Center for the Arts in Columbus, Ohio, which repeated the German formula of contrasting fragments of (in this case re-created) historic structures with abstract grids.[132] Charged, before his relationship with deconstruction had crystallized, with building a box whose shape was largely determined in advance, he responded by undertaking a mapping exercise, using the results to generate

Figure 3.24. Peter Eisenman, apartment block at Checkpoint Charlie, Berlin, 1985. Source: Livia Hurley.

not only the way in which the two volumes of the building collided at a slight angle but also the decorative grids he applied to their surfaces. Among the sources for the design was the original street grid of Friedrichstadt, the eighteenth-century extension to the city that had been bisected by the Wall, and the Wall itself, which ran almost directly behind the building, one of whose chief tenants is the Museum at Checkpoint Charlie.[133]

Although this was not strictly speaking a deconstructivist project, the approach appealed to Libeskind, who, like Eisenman and Gehry, had been included in the Museum of Modern Art's deconstructivism exhibition. A dozen years younger than Eisenman, Libeskind had not yet built anything when he competed for the extension of the Berlin Museum, although he had begun to establish a reputation for his projects and theory.[134] In his competition brief Libeskind described the way in which the irregular geometry of "Between the Lines" was generated by his own mapping exercise. Libeskind explained that he generated its ground plan from a diagram of an elongated Star of David, which he imposed upon a map of Berlin. The shape of

An Architecture of Fragmentation and Absence   127

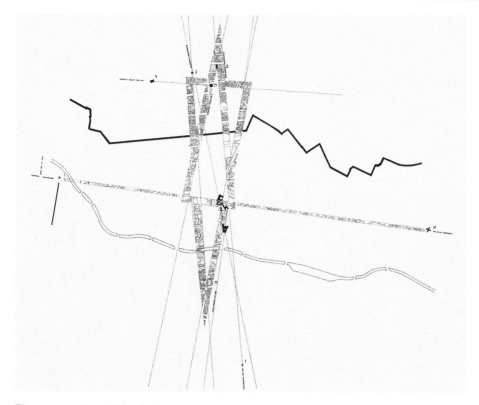

Figure 3.25. Daniel Libeskind, competition design, Jewish Museum, 1989. Source: Studio Daniel Libeskind.

the star and the placement of the other lines were, Libeskind claimed, influenced by places associated with key figures:

> Great figures in the drama of Berlin who have acted as bearers of an immense hope and anguish are traced into the lineaments of this museum: Heinrich Kleist, Rahel Varnhagen, Walter Benjamin, E. T. A. Hoffmann, Friedrich Schleiermacher, Arnold Schönberg, Paul Celan. They spiritually affirm the permanent human tension polarized between the impossibility of the system and the impossibility of giving up the search for a higher order. Tragic premonition (Kleist), sublimated assimilation (Varnhagen), inadequate ideology (Benjamin), and science (Hoffmann), displaced understanding (Schleiermacher), inaudible music (Schönberg), last words (Celan): these constitute the critical dimension that this work as discourse seeks to transgress.[135]

Left almost unmentioned was Mendelsohn, whose nearby office building for the Metal Workers' trade union lies at the south end of the block, clearly visible in 1989 across an expanse of empty lawn from the museum (Figure 3.26). In this diagram,

Figure 3.26. Erich Mendelsohn, rear facade, Metal Workers' Union Building, Berlin, 1930. Source: Livia Hurley.

Libeskind picked out the building's footprint in the same solid black as that of the museum. He has acknowledged that its acute angles inspired his own jagged lines.[136]

Although the way in which Libeskind derived the form of his building was closely connected to practices associated at the time with the new relationship between postmodern architecture and literary theory, the result was fully in keeping with well-established conventions regarding church and museum architecture in the Federal Republic. Here the historic building, an eighteenth-century courthouse, had been completely repaired after the war. Also crucial were new approaches to commemoration.

Eight years before Libeskind was awarded the commission for the extension to the Berlin Museum at the relatively young age of forty-one, Lin bested her competitors for the Vietnam War Memorial when she was only twenty-one. Informed by earth art and minimalism (Richard Serra was teaching at Yale when Lin was a student there), her V-shaped memorial, embedded into the Washington Mall and faced in polished black granite, into which the names of the individual dead were carved, initially triggered enormous controversy (Figure 3.27).[137] This was quelled upon its

An Architecture of Fragmentation and Absence

Figure 3.27. Maya Lin, Vietnam War Memorial, Washington, D.C., 1982. Source: Mario Roberto Durán Ortiz/Wikipedia Commons.

completion when veterans' groups, who had initially called for a more conventional design, embraced the finished design. Architectural historian Andrew Shanken captures the utility of minimalism, first recognized by Lin, for the design of memorials:

> Minimalism arose in the same years [as the Vietnam War] and gave a wide berth to these multiple viewpoints. It is an art that is assertive with space, not meaning. It sets a stage but leaves it empty for the spectator, who participates as an actor in the construction of meaning. . . . Lin used minimalism to restore some of the possibility of the cairn, boulder, or burial mound, those most ancient memorial traditions that transform landscape or liken the unfathomable forces and eons behind the appearance of an erratic boulder in a landscape to a life and its loss. The inconclusiveness of the Vietnam War and the upheaval associated with it lent themselves to such a vocabulary.[138]

Almost immediately memorials, which had been an increasingly minor feature of art and architecture since the emergence of abstraction in the early decades of the century, began to be built in large numbers again. Nowhere would the new memorial culture be so pervasive as in the United States and Germany.[139]

In both countries, it was closely associated from the beginning with the commemoration of the Holocaust. In the early decades after the Second World War, survivors and their supporters often shied away from constructing memorials. Early designs by Mendelsohn and Louis Kahn for memorials in New York were not realized, despite the city's large and generous Jewish community.[140] Jewish opponents of Mendelsohn's design for Riverside Park felt that efforts should focus instead upon taking care of the living; a member of the commissioning committee wrote Kahn that "not all present felt that your model totally fulfilled their longings, represented their thoughts or relieved their tragic memories."[141] Kahn, the twentieth century's most celebrated Jewish architect, had proposed a grid of glass cubes overlooking

Figure 3.28. Louis Kahn, project for a Memorial for Six Million, New York, 1967. Source: Louis Kahn Archives, Pennsylvania Historical and Museum Collections.

New York Harbor (Figure 3.28). He began work on the project in 1966, but it was canceled in 1972, two decades after the abandonment of Mendelsohn's project.[142]

By the 1980s, the situation was changing. The success of Lin's monument was one trigger; another may have been the Israeli invasion of Lebanon in 1982 and the massacres that followed from it, which encouraged some American Jews to focus more on remembering the Holocaust than on supporting Israel as the defining marker of their ethnic identity. In keeping with the precedent established by Lin, and by minimalism and postmodernism more generally, the new memorials, which were erected throughout the Federal Republic as well as across the United States, were generally abstract and deliberately antimonumental.[143] Although Erica Doss believes that "minimalism is the style of choice for many contemporary memorials precisely because of its theatricality, its emphasis on felt experience and audience engagement," Michael Kimmelman expressed a more widely held opinion in a 2002 article in the *New York Times*:

> Minimalism, of all improbable art movements of the last 50 years, [has] become the unofficial language of memorial art.... Once considered the most obstinate kind of modernism, Minimalism has gradually, almost sub rosa, made its way into the public's heart. And now these bare walls are blank slates onto which we project our deepest commonly held feelings.[144]

Even before the museum it housed officially opened to the public in 2001, the Jewish Museum proved by far the most popular as well as one of the most successful of these many attempts to forge a memorial culture capable of addressing the Holocaust.[145] This necessarily involved rejecting conventions developed in the context of patriotic nationalism but dovetailed with the way churches and museums had evoked absence in the Federal Republic for decades. In a book published to mark the museum's opening, Libeskind recounted his motivation far more clearly than he had at the time of his competition victory:

> Three basic ideas formed the foundation for the Jewish Museum design: first the impossibility of understanding the history of Berlin without understanding the enormous intellectual, economic, and cultural contribution made by its Jewish citizens; second the necessity to integrate the meaning of the Holocaust, both physically and spiritually, into the consciousness and memory of the city of Berlin; third, that only through acknowledging and incorporating this erasure and void of Berlin's Jewish life can the history of Berlin and Europe have a human future.[146]

The way in which Libeskind proposed to realize these goals drew directly upon Kahn's proposed New York memorial and upon Lin's recent success. The multiple sources for Libeskind's distinctive zigzags, and for the skill with which he manipulated the ground plane of his extension, including the link between it and the former courthouse, include Lin's monument as well as Mendelsohn's building. Libeskind's debt to Kahn's unbuilt memorial is even clearer, although its transparent character was more optimistic than the forest of concrete columns in Libeskind's disorienting Garden of Exile.

One enters the zinc-clad Jewish Museum by descending through an underground passage from what was the Berlin Museum and is now administrative facilities. Stairs crossed overhead by concrete beams lead up to the galleries, whose facades are slashed by irregularly shaped diagonal slits. At points at the path through the galleries one is confronted with views into inaccessible shafts, the voids set along an axis discernible only in plan, which Libeskind has described as "the space of Berlin, because it refers to that which can never be exhibited when it comes to the Jewish Berlin history. It has been reduced to ashes" (Figure 3.29).[147] At the end of one's journey one enters a tall concrete shaft known as the Holocaust Tower. The experience of being in this space, which is illuminated dimly by a thin clerestory opening, is obviously intended to recall the gas chambers, while the tilted ground in the Garden of Exile is even more physically unsettling. The obviousness of this symbolism, despite the abstract way in which it was expressed, led Kimmelman to dismiss the building as "the epitome of kitsch and mass sentiment," while acknowledging that "it has been a huge popular and critical success."[148]

Kimmelman wrote in the shadow of Libeskind's 2003 victory in the competition to design the successor to New York's World Trade Center, which cemented the architect's transformation from the enfant terrible of a nearly incomprehensible avant-garde into an architect easily able to communicate—albeit with the assistance

Figure 3.29. Void, Jewish Museum. Source: Livia Hurley.

of multiple publicity firms—with a public unfamiliar with the details of architectural theory but entranced, temporarily at least, with the rhetorical gesture of a tower that would rise exactly 1,776 feet.[149] All this remained well in the future when the Jewish Museum was under construction. The force of the building's symbolism was so compelling that an entirely new institution was created to fill its spaces.

Libeskind did not, like so many earlier architects working in Germany before him, contrast ruins with new construction executed in a modernist style. Instead, as Stirling had, he juxtaposed an intact historical structure with voids that invoked ruins. Like Stirling, he paid careful attention to the site and to the recent history of modern architecture in its environs. Aware of Rossi's evocation of Halbwachs's theory of collective memory, he was probably also familiar with Gehry's fragmentation of the facade of the Vitra. Libeskind's success at constructing an architecture that was both abstract and yet engaged with history was so great that the Jewish Museum has always been seen as the beginning of a new, specifically German approach to using architecture to confront the past, rather than as an heir to expressionism and the culmination of four decades of experimentation with voids.[150] Its progeny would join it among the most prominent symbols of the newly reunited city and country.

During the sixties, seventies, and eighties, museum buildings erected in the Federal Republic kept alive the approach to ruins inaugurated in the first years after the war in church construction. In his New National Gallery, Mies moved it from the edges of modernist orthodoxy into the international mainstream. For those unaware of the recent work of Mies's friend Schwarz, the connection between the gallery and the neighboring Matthew Church, and thus with the many churches that paired modern transparency with nineteenth-century masonry, went unnoticed. The same could be said of the impact of Oesterlen's church designs on his Historical Museum. The New State Gallery signaled that this fusion of abstraction and historicism could outlive a shift not only from sacred to secular construction but also from modernism to what was seen at the time as its postmodern antithesis. Indeed, it also proved possible to transpose this understanding of modern architecture as a series of fragments, possibly but not necessarily clustered around a preexisting historical building, to not one but two strands of the deconstructivist architecture that could be interpreted as either an extension of postmodernism or a rejection of it.[151]

The lines between these museums, and between them and the churches that preceded them, were difficult to draw when historians and critics focused on questions of style. Their architects were keenly aware of one another and, in the case of Mies, Oesterlen, and Stirling at least, of earlier examples of the key precedents for their approach. Moreover, although these few buildings represented only a small fraction of the new museums constructed in Germany during these decades, they garnered a disproportionate share of the international attention. The result was that each reinforced the next, as one foreign architect after another flying in to be considered for a highly charged and visible commission considered what it meant to work within the Federal Republic's very specific architectural circumstances.

By the time the Berlin Wall fell on 9 November 1989, although there was no body of criticism describing (much less one of theory defending) this strategy, it was well established and was championed by many of Germany's leading architects, including Bartning, Schwarz, and the Böhms, as well as international stars such as Mies, Stirling, and Gehry, and members of a younger avant-garde like Libeskind. In the years to come it would prove the point of departure for the talent that flooded into a newly reunited Berlin, as well as for Germans working in other parts of the country. Its impact was never limited to the Federal Republic. Even more than postwar German churches, the New National Gallery, the New State Gallery, and the Jewish Museum were some of the most prominent buildings of their time erected anywhere in the world, while the Vitra provided the point of departure for the Guggenheim in Bilbao. Their considerable resonance, however, was almost entirely detached from widespread awareness that they were anchored in a tradition. Acknowledging this would have eroded the degree to which each could be seen as an innovative new solution to the perpetual issue of how to address the Federal Republic's relationship with the architecture of the Second Reich, the Weimar Republic, and the Third Reich.

The similarity in approach mapped out here did not entail continuity in meaning, any more than it did in style. Between the reconstruction of the Alte Pinakothek and the design of the Jewish Museum, both of whose architects movingly evoked absence, there was a sea change in attitudes toward the Nazi past. Whereas in the 1950s German Christians considered themselves the victims of the Allied bombings that had damaged the Alte Pinakothek, the far younger public that greeted the Jewish Museum with such enthusiasm accepted that others had suffered even more at German hands and that this suffering merited public commemoration. Criticism of Libeskind's design, such as that voiced by Kimmelman, came more easily from American Jews for whom this understanding was already axiomatic.

A small but prominent cluster of museum buildings designed during the Federal Republic's first four decades thus provided useful ways of imagining the country's relation with multiple pasts. Respect for the neoclassicism of the early nineteenth century, a conservative position in the 1950s, was in the New National Gallery and the New State Gallery detached from nostalgia for the monarchies that had sponsored the construction of the country's original museum infrastructure. Indeed, in 1984 the Christian Democrat chief minister of Baden-Württemberg declared the importance of democracy having an even better sense of culture than had the monarchs who had established Stuttgart's original State Gallery.[152] To the degree that the New National Gallery was tinged by a sense of victimhood, it was the loss of the Altes Museum to the Communist east, more than the Third Reich's own demolitions or the bombing raids of the war, that bore the blame. The issue for Stirling was not how to memorialize loss but how to build upon the neoclassical past without invoking the monumentality associated with Nazi architecture. By the time Gehry designed the Vitra, fragmentation had become an aesthetic choice, largely devoid of political symbolism, although imbued with admiration for a particular expressionist strand of the New Building and its progeny as a fitting point of departure. Despite his allusion to the Metal Workers' Building, Libeskind was less dependent upon the example of the New Building than Mies, Stirling, or Gehry had been. Instead, he turned to the immediate past and the larger German confidence in architecture as a particularly effective means of communicating national identity. In so doing he also created a template for how the expanded Federal Republic could express its willingness to address the horrors of the Third Reich.

Four

Critical Reconstruction or Neomodernist Shards?
Postunification Berlin

Germany ceased being a monarchy as a result of the November Revolution of 1918, but Berlin once again has a queen (Figure 4.1). The famous statue of Nefertiti, the wife of the pharaoh Akhenaten, who ruled Egypt in the fourteenth century BCE, was excavated in Egypt in 1912 and put on display the following year on Berlin's famed Museum Island, where she stayed for twenty-seven years.[1] After having been moved for safekeeping during the Second World War and then installed in a modest outbuilding of West Berlin's Charlottenburg Palace, she has reigned since 2009 in considerable splendor from a perch in the center of an octagonal chamber that still bears the scars of the war.[2] Only patches of the Pompeian-style mosaic floor remain; the stone arches supporting the coffered, Pantheon-style dome are also patched, although the bold red-and-green wall painting has been mostly restored. None of this discourages tourists, who patiently wait for the chance to pay her homage; visitor numbers are much increased from what they were in Charlottenburg, where it was often possible to have a long private audience in her presence.

On 17 October 2009 a "new" museum, the New Museum, opened its doors on the island.[3] Despite the name, it was no longer new, as it originally opened in 1855. At that time, the adjective *new* was applied in comparison to its famous neighbor, designed by Schinkel, which at that point became the "Altes" or old museum. Like so many important mid-nineteenth-century Prussian buildings, the New Museum was the work of Schinkel's talented disciple, Friedrich August Stüler. It closed at the onset of the Second World War and was so badly damaged in the same raid that felled the Memorial Church that it stayed shut for another seven decades. For years, trees grew out of the ruins, which were scarcely tucked out of sight as the other museums on the island remained among East Berlin's most prominent tourist attractions, and

Figure 4.1. Friedrich August Stüler, Neues Museum, Berlin, 1855, renovated by David Chipperfield, 2009. Source: Ute Zscharmt for David Chipperfield Architects.

Critical Reconstruction or Neomodernist Shards? 139

a major rail route cut through the island just to the north. It is in this refurbished structure that Nefertiti now presides over the tourist throngs.

The headline in the *New York Times* when the renovated building went on view in March, before any art had been installed, announced, "For Berlin Museum, a Modern Makeover That Doesn't Deny the Wounds of War."[4] As had so often been the case since the unveiling in 1989 of Daniel Libeskind's design for the Jewish Museum, located just over a mile away, an architecture that juxtaposed fragments of a historic building with clearly modern insertions now served as a way of acknowledging the violence of war and, by implication, although it had not taken place at this site, of the terror unleashed by the Nazi state.

The "new" New Museum quickly became the new century's most prominent and popular example of the enduring appeal of this often jarring pairing of old and new.[5] As with other important museums in the Federal Republic over the course of the previous half century, its construction—or more exactly in this case reconstruction—was entrusted to a foreign architect, in this case David Chipperfield, an Englishman based in London.[6] Working closely with local preservation authorities, and amply funded by both the city and national government, he collaged salvaged elements of the original building with new construction sensitively executed in a firmly abstract, if far from high-tech, idiom. The result serves as one of the most powerful symbols of the rebirth of a united Germany as a country dedicated to culture and to acknowledging rather than escaping its checkered past. And yet there is very little that is new here, besides the unprecedented amount of money—more than 200 million euros—that it all cost.

This approach to building an identity specific to the Federal Republic of Germany was forged in the crucible of churches built in response to wartime destruction and chased in the far more comfortable circumstances of museums erected long after West Germany established itself as economically prosperous and politically stable. This reliance upon memories of modernism, often contrasted with historic fabric, survived major changes in architectural fashion, including the emergence of postmodernism, and was adopted by architects from abroad who sought to respond sensitively to particular German sites, including two located in West Berlin near the Wall. It is thus scarcely surprising that long before the Jewish Museum finally opened to the public in 2001, this had become the most successful architectural strategy for addressing the particular and peculiar circumstances of the historic core of a reunified Berlin following the fall of the Wall and that it continued to serve that purpose well into the new century.

There were alternatives, and for the first two decades after reunification these enjoyed the support of the city government and governed most new construction in Berlin's historical center. Planners adopted a strategy they termed "critical reconstruction" to govern the rebuilding of Mitte. This entailed a respectful recall of a decidedly classical past. Critical reconstruction's key principles were originally that the historical street plan should be revived and that no new building should occupy more than a single city block, be taller than thirty meters, or have more than 80 percent commercial space. Eventually, its adherents extended the planning approach espoused by the IBA to encompass a focus not on historicist architectural forms per se but on a respect for the urban fabric of a century earlier, including the limited scale of window openings.[7]

Nonetheless more original and attention-provoking recollections of a past that very specifically included modernism kept intruding upon and upstaging the official policy. One of the most effective ways they achieved this was by attracting more tourists. Reunification brought the infrastructure of a much larger country back to Berlin, but it also resulted across the course of the 1990s in the elimination of almost all of the city's manufacturing base. By the early twenty-first century, city marketing aimed at tourists would rival issues of national identity in importance in shaping those structures designed to stand out from the background architecture favored by adherents of critical reconstruction.[8] And it was to these buildings exhibiting the complexity of recent German history that tourists flocked.

The number of memory-related debates that erupted across the course of the redevelopment of Mitte is far too great to chronicle here. Four comparisons nonetheless clarify the difference between the two approaches as well as demonstrate the ways in which the creation of a new memory landscape helped alleviate the fears generated by reunification, especially among the victims of World War II and their descendants. The first pair includes two of the earliest and most prominent commercial buildings erected in the former east. For his Galeries Lafayette (1991–96), Jean Nouvel drew deeply from the well of the New Building; O. M. Ungers in the Friedrichstadt Passagen (1993–96), looked instead for inspiration to Schinkel's neighboring neoclassical theater, the Schauspielhaus. Although the Galeries Lafayette was an entirely new building, like Mies's New National Gallery, it began a dialogue with the architecture of a vanished past, in this case the modern commercial architecture erected nearby across the first third of the twentieth century and felled by a combination of aerial bombardment, Soviet invaders, and East German planners. Opened several years later and located several blocks to the northwest are Norman Foster's renovation of the Reichstag (1992–99) and the rebuilt Hotel Adlon (completed 1997) by Rüdiger Patzschke and Rainer Michael Klotz. With the Reichstag, an architectural strategy that had long served as the de facto face of the Federal Republic became its official one; the Adlon quickly emerged, as its predecessor had been, as Berlin's most prestigious hostelry. The Topography of Terror (2005–10), as configured by Ursula Wilms and Heinz Hallmann, as well as the previous project by Peter Zumthor (1997), creates a powerful contrast with Peter Eisenman's Memorial to the Murdered Jews of Europe (1997–2005), originally designed in concert with the sculptor Richard Serra. The Topography of Terror is a memory landscape with a strong grounding in a specific physical setting, while the Memorial to the Murdered

Jews of Europe not only lacks such a relationship but also appears to have been strongly influenced by critical reconstruction's planning precepts. Finally, the success of the New Museum (1997–2009) bears comparison with the efforts to reconstruct the former Hohenzollern royal palace or Schloss as the Humboldt Forum, still under way in 2018.

This list is by no means exhaustive. The chancellery by Charlotte Frank and Axel Schultes, for instance, which was completed in 2001, and the nearby federal office building named the Marie-Elisabeth-Lüders House and designed by Stephan Braunfels, of 2003, both borrow from another modernist source for the creation of *ex novo* ruins. The monumentality of both of these major civic buildings is consciously diminished by the presence of large geometric cutouts, like the ones inspired by the deep iwans of Mughal architecture that Louis Kahn adopted for the Indian Institute of Management in Ahmedabad (1962–74) and for his National Assembly Building in Dhaka, Bangladesh (1962–83), in an attempt to shield the core of his buildings from tropical heat and monsoon rains, conditions uncharacteristic of Berlin's more temperate climate.[9]

The battle over the appearance of Berlin's renewed center has ended in a nearly total victory for those who advocated integrating modernism's own past into the city's boldest new architecture. The antidote to critical reconstruction became one of the foremost examples of the revival of modernism that has occupied and reclaimed much of the forefront of international architectural culture since the late 1990s.[10] While employing modernist's abstract and often technologically inspired forms, this neomodernism does so in ways that admits that they can be ornamental and symbolic, rather than strictly functional, and thus flouts much of modernism's own original rhetoric about their purpose. Moreover, its emphasis on the fragmentary and the unstable broke, despite the precedent offered by Mossehaus, a gentle stroll to the south of Chipperfield's New Museum, with the modern German architectures on display at the Werkbund Exhibition in Cologne in 1914 and in Stuttgart in the late 1920s. Many of these featured dynamic, contrapuntal compositions, but all attempted to establish a holistic unity that by 2000 no longer seemed achievable or, indeed, desirable. And yet neomodernism acknowledges that the twentieth century happened and that its story includes the attempt to design buildings that both serve and express the emergence of new materials and new production processes. The triumph in Berlin of this approach over critical reconstruction in the competition to design meaningful symbols for a reunited Germany has been crucial in extinguishing international enthusiasm for historicism and in enabling deconstructionism to break free of its roots in postmodern theory and instead embrace a more explicit relationship with modernist precedent. Much more was built in Berlin according to the tenets of critical reconstruction, but it was the exceptions that resonated with both the international architectural profession and with the public in Berlin, nationally, and abroad.

The success of the revival of modernist forms in a handful of Berlin's most celebrated postunification buildings stands in contrast, not only to the reconstruction of the Schloss but also the rebuilding of Dresden's Church of Our Lady (Frauenkirche), one of Germany's most renowned and revered baroque buildings. Destroyed in the bombing that eviscerated the center of Dresden on 15 February 1945, and left by the Communist government as a pile of rubble memorializing the city's destruction, what had been the finest post-Reformation Protestant church in Germany was reerected, where possible, out of the original stones between 1993 and 2005. This grassroots effort, which was extremely successful in attracting private funding at home and abroad, especially in Britain, has prompted many further efforts to rebuild the parts of the city destroyed in 1945 along historicist lines. The Church of Our Lady could be rebuilt with so little controversy in part because, before sponsoring its construction Augustus the Strong converted to Catholicism to become king of Poland; he never worshipped in it. Thus, unlike the Memorial Church in Berlin, it never represented the state. Instead, reconstructing it became as much a means of expressing opposition to the Communist governments that had focused on rebuilding civic rather than sacred buildings or on expressing the suffering that Dresdeners and the refugees passing through the city had endured in 1945.[11] Moreover, unlike Berlin, or for that matter Cologne or Stuttgart, Dresden had been marginal to the emergence of modern architecture in Germany during the 1910s and 1920s; such architecture had first flourished there only in the 1960s. Never at stake here was how the public sphere of the Berlin republic would be imagined, nor its relationship to the crimes committed by the Third Reich or even to the achievements of the New Building. Consequently, despite Dresden's renewed popularity as a tourist attraction for those coming from beyond the Eastern Bloc, the audience for its urban and architectural strategies was less inclined to use them as barometers by which to judge the health of German democracy. Much more was always at stake in Berlin.

Tourism helped set the agenda there as well. Both East and West Berlin operated as showcases for communism and capitalism, respectively, rather than as linchpins of the economies of the Democratic and the Federal Republic. East Berlin was an administrative center; it also contained most of the city's historical architecture as well as the most important buildings representative of Communist rule from the Stalinallee to the Nikolaiviertel, created in the 1980s on the site of the former medieval city core and still a successful tourist attraction today.[12] West Berlin originally had a large garment industry as well as the factories of such firms as AEG and Siemens, but already by 1961, the year the Wall left it an isolated island, the five and a half million tourists a year who flocked to experience its unusual situation, and often to express solidarity with its residents, were a mainstay of the local economy. This was nonetheless heavily dependent on subsidies from the Federal Republic and from the countries responsible for its three sectors: France, the United Kingdom, and the United States.[13]

Reunification did little to improve Berlin's economic situation vis-à-vis the rest of former West Germany. Berlin, which like Hamburg and Bremen doubles as its own state within the Federal Republic, regularly ranks as one of the country's poorest states; its government is further burdened by the responsibility of maintaining the cultural infrastructure of both former rivals. It notoriously, for example, supports three opera houses. The three leading universities, while expensive to run, are rare bright spots, attracting young and talented people from across the country and indeed the world. Berlin's relatively low cost of living relative to other major German and European metropolises helps account for a lively artistic scene as well, although in recent years rents have risen precipitously. The factories that were a feature of the Cold War economy on both sides of the Wall have largely closed, however. The fact that most were owned by Germany's largest nonautomotive manufacturers, rather than by the smaller, more specialized, and agile businesses that drive most of the country's economy, hardly helped. These, like the garment business, have transferred most of their production to lower-wage countries in Eastern Europe and in Asia.[14]

In this context tourism's importance to the local economy has, if anything, increased. A huge wave of publicity accompanied the transfer of the capital to the city in 1999; this coincided with the opening of the Reichstag and of the new shopping and entertainment complex at Potsdamer Platz. These quickly became two of the city's most visited sites. Moreover, the role of tourism within the economy of most major cities has greatly expanded; it is now often their number-one industry. In this context Berlin's many new neomodernist attractions, which include several of the city's most visited sites, stand out for offering the "authenticity" travelers supposedly seek, even as many prove satisfied with simulacra like the Nikolaiviertel. Tourist figures are impressive; the Topography of Terror alone attracted nearly two million visitors between the opening in 2010 of its new quarters and the summer of 2012, and by 2015 the city as a whole drew well over twelve million. One-third of them come from abroad.[15]

In this context it is hardly surprising that Berlin's new memory landscapes now appear indivisible from the centrality of tourism to the city's economy. The marketing of individual cities, and particularly of their historic cores and new buildings designed by starchitects, is ubiquitous, and it is an arena in which a reunified Berlin has competed with great success.

Friedrichstrasse: Galeries Lafayette and the Friedrichstadt Passagen

The sleek glass curves of the Berlin flagship of the French department store chain Galeries Lafayette, picked out at night with bands of light, do not at first appear to have a strong relation to the local past (Figure 4.2). Instead, it remains one of the most up-to-date insertions into a neighborhood that has seen plenty of new construction in the two decades since its completion. There are no ruins in sight. And

Figure 4.2. Jean Nouvel, Galeries Lafayette, Berlin, 1995. Source: Jean-Pierre Dalbéra/Wikipedia Commons.

yet the Galeries Lafayette might be said to be haunted, above all by memories of the thriving department stores and luxury shops that once lined Leipzigerstrasse, four blocks to the south, clustered at its terminus at Potsdamer Platz, and wrapped up around Friedrichstrasse to where Nouvel's building stands today. What was often phrased in terms of a battle between the traditional European city and the forces of Americanization and globalization was also a fight over which past should serve as the model for the new Berlin, the neoclassical civic architecture designed by Schinkel for Prussian kings and their educated upper-middle-class subjects, or the Wilhelmine and Weimar-era commercial architecture commissioned by Jewish merchants from architects (many of them also Jewish) eager to employ new materials and forms and frequented by all who could afford their wares.

For all practical purposes, the Berlin Wall fell on the night of 9 November 1989; reunification followed within less than a year. Most of Berlin's defining physical artifact, the Wall that had for nearly three decades ringed West Berlin, disappeared quite quickly. With few exceptions Berliners were all too glad to see it gone; only years later did the lack of much of anything to show tourists begin to prompt regret in a few quarters that it had been so quickly demolished.[16] From the beginning it was clear that the return, really for the first time since 1939, of a capitalist real estate market across the city would result in a building boom (West Berlin had always been a protected outpost of consumer culture, rather than an example of an entirely free market).[17] The task of reknitting a divided city commenced even before the decision to move the capital from Bonn was made in 1991.

One of the first projects to be completed was the construction of three large blocks, termed "Quartiers" along Friedrichstrasse, the main artery running north–south perpendicular to Unter den Linden. Friedrichstrasse had been a key street in Cold War Berlin. To the south of the Quartiers Checkpoint Charlie had marked the place where it was bisected by the Wall; to the north the Friedrichstrasse elevated suburban railroad station had continued to serve as a transfer node for West Berlin's mass transport system, and was where the main crossing point for those who were not citizens of the four occupying powers had been located. Redevelopment plans for the site already under way in East Berlin before the fall of the Wall formed the basis for their capitalist successors.[18] Although only the third new building ran all the way through the block to Charlottenstrasse on the east, the side streets separating the middle block from its neighbors both terminated at the edge of the Gendarmenmarkt. This large public square is dominated by the eighteenth-century French and German cathedrals and by Schinkel's stark theater whose austere classicism provided a key precedent for many architects working in Berlin across the course of the twentieth century (Figure 4.3). Foreign architects, Jean Nouvel from Paris and the American firm of Pei Cobb and Fried, were responsible for two of the Quartiers, the Galeries Lafayette and one-half of the Friedrichstadt Passagen. A German, O. M. Ungers, designed the third for the American developer Tischman-Speyer.[19]

Although the three blocks also known as the Friedrichstadt Passagen stood, at least until the completed reconstruction of Potsdamer Platz began to open in 1998, for the return of capitalism to the former East Berlin, in fact, the development followed principles that had been pioneered in East Berlin in the 1970s independently of the introduction of postmodern urbanism to West Berlin by Ungers and Rob Krier.[20] Indeed, it was in part because much of the preliminary planning had already been completed before 1989 that the buildings were realized so quickly. All three blocks conformed to precedents established in the German Democratic Republic in the iconic Stalinallee and revived in the 1970s by preservation-minded East German architects. Each firmly met the street line and had the same height. In a new twist that to some extent rendered the respect for the street redundant, they were also threaded together by underground passageways. There was in addition a clear connection, however, to the IBA. Josef Paul Kleihues, who had organized it, chaired the jury for the 1990 competition that awarded the three Quartier sites to paired developers and architects.[21]

Hans Stimmann, who controlled much of the planning process in the city between 1991 and 2006, originally hailed the trio as examples of his policy of what he termed "critical reconstruction," even as he noted the differences between Nouvel's and Ungers's contributions. He wrote perceptively in 1993 that Nouvel, "in relation

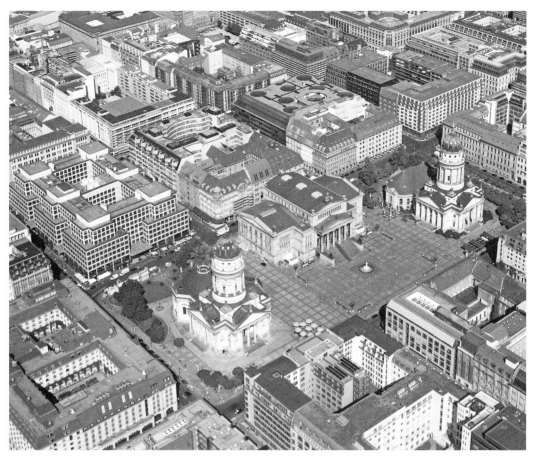

Figure 4.3. O. M. Ungers, Gendarmenmarkt, Berlin, with the Friedrichstadt Passagen (1996) at upper right. Source: Gunther Schneider.

to the tradition of the modern, ventured a look into the future and designed a new generation of department store, based entirely upon the symbolic working of glazed materials and the quality of light." He contrasted this with the approach taken by Ungers, who as "the German Rationalist, proposed a metropolitan stone-clad building in the tradition of Friedrichstraße."[22]

Stimmann was a native of the West German city of Lübeck. He had studied for his doctorate and then taught at the Technical University in West Berlin between 1975 and 1985, before being appointed in 1991 to the first of his two terms (1991–96 and 1999–2006; in between he held the lesser post of state secretary for planning in the city's ministry for urban development, the environment, and technology) as the head of planning for the city government.[23] Stimmann had contributed to grassroots planning initiatives in West Berlin since the 1970s. Ostensibly less concerned with the appearance of buildings than the way they were sited, he defined his approach to planning in an early essay by quoting his mentor Kleihues. It is, he wrote, "a dialogue between tradition and modern, which searches for the contradiction within the modern not in the sense of a breach, but as a visible lasting development of the relationship between place and time."[24] Stimmann was closely allied with the architect Hans Kolhoff and the architectural historian Fritz Neumeyer as well as Kleihues, all of whom had taught at the architecture school at the Technical University in Dortmund, where Stimmann was appointed an honorary professor in 2006.

How and what one would remember was key to the fissure that quickly opened up between the approach taken by Nouvel and that championed by Stimmann and Ungers. For Stimmann, who was associated with the English-speaking New Urbanists, the "plan of its streets contains the memory of the city. It imprints its physiognomy."[25] He thus transposed from buildings to city plans an understanding of collective memory pioneered by Aldo Rossi, who returned to Berlin to build the nearby Quartier Schützenstrasse (1994–97).[26] The tradition Stimmann prized had endured, he believed, up to the end of the nineteenth century but had then unraveled and became illegible. By the 1990s, however, the proponents of remembering modernism had adapted a technique initially developed to nurture nostalgia for the same past cherished by Stimmann in order to expose precisely the destructive capacities of both modernism and war that Stimmann wished to erase. They concurred that the urban fabric should be rewoven, but believed that the rents that had been torn through it should be left visible at the level of individual building sites, and that reviving the architecture of the New Building was the most effective way to achieve this. Their rather unlikely allies proved to be capitalist developers who wanted a less restricted say in how the center of the city was rebuilt. This approach consistently garnered more popular acclaim than critical reconstruction even before it became the basis for the new capital's infrastructure of history-oriented tourist attractions.

Stimmann's opponents sought to describe the debate over Berlin's architectural direction as being about whether or not to revive styles they perceived to be either democratic (the New Building of the Weimar Republic) or undemocratic (the neoclassicism of the Prussian monarchy, the Second Empire, and the Third Reich). In fact, Stimmann owed his position largely to his activist stance on the left wing of the local Social Democratic Party. Charged with reintroducing a real market into the city, he sought to control capitalist speculation through rules he believed would restore the specific kind of livability he associated with European cities (although not with Stuttgart, where freestanding buildings set into parks long predated the arrival of the modern movement, which in Stuttgart had been rather more respectful of the street; Stimmann described it as a place "where one can't really breath in European urban culture").[27] Ironically, he, like his modernist predecessors, stressed the formal qualities of buildings. It was left to the neomodernists to stress architecture's ability to communicate, above all through the symbolism of stylistic choices, even if the ways in which they did this owed almost nothing to Robert Venturi and Denise Scott Brown.

Stimmann quickly grew more critical of the entire Friedrichstrasse development. By 1994 he was complaining that the plots should have been broken into smaller pieces.[28] Its two opposite ends, by Nouvel at the north and Ungers at the south, nonetheless represent antithetical strategies regarding which aspects of the city's past to revive even as both were anchored in the architectural history of the immediate environs.

For most of the duration of the German Democratic Republic the Gendarmenmarkt lay in ruins. Only in 1984 did Schinkel's theater finally reopen as a concert hall; the renovation of the cathedrals was completed three years later. The quadrant framed by the elbow of the Wall, Unter den Linden, and the Spree River, had once been the center of official Berlin and included the many elegant shops and department stores erected along Leipzigerstrasse between the 1890s and the 1920s. After the war this badly damaged district was largely neglected until the rebuilding efforts of the 1970s, which filled a broadened Leipzigerstrasse with high-rise apartment buildings but left much of the rest of the neighborhood still in ruins.

Ungers took many of his cues from Schinkel's recently restored landmark. The predominately tan stone cladding of his building, accentuated at the base with brown, and lightened in the case of the recessed upper stories, where it turns to white, harmonized well with the warm sandstone of its historic neighbors. Although more strident, the grid of his windows nonetheless provided a sympathetic backdrop for the abstract, albeit rectangular, pattern of those lining the flanks of Schinkel's theater. Breaking his building up into three masses along the long facades and two along the short ones was a sympathetic gesture that hinted that the new shopping, office, and apartment complex might be considered as multiple structures instead of the one big block it in fact was. This was the template for critical reconstruction.

In comparison Nouvel's curtain wall, with its rounded corner and narrow bands marking the floor levels that were accentuated at night with ribbons of light, at first appears as an intrusion. Although smaller than the Ungers block (it is not visible from the Gendarmenmarkt), and with sleeker facades that appear less substantial, not least because of the way they reflect their neighbors, it is in many ways a bulkier building in that there is less variation along its street fronts. And yet Nouvel's approach was as solidly rooted in Berlin precedent as any aspect of Ungers's. As had been the case for Libeskind only two years earlier, Erich Mendelsohn provided Nouvel, who was not yet an international superstar although his Institut du Monde l'Arabe in Paris (1987–88) had been widely praised, with an important point of departure.[29] The degree to which he referred to the New Building was, however, ignored by those who preferred to regard a return to a modernism that had been out of fashion for two decades as a step into the future.

In 1928 Galeries Lafayette proposed opening its first German store on Potsdamer Platz eight blocks to the south and west of its later Nouvel building. It commissioned

Critical Reconstruction or Neomodernist Shards? 149

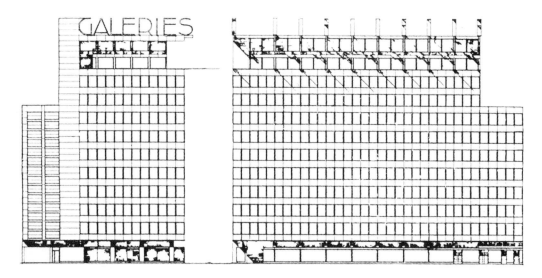

Figure 4.4. Erich Mendelsohn, project for Galeries Lafayette for Berlin, 1928. Source: *Erich Mendelsohn: Das Gesamtschaffen des Architekten* (Berlin: Rudolf Mosse Verlag, 1930).

a design from Mendelsohn (Figure 4.4). Although the French concern eventually pulled out, a smaller version of the original scheme opened as Columbushaus in 1932.[30] Nouvel did not cite Mendelsohn's project directly, but there are aspects of his design that relate directly to Mendelsohn's C. A. Herpich Furriers, which, until its destruction during World War II, was on Leipzigerstrasse, just to the south of Nouvel's site (Figure 4.5).[31] A midblock renovation of three existing townhouses, it featured what would come to be regarded as Mendelsohn's signature curves, as well as large areas of glazing. Its dramatic night lighting included glowing bands between stories.[32] Although this was achieved by indirect lighting of the travertine bands between the windows, which remained dark, the effect was similar to that adopted by Nouvel for his much larger store. There is no exact correlation here, but Nouvel did revive the spirit of Mendelsohn's commercial architecture: large areas of glass, sweeping curves, and dramatic night lighting, set atop a completely glazed ground story, and featuring recessed upper stories. Other Berlin precedents included the curtain wall of Bernhard Sehring's Tietz store, also formerly on Leipzigerstrasse, of 1899–1900, and Mies's project for a completely glazed skyscraper on Friedrichstrasse.[33] Throughout the 1990s, proponents of critical reconstruction defended stone-clad buildings as being in keeping with the city's specifically European traditions, purposely failing to acknowledge the degree to which the origin of the supposedly American and now global curtain wall office building could be traced back to Berlin.[34] Their opponents, meanwhile, insisted that these capitalist

Figure 4.5. Erich Mendelsohn, Herpich Store, Berlin, 1928. Copyright Bildarchiv Foto Marburg.

Critical Reconstruction or Neomodernist Shards?

Figure 4.6.   Atrium, Galeries Lafayette. Source: Yves Sucksdorf for Galeries Lafayette.

structures "embodied the spirit of the new Weimar democracy" and "expressed confidence without braggadocio."[35]

Nouvel's most significant departure from his Mendelsohnian model established a key precedent for the next key example of neomodernist architecture in Berlin. Mendelsohn famously eliminated the atrium that had been a central feature of most early department stores, including Alfred Messel's famous Wertheim store on Berlin's Leipziger Platz (1896–1906), which had two, from his examples of the type. He and his clients found it an outmoded waste of space now that consumers were used to ascending stairs and elevators to reach upper sales floors and that electric lighting could be used to provide even illumination across the depth of the block. Nouvel revived and yet transformed this characteristic feature of turn-of-the century department stores in a bold gesture that echoed the spectacular qualities of Bruno Taut's Glashaus (Figure 4.6). An atrium was indeed a requirement, as he needed to encourage pedestrian traffic not just to the upper floors but also to the basement level where his building connected to its neighbors to the south in what was intended to function as an enclosed indoor mall. But in place of the usual rectangular space, Nouvel inserted something entirely different. The American architectural critic Herbert Muschamp described it as "two cones of glass, touching base to base at the ground floor level. One points down, admitting natural light into the basement office [actually used as food hall] floors, the second, larger cone rises dramatically, punching holes through the seven selling floors. Like a compressed indoor version of Times

Square, the cone is a bombardment of light and color. Designer labels and other signs are projected as holograms onto the glass, which serves as a giant store directory."[36] This spectacular feature almost certainly encouraged Foster to place a similar—and equally unusual—cone atop the Reichstag.

Nouvel's own description of the building makes clear his self-conscious recall of effects long associated with expressionism:

> The dematerialization of the corner of the building enables motorists and pedestrians to see cones of light, the largest of which quivers, shimmers, scintillates with radiating lines and beams of color. . . . The two vast mirrored cones in the central space are objects of fascination. Depending on the theme of the various promotional campaigns, messages and images skim over their surfaces and, using the opposite process to anamorphosis (distorted image that resumes normal proportion in a curved mirror), a clear images is distorted and spread over all the mirrored surfaces—at once a veritable brain-teaser and visual feast. Complementing these distorted moving image-messages are other clear, perfectly controlled ones, projected on two large screens overlooking Friedrichstrasse and Französiche Strasse. The reflective, screen-printed glass façade reveals glimpses of these signs through triangular (echoing the cones) or rectangular (encasing the screens) haloes. The offices are pierced by cones of white light, veritable interior lamps. The floors, studded with transparent glass tiles around the cones, gradually become more opaque. All these effects of diffusing light through the interior characterize the building during the day, and are obviously even more apparent at night. Geometry and light create this architecture in all its infinite variations, closely linked to the weather, the time of day, and the nature of the images screened. Midway between the abstract and the figurative, artificial and natural light, we want to create an interplay, that subtle stagecraft that is the manipulating of seduction, a reflection upon what is shown and what is hidden, upon darkness and light, the intelligible and the perceptible.[37]

The overt recall of Taut's crystalline crowns within the blatantly commercial setting of a department store encompassed Nouvel's attempt in his first major international commission to work with the source of Germany's impressive tradition of modernist transparency and acknowledge, as in the original Glashaus, the economic utility of such spectacle. Here the boundary between commercial and civic was blurred not through the commercialization of public space for which postmodernism was often criticized, but through exactly the opposite: the development of something resembling a public sphere within a frankly capitalist setting.[38] The cone focuses attention not so much on the goods that can indeed be glimpsed through it as on the existence of the inhabitable space that rings it and of the activities taking place within it. In this rare example of the recall of modernism's rich history flourishing in a commercial rather than a civic setting, it acts to focus the building on a shared experience that is not primarily about selling but about the observation of open space.

Agreement over how to rebuild this corner of the city quickly fractured. Postmodernists favoring repair emphasized continuity with buildings that had been built over a century and a half earlier, that had only recently been restored to prominence, and even more recently made readily available to a formerly West German and Western European public (they had, of course, been on view to almost anyone from these places who converted the required number of marks, but the number of tourists from outside the Communist bloc who did so remained relatively small in the 1980s in comparison to those who would travel east to see them in the 1990s). Against this was posed the Galeries Lafayette. Here the focus of the respectful recall of the past shifted forward in time from the Wilhelmine, as in the debate over the Memorial Church, to the Weimar-era past, but remained fixed at a roughly six-decade interlude from the present. In the Galeries Lafayette a single aesthetic embodied both halves of what had in the Memorial Church been a jarring juxtaposition. The importance of memory was exacerbated in this case by the complete extinction of the original being remembered; the combination of wartime destruction and East German demolition had wiped out all physical traces of what had been Berlin's most fashionable shopping district. Nouvel replaced it with a building that was even more transparent and reflective than his model, and was thus capable of being read, as Ungers's block was not, as a void. Ironically it was Nouvel rather than Ungers who complained that those who favored critical reconstruction were forgetting the city's past. "I think they went about it as if nothing had happened, as if they were erasing history between 1933 and 1989," he declared in 1999.[39]

Around Pariser Platz: The Reichstag and the Hotel Adlon

The next battle would be fought over even more prominent real estate. At the end of the nineteenth century Pariser Platz, located where Unter den Linden meets the Brandenburg Gate, was one of Berlin's foremost urban spaces, a position it retained until the destruction wrought by World War II.[40] The Wall cut it off from the damaged Reichstag, the parliament building completed in 1894, which was located a half block into West Berlin. Restoring what had for nearly three decades been no-man's-land to its position as the civic and tourist heart of the city was one of the biggest challenges facing planners and architects in the 1990s, and one whose importance was only heightened by the decision to shift the capital from Bonn back to Berlin. In the end two very different strategies were applied. The renovation of the Reichstag, the second since the damage it endured from a fire in 1933 and during the war, was undertaken by the federal government and supervised by the Bundestag, the popularly elected lower house of the German legislature, which is the building's chief

Figure 4.7.   Paul Wallot, Reichstag, 1894. Source: Wikipedia Commons.

occupant. The reconstruction of the square was under the auspices instead of the city government.[41] The repaired Reichstag has become the symbol of the Berlin Republic and indeed the most powerful architectural icon the Federal Republic has ever possessed. Although Pariser Platz was the showcase for critical reconstruction, none of the new buildings framing the platz have been nearly as celebrated. In particular, the Hotel Adlon became a flashpoint for criticism of critical regionalism.

Discussions about renovating the Reichstag to serve as the parliament of a reunited Germany officially began in 1991. That the move back to Berlin was approved by a slim majority of only eighteen votes had more than a little to do with the largely negative reputation of the building to which the Bundestag would be returning. The first competition for the design of the parliament of a united Germany was held in 1872. It bore no fruit and a second was staged a decade later. The result, completed in 1892, was a rather pompous classical building designed by Paul Wallot (Figure 4.7). Typical of the large and lavishly detailed public edifices being erected across Europe and the Americas at the time, it was never much admired and was quickly considered out of date.[42]

A further problem was the degree to which the building became the symbol of the weakness of the institution it housed. Although there was universal male suffrage during the Second Empire, the power to appoint the chancellor remained with the emperor, a system that ensured there would never be a fully democratic government. When in 1912 the Social Democrats outpolled all their rival parties, stalemate

Critical Reconstruction or Neomodernist Shards? 155

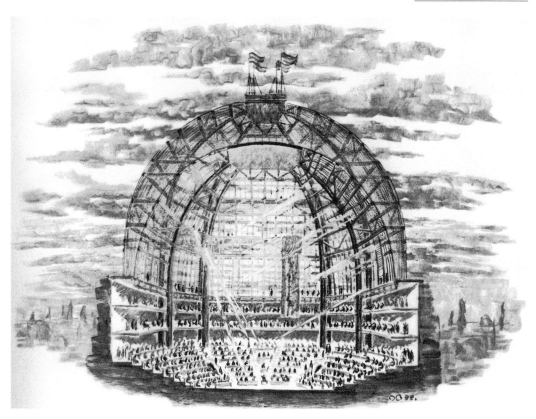

Figure 4.8. Gottfried Böhm, project for the Reichstag, 1988. Source: Deutsches Architektur Museum, Frankfurt.

ensued.[43] The institution of republican democracy in 1919 was a step forward, as was the enfranchisement of women, but political infighting, which reflected a lack of consensus among voters, ensured the new government commanded relatively little respect from either the left or the right.[44] The Reichstag fire on 28 February 1933 precipitated Hitler's consolidation of power.[45] In part because of this checkered past, neither the Federal Republic nor the government of West Berlin expended much effort on the building after the war. The ruins of the cupola were demolished in 1954. In 1961 Paul Baumgarten won a competition to restore what was left. This modest effort resulted, if anything, in a neutralization of a structure that, following an agreement signed in 1971, could only be used for meetings of political parties, not for the full Bundestag.[46]

Behind the scenes, considerable attention was paid to the Reichstag in the second half of the 1980s. Gottfried Böhm submitted a design in 1988 in which he reconstructed the cupola to serve as the roof over the plenary chamber, which he surrounded with galleries for the public (Figure 4.8). Although Böhm's entry in the 1992 competition won by Norman Foster proved unsuccessful, his design was

Figure 4.9. Behnisch and Partner, Bundestag, Bonn, 1992. Source: Qualle/Wikipedia Commons.

submitted to all the entrants, and Foster was eventually forced by his clients to adopt its basic approach, which he reworked in light, in particular, of the cone-shaped atrium of the Galeries Lafayette.[47]

The debate over the reconstruction of the Reichstag was complicated by the fact that in 1988 work had finally begun on the construction of purpose-built quarters for the Bundestag in Bonn, which for decades has been officially considered only a temporary capital and thus lacked much of the formal infrastructure of a nation-state. Commissioned from Günter Behnisch and Partner, this was the first occasion on which the Federal Republic had erected a civic building of such political or architectural significance (Figure 4.9). The new Bundestag was a stunning structure, a glass box that owed more than a little to Mies's New National Gallery. Its transparency was clearly intended to be an expression of democratic values and a critique of the old, discredited Reichstag. By the time the Bundestag moved into this building in 1992, it was already apparent that these were only temporary quarters; the return to Berlin took place a scant seven years later.[48]

The process of renovating the Reichstag began in 1992 with an architectural competition open to architects from around the world, who were mandated to incorporate transparency and sustainability into their designs. That none of the three prizewinners was German demonstrated the continued difficulty of shaping

Critical Reconstruction or Neomodernist Shards? 157

Figure 4.10.   Christo and Jeanne-Claude, Wrapped Reichstag, Berlin, 1971–95. Source: Wolfgang Vole/LAIF, Camera Press.

a national identity, nearly half a century after the end of World War II. Foster won the competition with a proposal to create a large glass roof that would extend well past the footprint of the original building. Its shape, if not the detail of its roof structure, seemed inspired in part by the New National Gallery. In the end, his Christian Democratic clients demanded that he restore the cupola.[49]

Before construction began, the building was ritually cleansed in the eyes of many observers, when the artists Christo and Jeanne-Claude wrapped it in aluminum-covered fabric in the summer of 1995 (Figure 4.10).[50] In a foretaste of the popular attraction Foster's renovated building would prove to be, millions flocked to the lawn in front of the building, which became for the first time in its history a genuinely popular and festive place to meet and relax. The critic Andreas Huyssen writes:

> Most agreed that the polypropylene-wrapped Reichstag, whose looks oscillated from shining silver in sunlight to muted gray on cloud-covered days to bluish purple under the spotlights at night, was serenely and at times uncannily beautiful, its spatial monumentality both dissolved and accentuated by a lightness of being that contrasted starkly with the visual memory of the heavy-set,

now veiled architecture. The wrapped Reichstag thus became a monument to democratic culture instead of a demonstration of state power.[51]

Four years later the reopened Reichstag quickly established itself as one of the most popular tourist attractions in the city, with locals initially numbering prominently among those who queued for hours for a chance to tour the building and particularly to visit the new cupola, which became a visual shorthand for the Berlin Republic.

The renovated Reichstag building proved so effective in part because Foster was careful to reveal rather than erase traces of the building's troubled past, including even graffiti scrawled by Soviet troops in May 1945, at the same time that he equipped it with all the infrastructure necessary for a modern legislative complex. It was the symbolism inherent in his approach, however, as much as the clean, high-tech insertions into the historic structure that commanded attention. Foster commented, in an article titled "The Reichstag Burns, This Time with Hope," "Our approach was based in the view that the history of the building should not be sanitized. And the fact that Germany accepted this approach shows to me what an extraordinarily progressive and open society it has become."[52] The American reporter Roger Cohen concurred, declaring, "Surely no other people would allow itself to be so grossly denigrated in its own Parliament! But then the modern Federal Republic probably places a greater value on the unabashed confrontation with the past than any other state."[53] The juxtaposition of old and new Foster employed had come a long way since being developed in the immediate aftermath of the war to express an expedient and almost covert nostalgia for Second Empire nationalism. Now it was praised for conveying authenticity and honesty, exactly what a generation earlier opponents had charged the Memorial Church and its supporters for lacking.

The cupola was key to the building's success (Figure 4.11). First, it symbolized that Germany had changed, that the Federal Republic was not the Reichstag of the Second Empire or the Weimar Republic, much less the Third Reich. Its explicit recall of the glass-and-steel architecture of Behnisch's Bundestag, as well as of Taut, Böhm, and Nouvel indicated as well continuity with the aspirations for a democratic Germany. Far more obvious was the public command of the space atop the legislative chamber. Although there is no actual view down on the legislators, the experience of being literally above the politicians while walking up the spiral ramp, accompanied by stunning views out across the government buildings and the rest of the city, conveys a sense of empowerment. The message of the contrast of an unsatisfactory but acknowledged past with a better present—and potentially also future—is clear.[54]

Key to the way this effect was accomplished was not only the form of the cupola but also the way in which Foster set an inverted mirrored glass cone inside it. Although its ostensible purpose was to make the building more energy efficient, in fact it operates above all to create a more memorable civic space, not least by reflecting views of the public back to themselves. Here, even more than in the Galeries

Critical Reconstruction or Neomodernist Shards?

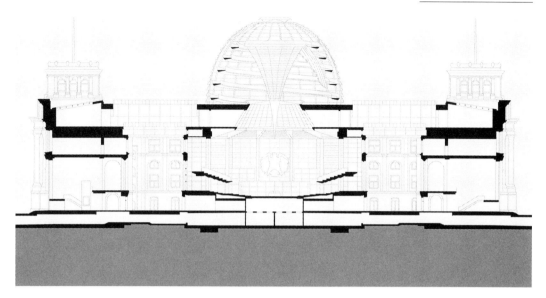

Figure 4.11. Section, Reichstag. Source: Conor Rochford.

Lafayette, the glass architecture of the 1990s explicitly recalls the Glashaus and Taut's schemes for visionary city crowns. There is no way to shift Berlin from the plains along the Spree to the pinnacles of the Alps, but Foster went even further than Nouvel, if not Böhm, in reviving expressionism's utopian dreams.

With the renovation of the Reichstag, the collage of old historicist and new neomodernist construction, employed across the Federal Republic for half a century, became the established face of the Berlin Republic. It was always, however, an architecture of exceptions, difficult if not impossible to apply across an entire urban district. It is thus not surprising that the rehabilitation of the center of Berlin, including of nearby Pariser Platz, proceeded along different lines (Figure 4.12). Here, with the key exception of the Brandenburg Gate, there were no authentic remains to integrate into new high-tech construction. Despite the array of international talent, which included Frank Gehry and Christian de Portzamparc, two winners of the prestigious Pritzker Prize (awarded as well to Foster in 1999), the architecture is rather bland. Gehry and Behnisch in particular chafed at the limitations imposed by the city's design guidelines, which mandated not only relatively low heights but also stone cladding and a high proportion of wall to window surface. After long negotiations Behnisch was granted more leeway than others, probably as a sop for the abandonment of his Bundeshaus in Bonn. It is in this context that the Hotel Adlon was rebuilt within its original footprint, but with simplified facades.

Pariser Platz's postunification significance was anchored by the restoration of traffic through the Brandenburg Gate and also by the prominent embassies, institutions, and memorials located in its immediate vicinity. The Adlon keeps company with a cluster of entirely new designs as well as reconstructions by an array of

160   *Critical Reconstruction or Neomodernist Shards?*

Figure 4.12. Pariser Platz with Hotel Adlon at center right. Source: Gunther Schneider.

celebrated architects. The buildings flanking the Gate were reconstructed as facsimiles, albeit with an extra story added. The one to the left of the Gate, once occupied by the Jewish impressionist painter Max Liebermann was reconstructed between 1996 and 1998 by Kleihues and serves as the headquarters of the Brandenburg Gate Foundation. The south flank of the square includes the American embassy (1996–2008), designed by Buzz Yudell of Moore Ruble Yudell, Gehry's DG (now DZ) Bank (1998–2000), and Behnisch and Partner's Academy of the Arts (1993–2005); the buildings facing them include Portzamparc's French embassy (1997–2002).[55] The British embassy, which opened just around the corner in 2000, was the work of James Stirling's former partner Michael Wilford.[56] The Allied embassies are clustered here; the former Soviet (now Russian) embassy, built between 1949 and 1951, is just to the east on Unter den Linden.

    The Hotel Adlon is located at the opposite end of Pariser Platz from the Reichstag. It stands on the platz's southeast corner, where it abuts Unter den Linden. A hotel of this name designed by Carl Gause originally opened in 1907 on the site, but its replacement is an entirely new construction (Figure 4.13). Built to replace Schinkel's Palais Redern, the original's elegant facades were closer to the architecture of Second Empire Paris than to Behrens's understated classicism. It had, as might be expected, palatial interiors equipped, of course, with all the most up-to-

Critical Reconstruction or Neomodernist Shards?

Figure 4.13. Carl Gause, Hotel Adlon, Berlin, 1907. Copyright Bildarchiv Foto Marburg.

date amenities. Most of the first building was destroyed by fire in May 1945 in the aftermath of the Soviet invasion; the rest was demolished in 1984.[57] Berlin's most celebrated hostelry until its partial destruction at the end of the war, this was always a place of capitalist spectacle spiced with political power. American visitors in 1961 described their visit to the truncated version that operated at the rear of the site:

> A driveway now led through waist-high weeds to the drab courtyard of the former servants' quarters; war had wrecked the main entrance. The reception room resembled a run-down country inn. Behind the desk an unshaven porter in shirt sleeves. A few seedy-looking travelers sat on cheap suitcases, waiting.[58]

The successor to the original Hotel Adlon trades on its name and reputation but is otherwise a new establishment. Unlike the refurbished Reichstag, this building, completed in 1997, conforms closely to the policy of critical reconstruction. This simulacrum of an authentic historical artifact quickly became the city's top address for wealthy and famous visitors.[59] This economic success did not translate, however, into the kind of architectural praise routinely accorded the Reichstag. Werner Sewing, one of the leading critics of critical reconstruction, might have been thinking of the Adlon when he wrote that "Wilhelmine urban planning [and in this case architecture] is being restaged as a liberating blow against socialism and modernism."[60] Indeed, the Adlon has come to stand, even more than Potsdamer Platz, as the showcase of the reintroduction of capitalist spectacle to Berlin, for the Disneyfication of the contemporary German cityscape.[61]

Not only does the Adlon serve tourists, but its location on Pariser Platz ensures that it forms part of the backdrop for the many tourist-friendly spectacles held within view of the Brandenburg Gate. From 1996 until 2003 and in 2006 one of the largest of these was the Love Parade, which was staged in the nearby Tiergarten. The techno music festival attracted up to a million people, many of whom spilled over into Pariser Platz.[62] The boisterous Christopher Street Day parades now conclude in Pariser Platz as well. Indeed, the route through the Tiergarten east to the Brandenburg Gate, designed to celebrate military victories, is now better known as "the fan mile," where enthusiasts gather to cheer on Germany's national football team, and for the huge dance party held every year on New Year's Eve. These events, like the city's stable of old and new architectural monuments, contribute to marketing it as a place for future-oriented businesses as well as for tourism.[63]

In the 1980s postmodern architecture and urbanism were widely associated with the neoliberal economic policies of Margaret Thatcher and Ronald Reagan.[64] The case of the Reichstag and the Hotel Adlon upends this pairing, however, despite the usefulness of event culture and city marketing to local businesses and developers. The long-standing relationship between a fragmentary modernism collaged with a historicist past and Christian Democratic politics assured that Helmut Kohl, who was chancellor from 1982 to 1998, and who was far more active as an architectural patron than either Thatcher or Reagan, consistently supported modernism. Behnisch's Bundeshaus in Bonn and I. M. Pei's addition to the German Historical Museum in Berlin (1998–2004) are just two examples of this.[65] So, often for similar reasons, did the rest of his party. It was the Social Democratic Party, in power from 1969 to 1982 and again from 1998 to 2005 at the national level, and at city level in a coalition with the Christian Democrats between 1991 and 2001, that remained more sympathetic to postmodern architecture and urbanism in general and critical reconstruction in particular. Socialists like Stimmann greatly respected the grassroots preservationists who had since the beginning of the 1970s routinely criticized modern architecture as the handmaiden of both big business and big government. This did not prevent critical reconstruction from being continually disparaged, however, as conservative, which, of course, it literally was.[66]

There was little room for informality, however, in the rebuilt center of Berlin. Instead, the rebuilt Pariser Platz highlighted the degree to which the formerly commercial spectacle of the Glashaus, the Herpich store, and the Galeries Lafayette had been transformed, first by Böhm and then by Foster, into an effective civic realm. If the cupola of the Reichstag was not really where important political discussions took place (and some of these undoubtedly did occur around the bar at the Hotel Adlon), it nonetheless effectively communicated reassuring messages about contemporary Germany's relationship to its past as well as the character of its present and future. In comparison, the Adlon's loose recall of a by no means undistinguished, but also tainted, past was rather vague. It lacked both the specificity of the Reichstag's scarred stones and the optimism of its transparency. Many of those who saw it, and even stayed there, presumed that it was a cherished survivor of an earlier era. Successful as a business, it failed to impress as a work of either historic or contemporary architecture or to become a widely recognized building.

None of this probably troubled proponents of critical reconstruction, as they were forthright about the importance of background buildings. The skirmishes fought over the architecture of Pariser Platz and other Berlin sites during the 1990s, including the generally unimpressive results of the much trumpeted redevelopment of nearby Potsdamer Platz, did much to tip the international balance away, however, from postmodern urbanism and toward a neomodernism that typically lacked the overt references to the past embedded in the Reichstag and even the Galeries Lafayette. The German architects committed to critical reconstruction may have controlled who did what in Berlin but they failed to garner international support; instead, the direction mapped out by Behnisch, Nouvel, and Foster dominated international practice well into the next century. The Berlin architecture wars were not yet over, however, but neomodernism increasingly proved more successful and influential than critical reconstruction in creating compelling new environments that addressed the ugliest chapters of the city's past.

Remembering Nazi Terror

The efficacy of neomodernism's memory landscapes, as demonstrated by the enthusiasm with which Berliners, other Germans, and tourists (not to mention reporters and newspaper critics) all greeted the Jewish Museum and the renovated Reichstag, as well as the wave of memorial building, particularly in relation to the Holocaust, that had been under way since the 1980s, combined to encourage a series of interventions in the urban fabric of a reunited Berlin. These were intended to remind contemporary inhabitants and visitors alike of the terror unleashed by the Third Reich, including the Holocaust, but also the persecution of Christian Germans and other Europeans.[67] The two most prominent Berlin environments created as a result of these efforts were the Memorial to the Murdered Jews of Europe, located on the rear side of the buildings lining the south flank of Pariser Platz, and the Topography of Terror, which stands on the site of the former headquarters of the Gestapo and the SS (Figures 4.14, 4.15, and 4.16). Although the first attracted by far the greatest amount of attention, the second now appears by far the more successful, not least because of how closely it hews to the well-established conventions pioneered in postwar churches of pairing fragments of nineteenth-century historicist architecture

Figure 4.14. Peter Eisenman, Memorial to the Murdered Jews of Europe, Berlin, 2005. Source: Schriebkraft/Wikipedia Commons.

Figure 4.15. Wilms and Hallmann, Topography of Terror, Berlin, 2010. Source: Manfred Brückels/Wikipedia Commons.

Critical Reconstruction or Neomodernist Shards?

Figure 4.16. Topography of Terror with Wall and Air Ministry at right. Source: N-lange.de/ Wikipedia Commons.

with new structures that draw upon expressionism and the New Building. Despite the apparent distance of both Eisenman, the architect of record, and the sculptor Richard Serra, who pulled out of the project in 1998, from postmodern historicism, their project is more closely tied than one might expect from critical reconstruction. By contrast, Wilms and Hallmann's intentionally low-key scheme highlights wounds particular to a specific location in a way that implicitly resists any such sense of a unified whole.[68]

Work on the Topography of Terror preceded the creation of most of the rest of Berlin's memoryscapes.[69] The site is located just south of where the Wall ran, to the east of Potsdamer Platz and the west of Checkpoint Charlie. This was where the School of Industrial Arts and Crafts, the Hotel Prinz Albrecht, and the Prince Albrecht Palais sat from their construction in the eighteenth and nineteenth centuries until they were badly damaged during the war. These were occupied during the Third Reich, respectively, by the Gestapo, the security service of the SS, and the leadership of the SS, in other words by the Nazi organizations most responsible for state-sponsored terror against civilian populations, including Jews. Of these structures, the palace had the most distinguished architecture. It was erected between 1737 and 1739; Schinkel undertook its renovation for Prince Albrecht, the son of King

Friedrich Wilhelm III. The Nazis used all three buildings for offices; the school also contained a prison in the basement. Damaged during the war, these structures were torn down afterward, when even the architectural quality of the Prince Albrecht Palais failed to mitigate against the desire to clear away the traces of where so many horrible deeds had been planned or taken place. During the 1980s, when the IBA focused attention on this part of Kreuzberg, attempts to address and expose its charged past finally began to be made. Spurred in part by outrage over Kleihues's dreams of having the Italian architect Giorgio Grassi rebuild the Prinz Albrecht Palais, these efforts culminated in 1987, the year of the city's 750th anniversary, with the installation of a temporary exhibition on the site.[70]

The effort to create a permanent documentation center atop the exposed ruins of the notorious buildings was closely tied to the decision to make Berlin the national capital. It did not proceed smoothly.[71] An architectural competition, organized in 1992 and held in 1993, resulted in the awarding of the commission to Zumthor (Figure 4.17).[72] His design was heralded for its sensitive relationship to the display of the ruins that had been uncovered during the 1980s. In an interview conducted three years after winning the competition, Zumthor recounted his initial experience of the site and the architectural response he crafted to it:

> My first reaction, when I saw the place for the first time, was that it was actually such a terrible thing that had happened there that I couldn't do a building there. The idea that there would be a building with all these ordinary features belonging to a museum or a cultural building or whatever is dreadful, like a Holocaust Museum with window shutters, and air conditioning, and lavatories.... It should be a meditative building. It should be simple and beautiful for this function. It's not going to be all black or rusty iron, or sad because of concentration camps. It should not reflect cruelty and terror. This doesn't work for me. The actual place and the documents the building houses will do that instead.[73]

In another account, Zumthor drew upon metaphors for the relationship between construction and integrity, transparency and openness that had by this time become clichés, without indulging in the specific allegories in which Libeskind had wrapped the nearby Jewish Museum. He described his approach to the site as "enclosing the remains of the building used by the National Socialists in an architectural envelope." This preserved the inexpertly excavated remains of its nineteenth-century predecessors. Zumthor's own contribution was to be, especially in comparison to the Jewish Museum, relatively mute, "pure structure, speaking no language but that of materials, composition and function." The architect equated honesty of construction with integrity toward the exposition of what had happened here. "Nothing plastered or concealed," he declared, "there is no way to disguise structural sins. From the

Critical Reconstruction or Neomodernist Shards?

Figure 4.17. Peter Zumthor, design for Topography of Terror, 1997. Source: Joachim Hofer for Atelier Peter Zumthor.

naked framework and concrete floor and ceiling panels to the light-weight non-load-bearing walls and sunlight-blocking draperies in the glazed hall, nearly everything in the building is laid, set, stood, or hung in full sight." Although he described the vertical members of the framework as louvers, he emphasized the relative transparency of what might have also been interpreted as prison bars, which in any case allowed views both in and out of the building.[74]

Construction of Zumthor's design began in 1997 but was paused after two years, as expenses rose. The fragments of this structure were finally demolished in 2004. Two years later Wilms and Hallmann won yet another competition, this time organized by the national government rather than the city. The brief to which they successfully responded explicitly declared, "There should not be an architectural exaggeration in the form of the future construction at the expense of an interest in the site.... The priority of the anticipated building is the provision of scholarly and teaching work, not a memorial."[75] The completed pavilion and the related reworking of the surrounding landscape finally opened four years later.

The new pavilion covers only a small part of the site, one end of which, running perpendicular to the remains of the Wall, ramps down to display the ruined cellars of the buildings put to such horrific purposes during the Third Reich. The square pavilion sits in a sea of particularly large gravel, whose overwhelmingly gray color harmonizes with the row of aluminum bars that form the outer of the building's two facades; the rear of the site is largely covered with trees. The entrance is located slightly off center in the facade. It faces the excavations and the Wall. From the galleries at this level, one can see out onto the rest of the site, through the double wall. This is composed of an interior glass skin fronted by a curtain of thin, horizontally arranged aluminum bars that recall, while reversing the orientation, Zumthor's strategy of alternating glass and concrete vertical bands of equal breadth across all four facades of his design.[76] The below-grade story devoted to administration and research is organized around a central square courtyard, which provides both daylight and an interior focus; one glazed exterior wall opens at this level onto a sunken rectangular courtyard, which provides additional light, but only a quasi-buried view out over the site.

The pavilion is a reserved, nearly neutral cousin of Mies's New National Gallery, located only a few blocks to the west. All of the structural expressiveness of that building has been purposely drained out here in order to focus attention instead on the exhibits, whether located within or outside its glass walls. Although the pavilion does not actually touch the entirely unmonumental archeological remains, the degree to which it rises above them is carefully controlled to be as unimposing as possible. The result does not create the strong sense of juxtaposition found in many postwar churches that pair fragments of historical buildings with new structures, but its impact certainly still comes from the contrast of nineteenth-century load-bearing construction and a modernist formal vocabulary.

The connection at the Topography of Terror between the memorial architecture that has been placed here and the physical traces of the location in which atrocities took place and were planned imbues the experience with a palpable sense of authenticity; that one of the last surviving stretches of the Wall borders it to the north further strengthens the connection between artifacts and history. (Located just across the street, along which the Wall once ran, looms the most imposing of all Nazi office blocks, the Air Ministry designed by Mendelsohn's former assistant Ernst Sagebiel for Hermann Goering).[77] Moreover, photographic documentation and text in both English and German located within the enclosure walls defining the site but outside the pavilion ensure that the sites's history is made clear even to those who do not enter the building. The somber character of this place is evident to all who come upon it.

The situation is very different at the Memorial to the Murdered Jews of Europe four blocks to the north.[78] The monument, which occupies a full city block, consists of a field, laid out in rows of dark-gray concrete slabs or stelae of uniform footprint but varying heights, all set upon an undulating ground plane. At one edge of the site is an underground information center, which in the words of the memorial's website "documents the persecution and extermination of European Jewry as well as the historic sites of the crime."[79] Trees have been planted among the blocks in another corner of the site.

Although Eisenman intended the blankness of his technique to communicate the impossibility of representing the Holocaust architecturally, many visitors fail to get the point. The first time I visited, French high school students were playing leap-frog over the stelae, while the arrangement also clearly appealed to younger children as a perfect place for a game of hide-and-seek. Every time I have returned in good weather I have found it serving above all as a playground, with laughter easily drowning out the speeches made by tour guides. Here the abstraction that was so successful in the Jewish Museum's much smaller garden of exile, experienced only once one has entered through the museum, is much less powerful, especially to young tourists in a festive mood who stumble upon it having wandered south on a sunny day from Pariser Platz. The buried documentation center is a far grimmer experience, but not everyone descends to view its sobering displays.

The process of commissioning and creating the Memorial was fraught with even more controversy than surrounded the creation of the Topography of Terror. Here, too, the initial idea preceded the fall of the Wall; as with the Jewish Museum, reunification provided a significant spur to the creation of what became an even more prominently located structure. What had begun as a grassroots initiative organized by the journalist and publicist Lea Rosh was adopted by a national government seeking to assuage international concern over the degree to which the constituent parts of the Berlin Republic were appropriately contrite about what an earlier united Germany had wrought. James A. Young, the American historian of Holocaust memorials who joined the jury for a second competition after criticizing the results of the previous one, sagely concluded, "Because the murdered Jews can respond to this gesture only with a massive silence, the burden of response now falls on living Germans—who in their memorial visits will be asked to recall the mass murder of a people once perpetrated in their name, the absolute void this destruction has left behind, and their own responsibility for memory itself."[80]

Eisenman and Serra reprised many aspects of the Garden of Memory from Libeskind's Jewish Museum, but the repetition at a larger scale in a less confined space often fails to have the same visceral effect upon visitors. Nor did the twinning of the American minimalist sculptor, whose father had been Jewish, with the Jewish American architect, survive the process of negotiating the details of the project's realization with the client. Serra, whose commitment to art over audience had been clear in the dispute over the removal of his sculpture *Tilted Arc* from Federal Plaza in New York, eventually withdrew when asked to revise his original design.[81] This left Eisenman as the public face of the memorial. In this role, he was easily upstaged by Libeskind, who had been born in 1946 in Poland to survivors of the Holocaust, whereas Eisenman had grown up in suburban New Jersey.[82]

The larger problem was not who had suffered more but what constituted an effective space in which to commemorate one of the darkest events of recent history, ideally in a way that would entice visitors to come and then provoke them to help ensure that nothing like this ever happened again. In lieu of the collage of historicist and modernist architecture employed in so many evocative German settings, Eisenman's design hews uncannily close to the design strategy associated with critical reconstruction.

Of course, critical reconstruction never encompassed a city with a shifting ground plane or wave-like variation in the heights of building blocks, but the regularity of the shape of the rectangular slabs, aligned along a firmly defined grid of footpaths, certainly resembled the cityscape produced by new planning regulations more than it did the angled, irregular spaces created by Serra's earlier sculptures or Eisenman's buildings of the 1980s and 1990s. Moreover, the opacity of the slabs, which are considerably thicker than the steel plates out of which Serra makes his sculptures, severed the direct relationship between Louis Kahn's project for a Holocaust memorial for New York and the crystalline character of much German expressionism. Berlin's most prominent memorial is tied neither to the physical presence of a fragmentary, ruined past nor, despite its abstraction, to the conscious recall of either expressionism or the modern architecture of the Weimar Republic. Here abstraction, shorn of an obvious relationship to history, becomes for too many observers simply meaningless. While Wilms's contribution to the Topography of Terror was once described as "wanting to reveal nothing," its very neutrality ends up saying more than this attempt at monumentality.[83]

That does not mean that the monument is not linked to its own moment in the history of the architecture and urbanism of the center of Berlin. Its regularity reads as an extension of Mitte's repetitiously dour office blocks, stripped of all ornamental detail, but still ponderous. The only apparent weight of the thin stone veneers cladding their closed facades lines the streets to the south and east. Erected across the last decade of the twentieth century and the first decade of the twenty-first, these were supposed to be the building blocks of a distinctively European city, but have instead been widely criticized for their lack of architectural flair.[84] Against the intentions of the planners and architects who shepherded its reconstruction, the new Mitte, including the glitzy new towers and shopping arcade at Potsdamer Platz, turned out to be composed of a rather dreary urban fabric, with the most highly regarded exceptions, such as the Galeries Lafayette, the Reichstag, and the Topography of Terror, created outside the purview of the tight regulations intended to ensure the quality of the whole.

Within the context of early twenty-first century Berlin both the Topography of Terror and the Memorial to the Murdered Jews of Europe are relatively conventional structures. Less powerful than the cupola of the Reichstag and less fresh than

Ungers's contribution to the Friedrichstadt Passagen originally was, these additions to the cityscape attracted attention largely because of the importance of their commemorative function and because of Eisenman's international reputation as an influential architectural theorist. The impact of the Topography of Terror derives above all from being located on such a poignant site. By virtue of its scale and prominent placement, the Memorial to the Murdered Jews of Europe demonstrates the earnest commitment of the government of the Federal Republic to keeping the worst about Germany's past in plain view, but it does little to build upon the considerable aesthetic achievement represented by earlier efforts to accomplish this worthy goal.

Centering the City: Museum Island and the Palace

The longest and most vociferous debate over architecture in postunification Berlin raged for more than two decades over the place once occupied by the Hohenzollern royal and later imperial palace or Schloss (Figure 4.18).[85] After years of discussion and widespread protests by members of the public from both halves of Berlin, and indeed around the world, the Communist-built Palace of the Republic (1973–76, Heinz Graffunder and Associates) was finally demolished between 2006 and 2008, setting the stage for the erection of a replica of the facades and interior courtyard of the palace, the war-damaged shell of which had been pulled down by the East German government in 1950 (Figure 4.19).[86] The cornerstone was finally laid in the summer of 2013 for the Humboldt Forum; construction of its reinforced concrete shell topped out in 2015; it is currently scheduled to open in 2019.[87] Featuring one facade and an interior designed by the Italian architect Franco Stella, it will include meeting rooms for cultural events, as well as quarters in which to exhibit the non-Western art now housed in museums located in Dahlem, a suburban district formerly part of the American sector of West Berlin (Figure 4.20).[88] Comparing the agonizing over the reconstruction of the palace with the painstaking and far less controversial neomodernist reconstruction of the nearby New Museum, demonstrates the degree of consensus that had emerged over this approach, which is now firmly identified with the admission of the darkest chapters of Germany's recent past, although admiration for the cultural accomplishments of mid-nineteenth-century Prussia also crept back into view (Figure 4.21).[89] The relentless attention to the details of the physical fabric paid by advocates of both projects should not be mistaken, however, for historical accuracy. There is to be plenty of twenty-first-century architecture in the projected Humboldt Forum as well as the New Museum. Moreover, accounts of both projects systematically exaggerate the importance of the original buildings.[90] The palace was not one of Europe's most important royal seats from the perspective of earlier architectural historians, nor did the New Museum figure prominently in previous accounts of either Prussian or international museum architecture.

Figure 4.18. Hohenzollern Palace (Schloss), Berlin, sixteenth through nineteenth centuries. Source: Wikipedia Commons.

Figure 4.19. Heinz Graffunder and Associates, Palace of the Republic, Berlin, 1976. Photograph by Dieter Schumacher. Source: Foto Marburg.

Critical Reconstruction or Neomodernist Shards?

Figure 4.20. Franco Stella, competition design for Humboldt Forum, Berlin, 2008. Copyright Stiftung Berliner Schloss—HumboldtForum/Architekt Franco Stella with RS HUF FG.

Figure 4.21. New Museum. Source: Janericloebe/Wikipedia Commons.

The hope already borne out in the case of the New Museum is that aggressive marketing campaigns can persuade a public composed even more of tourists than locals that these buildings constitute the heart of the city. "The Palace was not located in Berlin—Berlin was the Palace" announces an article written in 1992 by the journalist Wolf Jobst Siedler and featured prominently on the webpage of the group raising money for the completion of replicas of its original facades.[91] This emphasizes a conservative history of the city, in which culture is created or at least assembled by a well-educated elite clustered around the court and made available to an international mass public as a universal good. Were it not for the elegant interventions inserted by Chipperfield into the New Museum, it would thus be possible to ignore the degree to which twentieth-century Berliners, including Henry van de Velde, Walter Gropius, and Lilly Reich, as well as Taut, Mendelsohn, and Mies, all contributed to the emergence of alternatives whose global resonance resulted in part from their ability to represent a more diverse public.

The palace, built in stages from the fifteenth to the twentieth centuries, included facades by Andreas Schlüter and a dome added by Stüler according to a design originally envisaged by Schinkel. Its interiors were designed by a who's who of Prussian architects. Nonetheless, it never achieved the artistic quality or unity of baroque rivals such as Sans Souci in Potsdam or the Residence in Würzburg. Furthermore Wilhelm II had remodeled much of its interior in a way that had, except for the use of indirect electric lighting, little or nothing to do with progressive trends in German architecture of the period.[92] Following reunification, proponents of reconstructing the palace argued that a building with its massing, if not necessarily the same facades, needed to be restored to a site they saw as the centerpiece of the original city plan from which all later development spun out. Located on the edge of the medieval city, it had indeed governed the development of Unter den Linden and Museum Island, but the city expanded as well in other directions, albeit with less of the formality prized by these planners. Moreover it was only at the middle of the nineteenth century that the band of buildings fronting the water was finally removed, making its main facade visible from the west.

Stüler's New Museum, designed and built between 1841 and 1866, has been similarly lauded, especially on account of the technology involved in its construction and the complexity of the decoration of its interiors, neither of which was unusual in a wider European context.[93] As the quarter century it took to design, build, and decorate the building hints, the project had a complex and often troubled history; at least some of the solutions developed in order to erect such a large structure atop the marshy site were partly improvised as work slowly proceeded. Both iron girders, built by the local Börsig firm, and hollow clay "pots" helped lighten the load.[94] Most of the art originally housed in it, which included a large collection of plaster casts, would not today be considered very significant; key acquisitions, such as the bust of Nefertiti, were made only in the final years before World War I. In addition, none of the celebratory accounts that greeted its reopening dwelt on the degree to it, like its counterparts across Germany, was closely tied to the aims of the nation-state, in this case, Prussia.[95]

The erection of the Humboldt Forum is intended to be the linchpin in the strategy of critical reconstruction. Its proponents argue that the building, which features replicas of three of the external and two of the courtyard facades of the Hohenzollern Palace, will restore the key urban nucleus in relation to which Unter den Linden and Museum Island were both created. A statement on the homepage of the current website declares:

> The palace will restore the familiar picture of Berlin, complete its historic centre and heal the previously wounded cityscape. Its reconstruction is making Berlin once more the much-loved "Athens on the Spree." In this way a counterpoint is being created to the mass-produced modern areas of the city's centre.
>
> As a result, Berlin is now again becoming an exciting city in architectural terms as well. If it doesn't want to become boring, modernity has to face up to the city's history, allow itself to be judged against historic architecture and compete with it.[96]

The rebuilt royal palace will thus cement a vision of urban order based on historical precedent. For years the purpose it would serve remained vague. In 2009, the year after the competition for its design was concluded, the Humboldt Foundation (not to be confused with the federally financed Alexander von Humboldt Foundation that has long funded academic exchanges between the Federal Republic and the rest of the world or the nearby Humboldt University) was established both to build the structure and to be its tenant.

The foundation has "rebranded" the project; by 2012 its promotional materials paid relatively little attention to the history of the palace they seek to re-create. In particular the celebration of art from around the world, including tribal art from Germany's former colonies in Africa and Micronesia as well as from Islamic and East Asian courts, is intended to open the building's specifically Prussian past up to a world in which the Federal Republic respects the cultural achievements of its counterparts around the world, not least by exhibiting this material in prestigious proximity to Museum Island. The use of the name Humboldt conveys the same message of enlightened support for scientific inquiry across international boundaries; von Humboldt and his brother, Wilhelm, played a key role in the invention of the modern research university, one of nineteenth-century Prussia's most important cultural achievements.[97]

Meanwhile, the opening of the New Museum concluded the renovation of Museum Island as the tourist centerpiece of the reunified city (although a refurbishment of the Pergamon remains to be completed, the fact that this museum had been open, and thronged with tourists, without interruption since 1958 meant that this was really only a postscript). Added to the UNESCO list of World Heritage Sites in 1999, the five museums were originally conceived as part of the process of consolidating first a Prussian and then a German national state. They are now being reinterpreted as part of a shared international cultural heritage, an approach that overlooks continuing disputes about how some of the art currently or previously exhibited in them, including Nefertiti, was acquired.[98]

Figure 4.22. Korn and Bogatsky, State Council Building, Berlin, 1964. Source: SLUB/Deutsche Fotothek/Gerhard Hofert.

Museum Island is in fact only the northern tip of the island in the middle of the Spree occupied as well by the future Humboldt Forum and by the former State Council building of the German Democratic Republic. In a unique example of the use of ruins paired with modernism erected by the German Democratic Republic, one bay of the original palace was set into this building, erected between 1962 and 1964 by the architectural collective of Roland Korn and Hans Erich Bogatzky, in order to commemorate Karl Liebknecht's declaration of the first German republic from its window on 9 November 1918 (Figure 4.22).[99] This building also marked the official turn of the East German state away from socialist realism and toward the modernism that dominated civic architecture in most of the non-Communist world in the first decades after the war. The presence of the State Council Building just to the south of the Humboldt Forum site poses unusual questions about authenticity. While reconstructions of demolished buildings are not without precedent, few stand so close to fragments of the original.

No such issues are posed by the New Museum, where every effort was made to salvage as much as possible of the original structure and of its decoration. Chipperfield's building reprises the strategy originally adopted by Döllgast in his reconstruction of the Alte Pinakothek in Munich; indeed there are clear similarities between their two staircases (Figure 4.23). In addition to acknowledging the Alte Pinakothek as a precedent, Chipperfield has also cited the influences of "Egon Eiermann's articulate collage of ruin and modern intervention in the Kaiser Wilhelm

Figure 4.23. Stairhall, New Museum. Source: Ute Zscharnt for David Chipperfield Architects.

Gedächtniskirche."[100] The main difference between his building and these earlier examples was the degree to which the highest standards of conservation were now applied to nineteenth-century buildings and the resources that the Federal Republic could now bestow, as in the Reichstag, upon salvaging what would earlier have been seen as expendable remnants of the original structure. Chipperfield declared:

> Our vision was not to make a memorial to destruction, nor to create a historical reproduction, but to protect and make sense of the extraordinary ruins and remains that survived not only the destruction of the war but also the physical erosion of the last 60 years. This concern led us to create a new building from the remains of the old, a new building that neither celebrates nor hides its history but includes it.[101]

Such remains were not available a few hundred yards to the south. Much of the debate over whether or not to demolish the Palace of the Republic and replace it with a facsimile of its predecessor instead revolved around which memories merit expression through urban form. Many physical traces of the East German state have been erased from the heart of Mitte; others were viewed as endangered.[102] Although the former Stalinallee, renamed for Karl Marx in 1961, was probably the most politically tainted Communist-era urban ensemble in the former German Democratic Republic, it was never endangered because the planning paradigm adopted here accorded with critical reconstruction. Modernist East German landmarks, however, were vulnerable. Although the State Council Building was at one point threatened, it was retained and now houses a private business school. The Foreign Ministry, built on the site of Schinkel's former architectural academy, was quickly demolished, not least because the advocates of critical reconstruction hope to rebuild what was certainly one of nineteenth-century Germany's most original structures.[103]

The Palace of the Republic was vulnerable on three grounds. First, it stood on part of the land occupied by the former Hohenzollern palace; second, it was a relatively recent and by no means distinguished building. Its marble-and-dull-orange-mirror-glass facades made it appear more like a Third World luxury hotel than a major public building of a key Central European capital. There were many other more distinguished examples of East German architecture from the period nearby, including the State Council Building and the International Cinema. Third, like most buildings of its size on both sides of the former border between the Federal and the German Democratic Republics, the materials used in its construction, especially asbestos, posed significant health risks.[104]

On the other hand, the palace had incontrovertibly been the public face of the state. Sweeping it aside risked denying that there had ever been an East Germany, a Communist alternative to capitalism, and an attempt to build a workers' state, dependent as these may have been on a Soviet godparent. Moreover, the palace had been, or at the least certainly seemed in retrospect to have been, a particularly palatable public face for the regime. In addition to the rooms used by government functionaries it contained a wide variety of facilities open to the general public. That it hosted many popular functions, instead of being reserved for secretive government bureaucrats, certainly helped endear it to former East Germans. Many who expressed no fondness for the Communist regime recalled celebrating personal milestones at its numerous restaurants, cafés, and bars. And the Berlin city government had been willing to spend huge sums to decontaminate the convention center built in West Berlin at roughly the same time as the Palace of the Republic of many of the same hazardous materials. Finally, many who regretted that Walter Ulbricht, the first East German leader, had pulled down a building that had not been irrevocably damaged in the war, nonetheless felt it was dishonest to rebuild it or unbecoming to seek continuity with an undemocratic Prussian past (the sense in the 1960s that reconstruction was dishonest hampered efforts to rebuild Mies's Monument to Karl Liebknecht and Rosa Luxemburg).[105] The architect Matthias Sauerbruch wrote in 2009, "If the former Prussian palace is rebuilt as the simulacrum of Germany's architectural history, the 'Disneyfication' of the European city will have found its ultimate expression in Berlin."[106]

Thus the debate over the Palace of the Republic's fate was also over which memories matter in the Berlin Republic and the degree to which architecture is the appropriate means for expressing national consensus, if it indeed exists. Were the relatively recent personal experiences of the Federal Republic's newest citizens, as well as the political presence of their previous nation, deserving of recognition, or should the key position of the royal palace be restored either because of its significance as an architectural monument and urban linchpin or out of respect for the Hohenzollern dynasty? While the grounds for preservation of the palace remained relatively constant and garnered considerable support among West Berliners, West Germans, and people abroad, those who advocated its replacement oscillated between emphasizing the importance of a building that had similar massing to the royal palace and insisting on the literal re-creation of, at the least, its principal facades and one of its interior courts. Meanwhile, for several years early in the new century the shell of the communist palace, gutted of asbestos, served as one of the city's hippest forums for art and musical events. This endeared the structure to a new generation, many of whom discovered Berlin only after the fall of the Wall. Today steel recycled from it buttresses the Burj Khalifa in Dubai, the world's tallest building.[107]

The opening salvo in the discussion over the fate of the site occurred in the summer of 1993, when a temporary mock-up of the Hohenzollern Palace facades was erected alongside the Palace of the Republic. Sponsored by Thyssen Hünnebeck, a steel firm with its headquarters in western Germany, this full-scale model consisted of fabric printed with the details of the building's architecture and hung over steel scaffolding. Mirrors helped reduce the prominence of the Palace of the Republic and hinted at the appearance of a complete reconstruction.[108] The exhibition inside demonstrated that although there was no talk whatsoever of bringing back the monarchy, there was considerable nostalgia in some quarters for "the good old days." Highlights included fulsome coverage of the wedding of Wilhelm II's only daughter. The impression of many Berliners at the time was that this was a western German initiative with relatively little local backing.[109]

The following year a competition was announced for the erection of a new building on the site to house the foreign ministry. Already the presumption of both federal and city officials was that the Palace of the Republic would go. An early portent of the strength of critical reconstruction was established by the degree to which German entries were premiated in an anonymous international competition. Local architects were both more aware and more willing to offer designs that accorded with the taste of a carefully chosen jury. Not surprisingly, the winner, Bernd Niebuhr, proposed a structure that adhered to the footprint and massing of the royal palace. He refused, however, to imitate either the original facades or to echo the plans of the Hohenzollern Palace, instead placing a large oval courtyard at the center of his scheme.[110] This plan, however, came to naught. The expense associated with building new ministries for most federal departments quickly proved to be too great, as the weakness of the East German economy and thus the cost of reunification both became clearer. Instead, despite the message it sent, the foreign ministry moved into an expanded Imperial Bank. The Reichsbank had been built between 1934 and 1940 by Heinrich Wolff; Mies had been the alternate winner of the competition from which Mendelsohn, as a Jew, had been barred. The first and one of the most significant Third Reich public buildings in the city center, this had also been the place from which East Germany was actually governed.[111]

Subsequent attempts to rebuild the Hohenzollern Palace sought to replicate the fund-raising success of the effort to rebuild the Church of Our Lady in Dresden. Despite the strong relationship between critical reconstruction and Social Democratic politics at the local level in Berlin, efforts to raise money in the United States for the reconstruction of the Hohenzollern Palace embraced the Republican foreign policy establishment, with Henry Kissinger, Ronald Lauder, and the elder George Bush all attending a dinner organized in New York.[112] Publicity material targeted at wealthy Americans indulged in the nostalgia for a vanished Prussia, now associated above all with the quality of its architecture rather than the character of its government, that had infused the exhibition in the temporary replica erected in 1993. As of 2016 only fifty-nine million euros, half of the agreed-upon private contribution, had been raised.[113]

Another competition, held in 2008, resulted in the victory of the Italian architect Franco Stella, a former student of Rossi's. The brief demanded the reconstruction of three of the original four facades as well as part of Schlüter's interior courtyard; Stella's fourth facade, which replaced the single rather hodgepodge prebaroque one, is in the spirit of critical reconstruction. There was a further controversy when it proved that his office was not as large as originally reported and as required for competition entrants.[114] There was criticism at home and abroad of the project. Michael Kimmelman, for instance, wrote, "German officials, often inclined toward euphemism, have christened it the Humboldt Forum."[115] Describing the project as "a cultural misadventure from the start" and an example of "willed forgetfulness," Kimmelman joined many of his German counterparts in forcefully condemning the project.

The relative success of neomodernism in relation to critical reconstruction can be seen, however, by the near success of an alternative to Stella's scheme. The German architecture firm of Kuehn Malvezzi received an alternate first prize for an entry that adhered to the letter, but not always the spirit, of the competition by taking an incremental approach to the reconstruction of the facades of the original palace. They proposed re-creating the mass of the Hohenzollern Palace in brick, using government funds. The individual pieces of the masonry cladding constituting the replica of the historic facades would be added only as private donors contributed to the scheme. The expectation of the architects was that there was indeed much less popular support for the reconstruction than its supporters claimed, and that the building would retain a resemblance to the reconstruction of the Alte Pinakothek, with only a partial version of the historic facade rising along the exposed brick shell.[116]

Lack of enthusiasm for the reconstruction could be measured in other ways as well. When economic crisis struck at the end of 2008, funding for the project temporarily stalled, indicating that it was not a high government priority. Now cleared of the Palace of the Republic, the site returned to being the vacant lot it had been throughout the 1950s and 1960s. In early 2013, even the future of the small, high-modern information kiosk, called the Humboldt Box, designed by Bertram Vandreicke, erected in 2010, was temporarily endangered.[117] The presence of the kiosk demonstrated that the model here was private rather than public development; the bright red Infobox, perched lightly on pilotis, had between 1995 and 2001 played a similar role for the entirely capitalist redevelopment of Potsdamer Platz; in the summer of 2016 both the Humboldt Box and the completed facades were draped in enormous advertising banners for Samsung mobile telephones. Designed by Schneider and Schumacher the Infobox on Potsdamer Platz was a refreshing antidote to the banal corporate architecture actually built there. It proved so popular that there were calls to preserve it (there was also a whiff of irony about the degree to which this piece of advertising for Europe's largest capitalist real estate development of the period was clearly inspired by Soviet constructivism).[118]

The possible closure of the Humboldt Box threatened to give casual tourists unaware of the decades of debate over what had proved to be Germany's most highly charged place the impression that Germany was a country incapable of action. But more was at stake. Aleida Assmann, one of Germany's most prominent intellectuals and an expert on memory, has written that "reconstruction makes room not for a new future, but for a new past," in this case one suffused with nostalgia for a pre-democratic Prussia and Germany.[119]

Tellingly, there was no need for this degree of publicity, and thus implicitly also persuasion, on nearby Museum Island, where a related past was revived with much less controversy, in part because of the reverence paid here both to actual artifacts from the past and to contemporary architectural talent. The logic of refurbishing—to the point in the New Museum of partial reconstruction—nineteenth- and early twentieth-century cultural facilities attracted little opposition, despite the equally great expense involved. Indeed, much of the dissent that was voiced was over the fact that any modern design would be present. The city of Berlin, the Federal Republic, the European Union, and UNESCO all agreed to a policy of continuity with Prussian, imperial, Weimar, Nazi, and Communist uses of the site, all of which dovetailed in turn with the conscious emphasis the Federal Republic had placed since the late 1960s on the development of cultural infrastructure in general and art museums in particular. Critics uncomfortable with the message of respect for the Hohenzollern dynasty conveyed by the careful reconstruction of their city palace were much less likely to rue the preservation of the Altes Museum, although it was a key example of Hohenzollern patronage and had also, bedecked with banners emblazoned with swastikas, provided a backdrop for Nazi rallies, or the reconstruction and renovation of its sibling.[120] Germans writing about Museum Island recognized such events as chapters in a much longer history, whose focus was from the beginning the preservation of cultural treasures for the edification of the educated middle class and even potentially their empowerment. The circumstances in which many of these treasures reached Berlin, although controversial in the countries from which they had been taken, merited less mention, although this did not hinder curators at the New Museum from mounting an impassioned plea for the return of gold artifacts originally excavated in Turkey from Russia, to which they had been taken by the victorious Soviets.[121]

The New Museum succeeded at multiple levels where the reconstruction of the palace has apparently failed. Supporters of its reconstruction were able to leverage significant financial backing from a variety of public sources. They employed a celebrated architect from abroad. His position as a citizen of one of the countries that had defeated Germany in two wars, albeit before he was born, generated a sense of detachment from nationalist aims, even as it fostered contemporary national identity through the obvious symbolism of German integration into a community of nations that included the victors in those wars. Finally, the combination of crowds who thronged to visit the result and almost unanimously positive, as well as ample, media coverage at home and abroad served the larger purpose of highlighting the commitment a reunified Germany continued to make to the preservation of culture. This included artifacts from other parts of the world, heritage that had long been viewed by the curators and the Western publics for such museums as universal rather than national.[122] As an example of neomodernism that melded respect for the historical fabric with obviously modernist insertions, the New Museum belonged to a by now familiar and successful strategy.

By contrast, the failure of advocates of critical reconstruction to demolish the Palace of the Republic swiftly and to reconstruct a building whose massing at the least adhered to the precedent established by the Hohenzollern palace hampered their effectiveness. Not only did their scheme remain a flashpoint for those attempting to preserve the memory of the German Democratic Republic by reference to one of its most palatable and symbolic public buildings, but the twinning of international architectural culture with local German efforts, which had long been critical to the Federal Republic's self-presentation at home and abroad, increasingly unraveled as international architecture culture, not least because of the success of neomodernism in Berlin itself, moved away from the postmodernist historicism of which critical reconstruction was such a prominent example. Thus by the second decade of the twenty-first century, the rebuilding of the Hohenzollern Palace appeared increasingly provincial. This in turn left supporters of the project vulnerable to being seen as defenders of conservative nostalgia rather than as examples of the grassroots opposition to wholesale urban clearance on the part of capitalist real estate speculators and their big-government allies that had initially prompted Stimmann's embrace of Rossi's theories in the 1970s. It also opened the way to new interpretations of the reconstruction of the original palace, as well as of other high-profile sites in and near the city center, as pandering above all to what had long been one of the city's major industries: tourism.

The reconstruction of the palace will fill the city's most prominent architectural hole, but it is not clear that the Humboldt Forum will rival Museum Island, the Reichstag, the Jewish Museum, and the Topography of Terror, or even for that matter the Galeries Lafayette as one of central Berlin's most popular places. Its success will depend as much on public programming as on its architecture. As Berlin has multiple commercial, cultural, and governmental centers it is very unlikely, in any case, that the completed building will be perceived as the focal point of the entire city. Although it is always difficult to predict the future, it is equally unlikely that this will be more than the last gasp of an exhausted postmodernism, even if it is not necessarily the last reconstruction of a destroyed Berlin landmark. A new modernism, when it finally comes, that breaks free of the various precedents for contemporary architecture established in Germany during the Weimar Republic is likely to be based on conditions of its own time or on entirely different historical precedents, probably from another city and country.

The battles over Berlin have ended. Tourists flock to a memorial to the Wall at Bernauerstrasse, but elsewhere the physical evidence of its traces has largely been erased. The city government struggles to fund Berlin's substantial cultural facilities, certainly one of the most positive legacies of its Cold War importance, rather than erect more architectural showpieces. Initial predictions that Berlin would rival Frankfurt or even Düsseldorf as a national or even international center of commerce and capital have failed to materialize. In consequence, the pressure to build high-rise office towers has diminished. Berlin's unique mixture of the scruffy and the cosmopolitan attracts artists to settle there, but architects now come as tourists rather than to work. Berliners in particular and Germans in general have begun to debate the major political issues of the day with less and less recourse to the filter of architecture. While this shift may diminish the urgency of their architectural patronage, it is certainly healthy for their democracy.

Five

Manufacturing Memory in the Ruhr Region

On 15 December 2001 the inhabitants of Germany's Ruhr region awoke to find the front page of the local newspaper announcing proudly that a former mine north of the center of the city of Essen, the Zeche Zollverein (Customs Union Mine), had been placed on the UNESCO World Heritage List. The headlines compared the "Eiffel Tower of the Ruhr," as the tower over Pithead XII was labeled, with one of the most famous structures already on the list, the Pyramids (Figure 5.1).[1] Throughout the 1990s, geographers, city planners, architects, and arts administrators, working closely with the local political and business community, made this structure, abandoned in 1986 after just over fifty years of operation, the emblem of their efforts to revitalize the former heartland of continental Europe's coal and steel industry. For more than twenty years the steel latticework of Pithead XII's tower has graced the cover of almost every publication on the region.[2]

The transformation of the Zeche Zollverein, and of Pithead XII in particular, from a relatively obscure, outmoded mine into a widely recognized symbol of the region was part of the larger conversion in the 1990s and early years of the new century of disused industrial structures across the Ruhr region into emblems of local pride and potential regeneration. Crucial to this effort was the juxtaposition of existing structures with patently new insertions; visitors today to the Zeche Zollverein experience interiors designed by Norman Foster and Rem Koolhaas's offices and on their way in pass a building by the Japanese practice SANAA. In the first postwar decades the collage of old and new was a common approach to the reconstruction of churches, and in the second half of the twentieth century a number of West German museums made use of historicist as well as modernist sources to create an architecture of fragments evocative of absence. Across the two decades following reunification, architects, developers, planners, and politicians were among those who jostled in Berlin over the best way to create appropriate symbols for the Berlin Republic for

Figure 5.1. Schupp and Kremmer, Pithead XII, Zeche Zollverein, Essen, 1932. Source: Avda/Wikipedia Commons.

a public that included tourists, the business community, and those from around the world interested in how the country addressed its troubled twentieth century. In the capital what had been an unarticulated consensus about the efficacy of pairing references to historicism and modernism, a strategy originally infused with nostalgia for the years 1815 to 1914, as well as a strong sense of German victimhood, emerged as an unusually impressive way of instead evoking the pain Germans had caused.

In the same years that Friedrichstrasse and Pariser Platz were being rebuilt, the Reischtag renovated, and new memorial landscapes were being created in Berlin, what was happening in the Ruhr region was slightly different, however. Contrasting modernism's own past with its present was not a means of casting light on past horrors; instead, the conversion of the ruins of heavy industry into high culture quite purposefully overlooked the key role that precisely such infrastructure had played in rearming the Third Reich. The politics were also different. In Berlin acknowledging the Nazi past attracted praise from all corners, but doing so built quite specifically upon decades of structures erected with the tacit sponsorship of the Christian Democrats, while Social Democratic officials criticized modernism. In the Ruhr region, however, Social Democrats championed past and present modernism in the hopes of attracting tourists and creative industries. The region's effort enlisted top architectural talent from Germany and abroad, and the results had a real impact upon the profession of landscape architecture in particular. Unlike what happened in Berlin, however, they had almost no bearing on how those outside of these design-oriented fields viewed Germany.

The efforts in the Ruhr were largely prompted by the International Building Exhibition (IBA) Emscher Park, for which the Zeche Zollverein served as a centerpiece.[3] The goals of this decadelong project, which concluded in 1999, included the conversion of the region's industrial heritage into cultural landmarks that would serve as nodes for tourism and demonstrate to potential investors the region's long heritage of technical innovation.[4] This approach continued into the early twenty-first century in the successful campaign to make Essen the European capital of culture in 2010.[5] Although overshadowed by the reunification of Germany, the attempt to rejuvenate the economy of the Ruhr region by recycling its former steel mills and coal mines into a new cultural and recreational infrastructure, confirmed the importance of the ruins of modern industry, which were now far more pervasive in both halves of the country (and indeed throughout those parts of the world that industrialized successfully in the second half of the nineteenth century) than traces of the carnage of World War II.[6] The approach the IBA took toward their remains extended modernism's confrontation with its own past into the field of landscape architecture and transformed buildings that had previously been little appreciated into regional landmarks. As in Berlin, minimalist art of the 1960s, which had found early acceptance here, as well as the earth art that quickly followed from it, provided useful methods for creating memoryscapes.[7] At the same time, the deliberate manufacture of new cultural memories, to use Jan Assmann's term, through the preservation of physical artifacts paradoxically promoted forgetting, as many aspects of the region's history were swept under the carpet even as the literal traces were lovingly preserved.[8] Although these efforts to revitalize the region resulted in widespread favorable publicity at home and abroad (Lea Rosh, the Berliner publicist who instigated the Memorial to the Murdered Jews of Europe was involved in the effort), they failed to deliver the economic benefits forecast by their more enthusiastic promoters, who had hoped that drawing attention to the region's history of innovation would foster a new generation of entrepreneurship.[9]

The IBA Emscher Park and European Capitals of Culture initiatives attempted to create a comprehensive cultural infrastructure in an area that had in its economic prime lacked the range of bourgeois cultural institutions typical of other German cities of the size of Duisburg, Essen, Bochum, and Dortmund, as well as of vibrant avant-garde alternatives to them. The Landscape Park (Landschaftspark) in Duisburg, designed by Latz + Partner, which opened in 1994, and the ongoing refurbishment of the Zeche Zollverein in Essen, became the centerpieces of the region's effort to reinterpret its industrial heritage as politically and socially progressive art. These projects highlighted the continuing utility of Weimar and even Wilhelmine modernism to the identity of the Federal Republic, especially as reconstructed by its cultural elites. However, working-class memories of pollution, labor disputes, and the Third Reich undercut attempts to convey an uncomplicated interpretation of modernism as inherently progressive, and highlighted that effective advertising alone did not embed newly developed cultural memories in a community. Furthermore, the relatively peripheral location of both sites in relation to the centers of Duisburg and Essen, not to mention the relatively low national profile of these cities, hindered them from having the same impact as Berlin's new memory landscapes.[10]

Beginning in the middle of the nineteenth century the valley of the Ruhr River, which joins the Rhine in Duisburg, boomed as the region's coal was burned to produce iron and steel in some of Europe's most modern industrial installations.[11] Essen, where the Krupp family's steel empire was based, became the region's largest city; Duisburg gained the world's biggest inland harbor as well as a substantial steel industry of its own; Bochum and Dortmund also grew exponentially, and a number of smaller cities such as Hattingen, Gelsenkirchen, Oberhausen, Herne, and Witten also hosted important steel mills, mines, and other heavy industry. Development across the region was unusually decentralized. Throughout the region, many of the mines, mills, and furnaces lay outside or on the fringes of historic cities, towns, and even village centers. Today most of the region's cities are composed of communities gradually annexed over the course of the last century and a half and still separated from one another by green belts containing farms and woodlands.[12] Many of these nuclei grew up around the pitheads of coal mines or in relation to new rail lines.

For the first two-thirds of the twentieth century, the region was widely regarded as a cultural wasteland in which the raw brutality of capital trumped all else.[13] There were few theaters and publishing houses, no opera houses or universities. The rich were almost all nouveau and the poor, most of whom had rural roots, equally far removed from anything whose value was comprehensible to intellectuals. While the Krupp and Thyssen dynasties were wealthier and more powerful than many hereditary princes, they shared little of this success with their workforces. A small and inconsequential middle class did little to mediate between the two extremes; nowhere else in Germany was the threat of social unrest greater between the wars. Nor was it quickly quelled after Germany's second defeat. In the first postwar elections, held in 1949, more than 10 percent of the electorate in Essen voted Communist.[14]

The polarized politics of the first half of the twentieth century gradually eased in the 1950s as workers gained more political clout. The Social Democrats controlled the state government of North Rhine-Westphalia from 1966 to 2005 (they were re-elected in 2010 but lost in 2017), and remained in charge of many city halls for even longer stretches. Beginning with the establishment in 1962 of the Ruhr University Bochum, for several years Europe's largest construction site, higher education began to flourish across a region whose largest employers had once strenuously and successfully opposed its presence.[15] By the eighties, many of the new generation of Social Democrats had earned diplomas.

Social Democratic empowerment coincided, however, with the emergence of shifts in the global economy that, beginning in the 1950s, triggered the collapse of coal mining and the decline of steel production across the region. The pitheads and factories that had dotted the region for over a century began to vanish in the 1950s. Changes in both policy and taste combined, by the 1980s, however, to save many of those examples of the region's industrial heritage, which, like Zeche Zollverein or the blast furnace that became the Landscape Park, continued to function for their original purpose into that decade.

Evidence of a move toward preservation came in 1968 when the inhabitants of the Eisenheim housing estate in Oberhausen, the city immediately west of the Landscape Park and north of Zeche Zollverein, fought to restore their decrepit housing rather than move into new quarters.[16] This estate, the oldest purpose-built workers' housing in the region (it dates to 1845), was originally occupied mostly by miners and their families. Although dismissed by planners as outmoded because they lacked modern amenities, the small dwellings with their cottage gardens proved extremely popular with their inhabitants. Those who campaigned for the preservation of Eisenheim were interested above all in saving modest but cherished homes. They felt alienated from the apartment towers likely to supplant the story-and-a-half cottages, whose design, although standardized, remained imbued with nostalgia for village life, which indeed continued to flourish in the adjacent gardens, packed as they were with chickens and vegetable patches.

This grassroots campaign for renovation instead of replacement demonstrated the gap that was opening up between the aesthetics of the Social Democratic leadership, committed to a modernism that was by this time widely understood by educated Germans to be the antithesis of National Socialism, and that of actual workers, who cherished the craftsmanship that had gone into building and improving their houses as well as the community that had emerged around them. Although in the early twentieth-century industrial buildings engaged the talent of the German architectural profession, an industrial aesthetic applied to other purposes established little more than a toehold in the region until after World War II. Even during the Weimar Republic, mine owners and factory workers alike tended to wax nostalgic for an imagined agrarian utopia.[17] There are, for instance, few cousins of the Weissenhof here. Instead, despite increasingly rigorous attention to cost, which curtailed the use of superfluous ornament, garden city re-creations of premodern village life prevailed.[18]

Modernism's utility became widely acknowledged in the region only once modernity itself was threatened with obsolescence. Recognizing that the structural shift to a service economy could not be stopped dead in its tracks, political and economic leaders began in the late 1980s to provide the cultural facilities the region had always lacked in an attempt to enhance its appeal to investors and to the upper echelons of an increasingly mobile workforce. For them, the preservation of the region's outmoded industrial infrastructure demonstrated a historical commitment to state-of-the-art technology and created the cultural resources that might attract new, future-oriented businesses. Moreover, the establishment of new parks on brownfield sites helped cleanse the local air, land, and water. And even if the envisioned tourists seldom showed up, the parks did provide leisure opportunities to locals.

Under the imaginative leadership of the geographer and planner Karl Ganser, the IBA Emscher Park codified this cultivation of industrial culture *(Industriekultur)*.[19] By building upon the scaffolding of the region's industrial ruins, Ganser and his team hoped as well to nurture local pride. They began by knitting surviving sites together through the creation of the Route of Industrial Culture. In addition to the Landscape Park and Zeche Zollverein, other examples of recycling undertaken under IBA auspices include the gasometer in Oberhausen, which has been the site of both popular exhibitions and avant-garde art installations, and the Heinrichshütte, the mill in Hattingen where the steel for Richard Serra's earliest large works, several of which remain in nearby Bochum, was rolled. Although no economic resurgence materialized, this initially provincial approach to rustbelt landscape helped catapult neo-modernism into the mainstream of international landscape architectural practice.

Landscape Park

In the 1990s and the early years of the new century, none of the IBA Emscher Park projects attracted more attention, or spawned more imitations, than the Landscape Park (Figure 5.2).[20] In its use of nature to cleanse a contaminated industrial landscape and provide new leisure activities, in its reliance upon minimalism and earth art to transform industrial detritus into cultural landmarks, and in its creation of walkways that allowed visitors to experience mastery of sites that had long been off limits to the public, it pioneered strategies that would become characteristic of other brownfield parks created under IBA auspices. The pairing here of an early twentieth-century industrial installation with new references to later modern art, as well as to a prominent recent park in Paris, followed the approach employed by the architects who for more than four decades had been constructing a new identity for Germany in part out of memories of modernism, although the focus here was very much upon the region rather than the nation.

Opened in 1903, the Meiderich blast furnace that became the site of the Landscape Park was built atop a mineshaft that provided fuel with which to smelt iron. The required equipment was designed to function as efficiently as possible; aesthetics played no discernible role in the original arrangement, which was erected shortly before factory architecture became a central concern of the German architectural profession. Operated by Thyssen, it closed in 1985. Much of the furnace could have been quite literally scrapped, its components sold on the open market for their metal. Few parts of it were candidates for the adaptive re-use that has elsewhere

Figure 5.2. Latz + Partner, Landscape Park, Duisburg, 1994. Copyright Christa Panick. Courtesy of Latz + Partner.

in the region seen flourmills converted into art museums, pitheads into discos, and train stations into cinemas.[21] Instead, in 1991 the IBA sponsored a competition for a 750-acre park.

Latz + Partner won. Peter Latz was professor of landscape architecture and planning at the technical university in Munich-Weihenstephan. Since 1968 he has practiced in partnership with his wife, Anneliese. Their previous work included most notably a city park on the River Port Island in Saarbrücken, completed in 1989. Here they converted a clogged port into a public park that is in their words "the heart of an ecological urban renewal."[22] A series of waterfalls helps purify the water while providing a soothing sound, which dulls the roar of a nearby motorway. New, vaguely classical walls constructed out of debris scavenged from the site define the park's civic character. The rather postmodern air of this scheme distinguishes it from the more rugged character of the Landscape Park site. Other sources for the approach the Latzes took in Duisburg included the Westphalia Park in Dortmund, opened in 1959, and the Gas Works Park in Seattle, designed by Richard Haag, which opened in 1975, although there is far less integration of new plantings, environmental concerns, and existing architecture in either of these.[23]

The Latzes' approach proved perfectly suited to the goals and also the modest finances of the IBA, while their success in Duisburg helped prompt Peter Latz's emergence as one of the world's most influential landscape architects. Instead of demolishing the blast furnace, the Latzes advocated the preservation of as much as possible. The sintering plant, one of the most contaminated parts of the site, was one of the few installations to be destroyed (sintering is a metallurgical process in which powder is heated past the melting point in order to form objects). Nor did the Latzes espouse radical interventions. Their incremental strategy, and the sophisticated aesthetic sense that accompanied it, set the tone for the IBA's entire effort to refurbish the northern, poorer tier of the region by creating a network of new parks.[24] The impact of the paradigm established in Duisburg reached far beyond the region. The Landscape Park won the 2001 European Prize for Landscape Architecture; major French and American awards followed.[25] It has also been the centerpiece of a traveling exhibition of landscape design organized by the Museum of Modern Art in New York.[26] By providing a new template for effective responses to the interlinked problems of urban and environmental degradation, it has inspired the profession of landscape architecture to generate new and creative responses to both. The power of this example lies in its attentiveness to history and ecological concerns, and in the balance it attempts to create between emphatically popular pursuits and the more rarefied concepts of beauty that the Latzes share with those who admire minimalist art. It also lies in the pervasiveness of the problems it addresses.[27]

The most significant challenge the site posed was its literal filthiness. This was, as IBA organizers were all too aware, part of a larger problem with both the image and the reality of life in the region. Throughout its economic heyday, air and water

Manufacturing Memory in the Ruhr Region

Figure 5.3. Landscape Park. Source: Der Hexer/Wikipedia Commons.

pollution were pervasive.[28] Most mills burned coal from the seam that came almost to the surface in southern Bochum. For decades, a poisonous cloud of acrid brown smoke hung over cities and fields on all but the best days, penetrating lungs and living rooms alike, while at night the sky glowed red. The Dortmund-Ems and the Rhine-Herne Canal running parallel through the Emscher Valley were notoriously noxious. Despite the emergence in the early decades of the twentieth century of an industrial aesthetic, few contemporaries regarded the region's appearance with anything but disdain.

The Latzes relied on nature, and in particular on a German Romantic formulation of nature that emphasized its spiritual and even healing qualities, to purify an environment that they increasingly recast as a modernist garden and/or wilderness.[29] For instance, they channeled the poisoned water of the Rhine-Herne Canal through an underground concrete culvert, while creating a repository for rainwater at ground level (Figure 5.3). Although they retained the hard edges of the original industrial canal rather than softening them through creek restoration, they nonetheless created a place that is relatively tranquil and bucolic, one where it is possible to imagine boating, if not necessarily condone swimming. Their dual approach to plantings was equally significant. They balanced stately formality in key areas with a laissez-faire attitude in others. Particularly noteworthy was their relaxed attitude toward nonnative species, such as the wildflowers that arrived with iron ore from Sweden.[30] A whole discipline of industrial forestry has arisen in Germany through the deliberate conversion of parts of this and similar sites into quasi wilderness.[31] Although there is no real wilderness within the park's boundaries, there is certainly far greater biodiversity than had existed for well over a century.

The region's new parks double as locations for recreational activities ranging from walking and bicycling to more specialized sports such as rock climbing. One of the new bicycle paths that knit together towns along the Ems valley threads through the Landscape Park. These paths contribute to the provision of the recreational amenities the region had long lacked and that are now seen as critical to the creation of the quality of life needed to retain and attract professionals and managers.

Although much of the Landscape Park offers possibilities for contemplation, spots scattered throughout it are specifically designed as places to have fun. Over 220 events a year are staged in the park.[32] These include plays and dance performances as well as exhibits and open-air films. Some of the activities are more unexpected and eccentric. Rock climbers now use the walls of several bunkers, which have been transformed into an Alpine climbing wall, and scuba divers have staked a claim to the interior of the gasometer, which is now filled with water.

Simply beginning to cleanse the site and provide a backdrop for popular leisure activities was not enough. A "recycling economy," as the planner Thomas Sieverts termed the adaptation of the region's former manufacturing base to serve new economic purposes, depends as well on the "'recoding' of fallow land" that takes place "prior to the economic and material restoration."[33] Crucial to this recoding were art and culture; hence the repeated use of the term *industrial culture* to describe the transformation of the detritus of the region's original industrialization into the examples of challenging modern art the region had previously largely lacked. This creative reinterpretation built on German photography and American art of the previous three decades and was crucial to the favorable international reception of the Landscape Park.

Artists already steeped in modernism's industrial aesthetic were the first to effect this transformation. The conversion of industrial runs into art began in the 1950s, just as the mine pitheads and steel mills began to vanish from the local landscape. Bernd Becher and Hilla Becher began photographing such structures in 1957, when they were students at the Art Academy in nearby Düsseldorf, with Bernd switching from painting and graphic arts to photography, his wife's medium, in order to capture more objectively the standardization of the original artifact, as well as the decay that already engulfed many of them.[34] The Bechers' coolly rational work, which included an important series of depictions of pitheads from Britain, France, and Belgium, as well as the Ruhr, focused on typological similarities (Figure 5.4). For the Bechers, industrial architecture was in most cases vernacular design, which acquired artistic status largely through their carefully positioned lenses. The onset

Figure 5.4.   Bernd and Hilla Becher, *Pitheads*, 1974. Collection of Tate Gallery London. Courtesy of Sonnabend Gallery, New York. Copyright Estate Bernd and Hilla Becher/Tate London, 2016.

of what would become their life's work coincided with the codification in the Federal Republic of the association of an industrial aesthetic with liberal democracy.[35] Their eventual enormous success was one of the factors that encouraged local pride in what had until recently been viewed as a blight on the once picturesque landscape.

By the 1970s the precipitous decline of the Ruhr region's coal and steel industries was beginning to awaken admiration bordering on nostalgia for an environment that had earlier been more often denounced for the extraordinary degree to which it had been shaped solely by capital. The Bechers began to attract international attention during this decade, which was when they photographed both Zeche Zollverein and the site of the future Landscape Park. Bernd became professor of photography at the Art Academy in 1976; his tenure on the faculty overlapped with that of Josef Beuys. The Bechers' impact on photography was immense; many of the best-known German photographers active today, including Andreas Gursky, Candida Höfer, Thomas Ruff, and Thomas Struth, were their students.[36]

Equally crucial was the presence nearby of Max Imdahl.[37] Appointed the founding professor of art history at the Ruhr University in Bochum in 1965 at the age of forty, Imdahl pioneered the teaching of contemporary art in Germany. He was an early supporter of Serra. *Terminal*, installed outside the main Bochum train station in 1979, was one of Serra's first major public works; two years earlier a Serra piece had been installed in a Bochum gallery.[38] Although Serra, who himself worked in steel mills early in his career, is best known for the sculptures he created out of enormous and extremely heavy pieces of steel, much of his oeuvre is site specific. In this he was inspired in part by Robert Smithson, whom he had helped stake out *Spiral

Jetty, the iconic example of earth art constructed in the Great Salt Lake in 1970.[39] The interlinked legacy of Smithson and Serra as fostered by Imdahl, who died in 1988, would prove crucial to the creation of the Landscape Park in particular and to industrial culture in the Ruhr more generally. Serra contributed *Bramme für das Ruhrgebiets* to the IBA in 1998. A slab of steel, it sits atop the Schurenbachhalde slag heap in Essen.[40]

The Latzes' approach to the Landscape Park was clearly inspired in part by their admiration for Smithson. The American sculptor was raised amidst the industrial relics of Paterson, New Jersey, already memorialized by the poet William Carlos Williams, who was Smithson's pediatrician, before they became the subject of Smithson's own writings.[41] Moreover, the juxtaposition of minimalist artworks with ruined architecture, in this case a nineteenth-century train station, mounted in Berlin's Hamburger Bahnhof in 1989, gave further impetus to the Latzes' reinterpretation of the ruined blast furnace as modern art. Nowhere is this clearer than in the Piazza Metallica, an homage to the sculpture of artists like Carl Andre. Here in their words, "Iron plates that were once used to cover casting molds in the pig iron casting works form today the heart of the park."[42] In the Landscape Park the Latzes created a substitute for the city centers so far removed from industrial installations such as the blast furnace. The Piazza Metallica now serves as a site for temporary events that bring together larger publics than ever clustered in local village squares or marketplaces, blending inhabitants and visitors into a temporary community. Although this urbanity is short-lived, the piazza is nonetheless a compellingly bounded place at odds with the open-ended character of not only much of the rest of the park but also Duisburg's ill-defined cityscape.

Most successful were the raised walkways that facilitated the transformation of a working landscape into spaces for leisure, whether contemplation or play. Barriers such as train tracks were largely eliminated, although traces of their presence were preserved. These are best viewed from the walkway that now lines the edge of the rainwater canal. Such walkways have become one of the signature elements of the region's new parks, as well as of new landscape interventions elsewhere, such as New York's High Line, the first stretch of which opened in 2009.[43] The Zeche Zollverein in Essen, Nordsternpark in Gelsenkirchen, and Westpark in Bochum all feature them. Inspired by the ones Bernard Tschumi designed in 1982 for the Parc de la Villette in Paris, they provide the overview necessary to get a sense of a place whose organization was originally governed by technological efficiency rather than aesthetics, and which can thus be confusing (Figure 5.5). While Tschumi inscribed his paean to constructivism on a relatively blank field, the Latzes transposed this strategy of traces and raised walkways to an environment whose physical history they largely preserved. The aerial walkways also provide convenient pathways that offer the pretense of perching atop a largely untouched meadow and alleviate the flatness of the original landscape in which most projections are the residue of industrial activity.

Figure 5.5. Bernard Tschumi, Parc de la Villette, Paris, 1982. Source: Pline/Wikipedia Commons.

Above all, they imbue visitors with a sense of empowerment and control similar to that Foster accorded visitors to the Reichstag dome. This is a particularly significant inversion in sites that were long closed to all but their workforces, many of whom lacked access to and understanding of the complete installation.

Even more overtly popular was the lighting installation created in 1996 by Jonathan Park, best known for his lighting designs for performances by Pink Floyd and Roger Waters. Its bright green, blue, and red lighting of the blast furnaces is visible at night from a pair of adjacent highways as well as from within the park. Its spectacular character, rather removed from the quieter poetry espoused by the Latzes, makes this one of the iconic Ruhr region sights, included in almost all tourist guides and souvenir books about the region.

By insisting on an aesthetic approach to the ruined relics studded through the Landscape Park, the Latzes eschewed the insertion of didactic information that might have hindered its conversion. They chose largely to ignore the technological, social, and even the political context in which the rusting infrastructure was originally created and used. Focusing on the park's changing physical landscape helped to obscure less comfortable truths about its history. Memory is more often individual than collective and is far less durable than the steel that was once Duisburg's main contribution to the world economy. The memories evoked for visitors who come to the Landscape Park already schooled in the aesthetics of Smithson and Serra will inevitably be different from those of the descendants of people who worked here before, during, or immediately after World War II, which will differ in turn from those of the many guest workers who came to Meiderich from Southern Europe beginning in the mid-60s, and their families. Members of the first group are more apt to be conditioned not only by their education in the history of art, architecture, and the landscape but also by what locals have written about these places in order to attract precisely such visitors. The second and third groups instead draw to a greater degree upon either personal experience or oral history. No experience is more authentic than another, but those of the workers, their descendants, and their neighbors are less likely to be filtered by IBA publicity. Privilege, although more likely to facilitate the intellectual gymnastics that convert scrap metal into art, is not necessarily the bearer of truth.

The IBA's celebration of the Ruhr region's history of technological prowess was inevitably undercut by its simultaneous attentiveness to repairing the economy of the region. The issue of memory in post-1989 Germany has focused on the obvious horrors of the Third Reich, but the originality and the richness of the solutions pioneered in the Landscape Park were spurred by the complexity of a past in which the years 1933 to 1945 comprised only a single chapter, one moreover that was studiously overlooked in accounts of the park. The centrality of the region's heavy industry to Hitler's war machine was ignored in glowing reviews in which technological modernity was inevitably equated with artistic modernism and social progress. No visitor to the Landschaftspark would learn anything about this period in the site's history from a casual visit to the park or, for that matter, about the technology of the original infrastructure or its social and environmental costs. The memories promoted here are specific and selective.

Zeche Zollverein

Such lacunae are more glaring in the case of the Zeche Zollverein, located about ten miles to the east in Essen. The elevation of the pithead (that is, the top of a mine shaft, through which the products exacted below the earth are brought to the surface) of a defunct coal mine into the Ruhr region's other leading symbol of industrial culture exposes the inherent tensions between this idealization of form and the realities of its original use. The Zeche Zollverein, and especially Pithead XII—designed and built during the Weimar Republic, but embraced after 1933 as a model for both the artistry and the overt modernity of National Socialist industrial architecture—became the centerpiece of the region's ongoing effort to reinterpret its industrial heritage as politically and socially progressive art. The way in which this happened tells us a great deal about who manufactured memory, and why, in Germany during the 1990s and the opening years of the new millennium.

Official memory in Essen always had clear limits.[44] The particular form it took was often specific to the region, where opinion makers preferred to remember the oppositional (but not necessarily the Communist) politics of its workers rather than the tacit support that many industrialists had offered the Third Reich. Reinterpreted as testimony of cultural as well as technological innovation and reinvented as high art, the Zeche Zollverein pithead tower was a prominent component of first the IBA and then of Essen's successful entry for the honor of being designated as one of the cultural capitals of Europe.[45] New insertions have been key to this effort. Two prominent museums whose interiors are the work of internationally famous foreign architects—the Red Dot Museum (Norman Foster and Associates, 1992–97) and the Ruhr Museum (Rem Koolhaas's Office of Metropolitan Architecture, 2010)—have opened within it; a building by the Japanese firm SANAA, completed in 2006 to house a now-defunct school of management and design, sits on its edge.

For many years the ubiquitous publicity surrounding Pithead XII seldom failed to tie the elegant industrial installation, designed by the local firm of Fritz Schupp and Martin Kremmer, to the most enduring architectural symbol of progressive Weimar ideals, the Dessau Bauhaus, designed by Walter Gropius and completed in 1926.[46] An early draft of the UNESCO nomination equated "the strongly Cubist form of the individual buildings" with the "architectural ideals of the Bauhaus."[47] Misattributing Louis Sullivan's dictum "Form follows function" to the Bauhaus, the author of the UNESCO nomination, Udo Mainzer, the chief of conservation for the Rhineland, went on to imply that the dedication of Pithead XII, "the most modern and beautiful mine in the world" in the year "that the closing of the Bauhaus began," represented the continuation of the controversial school's precepts in the face of Nazi persecution.[48] After admitting that the mechanization and rationalization of Pithead XII contributed to the unemployment that helped bring the Nazis to power, the report proceeded to use architectural form to absolve the building itself of complicity:

> [Pithead XII] was much more intent on simultaneously accomplishing the humanization of the work world. Unquestionably the also somewhat revolutionary shift from feudal community to a socially reformed society, whose fulfillment depended a bit too much, however, on the different concerns of capital, is revealed in the design and hierarchical order of Zollverein XII's massing. The completion of the mine installation coincides by the way with the end of the German reparation payments to the Allies.[49]

This interpretation discounted miners, who remembered Pithead XII as ruthlessly rational.[50] Their accounts of visits by high-level Nazi officials were also purged from a history that equated architectural modernism with liberal democracy as well as economic development.[51]

The Zeche Zollverein is an emphatically modern building, but it was the product of a different aesthetic and political position from the Bauhaus and the New Building, which were almost certainly anathema to both its architects and their nominal client, the man for whom it was named, Albert Vögler, the head of United Steelworks (Vereinigte Stahlwerke AG).[52] This was at the time Europe's largest steel company. The strong sense of order and stability displayed in the choice of a brick infill, the steel grid that framed it, and the imposition of axial symmetry as much as possible upon the disposition of functional groups of buildings is at complete odds with cubism's rejection of Euclidean geometry as embodied in the Bauhaus's pinwheel plan. These features also clash with Gropius's choice of cantilevered stucco and glass planes that appeared to float as if suspended above the ground. Moreover, Pithead XII was an important template for Nazi industrial architecture, which was as much a showpiece for the regime as the more often cited neoclassical ensembles built or projected for Munich, Nuremberg, and Berlin.

Two generations of historians have reiterated that neither German nationalism in general nor National Socialism in particular were antimodern.[53] This enormous and sophisticated corpus of scholarship, much of it specifically grounded in architectural examples, has had little impact, however, upon the way in which many Germans continue to portray modern architecture as inherently antifascist. The conviction that the cultural values of urban planning, architecture, and design offer concrete solutions to political and economic problems was common across the political spectrum throughout the twentieth century in Germany.[54] The overwhelming identification since the war with institutionalized modernism has sheltered an elite, defined in a society in which the division between the intelligentsia and their counterparts in business and politics is often remarkably small, by taste as well as economic status, from admitting either the degree to which modernism's supposedly oppositional cultural positions have served to legitimize the political and economic status quo.

The case of the Zeche Zollverein is particularly interesting because there is no reason whatsoever to believe that those who reinvented Pithead XII's past to serve their own present had any sympathy whatsoever for the conservative nationalist politics it originally represented. On the contrary, their ability to ensure its preservation depended in large part upon their strong ties to city and state governments led by Social Democrats.[55] Despite these left-of-center political affiliations, their efforts implied that artistic form trumps political action as an expression of political dissent. This demeaned in particular the local working class, who throughout the twentieth century voted in large numbers for Roman Catholic, socialist, and Communist parties without ever expressing much enthusiasm for modern architecture and design.[56] This although the new histories created by the IBA and codified in 2010 in the inaugural exhibitions in the Ruhr Museum consistently focused on working-class experiences, which, however, they often sentimentalized.[57] The distortion of history in the memories manufactured for Pithead XII calls into question the degree to which other prominent examples of German "remembering" are shared by the society as a whole.

The Zeche Zollverein mine was established in what is now the northern Essen neighborhood of Katernberg in 1847. It was named after the customs union that at the close of the twentieth century was described by those who advocated the mine's preservation as a crucial first step toward German democracy. These preservationists also noted that the Zollverein was a crucial precedent for the establishment of the European Union, which helped finance the mine's restoration.[58] In 1928, two years after United Steelworks took over the mine, the local director, Friedrich Wilhelm Schulze Buxloh, commissioned Pithead XII. It opened four years later, replacing two earlier shafts.[59] The new pithead buildings were universally recognized to be the acme of industrial efficiency. Not only was the complex technologically up to date, it was also self-consciously beautiful.

Since the first decade of the twentieth century, German industry had turned to artist-architects to give their factories, the products produced in them, and the advertising for those products a gloss of culture. The intent was to make them more marketable, as well as redeem modern industrial society by ensuring the preservation of strictly cultural values. The first phase of this effort climaxed in Peter Behrens's work for the AEG and the founding in 1907 of the Deutsche Werkbund.[60]

The experiences of World War I, in which many of them fought, temporarily soured the excitement that young German architects, such as Walter Gropius, Bruno Taut, and Erich Mendelsohn, had about an architecture of demonstrable economic and industrial utility.[61] When their enthusiasm returned with the temporary stabilization of the German economy at the end of 1923, they were among those who romanticized mass production as a path to greater social equality, adopting industrial forms to critique not only nineteenth-century historicism but also the penchant for monumentality still on view in Paul Bonatz's Main Train Station in Stuttgart. Those who condemned this rejection of vernacular precedent as unpatriotic, even Bolshevist, resisted their efforts.[62] A middle group, to which Schupp and Kremmer belonged, were content to use new materials in the creation of buildings, often on what was for Germany unprecedented scale, closely associated with modernity. Others in the Ruhr region who adhered to this position included Emil Fahrenkamp, Jakob Koerfer, Edmund Körner, and Wilhelm Kreis. Although this group increasingly eschewed ornament, they continued to favor materials and compositions that created a reassuring aura of stability and permanence at a time of enormous social, economic, and political uncertainty.

Despite the frequent assertions made in the Ruhr region in the late 1990s and early twenty-first century that Schupp and Kremmer had been at the Bauhaus, they had actually studied in Stuttgart with Bonatz and Paul Schmitthenner.[63] Schmitthenner's deep respect for architectural tradition put him at complete odds with Gropius, who was appalled by his failure to acknowledge industrial technology, and campaigned successfully to prevent him being reappointed to his professorship after the war.[64] Schupp would ndoubtedly have been stunned if, as he was in the process of supervising Pithead XII's construction, he had heard it equated with the Bauhaus. In a 1930 interview he mockingly dismissed many of the architectural features associated with the school—including flat roofs, corner windows, and steel furniture—as "literary" and "romantic." Describing an encounter with a society lady who hoped to have met in him finally an architect who, presumably like Buckminster Fuller, could hang a rotating house from a mast, he noted, "So Eve tempted the poor architects with the apple, and thus also are designed the projects that smell of printing ink."[65] Instead of following what he dismissed in highly gendered terms as a fashion for novelty, he preferred to strike a balance between old and new, envisioning a modern church in which one could place a Renaissance altar by Tilman Riemenschneider, or a living room filled with Persian rugs and Gobelin tapestries. "We must try to win an absolute standard that finds the good in the old as well as in the new and rejects the rest."[66] Schupp, unlike most Bauhäusler, clearly associated good taste not only with respect for the past but also with luxury. Art, he implied, should be reserved for those who could afford it, rather than distributed to the masses, as many at the Bauhaus hoped, through industrially produced consumer goods.

Although they had nothing whatsoever to do with the Bauhaus, Schupp and Kremmer did number among Germany's leading interwar industrial architects. In contrast, Gropius received no new factory commissions after the middle of the 1920s, when he began to focus instead on the efficient production of mass housing. Schupp continued to be an important industrial architect after his partner's death in Berlin in 1945 at the hands of the Soviet invaders. Both Schupp and Kremmer were deeply indebted to the Werkbund's goals of integrating industry and culture. Although in the 1920s many of the group's members embraced the New Building, the Werkbund's original dedication to the ennoblement of industrial and graphic design, as well as of the architecture of both production and consumption, retained its appeal to cultured Germans who did not.

Vögler, for whom Pithead XII was originally named, was typical of the emphatically modern Germans who espoused this position without allying themselves with political liberalism or avant-garde design. As the leader of the United Steelworks, founded in 1926, he was one of Germany's leading businessmen. Although he never joined the Nazi party, his politics were consistently antidemocratic. After the November Revolution, he helped found the conservative German People's Party (Deutsche Volkspartei), led by Gustav Stresemann, before in 1924 moving to the short-lived National Liberal Union (Nationalliberale Vereinigung), a splinter party that opposed Stresemann's accommodation of parliamentary democracy. When it collapsed, he shifted his support to the German National People's Party (Deutschnationale Volkspartei). Vögler's decision in 1931 to close entire factories, leaving 6,900 workers jobless, contributed greatly to the political instability of the Weimar Republic's final years. Although his influence waned during the Third Reich, he committed suicide upon its defeat.[67]

Vögler's intellectual outlook was similarly conservative. He was friendly with Oswald Spengler and, during World War II, worked closely with Albert Speer. He was also a leading supporter of new psychologically based management techniques intended to ease the antagonism that politically engaged workers felt for their employers.[68] Above all, Vögler, whose name was originally emblazoned on Pithead XII in a Gothic script that represented the political as well as artistic antithesis of the sans serif associated with the Bauhaus, was committed to the rational organization of German industry. He envisioned a situation in which competition, whether between capitalists or between workers and management, would no longer impinge upon economic efficiency.[69]

The ubiquitous equation of modernity with a specific strand of architectural modernism epitomized by the Bauhaus and the New Building has hindered an understanding of the way in which interwar Germany's most technologically advanced industrial installations could be designed in a style that was at once entirely new and yet divergent from the representation of mass production. Modernity generated multiple modernisms, among them the fusion of high-tech with evocations of order and stability displayed in Pithead XII. The inhabitants of the Ruhr region may have welcomed this transposition of the wood-framed, brick infill vernacular agricultural buildings of the neighboring Münsterland into modern materials.

The Zeche Zollverein Pithead XII was not an example of Bauhaus architecture. Nor was it a Nazi building or for that matter, not least because of the small size of its workforce, an important site of slave labor during World War II.[70] In a telling example of the slipperiness of applying either stylistic or political labels to architecture, however, before being upheld as an example of Bauhaus modernism and thus of progressive rather than nationalist politics, Pithead XII was repeatedly published as a paradigmatic example of the architecture of the Third Reich. This confusion dates to 1938 when Gerdy Troost, the widow of Hitler's favorite architect, included it in her definitive survey of architecture in the Third Reich.[71] Pithead XII looked to both party loyalists, and to the later architectural historians who repeated the mistake, as if it had been built as part of Hitler's massive rearmament effort. Troost's assumption that it was built after 1933 also demonstrates the degree of enthusiasm the Nazis had for industrial aesthetics in what was understood to be their proper setting—actual factory architecture. Also crucial was that because of their solidity and symmetry, most Nazi factories, like Pithead XII, bore little resemblance to the New Building the Nazis and other conservative cultural critics had long termed "Bolshevist."[72]

The misinterpretation of Pithead XII as a Nazi-era building demonstrates the degree to which the study of twentieth-century architecture is dependent upon the examination of the published rather than the built record. It is unlikely that Troost or the postwar architectural historians who followed her example had seen Pithead XII for themselves, as all reproduce the same photograph of the powerhouse, which they describe as "a factory in Westphalia."[73] Troost used Pithead XII to illustrate her description of factories built since 1933 as "buildings of weight and order, effective through economic and clear lines, symbols of the precise clean work that is performed in them."[74] Ironically this mystification would fuse with confusion about the myth that the building had a Bauhaus lineage. After its closure, while the preservation of Pithead XII was well under way, but before the related publicity campaign had kicked into high gear, Werner Durth and Winfried Nerdinger, two of Germany's most respected historians of modern architecture, in groundbreaking accounts of the degree to which the architectural profession had collaborated with the Nazis republished Pithead XII as evidence of the degree to which "Bauhaus" aesthetics remained permissible after 1933.[75]

Yet workers' accounts stressed the connection between industrial efficiency and nationalist politics. The days after Pithead XII opened, an article in a local newspaper decried that it would leave 1,200 workers and employees to starve before noting the degree to which heavy industry was working with Hitler.[76] The dismissals pushed the total number of people in Essen looking for work to 78,951.[77] In 1992, Albert Bock, who worked at Pithead XII from the beginning, recalled the visits of Hermann Goering and other Nazi dignitaries, as well as the installation's importance to Hitler's rearmament policies.[78]

Although the pithead was not a Nazi building, the establishment of Hitler's dictatorship did nothing to alter the tone in which it was discussed. It continued throughout the thirties to be published as a model industrial installation in journals devoted to architecture and to industrial engineering.[79] It probably served as a prototype for the Beauty of Labor Bureau established in November 1933, as part of the Strength through Joy office of the German Labor Front.[80] Like Pithead XII, the campaign was inspired, as Speer himself admitted, by Werkbund-sanctioned precedents.[81]

It was left to Walter Buschmann, the author in 1987 of an early scholarly account of the Zeche Zollverein, to place Pithead XII in its proper place. Buschmann was an expert on the history of German industrial architecture. Seeking, as historians of peripheral subjects typically do, to defend the importance of his subject, he tied it to the mainstream of the modern movement in two ways. First, he described it as a descendant of Gropius's relatively conservative Wilhelmine writings about industrial architecture. Second, he pointed to the similarity between the framing system Schupp and Kremmer used at Pithead XII and that employed less than a decade later by Ludwig Mies van der Rohe for his buildings on the campus of the Illinois

Figure 5.6. Ludwig Mies van der Rohe, Perlstein Hall, Illinois Institute of Technology, Chicago, 1947. Source: Joe Ravi/Wikipedia Commons.

Institute of Technology in Chicago (Figure 5.6).[82] Both were legitimate claims; by suggesting Mies's awareness of mainstream German architectural practice during the 1930s, Buschmann placed himself in the forefront of establishing the architect's ties to the middle ground of the modern movement.[83]

The IBA organizers were well aware of the Zeche Zollverein's problematic political history.[84] At the same time that they began to describe Pithead XII as a Bauhaus building, their own enthusiasm for it stemmed largely from its deviance from canonical modernism. It was precisely this deviance that made it appear so interesting at a time when orthodox modernism was obviously outmoded. Just as Schupp and Kremmer established a middle ground between the New Building and the Third Reich's bombastic neoclassicism, so the rehabilitated Zeche Zollverein bridged the postmodernism of Aldo Rossi and O. M. Ungers, and the high tech of Jean Nouvel and Norman Foster, which by the turn of the millennium placed industrial imagery and symbolism once more at the forefront of international architectural culture. At the same time, the collapse of communism made the Marxist equation of capitalism and fascism, a chestnut of leftist history and cultural commentary since the Weimar Republic, far less tenable than it had been.

It proved easier to invent memories than to ensure that they were widely accepted. Finding appropriate uses for Pithead XII worthy of the grandiose claims now being made on behalf of a previously unappreciated landmark challenged both the organizers of the IBA and the supporters of bringing the Cultural Capital of Europe to the region. From the beginning the emphasis IBA planners placed on

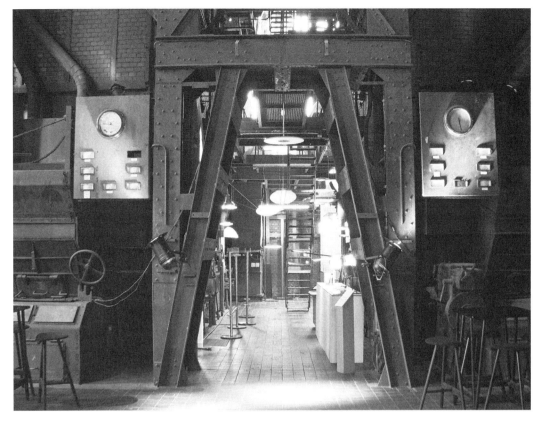

Figure 5.7. Norman Foster, Red Dot Design Museum, Essen, 1997. Source: Holger Ellgaard/ Wikipedia Commons.

its outstanding design encouraged consideration of art-related uses, but its location made it difficult to attract tenants of suitable standing. The region's most prestigious museum, the Folkwang, had little interest in moving from its site in prosperous south Essen, only minutes by foot from downtown, the main train station, and the opera house, to a remote and somewhat dingy neighborhood. Instead, in 2010 it acquired a new building by David Chipperfield.[85] Because design so effectively symbolized the transition the region had to make to a service economy, a series of design-related institutions were eventually, however, installed at Pithead XII.

Once again art offered state-sanctioned means of sanctifying capital. Although Ganser ensured that the actual physical restoration gave jobs and training to people who had long been unemployed, the local working class, many of Turkish origin, comprised only a marginal component of the audience for the direction taken by the IBA.[86] As attention gradually shifted from production to the service economy, from attracting high-tech industry to creating cultural programming, the IBA's efforts were increasingly targeted at those with larger disposable incomes and more obviously marketable talents.

Manufacturing Memory in the Ruhr Region

Figure 5.8. SANAA, School of Management and Design, Essen, 2006. Source: Myriam Thyes/ Wikipedia Commons.

The lingering impact of Werkbund-forged attitudes helped identify new uses. The Red Dot Design Museum upholds the Werkbund's original ideals of making German industry more competitive internationally by fostering good design. The design center for the state of North Rhine-Westphalia opened in the former powerhouse, shorn of its smokestack, in 1996.[87] Peter Zec, its first director, lamented the constrictions the building's status as a cultural monument placed on the use of the space, but the Foster-designed galleries continue the conflation of modernity and modernism inaugurated by Behrens in his work for the AEG (Figure 5.7). The carefully preserved traces of heavy industry, now clearly no longer in use, provide a powerful setting in which to display the abstract forms characteristic of contemporary design, many of them infused with an industrial aesthetic. The original installation continued to trumpet familiar clichés about modern design.[88] One exhibit began by contrasting giant photographs of Gropius's office at the Weimar Bauhaus with Mussolini's pompously traditional headquarters in Rome.[89]

A new EU-subsidized but private school of management and design moved in 2006 to premises designed by the internationally celebrated Japanese partners Kazuyo Sejima and Ryue Nishizawa of SANAA (Figure 5.8). The school's novel fusion of master's of fine arts and master's of business administration degrees also

Figure 5.9. Office of Metropolitan Architecture, interior, Ruhr Museum, Essen, 2010. Source: Rainer Hallama/Wikipedia Commons.

testified to continued faith in the Werkbund's original ideals, although its failure to thrive (it closed almost immediately; the building now houses the Folkwang University of the Arts) indicates the limits of this approach.[90]

More successful, and more closely aligned with the architecture of memory, was the adaptation of Pithead XII's coal-washing plant to serve as the Ruhr Museum (Figure 5.9). Unusually, instead of the local history museums common in most German cities, the region has long had a single institution, which was previously housed alongside the Folkwang Museum. In 2002, Rem Koolhaas and his Office of Metropolitan Architecture presented a master plan for the Zeche Zollverein site. The SANAA building was one result; the new Ruhr Museum, whose interior the Koolhaas office designed, a second.

Like the Red Dot Design Museum, the Ruhr Museum is as much an example of adaptive reuse as of neomodernism.[91] Nonetheless, throughout these structures the detritus of industrial processes is both harnessed as modernist ornament and juxtaposed with gleaming installations that employ a patently contemporary high-tech aesthetic. In the Ruhr Museum the public history of the immediate past developed in relation to the IBA has been enshrined in galleries that celebrate many aspects of the lives of workers, without including details about their political activities or the experiences that inspired such radicalism. The horrors of the Third Reich are not ignored. The museum is one of several in the region that have sponsored exhibitions devoted to the theme of slave labor during the Second World War. The relationship between the region's present "light houses" of industrial culture and nationalist politics of any stripe is seldom spelled out, however. Although the museum attracted relatively little attention in the architectural press, visitor numbers appear to be much greater than for many other industrial heritage–themed attractions in the region; since its opening the Zeche Zollverein site has finally buzzed with activity that had long been promised by those promoting its preservation. Nonetheless, Pithead XII is not yet as celebrated an attraction as the Tate Modern, a former London power plant converted into a modern art museum by the Swiss firm of Herzog and de Meuron. Their adaptive reuse of the Küppersmühle into a museum of modern art, also an IBA project, opened in Duisburg's Inner Harbor in 1999.[92]

Fame is not likely to promote a more complete understanding of the site's history. Interpreting Pithead XII as an example of Bauhaus architecture helped sanitize the crucial contribution that heavy industry and its architects made to the nationalism of both the Second and the Third Reichs. Attaching demonstrably untruthful narratives about the past to particular physical sites in order to enhance the position of ruling elites is neither new, however, nor, as David Lowenthal has demonstrated, uniquely German.[93] Equally importantly, offering design as a substitute for economic planning diverted resources from unemployed workers, already denigrated for their unwillingness to patronize the inevitably more expensive modernist objects that mistakenly symbolize opposition to fascism, to the offices of international architectural stars. It also enhanced the status of those locals for whom the project bought access to such celebrities. Although launched by socialist governments, the IBA is the most recent chapter in a century-long effort on the part of German intellectuals to put art at the service of economics in part to ensure their own continued relevance. The purported connection between the Zeche Zollverein and the Bauhaus enhanced the reputation not only of architects like Egon Eiermann who used their loyalty to modernism to rehabilitate themselves in the Federal Republic but also many of those who long afterward continue to base their claim to cultural authority upon "enlightened" taste.

The Ruhr's new cultural infrastructure has not generated the hoped-for economic rebirth. The region's population continues to decline and unemployment stubbornly remains the highest in western Germany.[94] The IBA attracted enormous international publicity, almost all of it immensely favorable, but closer to home attitudes were more mixed, and Essen's reign as a capital of culture was overshadowed internationally by sharing the title with Istanbul, and also with the Hungarian city of Pécs. The lack of local enthusiasm for the IBA, in contrast to the excitement that surrounded the closing of the region's chief highway for a picnic in the summer of 2010, was almost certainly because local perceptions of these sites as tainted by nationalist politics and industrial pollution were more resistant to the marketing campaigns that aim to increase local pride in the region and enhance its economic competitiveness than were travel writers and design aficionados based outside the region.[95] The relatively peripheral locations of many sites also hinder mass tourism. By the reckoning of its own administrators, the Landscape Park is a seven-minute walk from two different streetcar lines, themselves both remote from main train lines.[96] During the week, even in the summer, the park often feels abandoned unless something particular, like a rock concert, is on the schedule (in any case, the acoustics are problematic). Special events and facilities, however, combine to raise attendance to impressive levels. According to the park's own website, by 2003 the park was the most visited natural or cultural landscape in the state of North Rhine-Westphalia, but the city's, and indeed the region's promoters, are adept at manipulating such figures.[97]

By the last years of the new century's first decade a backlash against industrial culture as the principal strategy of regional economic development had begun to set in.[98] The question of how to retain the region's newer base of light industry had become far more urgent than the preservation of sites that had long lacked substantial workforces.[99] Avant-garde installations played a smaller role in Essen's year as a European capital of culture than the region's working-class heritage.

The comprehensive conversion of the means of production into avant-garde art faltered for several reasons.[100] Many natives of the region remained resistant to modernism. They refused to acknowledge the aesthetic qualities the Bechers and the Latzes recognized in the region's industrial infrastructure.[101] Only in the 1950s and 1960s had the local working class, encouraged by the leadership of the Social Democratic Party, briefly flirted with modern architecture, and by the eighties few were keen to repeat the experiment. There was little affection for the high-rise housing towers, banal office blocks, and concrete campuses of the postwar decades, none of which sported the handsome detailing of corporate skyscrapers in neighboring Düsseldorf. Moreover, nowhere in Germany was it more difficult to sustain the myth that tied modernism to antifascism. Almost everyone remembered that most local industrialists had opposed the establishment of the Weimar Republic and that many had tacitly supported the National Socialists. They also knew the contributions these factories had made to two war efforts. Nor did the return of prosperity in the fifties completely erase memories of the slave labor upon which many local firms had relied during the war. Finally the cleansing of the region's air was achieved only when the region's industrial base had largely collapsed; it will take much longer to redress other aspects of environmental degradation. Marc Treib, a landscape historian, notes the difficulty of incorporating these memories into the artistry of such parks:

> But unless we happen to have been the original inhabitants, I believe that we will always require some layer of explanation to make any historical structure or landscape truly relevant. And that layer becomes all the more necessary as the buildings drift further into the past. . . . The raw beauty of steel-making structures takes on a rather different aspect when we learn of lives lost and bodies maimed, and the mountains of pollutants it has injected into the soil and the atmosphere. These are the heavy aspects of history not readily evident in the structures themselves.[102]

Industrial culture nonetheless fulfilled important purposes. The ecological situation of the new parks and their immediate environs certainly improved enormously. In a period when sustainability and other environmental issues played a major part in German politics, this was enormously appreciated. These green lungs began to mitigate the enormous environmental damage wrought by the region's brief experience of prosperity while serving the still densely settled area's remaining inhabitants.[103] Furthermore, by refusing to erase the physical traces of the site's industrial past, the IBA organizers preserved the possibility of multiple types of memory. If some visitors find in the Piazza Metallica and Sinter Park echoes of Smithson and Serra, others, and not only those from the surrounding region, are free to be reminded of other details in the region's history, which may in turn be highlighted by later installations and/or refurbishments.

The IBA Emscher Park used a lingering attachment to technology to diminish the environmental and social damage wrought by industrial processes, while preserving the traces of those processes, which its organizers perceived as beautiful. This was distinct from harnessing the palimpsest to uncover previously ignored layers of potentially deeply disturbing meaning, as happened in Berlin at the Jewish Museum and the Topography of Terror. The use of fragments by modernists did not necessarily entail remembering the darkest chapters in German history. In the Ruhr region, however, the precedents set by expressionism and the New Building, which had achieved only a tenuous foothold, were less important than those established after the war. These included the churches throughout the region that paired ruined steeples with new construction, the installations photographed by the Bechers and the many local Serras. More than two decades of publicity have certainly deepened commitment to the new view of the region's recent history, especially as the numbers of those whose personal memories are at odds with it gradually diminish. Nonetheless, the manufacture of purportedly collective memories calls into question the degree to which ordinary Germans share the perspective on the past supposedly embedded in other memorial landscapes, especially the key examples of the architecture of memory created in Berlin since the fall of the Wall. Generations of use are likely here, too, to enhance the effectiveness with which these intentions are communicated, but the creation of a particular place intended to convey a set message on behalf of a region or a nation by no means ensures universal acceptance of even relatively uncontroversial points of view.

Six

Assimilating Modern Memory

On 4 March 2006 protestors took to the streets of the Cologne district of Ehrenfeld. Declaring "eliminate multiculturalism, stop the construction of the mosque," they objected to the construction by a Turkish religious organization of a monumental mosque in a city whose most famous building is its Gothic cathedral, finally completed in 1880 (Figure 6.1).[1] Although only about sixty people actually marched and many locals, including most left-of-center politicians, were warmly supportive, the combination of the protests and of inflammatory remarks by Ralph Giordano, a German Jewish intellectual who lived in Cologne, more than a year later eventually unleashed a media storm, during which polls showed a third of Cologne inhabitants supportive of the building and an equal number opposed, with a further 20 percent desiring a smaller mosque.[2] National and international coverage focused on the contentious position of immigrants within German culture and on a dispute that had parallels with arguments about the place of Islam in American as well as European suburbs and cityscapes.[3] Two years before their Swiss neighbors voted in 2009 to ban the construction of minarets and nearly a decade before hundreds of thousands of Syrian refugees and other migrants entered the country in the span of a few months, German opinion among the chattering classes was divided between supporters of multiculturalism, who believed that the country should celebrate difference, and those who preferred that immigrants should integrate by becoming as much like ethnic Germans as possible.[4] The debate highlighted that many Germans regarded themselves as living in a secular society; there were few traces left of the specifically Christian piety that had been so central to German architectural culture a half century earlier.[5]

Indeed, little attention was paid to the details of the proposed building's appearance, except to note that its architects had also designed Catholic churches, and to complain that its two minarets threatened the prominence of the cathedral's steeples, which—until the completion of the Eiffel Tower in 1889—had briefly been

Figure 6.1. Gottfried and Paul Böhm, DITIB Mosque, Cologne, photographed in 2015. Source: Raimond Spekking/Wikipedia Commons.

the world's tallest structures. Left unsaid as well was that the design of Diyanet İşleri Türk İslam Birliği (DITIB, the Turkish-Islamic Union of the Institution for Religion) Central Mosque, the first prominent mosque to be located so close to the center of a major German city, acknowledged that Muslims could be modern. More obviously historicist mosques, such as the Merkez Mosque completed in nearby Duisburg in 2008, generated far less controversy.[6] Although it was often faulted for its "Ottoman" design, and was shown as such on the placards carried by protesters, in fact the erosion of the central volume of the entirely abstract Cologne design established a delicate balance between modernist transparency and the evocation of a ruined imperial Ottoman mosque that was very much in keeping with the way in which German architects had for six decades been pairing or juxtaposing actual or implied incomplete, fragmented, or ruined historic form with the memory of a specifically expressionist modernism.[7]

This fluidity of reference in the design of the DITIB Mosque was hardly surprising considering that the architects were Gottfried Böhm and his son Paul, members of a dynasty known for nearly a century for their innovative Catholic churches, many of which, such as St. Anna, also in the Ehrenfeld district of Cologne, juxtaposed actual ruins with a glass architecture inspired by Bruno Taut's Glashaus (this church was designed by Gottfried in collaboration with his father, Dominikus, and completed in 1956).[8] Few were better positioned to integrate the DITIB Mosque into what was by this point a tradition used for a wide variety of mostly civic buildings but whose origins lay in the postwar design of sacred structures. By the first decade of the new millennium these architectural strategies had come to define the Federal Republic and were widely accepted by German citizens and by most international observers as offering trenchant evidence of the way in which Germans confronted their complex past.

Sharing this strategy with those not of ethnic German origin proved vexed, however, although this was never explicitly articulated in discussions of the proposed mosque for Cologne. The modern architecture pioneered at the Werkbund Exhibition in Cologne in 1914 that has constituted a key part of the Federal Republic's self-image since its founding in 1949 has remained current for an entire century largely because of support from outside Europe and for that matter the English-speaking world. Many Turks espoused modern architecture, and indeed for much of the twentieth century its abstract forms were more popular in cities like Istanbul and Ankara than they were with many Germans. Taut was among the German architects who found sanctuary there from the Third Reich. This story is better known in the English-speaking world than in Germany.[9] More recently Rudolf Stingel's installation staged in the upper floor of Berlin's New National Gallery in the spring of 2010 inadvertently spanned the distance that the country's cultural elites often continue to insist exists between German and "Oriental" material culture, which is not dissimilar from that between elite and working-class culture highlighted in the early installations at the Red Dot Design Museum in the Zeche Zollverein. And yet at precisely the same time that the inhabitants of Cologne were debating the appropriateness of the DITIB Mosque, two of Germany's leading automobile manufacturers, Volkswagen and BMW, turned to Zaha Hadid, an Arab Muslim woman who was born and raised in Baghdad, to convey their futuristic technological prowess.

The question of to whom modernism belongs remains fraught a decade later, as it becomes clear that there is no turning back on Angela Merkel's decision to admit record numbers of immigrants. Many of those who greeted the newcomers in the summer of 2015 remembered their own families' experience of displacement in and after World War II. At the same time, they understood that accommodating the influx of young men and families (very few women traveled alone) offered an opportunity to redeem the country's Nazi past in a way that went far beyond the construction of memorials.[10] Yet the increasingly authoritarian character of Recip Erdogan's leadership in Turkey, and its sponsorship of the revival of Ottoman forms, have changed the tenor of the reception of the DITIB Mosque, whose completion has also been stymied by problems with the construction of its unusual design.

The new arrivals joined an existing Muslim community whose origins are largely Turkish rather than Arab.[11] After the construction of the Berlin Wall in 1961 cut off the supply of East German refugees, German industry needed new sources of labor to feed the ongoing Economic Miracle (*Wirtschaftswunder*), which continued with little pause until the Arab oil embargo of 1973. Initially most immigrants came from Catholic and Orthodox communities in Southern Europe, but in 1961 the Federal Republic signed an agreement to import "guest workers" from Turkey. The expectation at first was that male factory workers, who arrived without their families, would quickly return to their own countries. Many stayed, however, and were eventually joined by their wives and children; originally most of the women worked as well.[12] German citizenship laws, which stress ethnicity over the place of birth, ensured that for decades most immigrants, regardless of their national origin, retained their foreign passports and were unable to vote. Citizenship laws were eased in 2000, but many residents, including people whose parents were born in Germany, are not legally German.[13] Furthermore, well into the twenty-first century many Germans did not (and still do not) regard neighbors who do not share their ethnicity and Christian religious background as German, regardless of what passport they carry. For instance, in 2007 a survey found that although relatively few ethnically Turkish migrants were comfortable with the idea of someone in their family marrying an ethnic German, the number of ethnic Germans who viewed being related by marriage to an ethnic Turk positively was far smaller.[14] Nonetheless, diversity is now a fact. By 2010 nearly one in five German residents was not of German descent; nearly half of these were not citizens, and 29 percent of families with children had at least one parent who was not ethnically German.[15]

A sympathetic account of the neighborhood surrounding the Zeche Zollverein written in 2008 gives a flavor of attitudes toward largely ethnically Turkish areas at that time and of the importance of mosques as an expression of pride in a specifically Muslim identity:

> Katernberg is a typical example of what is known as a problem area. The locals have even more drastic names for their area. For the Germans it has become "Turkish Katernberg"; and for the Turks "Little Chicago." . . . It is not possible to make a direct comparison with Polish emigration around 100 years before, because of religious and cultural factors and the different chronological conditions, but certain parallels can be seen. Despite the sometimes lengthy amount of time involved, developing self evident relationships between the majority society and minority population of foreigners and speakers of other languages has proved an extremely slow process. Germans still have not completely relinquished their somewhat rigid ideas of assimilation and, like the Poles, Turks are generally employed in the poorly paid, arduous, dirty and unhealthy occupations rejected by German workers. . . . The great majority of Turkish families live in former [factory] housing because it is almost impossible for them to find houses on the open market. . . . It was therefore almost inevitable that foreigners should turn in on themselves and form ghettos. . . . For this reason, in Kartenberg it is easy to see why the first generation of so-called guest workers have still not really arrived in Germany, and why their children and grand-

children did not integrate in the way politicians would wish.... Nevertheless there are signs that efforts to provide equal rights for all might yet prove successful. An expression of the self-confidence of the inhabitants of Turkish origin can be seen in the shape of the new Ayasofya mosque with its minaret and cultural centre on the Schalker Straße near shaft 4/5/11.[16]

For many years the main architectural issue related to immigration was the provision of housing; in the twenty-first century it shifted to being the articulation of public space for Islam.[17] The place of mosques in the German cityscape has, as in neighboring Switzerland and the Netherlands, as well as the United States, become key to discussions of the place of immigrants in German society.[18] Both Chancellor Merkel and former president Christian Wulff raised the hackles of many Christian Democrats by insisting in major speeches delivered in 2010 that Islam and mosques have a rightful place in Germany.[19] At the time the Social Democrats and the Greens were more consistently supportive of multiculturalism but were also more avowedly secular.

Paradoxically, although the debate in the first years of the new century over the role of guest workers and their descendants was often framed as being between the acceptance of difference and assimilation to German norms, when it came to architecture, at least, many Germans preferred that their neighbors remained recognizably exotic. While the country's many new synagogues have all been resolutely modern, the mosques that clearly demonstrated cultural difference garnered the greatest public support.[20] As the opposition to the Cologne mosque indicated, defining who has access to well-established German approaches to drawing upon multiple pasts, including that of modernism, remained controversial.

A Representative Mosque for Cologne

In 2005 the Turkish-Islamic Union of the Institution for Religion (known as DITIB after its Turkish acronym) sponsored a competition for the design of a congregational mosque.[21] Intended to be "representative," it was to be Germany's largest and most architecturally distinguished mosque.[22] Founded in 1984 in Cologne, where at least a tenth of the city population was by 2006 Muslim, DITIB is an umbrella organization representing nearly nine hundred mosques across the Federal Republic.[23] The Turkish government funds it, just as the German government provides the financial support for German Christians and Jews; before Erdogan's election as prime minister of Turkey in 2003, this was an offshoot of a secular government.[24] DITIB is the major sponsor of purpose-built mosques in Germany. Most German mosques are located in buildings originally built for other purposes. The previous DITIB Mosque in Cologne was, not untypically, in a former factory.[25] Although there are about forty-five mosques in Cologne and thousands throughout Germany, until the

2010s all but a handful remained almost invisible.[26] In the previous decade the apparent secrecy surrounding the location of German mosques helped foster distrust, as well as a sense of discrimination among those who worshipped in obscurity.

On 28 August 2008, more than two years after the first street protests erupted, the Cologne city council finally voted to approve construction.[27] Despite Christian Democratic complaints that it represented not integration but "a demonstration of power," the Christian Democratic mayor, Fritz Schramma, joined the Social Democratic, Green, Free Democratic, and Left members of the council in support of the project.[28] Josef Wirges, the Social Democratic vice-mayor of the district in which it is being built, predicted that eventually tourist buses will come to see it instead of taking visitors to the cathedral.[29] Construction proceeded slowly, however, with at least some of the delays apparently caused by the difficulty of erecting the overlapping shells that create the central space; in October 2011 DITIB fired the architects (they were rehired, although in the role of consultant rather than architect), and in March 2013 it won a seven-figure judgment against the builders.[30] Meanwhile a change of leadership within the mosque, which has brought it closer to Erdogan's Justice and Development Party (the AKP) in Turkey, has helped prompt the desire to have a more conventional interior; the prayer hall finally opened to the public in June 2017.[31]

Clearly one context for the reception of the Cologne mosque project were the events of 11 September 2001. Mohamed Atta, one of the organizers of the attacks that leveled the World Trade Towers in New York and damaged the Pentagon, just across the Potomac from Washington, D.C., studied architecture in Cairo before coming to Hamburg to pursue an advanced degree in city planning. It was there that he met two of the others who piloted planes used in an effort that was clearly structured around the enormous symbolic power of buildings.[32] Fears of terrorism have recently increased again following the attacks in Paris in 2015 and 2016, and subsequently in Brussels, Nice, and Berlin as well as the harassment of hundreds of women in Cologne on New Year's Eve 2015. This account, however, focuses on the architectural sources for the Cologne mosque and on the complexity of using modern architecture as a means of expressing the relationship between ethnic Germans and their Muslim neighbors, as well as on the reception of the two stages of the design.

Throughout the world, recent monumental mosques, like the one being completed in Cologne, have largely been built with funds from Saudi Arabia and the Gulf states in styles that quote from Islamic tradition, although not necessarily those of the places in which they are built or from which most of their congregations come.[33] In Germany, however, DITIB is the primary funder of new mosques, and both the political influence and the architectural forms instead come from Turkey, where conservative Salafi and Wahabi practices had until recently made few inroads.[34] The Cologne mosque was intended to be different, however, from the buildings that overtly reference Ottoman precedents.

To ensure acceptance, DITIB staged a competition in 2005 for the design of the Cologne mosque, with the results announced in March 2006; it also invited members of the city government and the architectural community to judge the entries. Representatives of each helped decide a blind competition entered by architects of varied ethnic and religious backgrounds.[35] This process almost certainly assured that the building would be in keeping with contemporary architecture in the city rather than resemble other recent German mosques. In what must have been seen as a perfect solution by both DITIB and many others, the victors, who had entered anonymously, were Paul Böhm, who continues to be the public face of the project, and his father, Gottfried.

The architects proposed locating the mosque atop an elevated quadrilateral base, itself anchored in one corner and near the end of its opposite extreme by minarets. Marking the area of the sanctuary was a dome-like feature, in which curved shells wrapped around large, irregularly shaped areas of glazing. Much of the rest of the structure was to be devoted to community activities and, following Muslim custom, commercial spaces whose rents are intended to help support the religious activities housed in the complex. Little advantage was taken of the corner site, abutting the intersection of Venloerstrasse, which hosts a neighborhood shopping district, and Innere Kanalstrasse, a multilane thoroughfare that is part of a ring road wrapping around the historic city center.

A more compelling revised design, issued in August 2007 to address public criticism as well as respond to the input of the clients, placed the two minarets, whose design but not height was altered, near the rear of the now nearly symmetrical mosque, in which the central circular feature, around which an L-shaped block wrapped at a discreet distance, morphed to absorb the rest of the original podium.[36] Although the sacred space remained raised, the exterior distinction between the two areas was largely erased as the enveloping shells acquired slightly more regular form, and the extent of the glazing between them increased to give passersby a clear view of the varied activities taking place within.

No other major Western European mosque belongs so emphatically to the history of the city and country in which it is to stand. This flexibility is possible because the only architectural requirement for a mosque is a niche, called a *mihrab,* in the center of the rear interior or *qibla* wall, which must be oriented toward Mecca.[37] A *minbar* or pulpit, and a minaret, the tower from which the faithful are called to prayer five times a day, are also customary, but minarets are rare in Germany; they more often serve as markers of identity than as platforms for actual chanting.[38] Mosque architecture has always varied enormously across space and time, accommodating local building traditions, available construction materials, and climate.

Press accounts of the Cologne mosque stressed the transparency of the winning design, which was substantially accentuated in the revised version.[39] Transparency has been a major theme in Cologne's architecture for well over a century; its use as a symbol of social equality and democracy also has deep local roots. The completion of Cologne's vast Gothic cathedral, whose flying buttresses allowed the walls to be filled largely with glass, symbolized the unification of Germany as much as, if not more than, the Catholicism of the Rhineland.[40] Its two towers were clearly the inspiration for the pair of minarets that frame the mosque (minarets are usually singular, although the status of imperial Ottoman mosques was marked by four). The idea of a glazed building large enough for the population of an entire city to assemble within and dedicated to a disinterested if not necessarily sacred purpose haunted German architects for decades to come. Bruno Taut's Glashaus and Otto Bartning's Steel Church, erected on the same fairgrounds in 1914 and 1928, respectively, although not built on the scale of cathedrals, demonstrated that such dreams could be expressed from within modernism's synthesis of technologically advanced construction and abstract form.[41] Hans Schwippert and Gunter Behnisch's quarters for the Bundestag in nearby Bonn, although taking a different shape, relied for much of their effect upon the equation of transparency with democratic government.

Although Dominikus and Gottfried Böhm typically favored an emphasis on sculptured form, most often executed in reinforced concrete, over transparency, their work provided the key formal precedents for the translation of the Ottoman imperial mosque prototype into German. Like Dominikus's Church of St. Engelbert (1932) in Cologne-Riehl, Gottfried's Mariendom in Velbert-Neviges (1968) and his St. Gertrud in Cologne-Ehrenfeld (1965), and Paul's St. Theodor in Cologne-Vingst (2002), the DITIB Mosque is a centralized structure; all but the last also feature a cap-like roof structure. As at St. Engelbert, the architects placed the roughly oval prayer hall atop a platform containing community-oriented activities.[42] The form of the mosque's roof structure alludes, albeit obliquely, more to imperial Ottoman mosques than Taut's city crowns, but the relationship to the Mariendom is also obvious, although the mosque, which sits on a busy corner formed by the inner ring road and a neighborhood commercial artery, completely lacks the complex setting into which Gottfried was able to place that cathedral-sized pilgrimage church. St. Gertrud, just over a mile away from the mosque, is a miniature variant of the Mariendom. On a midblock site, it is set just slightly back from the street and marked by a single irregular steeple (Figure 6.2).[43] Just a few kilometers to the east Paul's St. Theodor is another circular concrete church, in this case with a processional ramp containing the Stations of the Cross wrapping around the exterior in a way that also creates a spiral slot of overhead lighting on the interior (Figure 6.3). Built on the site of an early twentieth-century parish church that was destroyed in the war, it replaced a provisional postwar church.[44] The sense of sliding volumes here, while in no way evoking a ruin, does anticipate the larger gaps between the volumes of the DITIB Central Mosque.

The two sides of the roughly rectangular site that do not face the street are composed of slightly angled but otherwise conventional office blocks that would have

Assimilating Modern Memory 221

Figure 6.2. Gottfried Böhm, St. Gertrud, Cologne, 1965. Source: Elya/Wikipedia Commons.

won easy approval in Berlin from Hans Stimmann. The volume of the mosque itself, however, comprises six concrete shells, flanked toward the rear of each side by a minaret, that together create a dome-like structure. Split to allow light in at two stages on each side as well as from above and again at the center, these complexly curved surfaces evoke the form of a domed Ottoman mosque while being constructed of entirely different materials and in a frankly modern style. The result not only allows views through the building but also creates the sense that it is composed of fragments in a way that is not entirely dissimilar from Stirling's New State Gallery.

None of these nods to a mix of local and other German examples of modern sacred and civic architecture eased the approval process. Public opposition focused on the height of the minarets (which at 55 meters were nowhere near as tall as the 157-meter-high twin steeples of the cathedral), and on issues regarding integration,

Figure 6.3. Paul Böhm, St. Theodor, Cologne, 2002. Source: Livia Hurley.

primarily on the role of women in Muslim society, as well as the extent to which Turkish migrants spoke German. Concern was particularly high that the sermons at Friday prayers be delivered in German.[45] Many observers simply refused to accept that the building was modern. Local Christian Democrats complained at a meeting held in April 2006, shortly after the winning design was announced, that it was "a very traditional Islamic form," which represented "a national ethnic character instead of an international space for Muslims of different backgrounds. It would be better to plan a building with which non-Muslims could identify."[46] Sabine Kraft, an architectural historian who wrote her doctoral thesis on German mosques, lamented that the presence of a dome and minarets, which she saw as imperial gestures representing the strength of Islam in Germany, prevented this from being a really experimental building. Although fully aware of the Böhm dynasty's position in the history of modern German sacred architecture, Kraft saw the mosque design as lying outside it.[47]

But the issue was not just how modern its architecture would or would not be.

Comments on the website of Pro-Cologne, the citizens' initiative that organized antimosque demonstrations, give a sense of a hostility that had little to do with architectural style:

> Now the cat is out of the bag. If the jury for the architectural competition for the DITIB mosque has its way, Ehrenfeld will soon be dominated by two fifty-five-meter-tall minarets and a prominent mosque dome. The prizewinning design is an unmistakable sign of the Islamic missionary work in the tradition-rich cathedral city of Cologne.[48]

The text goes on to warn that if the building were not stopped, more mosques might be built. Why were so many commentators, including at least one with a sophisticated grasp of the history of recent German sacred architecture, so unwilling to see the design as belonging to what was by this point an indigenous tradition, albeit one that was being almost literally deconstructed to provide the openness demanded by so many? In the nineteenth century the construction of Protestant churches and of synagogues in Cologne had prompted little of the debate triggered by the mosque.[49] What had changed?

Above all, the former centrality of the church had been substantially eroded in an increasingly secular country. Those who supported this development were not necessarily inclined to welcome the presence of a monumental sacred structure of any kind, while those who were distressed by it were uneasy about a foreign faith that was successfully carving out a place for itself in German public life.[50] One would have little sense from the many criticisms of DITIB as being supported by the Turkish government that German churches (and for that matter synagogues) were dependent on a state funding mechanism not available to Muslims, who thus turned to their primary country of origin for support. Although many individuals and even parishes supported the mosque out of a feeling of shared religiosity, few local Christian leaders were unequivocal in their support; Joachim Cardinal Meisner admitted to having a "bad feeling" about the project.[51] The controversy over the construction of the mosque encouraged Christian leaders to complain repeatedly about the difficulty of maintaining churches in predominately Muslim countries, although this was a foreign policy issue with no legal influence upon the rights of Germany citizens and residents to practice their own faith. And the grounds for jealousy were real at a time when the neighboring archdiocese of Essen was closing down over a hundred churches, including distinguished examples of postwar modern architecture.[52] One German commentator summarized the Turkish reaction as, "See here what we have achieved. We build, and the Germans don't even have the money to maintain their own churches."[53]

At the same time, there were few Muslim spokespersons familiar with the churches the Böhms had built and even fewer willing to describe the degree to which the mosque had its origins in those rather than in Islamic precedent; indeed, the scope of their accomplishments was no longer familiar to many Germans who were not specialists in the subject. Nor was the creative tension between the much-lauded openness of the mosque and the voids of the Jewish Museum in Berlin, which sits on the edge of a neighborhood with a large proportion of ethnically Turkish residents, likely to be any more welcome.[54]

That opposition to the first German mosque whose design was firmly rooted in German architectural precedent suggested as well that a real focus of discontent was the degree to which newcomers were mastering and manipulating local culture, including memories of modernism, which were perceived to be specifically Judeo-Christian (the new wave of German synagogues have been greeted with very little public opposition, and have received a great deal of support from a variety of public and private organizations, but security remains a concern and there has also been an attack upon a Sikh *gurdwara* in Essen).[55] The builders of the Cologne mosque faced many more obstacles, for instance, than their counterparts some forty miles away in Duisburg-Marxloh.

The largest mosque in Germany opened in 2008 less than three miles from the Landscape Park.[56] The first German mosque to be built in part with public funds, the Merkez Mosque stirred up none of the controversy unleashed in Cologne, although it was an obviously historicist building, clearly modeled on the Ottoman mosques erected across Eastern Europe and Anatolia in the fifteenth through the seventeenth centuries (Figure 6.4). That the principal difference between the Cologne and Duisburg mosques was stylistic, rather than functional, suggested that opposition to mosques, although phrased in terms of their foreignness, was actually ameliorated when they were obviously exotic imports. The Merkez Mosque contains, as its Cologne counterpart also will, a large variety of public spaces in which people of other faiths or no faith at all will be welcome.[57] Tenants of the DITIB Central Mosque will not be allowed to sell pork or alcohol, but there will be no other restrictions placed on their commercial activities, which are intended to encourage interfaith dialogue and reach out to the surrounding community.

Despite the amount of controversy it precipitated over the course of more than a decade, the DITIB Mosque has not been widely discussed upon its completion, which has occurred in a very different political climate from the one in which it was initially designed.[58] Those focusing primarily upon the aesthetic quality of its architectural form are likely to be unimpressed by the rather awkward relationship between the gridded glass voids and the more supple curves of the concrete envelope. Its interior, which due to a change of leadership within the mosque features a modicum of the ornament absent on the facades, is not as impressive a space as that of the Mariendom. Whether or not it can be integrated into German accounts of modern sacred architecture will say as much about the segment of the society that writes about such topics and their audience as about the building itself. It is very likely to

Figure 6.4.   Cavit Sahin, DITIB Merkez Mosque, Duisburg, 2008. Source: Ani/Wikipedia Commons.

win widespread recognition as the architectural emblem of Germany's ethnic Turks, if not necessarily of other Muslims, at least until something equivalent at least in scale is erected in Berlin.

Muslims and Modernism

The criticism of Böhm's mosque design in 2006–7 by a vocal minority from across the political spectrum highlighted that many Germans identify their modernist heritage as one of the things that separates them and those of European descent from the rest of the world, including Muslims at home and abroad. Modern architecture and design are typically used in Germany to differentiate an elite shaped by education and taste from workers of all ethnic backgrounds. Yet from the beginning these have been one of the country's most successful exports, and it is precisely the interaction with other cultures that has kept modernism fresh over the course of the last eighty years.[59] Since the 1930s the urban middle classes in Africa, Asia, and Latin America have arguably been far more enthusiastic supporters of modern architecture than their European counterparts.[60] The apparent homogeneity of abstract architecture and the ubiquity of concrete skeletal construction mask the degree to which the European and North American architectural community depended on "the other" to realize what continues often to be mistaken for an exclusively western conception of modernity.[61]

Haunting much of the commentary on the mosque was the presumption by Germans of Christian and Jewish descent that the people who worship at DITIB mosques were less modern than ethnic Germans. Except for a few references to the origins of the Ottoman imperial mosque in the Turkish conquest of Istanbul in 1453, and thus its inappropriate triumphalism for a historically Christian city, the historical specificity of the Turkish precedents for the building was as widely overlooked as the German ones. And yet Turkey, like a number of other predominately Muslim countries, has often actively promoted modern architecture. Beginning in the 1930s both national governments and the urban middle class in these places found in its inexpensive, abstract forms and equally obviously modern materials a useful shorthand for their aspirations for economic and social advancement.[62] Although this is no longer reliably the case under the governments formed since 2003 by the AKP, which has revived Ottoman rituals and welcomed allusions to Ottoman architecture, many people of Turkish origin in Germany, even when they come from rural hinterlands, are more aware of modern architecture from lived experience in Turkey as well as access in Germany to Turkish television and films than their German neighbors realize.[63]

Nor was the Turkish enthusiasm for modern architecture unique in the region. The situation was little different in Baghdad in the 1950s, when Hadid was growing up there in a modern house designed by the Syrian architect Badri Quadah. Criticism of the position of women in the Islamic faith and in Muslim society was at the core of the debate over the DITIB Mosque in Cologne, and yet at the same time an Arab woman was providing some of Germany's biggest businesses with bold expressions of futuristic form. Hadid's fame in design circles did nothing, however, to make ethnic Germans, including those engaged in the visual arts, more familiar with the material culture of their Muslim neighbors, as Stingel's installation in Berlin demonstrated.

Credit for the international dissemination of modernist architecture has usually been given to exiles from Nazi Germany, especially Gropius and Mies.[64] This emphasis on Western European agency ignores, however, the degree to which it satisfied the needs of clients, as well as to which immigrant architects needed to adapt their designs in order to become successful in their new homes, not something that all were easily able to do. It also draws disproportionate attention to the interaction between Europe and the United States, at the expense of the contributions made by architects and clients in countries like Turkey and the three former Ottoman provinces that now compose Iraq. In reclaiming for European-born men of genius what was actually a more complex set of alliances shared among a web of architects and patrons reaching well into the developing world, the emphasis on Europe helped sustain the idea that modernity itself was specifically western.[65]

Turkey played a key role in the transfer of modern architecture from German-speaking Europe to less industrialized areas of the world. To most of its original adherents, the modern movement must have seemed a doomed cause during the 1930s. The style's popularity waned in all of the places it had originally flourished. Although often blamed on the rise of political extremism on both the left and the right, shifts in fashion were equally responsible, as modernism lost the ability to convey the new in places where it was now too familiar to shock. The modern movement proved sustainable during these years only where it was truly new, above all on the non-Soviet fringes of Europe.[66] Its optimistic message of progress, especially after the global economic crisis called into question the degree to which an industrial economy did indeed operate rationally, was key to this success. The new style survived above all because it promised a technological modernity that many of the places in which it now flourished did not yet possess. This was true above all in the eastern Mediterranean, especially in the British Mandate of Palestine and in the Republic of Turkey.[67]

Kemal Atatürk, Turkey's founder and first president, reinvigorated what had been the core of the Ottoman Empire, which had in the century before the Treaty of Lausanne been denuded of, first, its North African, then its European, and finally its Arab provinces. For Atatürk, employing abstract architectural forms was central to his transformation of the truncated Ottoman Empire into a modern nation-state. Moreover, he turned specifically to German-speaking architects for technical assistance in attaining this goal; at the same time many of Turkey's best local architects, including Sedad Eldem, had trained in Germany or made study visits there during the 1920s. Indeed, the history of German architecture of this period can hardly be written without reference to Turkey. In the 1930s and 1940s German architects were as likely to find refuge and work in Turkey as in the United States; after the war their work there and that of their Turkish counterparts was held up as an example for West German architecture. The Germans who went to Turkey ranged from bourgeois reformers to avant-garde radicals. While the Austrian Clemens Holzmeister garnered the most prestigious commissions in the new capital of Ankara, including that for the Parliament, the two most important Germans to move to Turkey were Taut, who arrived in 1936 and died there two years later, and Paul Bonatz, who came in 1943 and stayed until 1954.[68] Not all of their work was designed in the spirit of the New Building, but all was part of a concerted effort to modernize Turkey.

The lack of an impressive industrial infrastructure did not mean that Turks had no experience of modernity. Nationalism was central to modernity and to the deployment of modernism in architecture as it created the need to make visibly decisive breaks with immediate imperial precedents that had by definition been trans- or international.[69] Alternatives had to be created for which no or limited precedents existed, as the infrastructure of a nation-state was by definition modern. It could not easily be based entirely on the sacred or the secular architecture of an actual or an imagined past that, moreover, did not communicate the sense of optimistic possibility inherent in new architectural forms.

Atatürk's use of modern architecture in the service of both nationalism and modernization had a strong impact in the region, including in neighboring Iraq, which had been created by the British after World War I out of former Ottoman provinces. In the 1950s, its capital aspired to be far more of a showcase in this regard than any city in the Federal Republic. Baghdad grew rapidly as petroleum challenged coal's popularity and price on the international market (this is what prompted the decline of the Ruhr region) and as Arab countries were able to secure an increasing share of the profits from the wells sunk within their borders by European and American multinationals. Although Frank Lloyd Wright's opera house was never built, Walter Gropius's firm, the Architects' Collaborative, designed much of the university and the Greek planner Constantinos Doxiadis laid out new model districts.[70]

As modern architecture morphed from being the province of a European avant-garde to that of the political elites in places like Turkey and Baghdad, its content shifted. What had once been identified, albeit often erroneously, with the socialist empowerment of the working classes now served a new middle class involved in governing new or aspiring nation-states. Its optimistic message that mass production, organized as often by state planners as by private capital, could generate a better future had always been lost on most factory workers, but it immediately struck a chord with those who, like their more socially marginal (because often Jewish) German predecessors during the 1920s, wished to distinguish themselves from both earlier imperial or aristocratic rulers on the one hand and from rural peasants on the other. Moreover it did so at relatively little cost.[71]

While the fusion of historic structures or historicism with the deliberate recall of modernism seen in the design of the DITIB Mosque for Cologne is part of an approach to architecture rooted in the specific circumstances of the Federal Republic, the international emergence of neomodernism at the end of the twentieth century, which confirmed the global relevance of buildings like the Jewish Museum and the dome of the Reichstag, depended as well on the continued enthusiasm that Arab and Asian clients displayed for modernism. Two key examples were Norman Foster's Hong Kong and Shanghai Bank (1979–86) in Hong Kong and Jean Nouvel's Institute of the Arab World (1981–87) in Paris (Figure 6.5).[72] These are hybrid designs, which graft the latest technology onto a creative recall of Chinese spatial and Arab ornamental strategies respectively. Although Foster was hardly unknown when he was commissioned to design what was then the most expensive building in the world, Nouvel made his reputation on the back of the simultaneously ornamental and high tech apertures which he employed as an up to date version of the pierced screens that traditionally filtered light in many Arab buildings. It was these specific commissions that garnered both architects the reputation required to obtain their Berlin commissions.

Only a small minority of Germany's original Turkish "guest workers" came from the urban middle class that adopted modern architecture with such enthusiasm in

Assimilating Modern Memory

Figure 6.5.   Jean Nouvel, Institute of the Arab World, Paris, 1987. Source: Livia Hurley.

the 1930s and repeatedly returned to it in the decades that followed. Nonetheless, increasingly easy access to Turkish media, especially satellite television, as well as their own rising standards of living, helped encourage many of those of Turkish background residing in Germany at the end of the twentieth century and the beginning of the twenty-first to identity with modernism, sometimes to a far greater degree than the many Germans who had throughout the postwar period preferred to dwell in houses with gabled roofs, no matter what the contemporary architectural fashion might be.[73]

The details of the taste of ethnic Turks resident in Germany, and the history of modern Turkish architecture and design remain nearly invisible to most ethnic Germans. An almost accidental dialogue between the two was triggered by an installation by the artist Rudolf Stingel, a native of the South Tyrol, a German-speaking district of northern Italy, that filled the upper floor of the New National Gallery in Berlin in the spring of 2010 (Figure 6.6). Stingel placed a carpet printed with a black-and-white reproduction of the design of an Agra carpet in his own collection on the floor of the entrance level of Mies's building and hung a large crystal chandelier from the ceiling. The handout accompanying the exhibition emphasized the dialogue between the Indian-made carpet, which was to stand simultaneously for the "orient" and for the European bourgeois taste against which architects like Mies had reacted,

Figure 6.6. Rudolf Stingel, installation, New National Gallery, Berlin, 2010. Copyright bpk Photo Agency/David von Becker.

and the explicitly European, albeit baroque, style of the chandelier with which he paired it. As several commentators, including the writers of the museum's own press releases, quickly noticed, however, both imbued a space many museumgoers already experienced as a temple with the character of a contemporary German mosque; similar chandeliers (and in some cases better carpets) grace many German ones.[74] Thus what was meant to be a dialogue between premodern European and Asian ornament and modern minimalism in fact collapsed much of the distance between the "sacred" spaces of German secular intellectuals and the more pious of their Muslim neighbors.

Far from these ordinary neighborhood mosques, several of the new German temples of high design were the work of Hadid, who, like the architects and patrons of the DITIB Mosque for Cologne, asserted the possibility of Muslim modernity in a society that often articulates its doubts about the possibility of such a thing in terms of the way in which it perceives Islam treats women. Much German criticism of Islam during the debate over the DITIB Mosque and subsequently has focused on the supposedly inferior position of women in Islamic societies. Indeed, those anxious to defeat such stereotypes initially hoped she might design the mosque in Cologne.[75] While most of the local opposition to the building came from the right and focused on the height of the minarets as well as the prominent presence of a mosque in relation to a Gothic cathedral, much of the international attention paid to the dispute was triggered by the criticism emanating from the left, where a central concern was how many Muslim women dress.[76]

German discussions of the status of women under Islamic law and social practices typically focused more on issues of sartorial modesty than violence against women, which although relatively rare, certainly did and does occur, or, for that matter, educational or economic opportunity.[77] In 2007 Ralph Giordano, a prominent German Jewish intellectual and an opponent of the mosque, commented, "I don't want to see women on the street wearing burqas. I'm insulted by that—not by the women themselves but by the people who turn them into human penguins."[78] Although many Muslim women in Germany chose to cover some or all of their hair (as do Orthodox Jewish women, who more typically wear wigs) with scarves in the first years of the twenty-first century, almost none wore burqas or veils.[79] Hadid's dramatic style of self-presentation belied such facile stereotypes, even as it helped enable her to define modernity on her own terms.[80]

Hadid credited her desire to become an architect to a childhood visit to the great mosque of Córdoba.[81] Her parents belonged to exactly the Muslim upper middle class that had fostered modern architecture in Turkey and did the same in Iraq. Her father, a prominent politician who rose to become minister of finance, was a graduate of the London School of Economics; her mother was an artist. The family lived in a modern villa on what were then the outskirts of Baghdad.[82] Their daughter, although schooled abroad in Switzerland, Beirut, and the United Kingdom, nonetheless was raised in an environment in which many of the world's leading architects hoped to build.

In tandem with her education at the Architectural Association in London and her own outsize talents, growing up in Baghdad helped position Hadid as the person to whom German companies regularly turned at the turn of the century when they wanted to demonstrate their own modernity, not least to an international audience.[83] In the 1970s and eighties she experimented with the revival of suprematism, an offshoot of constructivism. This led in 1988 to her inclusion, alongside Frank Gehry and Daniel Libeskind, in the Museum of Modern Art in New York's exhibition of deconstructivist architecture, although—like Gehry—she displayed little interest in the theoretical underpinnings of the style.[84] That this was now detached from any social program was made clear in her breakthrough competition design for a commercial development, including apartments as well as a fitness studio, for a site atop Hong Kong's "Peak." Hadid's powerful renderings, whose forced perspectives developed in advance of computer-aided design programs, made this one of the most remarked upon unbuilt projects of the 1980s.[85]

For many years Hadid built almost nothing; her considerable reputation was derived instead from a mix of unpublished projects, lectures, and teaching. Her first

Figure 6.7.   Zaha Hadid, Vitra Fire Station, Weil am Rhein, 1993. Source: Livia Hurley.

realized buildings were both in Germany. They included a fire station in Weil am Rhein, just across the German border from Basel, which was commissioned in 1990 by the Vitra furniture firm and completed three years later (Figure 6.7). From the beginning, this unusual structure, whose acutely angled planes included sloping wall slabs, was as much a demonstration of the company's commitment to adventuresome design as a practical guard against fires like the one that had ravaged its complex in 1981.[86] The building was eventually converted to serve as a gallery, a use that facilitated its access to architectural pilgrims who came in increasing numbers to tour the company's campus-like plant. Hadid also erected a sharply angled apartment block on Stresemannstrasse to the IBA in Berlin.

Hadid demonstrated her continuing ability to supply German industry with compelling imagery of the new in her Phaeno Science Center in Wolfsburg and her factory for BMW in Leipzig, both finished in 2005 (Figures 6.8 and 6.9). A tourist brochure described the Phaeno as the culmination of a tradition of innovative architecture in the city that dates back to the 1950s, when both Alvar Aalto and Hans Scharoun built there.[87] "From then until the Phaeno," concludes the publicist, "practically every ten years a trailblazing cultural project has been realized here that stands as a pioneering architectural impulse."[88] The museum's own brochure highlights the utility of commissioning the largest structure yet built by this unconventional architect in drawing attention to itself, stated proudly that the Phaeno has been recognized by the British newspaper the *Guardian* as one of the world's twelve most important modern buildings, a list that also included the Empire State Building and the Sydney Opera House.[89]

Figure 6.8. Zaha Hadid, Phaeno Science Center, Wolfsburg, 2005. Source: Richard Bartz/Wikipedia Commons.

Figure 6.9. Zaha Hadid, BMW Central Building, Leipzig, 2005. Source: BMW Werk Leipzig/Wikipedia Commons.

The BMW factory, in which the production line snakes through the offices, bringing white- and blue-collar workers within sight of one another, garnered similar praise.[90] Catherine Slessor, writing in *Architectural Review,* declared it "a genuinely radical building, formally and spatially, that re-envisages the conventions, activities and hierarchies of the industrial workplace and recasts them as an efficient, flexible and dynamic organism."[91] In Leipzig, a city in the formerly Communist east, the equality with which each employee is treated appears to be particularly appreciated. The building does not simply display the image of future. Like the Phaeno, the BMW Center is built of self-compacting concrete; the two buildings were the first time this material had been employed in Germany. The factory is enough of an attraction that the company is able to charge hefty fees for guided tours, applying a surcharge to those particularly interested in its architecture rather than the manufacture of automobiles.[92]

These two Hadid buildings represent a different phase of her career than her earliest German buildings. They are more plastic in form, and engage their users in a more welcoming yet dynamic way than the sharp angles of the Vitra Fire Station and her contribution to the IBA. Unlike other foreigners building in Germany, including Stirling, Gehry, Libeskind, Foster, Eisenman, and Chipperfield, Hadid remained entirely herself, however.[93] Unlike them, or for that matter the Böhms, she did not need to integrate herself into the local ways of working. Although she initially favored sharp angles, she never invoked a relationship to shards of expressionist glass, and she certainly never created a dialogue within her buildings between modernism and historicism; only modernism mattered to her. She was certainly aware of its past, even as she sculpted its future. The Phaeno and the BMW Center were made possible by a combination of new digital tools and ways of building with concrete, and they appear futuristic. They evoke some of the same energy as Erich Mendelsohn's visionary drawings, just as her earlier work drew on suprematism.[94] And yet she felt no need to reach further back, and no need to develop a modernism that was fragmented, incomplete, or ruined. Instead, her buildings in Wolfsburg and Leipzig seem to embody a tremendous energy that is moving forward without restraint.

Hadid's success may yet prove to be the template for a new, more open German society. If that goal is achieved, the early intentions for the mosque in Cologne, however the interior of the final building appears, and whatever the character of the institution it houses proves to be when the building is finally dedicated, will also be part of the story. In the Böhms' design for the DITIB Central Mosque the juxtaposition of historicism and modernism in postwar German architecture shifted from balancing the trauma of the specifically German past with the possibility of a better future to acknowledging both the historic architecture left behind by its largest group of immigrants and their potential integration into German society. And yet, in part because the process it is supposed to represent has not been fully achieved, it remains very difficult for its target audience, which very much includes Germans who are Christians or who have no faith at all, to recognize, much less celebrate, this accomplishment. What began as a specifically religious response to the destruction wrought by World War II has become so completely a secular practice that it is challenging for even those who assisted in its original creation to employ it for a sacred purpose.

Conclusion

The Kolumba Museum in Cologne

On 15 September 2007, in the middle of the controversy over the DITIB Central Mosque, a new museum opened scarcely a mile to the east in what had once been the heart of medieval Cologne (Figure C.1). In it Peter Zumthor was able to realize what he had been unable to build in Berlin. Joachim Cardinal Meisner proudly presided over the dedication of the Kolumba, which serves as the archdiocese's art museum, declaring, "Wherever culture is uncoupled from worship *(Kultus)* and separated from the worship of God, worship stiffens into ritualism and culture degenerates" (he controversially used the German verb *entartet,* the derogatory word employed by the Nazis in their condemnations of modern art).[1] Yet arguably nothing better demonstrated the ossification of both religion and an architectural strategy devised to support it than this layering of a museum atop what had been a site of Christian worship for over a thousand years. Despite the lively debate over the Central Mosque, the usefulness of the architecture of modern memory was reaching its limits, as a secular German democracy no longer in denial about the crimes committed by an earlier generation finally moved on. Although greeted by many as one of Germany's most handsome new buildings, the Kolumba has never been seen as in any way symbolizing the Federal Republic. Moreover, it was widely condemned by preservationists as a desecration of a modern monument, Gottfried Böhm's construction of a chapel around a medieval statue of the Virgin that had (many said miraculously) survived the destruction of the late medieval church during World War II.[2] This highlighted the difficulty of reading Zumthor's abstraction as new, nearly a century after it had been showcased so effectively just across the Rhine in the Werkbund Exhibition.

The sheer number of Cologne's medieval churches and the extent of the damage inflicted on them during World War II ensured that not every one of them would be required to serve the regular parish needs of worshippers who increasingly lived outside the original heart of the city. Because of the comprehensiveness of the erasure of what was never one of the city's most important works of sacred architecture,

Figure C.1. Peter Zumthor, Kolumba Museum, Cologne, 2010. Source: Livia Hurley.

St. Kolumba was particularly vulnerable to being left out of, or at the least placed at the end of, the reconstruction of the city's Catholic infrastructure. The survival of the so-called Madonna of the Rubble, ensured a special role for the site, however, perhaps as a distinctly uncelebratory war memorial.[3]

The chapel that now houses the statue, erected in 1949–50 and expanded in 1956–57, was Gottfried Böhm's first independent commission (Figure C.2). An early, but small and not immediately influential, example of the approach to architecture documented in this book, it continues to be one of the city's most cherished places to pray. Onto a surviving stump of the medieval nave Böhm appended an octagonal chancel with a freestanding circular altar. On sunny days, light floods through two sets of four tall abstract stained glass windows designed by Ludwig Gies. These frame the sliver of wall on axis with the nave on which Böhm placed the Madonna and a fragment of her medieval protective canopy (Figure C.3). Later he appended a small, explicitly modern structure to the north of the main body of the church.[4]

Archaeological excavations conducted between 1974 and 1976 complicated matters by revealing evidence of previous structures dating back to Roman times. They also made it more difficult to use the site as Böhm intended. Although Böhm was active in discussing alternatives, in 1997 Zumthor won a competition to wrap the chapel and the excavated remains in a museum. Only a few fragments of Böhm's

Conclusion

Figure C.2.   Gottfried Böhm, Kolumba Chapel, Cologne, 1950. Source: Arved von der Ropp.

building are now visible from the street, although the medieval remains have been scrupulously preserved. The character of the chapel has been completely transformed, however, since the amount of light penetrating the open brickwork in which Zumthor partially enclosed this volume is limited. Zumthor reserved for himself the daylight that once warmed Böhm's chapel. Only the museum galleries, located above and to the north of Böhm's structure, feature large, fully glazed openings.

Zumthor's building has been justly lauded as a carefully crafted structure in which to recover the contemplative ambience in which the exhibited works, many gathered from Cologne's churches, were originally seen.[5] At the same time, however, the musealization of the medieval remains and the partial destruction and otherwise entombment of the modern chapel constructed out of them accentuate the limited role the Christian faith plays in the Federal Republic today. More people probably come to see the building and the works of art it houses than attend Mass in most of the city's churches (the chapel itself continues, however, to draw a considerable public). No building erected by the archdiocese has garnered so much praise since the completion of the Mariendom nearly forty years earlier. That church, however, was the focus of active pilgrimage rather than the exhibition of works of art.

Nor has the reception of the museum been entirely positive. The callous approach

Figure C.3. Interior, Kolumba Chapel. Source: Arved von der Ropp.

Zumthor and his clients took to Böhm's chapel dismayed those who prized this earlier encounter between abstract structure and religious faith.[6] As the establishment in 1988 of DOCOMOMO, an advocacy group dedicated to the preservation of modern architecture, demonstrates, modernism has long since ceased to be new.[7]

The architects, many of them based in Cologne, who invented the approach to architecture chronicled in these pages, in which modernism embodied memory as much or more than it represented the present or the future, witnessed the creation of modernism but they became aware after World War II that much of its effectiveness lay in the references it made to the Weimar Republic. They tempered their own work, stripping it of much of the radicalism on display at the Werkbund Exhibition in 1914, as well as in their churches in Cologne and nearby Aachen, in order to build the underpinnings for a more successful, because in many ways less ambitious, state, the Federal Republic, whose nationalism was tamed by being embedded in international institutions, of which the first were the Catholic and Protestant churches. Their goals harmonized with those of their religious and political leadership, Josef Cardinal Frings, Konrad Adenauer, and Otto Dibelius.

These architects and clerics could hardly have imagined the creative use to which an increasingly secular society would put the results. Rudolf Schwarz, who died in 1961, did not live to see his friend Mies commissioned to design the New National Gallery; nor did Otto Bartning. And Gottfried Böhm may not always have cherished the ways in which James Stirling, Frank Gehry, and Daniel Libeskind deploye d the dramatization of the relationship between past and present that he often imbued with sacred meaning and always with a deep respect for the built heritage of particular places. Nor could Böhm have easily imagined in the 1980s, when he developed the prototype for Norman Foster's dome for the Reichstag, the nearly immediate reunification of Germany or the revival of modernism it would help spark.

Just as the Economic Miracle of the postwar years must have astounded Schwarz, who had been so despairing in the letters he sent Mies in the late 1940s, so, too, the equally rapid collapse of the industrial economy in the Ruhr region, where he had built so many churches, would have amazed him. He would undoubtedly be disappointed to see so many of his churches made redundant, as a result of the industrial decline and the enormous social changes the subsequent decades have brought with them. It is unlikely that he would appreciate the Industriepark in Duisburg, although he might always have admired the Zeche Zollverein, as Mies almost certainly did. And while Schwarz would probably have dismissed the DITIB Central Mosque as unnecessarily flamboyant, it is likely that his mentor Dominkus Böhm would have viewed it with considerable pride, as might have Henry van de Velde, whose penchant for curves it shares. And just as Zumthor mourns the destruction of parts of the Main Train Station in Stuttgart, so Paul Bonatz might well have applauded the Kolumba Museum's exquisite construction and monumental abstract massing.[8]

And yet is there any need for contemporary German architecture to please its rather distant ancestors? Direct experience of the Third Reich is no longer the norm; the pain it caused to the living has almost been exhausted. The commemoration of its terror has been firmly inscribed in the landscape, particularly in the heart of Berlin. German democracy has been achieved, and Germany is once again powerful as well as whole. There may be other ways of imagining its present and its future than the ones employed for a century; Zaha Hadid and her clients certainly thought so. Perhaps the architecture of the twentieth-first century should address concerns particular to it. It is likely that residents of the Federal Republic will continue to use architecture to frame struggles over individual and collective identity; it is a medium with which intellectuals are familiar and one loaded with popular associations, no matter that not all of them are accurate. It is not, however, so certain that either modernism or memory, the themes that have obsessed many educated Germans for nearly three-quarters of a century, will continue to play such a central role in these debates. Already Berlin's memory landscapes appeal more to tourists than to inhabitants, especially the youth who flock to the city to study and to work in information technology and the arts. Their elders, the residents who struggled so hard to establish these spaces of commemoration, have long since achieved their goal.

Not all societies fight about the appearance of strategically positioned buildings. Turf wars are more likely to be about the control of space, and of the money it can bring, than about style, although these struggles, too, have occurred before. Identity can be played out, instead, through literature or music, as in twentieth-century Ireland, for instance, in which experimentation in the visual arts was for a long time largely left to Protestant women, an otherwise doubly marginalized group.[9] And not all collective or individual memories are transmitted through buildings; photographs have long been key in the United States.[10] Yet neither the way in which ordinary citizens or the intelligentsia have participated in debates over buildings since German unification in 1989 was as unprecedented as many scholars, detached from history by the theoretical perspectives of other disciplines, believed.

The debates and the results may not have been unique, but the buildings they engendered have certainly been widely heralded, with an impact that has stretched far beyond the Federal Republic. This architecture has produced some of the most meaningful experiences of their time, as well as some of the most widely disseminated and discussed images of buildings. Examining its history prompts a deeper understanding of both what it has achieved and what it has failed to accomplish. It is not the buildings themselves that have forced Germans to address the mix of commemoration and utopianism captured in these schemes but the act of creating them that has focused public awareness on a wide variety of intentions. Nor can one be sure that these buildings will continue to convey the meanings embedded in their creation. Even the Jewish Museum may eventually be experienced quite differently from the way Libeskind intended.

What persists instead is the ability of the historian to reconstruct the ways in which built form triggered debate and acquired meaning in what became the Federal Republic of Germany between 1945 and the early twenty-first century. These struggles were some of the most fruitful ways in which citizens learned to make democracy work as they slowly acquired faith in its institutions. This, it may be hoped, is a legacy that will also endure.

Acknowledgments

This book has deep roots in many visits I have made to Germany and the years I have lived there. I have acquired many debts along the way. The most obvious are to the Deutsche Akademische Austauschdienst and the Irish Research Council for Research in the Humanities and Social Sciences, which generously funded this project. But people matter most. The late Klaus Tenfelde was an exemplary host at the Bibliothek des Ruhrgebiets; the IRCHSS grant enabled me to hire Livia Hurley, who was an extraordinarily able research assistant. I benefited greatly from her familiarity with this material.

Parts of this project were presented at events hosted by Dublin City Council, the Free University Berlin, Mount Street Jesuit Centre in London, the School of the Art Institute of Chicago, University College Dublin, Washington University in St. Louis, Wesleyan University in Middletown, and Yale University in New Haven, as well as a number of meetings of the Society of Architectural Historians. I thank my hosts and session chairs, who included Charles Duggan, Ole Fischer, Mary Jane Jacobs, Paul Jaskot, Katherine Kuenzli, Eric Mumford, Robert Proctor, Gillian Pye, Gavriel Rosenfeld, Ellen Rowley, Sabine Strümper-Krobb, Jörn Schafaff, Joseph Siry, Robert Stern, Leslie Topp, Benjamin Wihstutz, and Robert Wojtowicz, as well as my audiences. The local Goethe Institut generously funded two of the Dublin conferences. Finally, I thank Amin Alsaden for identifying the architect of Zaha Hadid's family home in Baghdad for me.

I have been particularly fortunate to have outstanding colleagues in Dublin. For this project the most critical have been Hugh Campbell, Anne Fuchs, Lisa Godson, JoAnne Mancini, Emily Mark-FitzGerald, John Tuomey, and the late Richard Hurley. Elsewhere Karl Keim, Mary Pepchinski, and the late Werner Sewing in Berlin, Barbara Miller Lane in Bryn Mawr, Steve Perry in Cambridge, Ruth Hanisch and Wolfgang Sonne in Dortmund, Carsten Ruhl and Wolfgang Voigt in Frankfurt, Florian Urban in Glasgow, Esra Ackan in Ithaca, Jan Frohburg in Limerick, Richard Etlin in New York, Dietrich Neumann in Providence, and Patrick Quinn in Troy have been among the many others whose challenges, insights, and hospitality have mattered enormously. Florian Dreher in Karlsruhe and Susanne Kohlheyer and Peter Daners in Stuttgart kindly made available material of which I would otherwise have been unaware. The way I understand Germany is inevitably bound to my experiences as the wife of Sumit Chakraborty, who brought me to Bochum; the mother of Shomik Chakraborty, who was born there; and Rachel Thoma, Gönül Yelsin, and the late Luise Gritto, all of whom I met there. Once again the indomitable Pieter Martin and the superb staff of the University of Minnesota Press, as well as Mary Byers, have shepherded my project through to completion with a welcome finesse I have never experienced elsewhere; many thanks as well to the exceedingly helpful anonymous reviewers.

Finally, this book is dedicated to two dear friends I have known for much longer than any of those mentioned above. One introduced me to the subject of modern German architecture, and the other ensured that it continued to fascinate me. I first visited many of the buildings in these pages in the summer of 1985 in the company of Oliver Radford. Without him I would have spent my time looking only at medieval cathedrals and Old Master paintings; his enthusiasm (coupled with his driving skills) carried us across the autobahns, bridges, walls, and even farm paths of a still divided country. Friedegund Holzmann walked much of the way to Berlin at the end of the war. Since 1988 her Dahlmannstrasse apartment has been my home there and the perch from which I have joined her in witnessing the latest chapters in the city's history and in trying to make sense of them as they unfolded, while welcoming the next generation of our families into the world.

Notes

Introduction

Except where indicated, translations from German-languages sources are mine.

1. Michael Cullen, *Der Reichstag: Parlament, Denkmal, Symbol* (Berlin: be.bra verlag, 1995), and David Jenkins, ed., *Norman Foster: Works 4* (Munich: Prestel, 2004), 248–351.
2. As quoted in Jenkins, *Norman Foster: Works 4*, 302.
3. Ibid., 259.
4. Ibid.
5. Andreas Huyssen, *Present Pasts: Urban Palimpsests and the Politics of Memory* (Stanford, Calif.: Stanford University Press, 2003), 7, 9. This view is ubiquitous in discussions of Berlin since 1989. Other examples include Lutz Koepnik, "Forget Berlin," *German Quarterly* 74 (2001): 347.
6. As well, one might add, as those that address these buildings as revisions of modernism. See, for instance, Hal Foster, *The Art-Architecture Complex* (New York: Verso, 2011).
7. A key text for such a view is Colin Rowe and Fred Koetter, *Collage City* (Cambridge, Mass.: MIT Press, 1978).
8. For instance, Brian Ladd, *Ghosts of Berlin: Confronting German History in the Urban Landscape* (Chicago: University of Chicago Press, 1998); Jennifer Jordan, *Structures of Memory: Understanding Urban Change in Berlin and Beyond* (Stanford, Calif.: Stanford University Press, 2006); Karen Till, *The New Berlin: Memory, Politics, and Place* (Minneapolis: University of Minnesota Press, 2005); and James E. Young, *At Memory's Edge: After-Images of the Holocaust in Contemporary Art and Architecture* (New Haven, Conn.: Yale University Press, 2002).
9. It has also been important elsewhere. See Mark Crinson, *Stirling and Gowan: Architecture from Austerity to Affluence* (New Haven, Conn.: Yale University Press, 2012), 285.
10. Aldo Rossi, *L'architettura della città* (Padua, Italy: Marsilio, 1966), which appeared in German as *Die Architektur der Stadt: Skizze zu einer grundlegen Theorie des Urbanen*, trans. Arianna Giachi (Düsseldorf: Bauwelt Fundamente, 1973), and in English as *The Architecture of the City*, trans. Diane Ghirardo and Joan Ockman (Cambridge, Mass.: MIT Press, 1982). For the dating of the memory boom to the 1970s see Jeffrey K. Olick, Vered Vinitzky-Seroussi, and Daniel Levy, eds., *The Collective Memory Reader* (Oxford: Oxford University Press, 2011), 3. Rossi is mentioned nowhere in this otherwise comprehensive account.

11. See Marie Moran, *Identity and Capitalism* (London: Sage, 2014), for the recent history of this key word.
12. Contrast the inclusive history told by Wolfgang Pehnt in *Deutsche Architektur seit 1900* (Munich: Deutsche Verlags-Anstalt, 2005) and *Die Architektur des Expressionismus* (Ostfildern: Hatje Cantz, 1998), or in the 1920s in Gustav Adolf Platz, *Die Baukunst der neuesten Zeit* (Berlin: Propyläen Verlag, 1927), with narrower accounts given in Walter Gropius, *Internationale Architektur* (Weimar: Bauhaus Bücher, 1925), Nikolaus Pevsner, *Pioneers of the Modern Movement* (London: Faber & Faber, 1936), and Sigfried Giedion, *Space, Time, and Architecture: The Growth of a New Tradition* (Cambridge, Mass.: Harvard University Press, 1941). Although Frederick Kiesler used this term in *Contemporary Art Applied to the Department Store and Its Display* (New York: Brentano's, 1930), 39, it remains widely associated with Henry-Russell Hitchcock and Philip Johnson, *The International Style* (1932; repr., New York: Norton, 1966).
13. David Kim, *The Traveling Artist in the Italian Renaissance: Geography, Mobility, and Style* (New Haven, Conn.: Yale University Press, 2014), describes this for a different era.
14. For Dresden and Nuremberg, see Susanne Vees-Gulani, "The Politics of New Beginnings: The Continued Exclusion of the Nazi Past in Dresden's Cityscape," in *Beyond Berlin: Twelve German Cities Confront the Holocaust,* ed. Gavriel D. Rosenfeld and Paul B. Jaskot (Ann Arbor: University of Michigan Press, 2008), 25–47; and Paul Jaskot, *The Nazi Perpetrator: Postwar German Art and the Politics of the Right* (Minneapolis: University of Minnesota Press, 2012), 167–204.
15. Paul Fussell, *The Great War and Modern Memory* (New York: Oxford University Press, 2000).
16. Kathleen James-Chakraborty, "Beyond the Wall: Reunifying Berlin," in *Debating German Cultural Identity since 1989,* ed. Anne Fuchs and Kathleen James-Chakraborty (Rochester, N.Y.: Camden House, 2011), 100–116.
17. Maurice Halbwachs, *On Collective Memory,* ed. and trans. Lewis A. Coser (Chicago: University of Chicago Press, 1992); Jan Assmann, "Collective Memory and Cultural Identity," *New German Critique* 65 (1995): 125–33; and Aleida Assmann, *Der lange Schatten der Vergangenheit: Erinnerungskultur und Geschichtspolitik* (Munich: C. H. Beck, 2014). See also David Lowenthal, *The Past Is a Foreign Country* (Cambridge: Cambridge University Press, 1985), and Lowenthal, *The Heritage Crusade and the Spoils of History* (Cambridge: Cambridge University Press, 1996), as well as Anne Fuchs, Mary Cosgrove, and Georg Grote, *German Memory Contests: The Quest for Identity in Literature, Film, and Discourse since 1990* (Rochester, N.Y.: Camden House, 2010).
18. "Das Gutenberghaus," *Blätter für Architektur und Kunsthandwerk* 17 (1904): 91 and Plate 120; and "Geschäftshaus Rudolf Mosse," *Berliner Architekturwelt* 7 (1905): 95–96 and Figures 140–43.
19. Joseph Siry, *The Chicago Auditorium Building: Adler and Sullivan's Architecture and the City* (Chicago: University of Chicago Press, 2004); and Leonard Eaton, *American Architecture Comes of Age: European Reaction to H. H. Richardson and Louis Sullivan* (Cambridge, Mass.: MIT Press, 1972).

20. Kathleen James, *Erich Mendelsohn and the Architecture of German Modernism* (Cambridge: Cambridge University Press, 1997), 88–102; and Sabine Hake, *Topographies of Class: Modern Architecture and Mass Society in Weimar Berlin* (Ann Arbor: University of Michigan Press, 2008), 181–96.
21. Manfredo Tafuri and Francesco Dal Co, *Modern Architecture*, trans. Robert Erich Wolf (New York: Rizzoli, 1986), 143; and Maud Lavin, *Cut with the Kitchen Knife: The Weimar Photomontages of Hannah Hoch* (New Haven, Conn.: Yale University Press, 1993).
22. For the destruction that did occur and its impact on the New Building see Susan Henderson, "Ernst May and the Campaign to Resettle the Countryside: Rural Housing in Silesia, 1919–1925," *Journal of the Society of Architectural Historians* 61 (2002): 188–211.
23. An important early exploration of this theme can be found in Barbara Miller Lane, *Architecture and Politics in Germany, 1918–1945*, rev. ed. (Cambridge, Mass.: Harvard University Press, 1985).
24. The coupling of pre– and post–World War I examples is an important theme of Geoff Eley, Jennifer L. Jenkins, and Tracie Matysik, *German Modernities from Wilhelm to Weimar: A Contest of Futures* (London: Bloomsbury, 2016).
25. Pehnt, *Deutsche Architektur seit 1900* and *Die Architektur des Expressionismus*.
26. William Jordy, "The Symbolic Essence of Modern European Architecture of the Twenties and Its Continuing Influence," *Journal of the Society of Architectural Historians* 22 (1963): 177–87. See also Adrian Forty, *Objects of Desire: Design and Society since 1750* (London: Thames and Hudson, 1986).
27. Alan Colquhoun, *Modern Architecture* (Oxford: Oxford University Press, 2002), 9.
28. Rolf J. Goebel, "Berlin's Architectural Citations: Reconstruction, Simulation, and the Problem of Historical Authenticity, *PMLA* 118 (2003): 1268–89, recognizes the importance of this church for postunification architecture in the city.
29. For an exception see Rosenfeld and Jaskot, *Beyond Berlin*.
30. Aleida Assmann, "Rekonstruktion—Die zweite Chance; oder, Architektur aus dem Archiv," in *Geschichte der Rekonstruktion: Konstruktion der Geschichte*, ed. Winfried Nerdinger with Markus Eisen and Hilde Strobl (Munich: Prestel, 2011), 16.

1. Making German Architecture Modern

1. David Gordon Smith and Josie Le Blond, "Germany Shocked by 'Disproportionate' Action in Stuttgart," *Spiegel Online International*, 1 October 2010.
2. Ibid.
3. Roland Nelles, "Merkel's Water Cannon Politics," *Spiegel Online International*, 1 October 2010.
4. Kate Connelly, "Why German Trains Don't Run on Time Any More," *Guardian*, 11 June 2016.
5. Nikolaus Pevsner, *Pioneers of the Modern Movement* (London: Faber & Faber, 1936); Giedion, *Space, Time, and Architecture*, downplayed expressionism; for accounts that include it see Karl-Heinz Hüter, *Architektur in Berlin 1900–1933* (Stuttgart: Kohlhammer, 1989), and Pehnt, *Deutsche Architektur seit 1900*.

6. Norbert Huse, *"Neues Bauen" 1918–1933: Moderne Architektur in der Weimarer Republik* (Munich: Moos, 1975).
7. Joan Campbell, *The German Werkbund: The Politics of Reform in the Applied Arts* (Princeton, N.J.: Princeton University Press, 1978); Frederic J. Schwarz, *The Werkbund: Design Theory and Mass Culture before the First World War* (New Haven, Conn.: Yale University Press, 1996); and John Maciuika, *Before the Bauhaus: Architecture, Politics, and the German State, 1890–1920* (Cambridge: Cambridge University Press, 2008). See also Kevin Repp, *Reformers, Critics, and the Paths of German Modernity: Anti-Politics and the Search for Alternatives, 1890–1914* (Cambridge, Mass.: Harvard University Press, 2000).
8. Ferdinand Tönnies, *Community and Society*, trans. Jose Harris and Margaret Hollis (Cambridge: Cambridge University Press, 2001).
9. Johannes van Acken, *Christozentrische Kirchenkunst: Ein Entwurf zum liturgischen Gesamtkunstwerk* (Gladbeck: A. Theben, 1923).
10. Wulf Herzogenrath, Dirk Teuber, and Angelika Thiekötter, eds., *Der westdeutsche Impuls 1900–1914: Kunst und Umweltgestaltung im Industriegebiet; Die Deutsche Werkbund Ausstellung Köln 1914* (Cologne: Kölnischer Kunstverein, 1984).
11. Pevsner, *Pioneers of Modern Design: From William Morris to Walter Gropius* (New York: Museum of Modern Art, 1949), 135.
12. Karin Wilhelm, "Die 'Musterfabrik'—Büro und Fabrikgebäude von Walter Gropius," in Herzogenrath, Teuber, and Thiekötter, *Der westdeutsche Impuls*, 143–54. See also Karin Wilhelm, *Walter Gropius, Industriearchitekt* (Braunschweig: Vieweg, 1983), 50–59. Reyner Banham, *A Concrete Atlantis: U.S. Industrial Building and European Modern Architecture* (Cambridge, Mass.: MIT Press, 1986); Kathleen James-Chakraborty, *German Architecture for a Mass Audience* (London: Routledge, 2000), 30–31. For the Wasmuth Portfolio see Anthony Alofsin, *Frank Lloyd Wright: The Lost Years, 1910–1922* (Chicago: University of Chicago Press, 1993), 1–3. See Reginald Isaacs, *Walter Gropius: An Illustrated Biography of the Creator of the Bauhaus* (Boston: Little, Brown, 1991), 25, and Anthony Alofsin, "Frank Lloyd Wright und das Bauhaus," in *Bauhaus Global: Gesammelte Beiträge der Konferenz Bauhaus global vom 21. bis 26. September 2009*, ed. Bauhaus Archiv Berlin (Berlin: Mann Verlag, 2010), 49–54, for dismissals of Meyer's contribution, and Annemarie Jaeggi, *Adolf Meyer—der zweite Mann: Ein Architekt im Schatten von Walter Gropius* (Berlin: Argon, 1994), for a convincing counterargument. Isaacs's argument is undoubtedly based upon Gropius's letter to Vincent Scully of 31 January 1962, a copy of which can be found in carton 11, Reginald Isaacs Papers, Archives of American Art, Washington, D.C. Gropius spent the last years of his life trying to adjust the historical record in multiple ways in order to enhance the importance of what he had accomplished in Germany.
13. Adolf Behne, "Die Kölner Werkbundausstellung," *Die Gegenwart* 86 (1914): 503–4, as cited in Katherine Kuenzli, "Architecture, Individualism and Nation: Henry van de Velde's 1914 Werkbund Theater Building," *Art Bulletin* 94 (2012): 251–73.
14. Kuenzli, "Architecture, Individualism and Nation"; and Klaus-Jürgen Sembach and Birgit Schulte, eds., *Henry van de Velde: Ein europäischer Künstler seiner Zeit* (Cologne: Wienand, 1992).

Notes to Chapter 1

15. Erich Mendelsohn to Luise Maas, 14 September 1914, in *Eric Mendelsohn: Letters of an Architect,* ed. Oscar Beyer (London: Abelard-Schuman, 1967), 33, and Hans Josef Zechlin, "Über das Organische und das Malerische in der Baukunst," *Neue Bauwelt* 4 (1949): 103.

16. Le Corbusier, *Towards a New Architecture,* trans. Frederick Etchells (New York: Dover 1986), 289; and Walter Gropius, *Monumentale Kunst und Industriebau,* as reprinted in Wilhelm, *Gropius, Industriearchitekt,* 119.

17. See Debora Silverman, *Art Nouveau in Fin-de-Siècle France: Politics, Psychology, and Style* (Berkeley: University of California Press, 1989), for this rosy-eyed view. For a more realistic appraisal see Ursula Muscheler, *Möbel, Kunst und feine Nerven: Henry van de Velde und der Kultus der Schönheit 1895–1914* (Berlin: Berenberg Verlag, 2012).

18. *Henri van de Velde: Theatre Designs 1904–1914* (London: Architectural Association, 1974); and Edward Gordon Craig, *On the Art of the Theatre* (London: William Heinemann, 1911). The Werkbund Theater bears comparison with Heinrich Tessenow's Festhalle completed in Hellerau in 1911 for Jacques Dalcroze, where Adolphe Appia was responsible for the inaugural production, and the Jahrhunderthalle by Max Berg in Breslau, which opened in 1913 with a pageant staged by Max Reinhardt. See James-Chakraborty, *German Architecture for a Mass Audience,* 73–82; and Margaret Maile Petty, "Illuminating the Glass Box: The Lighting Designs of Richard Kelly," *Journal of the Society of Architectural Historians* 66 (2007): 195.

19. Dirk Teuber, "Henry van de Veldes Werkbund Theater: Ein Denkmal für Friedrich Nietzsche," in Herzogenrath, Teuber, and Thiekötter, *Der westdeutsche Impuls,* 115.

20. Historians have been slow to realize this impact. For the evolving view of expressionism and of the place of the Glashaus within it see Denis Sharp, *Modern Architecture and Expressionism* (London: Longman, 1966); Wolfgang Pehnt, *Expressionist Architecture,* trans. J. A. Underwood and Edith Küstner (New York: Praeger, 1973), expanded into *Die Architektur des Expressionismus*; Rosemarie Haag Bletter, "The Interpretation of the Glass Dream—Expressionist Architecture and the History of the Crystal Metaphor," *Journal of the Society of Architectural Historians* 40 (1981): 20–43; and Bletter, "Paul Scheerbart's Architectural Fantasies," *Journal of the Society of Architectural Historians* 34 (1975): 83–97; Kai Gutschow, "From Object to Installation in Bruno Taut's Exhibit Pavilions," *Journal of Architectural Education* 69, no. 3 (2006): 63–70; Dietrich Neumann, "'The Century's Triumph in Lighting': The Luxfer Prism Companies and Their Contribution to Early Modern Architecture," *Journal of the Society of Architectural Historians* 54 (1995): 24–53; and Angelika Thiekötter, ed., *Kristallisationen, Splitterungen: Bruno Tauts Glashaus* (Basel: Birkhäuser, 1993).

21. Angelika Thiekötter, "Der Werkbund und seine Ausstellung," in Herzogenrath, Teuber, and Thiekötter, *Der westdeutscher Impuls,* 78–94; Schwarz, *Werkbund*; and Maciuika, *Before the Bauhaus,* 274–82.

22. As published in translation in *German Expressionism: Documents from the End of the Wilhelmine Era to the Rise of National Socialism,* ed. Rose-Carol Washton Long (Berkeley: University of California Press, 1993), 193, 248.

23. Iain Boyd Whyte, *Bruno Taut and the Architecture of Activism* (Cambridge: Cambridge University Press, 1982); Iain Boyd Whyte, ed., *The Crystal Chain Letters: Architectural*

Fantasies by Bruno Taut and His Circle (Cambridge, Mass.: MIT Press, 1985); Bruno Taut, *Alpine Architecture: A Utopia,* ed. Matthias Schirren (Munich: Prestel, 2004), and Bruno Taut, *Die Stadtkrone* (Jena: E. Diedrichs, 1919).

24. Mies, copy of letter to Gropius, 4 October 1923, container 1; and Mies, copy of letter to van de Velde, 29 September 1923, container 2, Ludwig Mies van der Rohe Papers, Manuscript Division, Library of Congress, Washington, D.C. (hereafter cited as Mies Papers). For more on the relationship between Gropius and van de Velde see Kathleen James-Chakraborty, "Fragile Allianz: Über die Beziehung zwischen Henry van de Velde und Walter Gropius," in *Mythos Bauhaus: Zwischen Selbsterfindung und Enthistorisierung,* ed. Anja Baumhoff and Magdalena Droste (Berlin: Reimer, 2009), 35–52, and Kathleen James-Chakraborty, ed., *Bauhaus Culture: From Weimar to the Cold War* (Minneapolis: University of Minnesota Press, 2006), 26–42.

25. Otto Bartning, copy of letter to Gropius, 2 November 1955, carton 6, Reginald Isaacs Papers.

26. Gropius, copy of letter to Udo Kulturmann, 28 February 1962, carton 11, Reginald Isaacs Papers.

27. Roland May and Wolfgang Voigt, eds., *Paul Bonatz 1877–1956* (Berlin: Wasmuth, 1910).

28. It was included, for instance, in Henry-Russell Hitchcock, *Modern Architecture: Romanticism and Reintegration* (New York: Payson and Clark, 1929), 138, and *Architecture: Nineteenth and Twentieth Centuries* (1958; repr., Harmondsworth: Penguin, 1977), 462. For a contrasting view see H. E., "Zum Tode von Paul Bonatz," *Bauen + Wohnen* 12 (1957): 33.

29. The station is not vernacular, but it nonetheless conforms in many ways to the approach described in Maiken Umbach, *German Cities and Bourgeois Modernism, 1890–1924* (Oxford: Oxford University Press, 2009).

30. Marc Hirschfell, "The Baghdad Station: Oriental Elements in the Stuttgart Railway Station," in May and Voigt, *Paul Bonatz,* 63–68.

31. http://www.bahnprojekt-stuttgart-ulm.de/projekt/stuttgart-filder-s21/neue-bahnhoefe/hauptbahnhof-stuttgart offers a defense of this project; see http://www.kopfbahnhof-21.de for a critique. Both consulted 29 January 2012.

32. Nicolai Ouroussoff, "Last Call for an Elegant Rail Station," *New York Times,* 3 October 2009.

33. James, *Erich Mendelsohn,* 178–93, and Regina Stephan, *Studien zu Waren- und Geschäftshäusern Erich Mendelsohns in Deutschland* (Munich: Tudev, 1992), 108–23.

34. Simone Förster, *Masse braucht Licht: Arthur Kösters Fotografien der Bauten von Erich Mendelsohn; Ein Beitrag zur Geschichte Architekturfotografie der 1920er Jahre* (Berlin: Winter Industries, 2008), 137–49.

35. Erich Mendelsohn, *Amerika: Bilderbuch eines Architekten* (Berlin: Rudolf Mosse, 1926). See also James, *Erich Mendelsohn,* 57–70.

36. Erich Mendelsohn, *Complete Works of the Architect,* trans. Antij Frisch (New York: Princeton Architectural Press, 1992), 9–10, for Mendelsohn on Taut.

37. Gropius to Mies, 4 June and 15 October 1923, container 1, Mies Papers.

38. For Schocken, who was also an important book collector and publisher, see Anthony

Notes to Chapter 1

David, *The Patron: A Life of Salman Schocken, 1877–1959* (New York: Metropolitan Books, 2003). Mendelsohn's death was hardly mentioned in German architectural journals. Oskar Beyer, "Erich Mendelsohn starb vor zehn Jahren," *Baumeister* 60 (1963): 977–84, for the commemoration of the tenth anniversary.

39. "Kaufhaus 'Schocken' in Stuttgart," *Bauwelt* 50 (1959): 941; Stephan, *Studien zu Waren- und Geschäftshäusern Erich Mendelsohns in Deutschland*, 235–47; and Petra Ralle, *Konsequenz Abriss: Das (un)vermeidbare Ende des Kaufhaus Schocken in Stuttgart* (Stuttgart: Hohenheim, 2003).

40. Fachschaft Architektur der TH Stuttgart, "Kaufhaus Schocken in Stuttgart," *Bauwelt* 50 (1959): 1025.

41. Wolfgang Voigt and Hartmut Frank, *Paul Schmitthenner 1884–1972* (Tübingen: Wasmuth: 2003).

42. Egon Eiermann to Prof. Hoss, 16 December 1968, in Südwestdeutschen Archiv für Architektur und Ingenieurbau, Universität Karlsruhe, *Egon Eiermann: Briefe des Architekten 1946–1970* (Stuttgart: Deutsche Verlag, 1994), 146–47; and Werner Hebebrand, "Kaufhaus Schocken in Stuttgart," *Bauwelt* 50 (1959): 1025; "Kaufhaus 'Schocken' in Stuttgart," 941. Eiermann was no fan of department stores. See his letter to Gerber, the Oberbaurat of Heilbronn, 22 June 1951, in Südwestdeutschen Archiv, *Egon Eiermann: Briefe*, 24–25.

43. Robin Schuldenfrei has repeatedly pointed out the luxurious character of much of the New Building. See her "Sober Ornament: Materiality and Luxury in German Modern Architecture and Design," in *Histories of Ornament: From Global to Local*, ed. Alina Payne and Gülru Necipoglu (Princeton, N.J.: Princeton University Press, 2016), 334–48, and "Luxus, Produktion, Reproduktion," in *Mythos Bauhaus: Zwischen Selbsterfindung und Enthistorisierung*, ed. Anja Baumhoff and Magdalena Droste (Berlin: Reimer Verlag, 2009), 70–89.

44. Karin Kirsch, *The Weissenhofsiedlung: Experimental Housing Built for the Deutscher Werkbund, Stuttgart, 1927* (Stuttgart: Deutsche Verlags-Anstalt, 1994); and Richard Pommer and Christian F. Otto, *Weissenhof 1927 and the Modern Movement in Architecture* (Chicago: University of Chicago Press, 1991).

45. Kirsch, *Weissenhofsiedlung*, 47–48. See also Pommer and Otto, *Weissenhof 1927*. Three years earlier Mies had optimistically written, "I view the industrialization of the building trade as the key problem of building in our time. If we achieve this industrialization, then the social, economic, technical and even artistic questions can be resolved relatively easily." Ludwig Mies van der Rohe, "Industrial Building," in *G: An Avant-Garde Journal of Art, Architecture, Design and Film, 1923–26*, ed. Detlef Mertins and Michael W. Jennings (London: Tate Publishing, 2010), 120.

46. Matilda McQuaid and Magdalena Droste, *Lilly Reich Designer* (New York: Museum of Modern Art, 1996); Caroline Constant, *Eileen Gray* (London: Phaidon, 2007); Jennifer Goff, *Eileen Gray: Her Work and Her World* (Dublin: Irish Academic Press, 2015); Mary McLeod, ed., *Charlotte Perriand: An Art of Living* (New York: Harry N. Abrams, 2003), Anne Montfort, ed., *Sonia Delaunay* (London: Tate, 2015); Sigrid Wortmann Weltge, *Women's Work: Textile Art from the Bauhaus* (San Francisco: Chronicle Books, 1993); Ulrike Müller, ed., *Bauhaus Women: Art, Handicraft, Design*

(Paris: Flammarion, 2009); and T'ai Smith, *Bauhaus Weaving Theory: From Feminine Craft to Mode of Design* (Minneapolis: University of Minnesota Press, 2014).
47. Kirsch, *Weissenhofsiedlung*, 62.
48. Christiane Lange, *Ludwig Mies van der Rohe & Lilly Reich: Furniture and Interiors* (Ostfildern: Hatje Cantz Verlag, 2007). See also Kathleen James-Chakraborty, "Ausstellungen erleben: Lilly Reichs Produktdisplays, 1927–1931," in *Sowohl als auch dazwischen: Erfahrungsräume der Kunst,* ed. Jörn Schafaff and Benjamin Wihstutz (Paderborn: Wilhelm Fink, 2015), 56–76.
49. James, *Erich Mendelsohn*, 203.
50. Ibid., 184–85. Many years later, Bonatz would weigh in on Eiermann's design for a department store in Heilbronn. See Egon Eiermann to Fritz Müller, 19 March 1952, in Südwestdeutsche Archiv, *Egon Eiermann: Briefe,* 25.
51. Eric Mumford, *The CIAM Discourse on Urbanism, 1928–1960* (Cambridge, Mass.: MIT Press, 2000), 9–27. *Neues Bauen* was nonetheless the term Gropius used when translating "Congrès Internationale d'Architecture Moderne" from the French. See copy of a draft of a letter he wrote to the organizers of the Milan esposizione triennale internazionale, enclosed in a letter to Mies of 1 February 1933, container 1, Mies Papers.
52. http://www.weissenhof.ckom.de/01_allgemein/index.php?thema=1&kategorie=0&lang=de, consulted 7 February 2012.
53. Förster, *Masse braucht Licht*; Michael Stöneberg, *Arthur Köster: Architekturfotografie 1926–1933; Das Bild vom Neuen Bauen* (Berlin: Gebr. Mann Verlag, 2009); Claire Zimmerman, *Photographic Architecture in the Twentieth Century* (Minneapolis: University of Minnesota Press, 2014).

2. Inserting Memory into Modern Architecture

1. Kristin Feireiss, ed., *Egon Eiermann: Die Kaiser-Wilhelm-Gedächtniskirche* (Berlin: Ernst & Sohn, 1994); and Kai Kappel and the Evangelische Kaiser-Wilhelm-Gedächtnis-Kirchengemeinde Berlin, eds., *Egon Eiermann—Kaiser-Wilhelm-Gedächtnis-Kirche Berlin: 1961/2011* (Lindenberg im Allgau: Kunstverlag Josef Fink, 2011).
2. Ulrich Conrads, "Die neue Kaiser Wilhelm Gedächtnis Kirche in Berlin," *Bauwelt* 53 (1962): 95. Friedrich Fürlinger had established the importance of the area around the church as a substitute for the lost "Mitte" even before the construction of the Wall. See his "Stadtplanung in Berlin," *Bauen + Wohnen* 12 (1957): 230. For more on Conrads and his activities during these years see Stephanie Warnke, *Stein gegen Stein: Architektur und Medien in geteilten Berlin, 1950–1970* (Frankfurt: Campus Verlag, 2009), 186–96.
3. G. E. Kidder Smith, *The New Churches of Europe* (New York: Holt, Rinehart and Winston, 1964), 123.
4. Frederick Kempe, *Berlin 1961: Kennedy, Khrushchev, and the Most Dangerous Place on Earth* (London: Penguin, 2012).
5. Wolfgang Pehnt, "To the Limits of the Rules: Egon Eiermann's Gedächtniskirche in Its Own Day," in Feireiss, *Egon Eiermann,* 7.
6. For an opposing view see Adrian von Buttler, "New Urban Spaces in West Berlin:

Breitscheidplatz and Kulturforum," in *Radically Modern: Urban Planning and Architecture in 1960s Berlin,* ed. Thomas Köhler and Ursula Müller (Tübingen: Wasmuth, 2015), 65.

7. Südwestdeutschen Archiv, *Egon Eiermann: Briefe,* 124.
8. Kai Kappel, *Memento 1945? Kirchenbau aus Kriegsruinen und Trümmersteinen* (Munich: Deutsche Kunstverlag, 2007). For the Kaiser Wilhelm Memorial Church in particular see 136–44.
9. *Germany Reports* (Bonn: Press and Information Office of the German Federal Government, 1953), 287–90; *Modern Architecture in Germany,* intro. Ulrich Conrads, trans. James Palmes (London: Architectural Press, 1962), 202–9; Wolfgang Pehnt, *German Architecture 1960–1970* (New York: Praeger, 1970), 207–27. See also Dennis L. Bark and David R. Gress, *A History of West Germany 1945–1963: From Shadow to Substance* (Oxford: Basil Blackwell, 1989), 145–54; and *Modern Churches in Germany* (Dublin: Municipal Gallery, 1962), the catalog of an exhibition that had an attendance of forty-three thousand and a major impact upon subsequent Catholic church design in Ireland.
10. W. G. Sebald, *On the Natural History of Destruction* (London: Hamish Hamilton, 2003). These buildings should also be viewed in the context of new scholarship about the impact upon architecture of World War II. See in particular Jean-Louis Cohen, *Architecture in Uniform: Designing and Building for the Second World War* (Paris: Éditions Hazan, 2011); Beatriz Colomina, *Domesticity at War* (Cambridge, Mass.: MIT Press, 2007); Sheila Crane, *Mediterranean Crossroads: Marseilles and Modern Architecture* (Minneapolis: University of Minnesota Press, 2011); and Andrew Shanken, *194x: Architecture, Planning, and Consumer Culture on the American Home Front* (Minneapolis: University of Minnesota Press, 2009).
11. Max Taut to Mies, 30 June 1948, carton 7, Mies Papers. See also Südwestdeutschen Archiv, *Egon Eiermann: Briefe,* 7–9.
12. Jeffry M. Diefendorf, *In the Wake of War: The Reconstruction of German Cities after World War II* (Oxford: Oxford University Press, 1993); Werner Durth and Niels Gutschow, *Träume in Trümmern: Planung zum Wiederaufbau zerstörter Städte im Westen Deutschlands 1940–1950* (Braunschweig: F. Vieweg & Sohn, 1988); and Klaus von Beyme et al., eds., *Neue Städte aus Ruinen: Deutscher Städtebau der Nachkriegszeit* (Munich: Prestel, 1991).
13. Benedikt Boucsein, *Graue Architektur* (Cologne: Walther König Verlag, 2010).
14. Pamela M. Potter, *The Art of Suppression: Confronting the Nazi Past in Histories of the Visual and Performing Arts* (Berkeley: University of California Press, 2016); and John Zukowsky, ed., *The Many Faces of Modern Architecture: Building in Germany between the World Wars* (Munich: Prestel, 1994), for two accounts that challenge the primacy of state architecture to interpretations of Third Reich architecture as a whole; see Deborah Ascher Barnstone, *The Transparent State: Architecture and Politics in Postwar Germany* (London: Routledge, 2005), 61–86, on the Bundeshaus in Bonn.
15. Greg Castillo, "Making a Spectacle of Restraint: The Deutschland Pavilion at the 1958 Brussels Exhibition," *Journal of Contemporary History* 47, no. 1 (2011): 97–119; and Greg Castillo, *Cold War on the Home Front: The Soft Power of Midcentury Domesticity* (Minneapolis: University of Minnesota Press, 2010), 183–88.

16. Paul Betts, "The Bauhaus as Cold War Legend: West German Modernism Revisited," *German Politics and Society* 14 (1996): 75–100; and Paul Betts, *The Authority of Everyday Objects: A Cultural History of West German Industrial Design* (Berkeley: University of California Press, 2004).
17. At the time, these churches fell outside the definition of a historic monument. See Françoise Choay, *The Invention of the Historic Monument,* trans. Lauren O'Connell (Cambridge: Cambridge University Press, 2001), 82–116.
18. Frederic Spotts, *The Churches and Politics in Germany* (Middletown, Conn.: Wesleyan University Press, 1973), 48–50; Maria D. Mitchell, *The Origins of Christian Democracy: Politics and Confession in Modern Germany* (Ann Arbor: University of Michigan Press, 2012), 33–35.
19. Jürgen Joedicke, "Kirchenbau in unserer Zeit," *Bauen + Wohnen* 13 (1958): 354.
20. Ibid., 357.
21. Robert P. Ericksen, *Complicity in the Holocaust: Churches and Universities in Nazi Germany* (Cambridge: Cambridge University Press, 2011), 24–60, 94–138; on the importance of community in German church design during the Weimar Republic, Kathleen James-Chakraborty, *German Architecture for a Mass Audience* (London: Routledge, 2000), 41–69.
22. Spotts, *Churches and Politics in Germany,* 47–88, and Mitchell, *The Origins of Christian Democracy,* 33–55.
23. Jörg Arnold, *The Allied Air War and Urban Memory: The Legacy of Strategic Bombing in Germany* (Cambridge: Cambridge University Press, 2011), 90.
24. Neil Gregor, *Haunted City: Nuremberg and the Nazi Past* (New Haven, Conn.: Yale University Press, 2008), 80; Norbert Frei, *Adenauer's Germany and the Nazi Past: The Politics of Amnesty and Integration,* trans. Joel Golb (New York: Columbia University Press, 2002), 94–99, 110, 113, 184.
25. Frei, *Adenauer's Germany,* 99; and Ericksen, *Complicity in the Holocaust,* 170–79, who notes, "Postwar Germany almost immediately and almost entirely jettisoned the Nazi ideology. In other words, despite whatever problems might have existed in concept or implementation, denazification somehow seems to have achieved its primary goal" (187).
26. Mitchell, *Origins of Christian Democracy,* 73–104.
27. Ronald J. Ross, *Beleaguered Tower: The Dilemma of Political Catholicism in Wilhelmine Germany* (Notre Dame, Ind.: University of Notre Dame Press, 1976); and Margaret Stieg Dalton, *Catholicism, Popular Culture, and the Arts in Germany, 1880–1933* (Notre Dame, Ind.: University of Notre Dame Press, 2005).
28. Jeffrey Herf, *Divided Memory: The Nazi Past in the Two Germanys* (Cambridge, Mass.: Harvard University Press, 1997), 221–24; Bark and Gress, *History of West Germany*; and Gregor, *Haunted City.*
29. Spotts, *Churches and Politics in Germany,* 153, 183–207, 212–13.
30. Pehnt, *German Architecture 1960–70, Deutsche Architektur seit 1900,* and *Rudolf Schwarz und seine Zeitgenossen: Die Plangestalt des Ganzen* (Cologne: Verlag der Buchhandlung Walther König, 2011); see also Wolfgang Pehnt and Hilde Strohl, *Rudolf Schwarz 1897–1961: Architekt einer anderen Moderne* (Ostfildern: Hatje Cantz, 1997).

Notes to Chapter 2

31. G. Kohlhaus, "Kirchenbau gestern und heute," *Bauwelt* 47 (1956): 1204.
32. Robert G. Moeller, *War Stories: The Search for a Usable Past in the Federal Republic of Germany* (Berkeley: University of California Press, 2003); Gregor, *Haunted Cities*; Jaskot, *Nazi Perpetrator*.
33. Unless otherwise noted this account follows Chris Gerbing, *Die Auferstehungskirche in Pforzheim (1945–1948): Otto Bartnings Kirchenbau im Spannungsfeld zwischen Moderne und Traditionalismus* (Regensburg: Schnell + Steiner, 2001); and Kappel, *Memento 1945?*, 200–204. See also Hermann Hampe, "Die erste der deutschen Notkirchen im Montagebau," *Bauwelt* 5 (1950): 61–63; and *Bauwelt* 3 (1948): 439.
34. Hampe, "Die erste der deutschen Notkirchen im Montagebau," 61–62.
35. Ursula Moessner, *Pforzheim Code Yellowfin: Eine Analyse der Luftangriffe 1944–1945* (Sigmaringen: Thorbecke, 1991).
36. Kappel, *Memento 1945?*, 12, notes that salvaged bricks are usually more expensive than new because of the manual labor involved in collecting them, but that may not have been true in the immediate postwar years for the bricks and stones used to construct this church.
37. http://www.otto-bartning.de, consulted 15 February 2012.
38. Wolfgang Jean Stock, ed., *European Church Architecture 1900–1950: Towards Modernity* (Munich: Prestel, 2006), 155. This book and the accompanying volume, *European Church Architecture 1950–2000* (Munich: Prestel, 2003), offer the most recent comprehensive treatment of twentieth-century German church architecture.
39. Hampe, "Die erste der deutschen Notkirchen im Montagebau," 61.
40. The subject of the degree to which Nazi architecture broke with earlier and later German architecture remains a fraught one, with popular belief resolutely diverging from established scholarship. Examples of the latter include Lane, *Architecture and Politics in Germany*; Winfried Nerdinger, ed., *Bauhaus Moderne in Nationalsozialismus* (Munich: Prestel, 1999); and Zukowsky, *The Many Faces of Modern Architecture*, for prewar continuity; Betts, *The Authority of Everyday Objects*, for postwar continuity; and Pehnt, *Deutsche Architektur seit 1900*, for both.
41. Manfred Sack, introduction to Gerhard G. Feldmeyer, *The New German Architecture* (New York: Rizzoli, 1993), 19; echoed in Südwestdeutschen Archiv, *Egon Eiermann: Briefe*, 9–11.
42. Otto Bartning, *Vom neuen Kirchenbau* (Berlin: Bruno Cassirer, 1919).
43. Jürgen Bredow and Helmut Lurch, *Materiellen zum Werk des Architekten Otto Bartning* (Darmstadt: Das Beispiel, 1983); and Stock, *European Church Architecture 1900–1950*, 118–23.
44. Otto Bartning, *Die Stahl Kirche* (New York: Copper and Brass Research Institute, 1930); Albert Christ-Janer and Mary Mix Foley, *Modern Church Architecture: A Guide to the Form and Spirit of 20th Century Religious Buildings* (New York: McGraw-Hill, 1962), 129; JH, "The Church in a Modern World," *Architectural Forum* 109 (December 1958): 82–89; and *German Church Architecture of the 20th Century* (Munich-Zurich: Schnell & Steiner, 1964), unpaginated. See also Christian Welzbacher, *Monumente der Macht: Eine politische Architekturgeschichte Deutschlands 1920–1960* (Berlin: Parthas, 2016), 93–102.

45. Dörte Nicolaisen, *Das andere Bauhaus: Otto Bartning and die Staatliche Bauhochschule Weimar 1926–1930* (Berlin: Kupfergraben, 1996).
46. Hans Schoszberger, "Der Herr Präsident wird 70 Jahre," *Bauwelt* 44 (1953): 295.
47. The web page of the organization credits Bartning with having launched "the moral new beginning" of the organization. http://www.bda-bund.de/der-bda/chronik.html, consulted 31 July 2011.
48. Editorial comment accompanying Otto Bartning, "Vom Bauen," *Werk* 39 (1952): 240.
49. Otto Bartning and Willy Weyres, *Kirchen: Handbuch für den Kirchenbau* (Munich: G. D. W. Callway, 1959).
50. Otto Bartning, ed., *Darmstädter Gespräche ("Mensch und Raum")* (Darmstadt: Neue Darmstädter Verlag, 1952); and Ulrich Conrads and Peter Neitzke, eds., *Mensch und Raum: Das Darmstädter Gespräche 1951* (Wiesbaden: Vieweg + Taubner, 1991). See also Martin Heidegger, "On Dwelling," in *Rethinking Architecture*, ed. Neil Leach (London: Routledge, 1997), 100–124; and Günter Figal, ed., *The Heidegger Reader* (Bloomington: Indiana University Press, 2009).
51. Kappel, *Memento 1945?*, 235–41; Pehnt and Strohl, *Rudolf Schwarz*, 70–77, 126, 146–49; Pehnt, *Die Plangestalt des Ganzen*, 64–84; and Richard Kieckhefer, *Theology in Stone: Church Architecture from Byzantium to Berkeley* (Oxford: Oxford University Press, 2004), 229–64. For the continued high regard shown for the Aachen church in postwar Germany see Joedicke, "Kirchenbau in unserer Zeit."
52. Rudolf Schwarz, *Kirchenbau: Welt vor der Schwelle* (Heidelberg: F. H. Kerle Verlag, 1960), 225.
53. Romano Guardini, *The Spirit of the Liturgy* (London: Sheed and Ward, 1937).
54. Schwarz to Mies, 9 October 1948, container 53, Mies Papers. The Mies Papers are full of evidence of the men's mutual respect. For instance, on 4 September 1947, Alfons Leitl wrote Mies to tell him of the warm words Schwarz had spoken about him at a Cologne meeting reestablishing the Werkbund; container 5, Mies Papers. See also Detlef Mertins, *Mies* (London: Phaidon, 2014), 134–35, 157–61, 398–99, 417–18.
55. Schwarz, *Kirchenbau*, 233.
56. *Modern Architecture in Germany*, 206–7; Peter Hammond, ed., *Towards a Church Architecture* (London: Architectural Press, 1962), 129; Robert Maguire and Keith Murray, *Modern Churches of the World* (London: Studio Vista Limited, 1965), 82–95; Joseph Picard, *Modern Church Architecture*, trans. Ellen Callmann (New York: Orion Press, 1960), 87–89; and Kidder Smith, *New Churches of Europe*, 160–71. For an enthusiastic American report on German churches, although it does not include this particular Schwarz church, see also John Burchard, *The Voice of the Phoenix: Postwar Architecture in Germany* (Cambridge, Mass.: MIT Press, 1966), 122–35.
57. Kidder Smith, *New Churches of Europe*, 164.
58. Ulrich Conrads, Magdalena Droste, and Winfried Nerdinger, eds., *Die Bauhaus-Debatte 1953: Dokumente einer verdrängten Kontroverse* (Braunschweig/Wiesbaden: Vieweg, 1994).
59. Rudolf Schwarz, "Bilde Künstler, rede nicht," in ibid., 44–45.
60. *Bauwelt* 49 (1958), cunningly paired "Walter Gropius 75 Jahre Alt," 442, with Rudolf Schwarz, "Kirche zum Heiligen Kreuz in Bottrop/Westfalen," 448–50. See also Ulrich Conrads, "Gedenken an Rudolf Schwarz," *Bauwelt* 52 (1961): 460.

Notes to Chapter 2

61. The January issue of *Baumeister* 49 (1952) featured an article and a number of churches by Steffann, including one designed in collaboration with Schwarz.
62. Schwarz to Mies, 21 May 1947, container 53, Mies Papers.
63. Schwarz to Mies, 9 October 1948, container 53, Mies Papers. Mies for his part telegrammed Schwarz's widow, Maria, on 21 April 1961, saying, "I am deeply erschuettert over the news of the death of your husband, my old friend, a deep thinker and great artist"; container 53, Mies Papers.
64. Rudolf Schwarz with an introduction by Ludwig Mies van der Rohe, *The Church Incarnate: The Sacred Function of Christian Architecture* (Chicago: Regnery Press, 1958).
65. Hans-Peter Schwarz, *Adenauer: Der Aufstieg 1876–1952* (Stuttgart: Deutsche Verlags-Anstalt, 1986), and *Adenauer: Der Staatsmann 1952–1967* (Stuttgart: Deutsche Verlags-Anstalt, 1991). See also Jeffrey Herf, *Divided Memory*, 209–26.
66. Pehnt and Strohl, *Rudolf Schwarz*, 79–111. Schwarz wrote Mies afterward: "It was clear to me in the first months of the war, what must happen, and I prepared for it with zeal like a student for a big exam. Luckily, although I had already been denounced in Aachen for political unreliability and was being watched by the Gestapo, I was charged with the reconstruction of a large area that included Maginot-Linie, Lorraine, the Pfalz, and the Saar region." He added that he didn't regret the year afterward he spent in jail reading Goethe. Schwarz to Mies, 21 May 1947, container 53, Mies Papers.
67. Schwarz to Mies, 21 May 1947, container 53, Mies Papers.
68. This account of the original building follows Vera Frowein-Ziroff, *Die Kaiser Wilhelm-Gedächtniskirche: Entstehung und Bedeutung* (Berlin: Gebr. Mann, 1982), 312–20, for the funding, and Günther Kühne, "Die Zukunft der Kaiser Wilhelm Gedächtniskirche," *Bauwelt* 48 (1957): 315, for that of its successor. See also Markus Dröge, "Das geknickte Rohr wird er nicht zerbrechen," in Kappel and the Evangelische Kaiser-Wilhelm-Gedächtnis-Kirchengemeinde Berlin, *Egon Eiermann*, 4, which highlights its importance as a memorial against war and destruction, as does Horst Gunter, "Church Life," in Feireiss, *Egon Eiermann*, 73, who also points out (80) that Eiermann's building was funded in part by the conservative publisher Axel Springer.
69. Leonard Eaton, *American Architecture Comes of Age: European Reaction to H. H. Richardson and Louis Sullivan* (Cambridge, Mass.: MIT Press, 1972); Barbara Miller Lane, *National Romanticism in Germany and the Scandinavian Countries* (Cambridge: Cambridge University Press: 2000), 73–78, 202–6, 214–15.
70. James O'Gorman, *H. H. Richardson: Architectural Forms for an American Society* (Chicago: University of Chicago Press, 1987).
71. Peter Hutter, *"Die feinste Barberei": Das Völkerschlachtdenkmal bei Leipzig* (Mainz: P. von Zabern, 1990); and Julius Posener, *Berlin auf dem Wege zu einer neuen Architektur: Das Zeitalter Wilhelms II* (Munich: Prestel, 1979). See also Lane, *National Romanticism*, 223–28.
72. "The Sedan Celebration," *New York Times*, 2 September 1895.
73. As quoted in Frowein-Ziroff, *Die Kaiser Wilhelm-Gedächtniskirche*, 317.
74. He particularly despised Peter Behrens's German Embassy in St. Petersburg. See Olaf Asendorf, Wolfgang Voigt, and Wilfried Wang, *Botschaften: 50 Jahre Auslandsbauten der Bundesrepublik Deutschland* (Bonn: Bundesamt für Bauwesen und Raumordnung, 2000), 78.

75. Frowein-Ziroff, *Die Kaiser Wilhelm-Gedächtniskirche,* 333–35; and Enno Kaufhold and Jürgen Hohmuth, *Berlin Zeitsprünge: Die Entwicklung der Stadt* (Berlin: Nicolai, 2010), 153–56.
76. Walter Maas, *Der Aachener Dom* (Cologne: Greven, 1984), 19–20.
77. Frederic Schwartz, *The Werkbund: Design Theory and Mass Culture before the First World War* (New Haven, Conn.: Yale University Press, 1996).
78. Jacobi's opposition to the regime was a frequent topic of *New York Times* dispatches from Berlin from 1933 until 1937. See also Marc Zirlewagen, "Jacobi, Gerhard," in *Biographisch-Bibliographisches Kirchenlexikon,* 37 vols. (Nordhausen: Bautz, 2005), 24:887–92; and Kappel, *Memento 1945?,* for the degree to which pastors and priests who had opposed the Third Reich disproportionately numbered among the leaders of congregations in which ruins of prewar churches were preserved.
79. Hans Eckstein, "Zur Würdigung und Kritik des Gedächtniskirchen-Wettbewerbs," *Bauen + Wohen* 12 (1957): 211–13; and F. Müller-Merkstein, "Notwendige Worte zu Frage 'Gedächtniskirche,'" *Bauen + Wohnen* 12 (1957): 168–70, for two early expressions in the architectural literature of this memorial function.
80. [Günter] P[ohl], "Um die Kaiser-Wilhelm-Gedächtniskirche in Berlin," *Baumeister* 53 (1956): 174, which reprints remarks that appeared on 15 January 1956 in the popular publication *Die Welt am Sonntag.*
81. C.-H. Schwennicke, "Der Turm," undated clipping, Eiermann Papers, Südwestdeutschen Archiv für Architektur und Ingenieurbau, University of Karlsruhe, equates democracy with the effectiveness of the protests against the proposed demolition.
82. Eiermann to Elisabeth Kaufmann, 14 February 1958, Eiermann Papers.
83. Warnke, *Stein gegen Stein,* 220–31.
84. Gregor, *Haunted City,* 4, 13.
85. Kaufhold and Hohmuth, *Berlin Zeitsprünge,*153–56, and Karl-Heinz Metzger and Ulrich Dunker, *Der Kurfürstendamm: Leben und Mythos des Boulevards in 100 Jahren deutscher Geschichte* (Berlin: Konopka, 1986), 38–44, 225–28.
86. "Berlin to Rebuild War-Torn Memorial Church," *New York Times,* 10 April 1954, reported that this scheme would seat fifteen hundred worshippers and cost five hundred thousand dollars, a quarter of what a more accurate reconstruction would require, and a third of what a subsequent article ("Cornerstone Laid for Berlin Church," *New York Times,* 10 May 1959, 86) described as the price tag for Eiermann's building. The church was hoping for American donations. Jacobi was quoted as saying, "The tower should remain in its present form for two or three decades as a reminder of the heavy fate which befell Berlin."
87. Günter Pohl, "Der Wettbewerb für den Neubau der Kaiser-Wilhelm-Gedächtniskirche in Berlin," *Kunst und Kirche* 20, no. 2 (1957): 52.
88. This account is based largely on articles published in the journal *Bauwelt* between 1947 and 1962. For Bartning's presence on the jury, see "Kaiser-Wilhelm-Gedächtniskirche," *Bauwelt* 47 (1956): 1114; for the Matthäuskirche see Kappel, *Memento 1945?,* 268–70; Wulf Schirmer, *Egon Eiermann 1904–1970: Bauten und Projekte* (Stuttgart: Deutsche Verlags-Anstalt, 2002), 105–8; and Wulf Schirmer, "Die Matthäuskirche in Pforzheim," *Bauwelt* 44 (1953): 754. Critics at the time also noted the

Notes to Chapter 2

importance of Eiermann's entry in the 1953 competition for the St. Nikolai Church in Hamburg. See Shirmer, *Egon Eiermann*, 112–13, and Kühne, "Die Zukunft der Kaiser-Wilhelm-Gedächtniskirche," 314. The fullest account of the competition appears in Pohl, "Der Wettbewerb," 50–64.

89. Kühne, "Die Zukunft der Kaiser-Wilhelm-Gedächtniskirche," 313–17; and U[lrich] C[onrads], "Zweierlei Maß," *Bauwelt* 48 (1957): 854–55. See also "Berlin Protests Plan to Raze Kaiser Wilhelm Church," *New York Times,* 23 March 1957, 21, and Frohwein-Ziroff, *Die Kaiser Wilhelm Gedächtniskirche,* 338. Eiermann and his supporters maintained that some of the damage had been done by the publication of an unflattering photograph of his model. See Eiermann to Heinzel, 10 April 1957, Eiermann Papers.

90. Kühne, "Die Zukunft der Kaiser-Wilhelm-Gedächtniskirche," 316; for Brandt's comments see Uwe A. Oster, "Streit um die Gedächtniskirche: Rettet den Turm!," *Damals,* http://www.damals.de/de/16/Rettet-den Turm.html?issue=116916&aid=116879&cp=1&action=show, consulted 6 October 2011. See Hilde Hermann, "Echtes und falsches Ärgernis," *Echo der Zeit,* 14 April 1957, clipping, Eiermann Papers, for an argument for the demolition of the steeple, which criticized the representation of those who wrote in to save it as representing the majority of Berliners.

91. Mies wrote about Eiermann and Otto Firle in an affidavit to Hannes Luerhsen dated 6 October 1950, stating that they "both play an important part in the architectural development of Europe today and are professionals of high standing." Container 5, Mies Papers. See also Südwestdeutschen Archiv, *Egon Eiermann: Briefe,* 46.

92. Hans Eckstein, "Egon Eiermann zum 60. Geburtstag," *Bauen + Wohnen* 19 (1964):15.

93. Winfried Nerdinger, "Bauhaus Architecture in the Third Reich," in James-Chakraborty, *Bauhaus Culture,* 139–52. For Eiermann's own view see Südwestdeutschen Archiv, *Egon Eiermann: Briefe,* 28–31. See also Welzbacher, *Monumente der Macht,* 201–39.

94. Südwestdeutschen Archiv, *Egon Eiermann: Briefe,* 87.

95. Ibid., 158.

96. Günther Kohlhaus, "Der kirchliche Raum in Gestalt und Bedeutung," *Bauwelt* 47 (1956): 1010. See also Immo Boyken et al., *Egon Eiermann 1904–1970: Bauten und Projekte* (Stuttgart: Deutsche Verlags-Anstalt, 1984); Annemarie Jaeggi, ed., *Egon Eiermann (1904–1970): Architect and Designer* (Ostfildern: Hatje Cantz Verlag, 2004); and Südwestdeutschen Archiv, *Egon Eiermann: Briefe,* 240.

97. Castillo, "Making a Spectacle of Restraint," 97–119; and Paul B. Jaskot, *The Architecture of Oppression: The SS, Forced Labor and the Nazi Monumental Building Economy* (London: Routledge, 2000), 34–46.

98. J. Alexander, Jerry Hecht, and Immo Boyken, *Egon Eiermann, German Embassy, Washington* (Stuttgart: Edition Axel Menges, 2005).

99. P[ohl], "Um die Kaiser-Wilhelm-Gedächtniskirche in Berlin," 174.

100. Richard Evans, *The Third Reich in Power* (London: Penguin, 2005), 220–33.

101. "Eiermann: 'Ein fauler Zahn,'" *Der Tag,* 2 April 1957, clipping, Eiermann Papers.

102. Spotts, *Churches and Politics in Germany,* 119.

103. Frei, *Adenauer's Germany and the Nazi Past,* 98; and Ericksen, *Complicity in the Holocaust,* 190–91.

104. Spotts, *Churches and Politics in Germany*, 7, 15, 17, 119–20, 127–29, 255, 294–96, 313; and Gregor, *Haunted City*, 256.
105. Elsewhere, historic congregations occasionally rebuilt on different sites. See Hermann Hampe, "Die neue evangelische Ludwigskirche in Freiburg," *Bauwelt* 45 (1954): 1026–27.
106. H. J. Z[echlin], "Akropolis, Cranach, Schinkel und die Kaiser-Wilhelm-Gedächtniskirche," *Bauwelt* 45 (1954): 251; Hampe, "Die neue evangelische Ludwigskirche in Freiburg," 1026; and Ernst Runge, "Neue Vorschläge zu: 'Rund um den Zoo,'" *Bauwelt* 46 (1955): 230, all comment negatively on the traffic situation surrounding the church.
107. Hans Eckstein, "Zur Würdigung und Kritik des Gedächtniskirchen-Wettbewerbs," *Bauen + Wohnen* 12 (1957): 211; and P[ohl], "Um die Kaiser-Wilhelm-Gedächtniskirche in Berlin," 174.
108. After the erection of the Wall, Dibelius and his successor were barred from entering East Berlin. "Dibelius, 85, Steps Down as Berlin's Lutheran Head," *New York Times*, 11 April 1966.
109. H. J. Zechlin, "Der Werkbund und die Kaiser-Wilhelm-Gedächtniskirche," *Neue Bauwelt* 5 (1950): 819; Zechlin, "Die Zukunft der Kaiser-Wilhelm-Gedächtniskirche," *Neue Bauwelt* 7 (1952): 337; and Z[echlin], "Akropolis, Cranach, Schinkel."
110. Gustav Adolf Platz, "Die Gedächtniskirche," *Neue Bauwelt* 2 (1947): 329.
111. Zechlin, "Der Werkbund und die Kaiser-Wilhelm-Gedächtniskirche," 819.
112. Eckstein, "Zur Würdigung und Kritik des Gedächtniskirchen-Wettbewerbs," 211.
113. "Berlin to Rebuild War-Torn Memorial Church," *New York Times*, 10 April 1954, 3; and Z[Echlin], "Akropolis, Cranach, Schinkel," 251.
114. For exceptions, often related to monastic orders see Kappel, *Memento 1945?*, 223–32.
115. r., "Problematik im Kirchenbau," *Baumeister* 52 (1955): 836–39.
116. Z[echlin], "Der Helgoländer Kirchenwettbewerb," *Bauwelt* 48 (1957): 207; and Ulrich Conrads, "Gefallen moderne Kirchen?," *Bauwelt* 50 (1959): 1412.
117. Metzger and Dunker, *Der Kurfürstendamm*, 38–44, 225–28.
118. Pehnt, "To the Limits of the Rules," in Feireiss, *Egon Eiermann*, 9.
119. Eckstein, "Zur Würdigung und Kritik des Gedächtniskirchen-Wettbewerbs," 211.
120. "Nur eine Ruine ...," *Spandauer Volksblatt*, 22 March 1957, clipping, Eiermann Papers.
121. "Wahrzeichen Berlins weicht starrem Beton," *Der Tag*, "Die Gedächtnis-Kirche wird völlig abgerissen," *Berliner Morgenpost*, and Heinz Tiede, "Der Turm verschwindet," *Telegraf*, all 21 March 1957, clippings from Eiermann Papers.
122. "Berlins 'schönste Ruine' muss nun doch verschwinden," *Der Kurier*, 21 March 1957, clipping, Eiermann Papers.
123. "Der Turm muß bleiben!," *Telegraf*, 24 March 1957, clipping, Eiermann Papers.
124. Südwestdeutschen Archiv, *Egon Eiermann: Briefe*, 95.
125. Ibid., 102.
126. Egon Eiermann to Otto Schmidt, editor of *Der Abend*, 22 March 1957, Eiermann Papers.
127. Castillo, *Cold War on the Home Front*.
128. "In Ost-Berlin sieht es anders aus," *Bauwelt* 48 (1957): 580–81, for a West Berlin Cold War perspective.

Notes to Chapter 2

129. Henriette von Preuschen, "Kirchliche Erinnerungsorte in der DDR," in *Moderne Kirchenbauten als Erinnerungsräume und Gedächtnisorte*, ed. Kai Kappel, Matthias Müller, and Felicitas Janson (Regensburg: Schell + Steiner, 2010), 70–78.
130. For examples of Western reactions to these demolitions, see Edgar Wedepohl, "Abbruch des Stadtschlosses Potsdam? Offener Brief an Herrn Oberbürgermeister Paul, Potsdam," *Neue Bauwelt* 4 (1949): 87–89; Erich Schonert, "Was wird aus dem Berliner Schloss," *Neue Bauwelt* 5 (1950): 590–91; "In Ost-Berlin sieht es anders aus," *Bauwelt* 48 (1957): 580–81; "Geradeaus-Moderne," *Bauwelt* 49 (1958): 176–77; and Friedrich Mielke, "Der Wiederaufbau Potsdams und das Stadtschloss," *Bauwelt* 49 (1958): 812–17. See also Detlev Heikapm, "Demolition in Berlin," *Architectural Design* 25 (1986): 52–57.
131. "Eiermann will weiter entwerfen," *Der Kurier*, 4 April 1957, clipping, Eiermann Papers.
132. "Ein einziger Proteststurm geht durch Berlin," *Der Tag*, 23 March 1957, clipping, Eiermann Papers.
133. This was echoed in "An Ost und West," *Telegraf*, 24 March 1957, clipping, Eiermann Papers, where Eiermann's model was compared to a crematorium.
134. "Der Turm muß bleiben!," *Telegraf*, 24 March 1957, clipping, Eiermann Papers. See also C.-H. Schwennicke, "Der Turm," undated clipping, Eiermann Papers.
135. m., "Der umstrittene Turm," *Telegraf*, 2 April 1957, clipping, Eiermann Papers.
136. Eiermann to Pohl, 12 August 1957; Eiermann to Bartning, 2 November 1957; Eiermann to Bartning, 10 March 1958; and Bartning to Eiermann, 12 March 1958; all Eiermann Papers.
137. "Christuskirche in Bochum," *Bauwelt* 50 (1959): 1410–12; "Zwei Beispielen von Kirchen-Neubauten mit erhaltenem neoromanischen Turme," *Bauwelt* 49 (1958): 176; and Kappel, *Memento 1945?*, 132–36. See also Kai Kappel, "Das Ringen um den Neubau—Planungsgeschichte, Wettbewerbe und Presse-Echo," in Kappel and the Evangelische Kaiser-Wilhelm-Gedächtnis-Kirchengemeinde Berlin, *Egon Eiermann*, 23–26, for Eiermann's examination of these churches and of work by Schwarz, and for his conversation with his friend Schneider-Esleben.
138. St. Anna is also featured in "Zwei Beispielen," 175. For St. Bonifatius see Markus Jager, "Einfach zeitlos: St. Bonifatius, Dortmund, 1952–1954 von Emil Steffann," in *Auf den zweiten Blick: Architektur der Nachkriegszeit in Nordrhein-Westfalen*, ed. Sonja Hnilica, Markus Jager, and Wolfgang Sonne (Bielefeld: transcript, 2010), 124–31. See also Kappel, *Memento 1945?*, 188–93.
139. Pehnt, *Deutsche Architektur seit 1900*, 256–78.
140. Anne Fuchs, *After the Dresden Bombing: Pathways of Memory, 1945 to the Present* (Basingstoke: Palgrave Macmillan, 2010), 32–80.
141. Pehnt, "To the Limits of the Rules," in Feireiss, *Egon Eiermann*, 7. See also George Demidowicz and Heather Gilderdale Scott, *St. Michael's Coventry: The Rise and Fall of the Old Cathedral* (London: Scala, 2015); Nigel F. Swift and David Paisey, "Dominikus Böhm, Sir Basil Spence and the Dream in the Dentist's Chair: A German Source for Coventry Cathedral," *German Life and Letters* 64 (2011): 235–54; and Louise Campbell, *Coventry Cathedral: Art and Architecture in Post-war Britain* (Oxford: Clarendon, 1996).

142. D. K., "Jüdisches Gemeindehaus Berlin, Fasanenstraße," *Baumeister* 58 (1961): 96–100.
143. Gavriel D. Rosenfeld, *Building after Auschwitz: Jewish Architecture and the Memory of the Holocaust* (New Haven, Conn.: Yale University Press, 2011), 90–91; Harold Hammer-Schenk, "Die Architektur der Synagoge von 1780 bis 1933," in *Die Architektur die Synagoge,* ed. Hans-Peter Schwarz (Stuttgart: Ernst Klett Verlag, 1988), 265–69; and Salomon Korn, "Synagogenarchitektur in Deutschland nach 1945," in Schwarz, *Die Architektur die Synagoge,* 312–13.
144. For example, U[lrich] C[onrads], "Ceterum," *Bauwelt* 49 (1958): 171–76.
145. Schirmer, *Egon Eiermann,* 164–71.
146. http://www.gedaechtniskirche-berlin.de/KWG/dateien/gebaeude/neuekirche.php, consulted 13 March 2012.
147. Reinhard Gieselmann, *Contemporary Church Architecture* (London: Thames and Hudson, 1972), 12; Schirmer, *Egon Eiermann,* 64; Kai Kappel, "Das Ringen um den Neubau—Planungsgeschichte, Wettbewerbe und Presse-Echo," in Kappel and the Evangelische Kaiser-Wilhelm-Gedächtnis-Kirchengemeinde Berlin, *Egon Eiermann,* 20–21, for exceptions. Pehnt, "To the Limits of the Rules," in Feireiss, *Egon Eiermann,* 12, points to the possibility of Karl Moser's St. Antonius in Basel, downriver far from Eiermann's base in Karlsruhe, as an intermediary source.
148. Hope M. Harrison, *Driving the Soviets up the Wall: Soviet–East German Relations, 1953–1961* (Princeton, N.J.: Princeton University Press, 2005), 96–138.
149. Kempe, *Berlin 1961,* 314.
150. G. Kohlhaus, "Kirchenbau gestern und heute," *Bauwelt* 47 (1956): 1204.
151. Conrads, "Die neue Kaiser Wilhelm Gedächtnis Kirche in Berlin," 95–98. See also Südwestdeutschen Archiv, *Egon Eiermann: Briefe,* 143.
152. Südwestdeutschen Archiv, *Egon Eiermann: Briefe,* 135.
153. See Arnold, *The Allied Air War,* 98–137, for the degree to which such feelings were widespread, particularly in the Federal Republic.
154. Rolf J. Goebel, "Berlin's Architectural Citations: Reconstruction, Simulation, and the Problem of Historical Authenticity," *PMLA* 18 (2003): 1269.
155. This despite what the architect himself would later claim. See Egon Schirmbeck, "Gottfried Böhm: Anmerkungen zum architektonischen Werk," *Bauen + Wohnen* 32 (1977): 421. The visual evidence clearly belies anything Böhm said on the subject, however, as Schirmbeck all but admits later in the article. See also Gieselmann, *Contemporary Church Architecture,* 16–63, for its scale and an important early publication of the building in English.
156. Wolfgang Voigt, ed., *Gottfried Böhm* (Berlin: Jovis, 2007), especially Karl Keim, "The Multi-layered Concrete Rock: The Pilgrimage Church in Neviges," 60–79; and Wolfgang Pehnt, *Gottfried Böhm* (Basel: Birkhäuser, 1999), 75–79.
157. James-Chakraborty, " From Isolationism to Internationalism," in James-Chakraborty, *Bauhaus Culture,* 153–70. See also Schirmbeck, "Gottfried Böhm."
158. H. Klumpp and E. Schirmbeck, "Interview mit Gottfried Böhm," *Bauen + Wohnen* 32 (1977): 427.
159. Josef Cardinal Frings, Einleitung [introduction], *Dominikus Böhm* (Munich: Schell & Steiner, 1962), 11.

Notes to Chapter 3

160. Giles MacDonogh, *After the Reich: From the Liberation of Vienna to the Berlin Airlift* (London: John Murray, 2008), 368–69. For St. Engelbert see Wolfgang Voigt and Ingeborg Flagge, eds., *Dominikus Böhm 1880–1955* (Frankfurt: Deutsches Architektur Museum, 2005), esp. 145–47.
161. Klumpp and Schirmbeck, "Interview mit Gottfried Böhm," 425.
162. Voigt, *Gottfried Böhm*.
163. Van Acken, *Christozentrisches Kirchenkunst*; and Voigt and Flagge, *Dominikus Böhm*.
164. Böhm received the prestigious Pritzger Prize in 1986, but he is far less well known than most others who have garnered this honor.
165. Schirmbeck, "Gottfried Böhm," 422.
166. As quoted in Voigt, *Gottfried Böhm*, 201–4.
167. Kieckhefer, *Theology in Stone*, 280–81.
168. Pehnt, *Gottfried Böhm*, 13.
169. Voigt, *Gottfried Böhm*, 254–55, for a bibliography. See also Edwin Heathcote, *Contemporary Church Architecture* (Chichester, UK: Wiley, 2007), 47–49; and Stock, *European Church Architecture 1900–1950*, 142–45.
170. Conversely, see Lothar Kettenacker, *Germany 1989: In the Aftermath of the Cold War* (New York: Pearson Longman, 2009), for an interpretation that stressed the importance of the Protestant church to the opposition movement in the German Democratic Republic.

3. An Architecture of Fragmentation and Absence

1. Mark Girouard, *Big Jim: The Life and Works of James Stirling* (London: Chatto and Windus, 1998), 209–10.
2. The museum recorded 500,000 visitors within less than four months of its opening; within a year 1,300,000 people came, compared to the 210,000 who had visited the old building in 1982, when the State Gallery ranked eighth among West German art museums in attendance. Gerhard Eigel, "Die Staatsgalerie meldet neuen Besucherrekord," *Stuttgarter Zeitung*, 23 June 1984; and Barbara Erbsen-Haim, "Ungewöhnliches Museum ist ungewöhnlich gefragt," *Cannstatter Zeitung*, 3 June 1985.
3. Heinrich Klotz, *New Museum Buildings in the Federal Republic of Germany* (Frankfurt: DAM, 1985), 7. Pehnt, *Gottfried Böhm*, 31, makes the same point.
4. Wolf Lepenies, *The Seduction of Culture in German History* (Princeton, N.J.: Princeton University Press, 2006), for a critique of this role.
5. André Bideau, *Architektur und symbolisches Kapital: Bilderzählungen und Identitätsproduktion bei O. M. Ungers* (Basel: Birkhäuser, 2012).
6. Ra, "Museumsneubau für Staatsgalerie," *Stuttgarter Zeitung*, 7 September 1976.
7. Wolfgang Rainer, "Feste Zukunft für die Staatsgalerie," *Stuttgarter Zeitung*, 8 September 1976.
8. Klotz, *New Museum Buildings*, 7.
9. James Sheehan, *Museums in the German Art World: From the End of the Old Regime to the Rise of Modernism* (Oxford: Oxford University Press, 2000).
10. Michael Eissenahuer, Astrid Bähr, and Elisabeth Rochau-Schalem, eds., *Museum

Island Berlin (Berlin: Hirmer Publishers, 2012), especially Peter-Klaus Schuster, "Berlin's Museum Island—a German Educational Landscape," 129–55.

11. The Bundestag's Committee for External Cultural Policy was established in 1969 by the new SPD government, as was the independent Zentrum für Kulturforschung. Gerard Braunthal, "The Policy Function of the German Social Democratic Party," *Comparative Politics* 9 (January 1977): 127–45; Gregory Paschalidis, "Cultural Outreach: Overcoming the Past," in *The Routledge Handbook of German Politics and Culture*, ed. Sarah Colvin (Abingdon: Routledge, 2015), 457–72.

12. g, "Als 'kulturelles Jahrhundertwerk' gepriesen," *Schwäbische Zeitung*, 10 March 1984; "Big Jims Bau proviziert Bürger in Stuttgart," *Neue Hannoversche Presse*, 10 March 1984.

13. Gerhard G. Feldmeyer, *The New German Architecture* (New York: Rizzoli, 1993), 13.

14. Rossi, *Architecture and the City*, 130. For a negative assessment of Rossi's discussion of collective memory see Adrian Forty, *Words and Buildings: A Vocabulary of Modern Architecture* (London: Thames and Hudson, 2004), 217–18.

15. Halbwachs, *On Collective Memory*.

16. Manfredo Tafuri, "L'architecture dans le boudoir: The Language of Criticism and the Criticism of Language," *Oppositions* 3 (May 1974): 37–62, and Francesco Dal Co, "Criticism and Design," *Oppositions* 13 (Summer 1978): 17–21.

17. Pierre Nora, ed., *Realms of Memory: The Construction of the French Past*, 3 vols. (New York: Columbia University Press, 1996–98); and Jan Assmann, *Cultural Memory and Early Civilization: Writing, Remembrance, and Political Imagination* (Cambridge: Cambridge University Press, 2011).

18. Gavriel D. Rosenfeld, "The Architect's Debate: Architectural Discourse and the Memory of Modernism in the Federal Republic of Germany, 1977–1997," *History and Memory* 9 (1997): 189–225.

19. Hans Kiener, "Die Alte Pinakothek in München," *Baumeister* 47 (1950): 732. Kiener was the author of *Neue deutsche Baukunst* (Munich: Allgemeine Vereinigung "die Kunst dem Wolfe," 1936) in the Die Kunst dem Volke series. Doris Schmidt, "Das umgebaute Städelsche Kunstinstitut in Frankfurt am Main," *Baumeister* 61 (1964): 1087–95, for the reconstruction of the Städel in Frankfurt, whose unusually clear separation of spaces for permanent and temporary exhibitions may have influenced Mies's New National Gallery.

20. Gavriel D. Rosenfeld, *Munich and Memory: Architecture, Monuments, and the Legacy of the Third Reich* (Berkeley: University of California Press, 2000), esp. 41–45, 186–87; and Klotz, *New Museum Buildings*, 8–11, 37–40.

21. Rüdiger an der Heiden, *Die Alte Pinakothek: Sammlungsgeschichte, Bau und Bilder* (Munich: Hirmer Verlag, 1998).

22. Sheehan, *Museums in the German Art World*, 62.

23. Kappel, *Memento 1945?*, 180–86, 259–63, and 344; and *Das Münster* 27, no. 3 (July 1974): 214.

24. Franz Herre, *Ludwig I: Ein Romantiker auf Bayerns Thron* (Stuttgart: Hohenheim, 2005).

25. "Hanover: Historisches Museum am Hohen Ufer," *Bauwelt* 58 (1967): 217–23; and Klotz, *New Museum Buildings*, 11, 53–56.

Notes to Chapter 3

26. Kidder Smith, *New Churches of Europe,* 130–41; and Kappel, *Memento 1945?,* 85–88.
27. Kappel, *Memento 1945?,* 350.
28. Mertins, *Mies,* 384–99.
29. Winfried Nerdinger, *Bauhaus-Moderne in Nationalsozialismus: Zwischen Anbiederung und Verfolgung* (Munich: Prestel, 1999), 156–65.
30. Philip C. Johnson, *Mies van der Rohe* (New York: Museum of Modern Art, 1947).
31. Wolf Tegethoff, "From Obscurity to Maturity: Mies van der Rohe's Breakthrough to Modernism," in *Mies van der Rohe: Critical Essays,* ed. Franz Schulze (Cambridge, Mass.: MIT Press, 1990), 28–94.
32. Henry B. Ryan, "A New Look at Churchill's 'Iron Curtain' Speech," *Historical Journal* 22 (December 1979): 895–920.
33. Barry Bergdoll and Terrence Reilly, *Mies in Berlin* (New York: Museum of Modern Art, 2002).
34. Frei Otto, "Mies van der Rohe," *Neue Bauwelt* 6 (1951): 594.
35. Text of speech by Friedrich Baron von Lupin, German consul general at Chicago, on 2 April 1959, at the Arts Club of Chicago on the occasion of the presentation of the Commander's Cross of the Order of Merit of the Federal Republic of Germany to Professor Ludwig Mies van der Rohe, 1–2, container 29, Mies Papers.
36. S. Giedion, "Der moralische Einfluß der Architektur Mies van der Rohes," *Bauen + Wohnen* 11 (1956): 228–29.
37. Werner Harting, "Das Mannheimer Nationaltheater und die Baukunst," *Bauwelt* 44 (1953): 401–4; Franz Schulze and Edward Windhorst, *Mies van der Rohe: A Critical Biography* (Chicago: University of Chicago Press, 2012), 313–15.
38. Mies, English draft of German letter to Otto Bartning, 4 July 1955, container 19, Mies Papers.
39. Peter Metz to Mies, 7 April 1961, and Rolf Schwedler to Mies, 6 July 1961, both container 19, Mies Papers.
40. Warnke, *Stein gegen Stein,* 119–40.
41. See Gropius, copy of letter to Serge Chermayeff, 23 March 1950, carton 7, Raymond Isaacs Papers, for critical remarks about Mies's teaching at IIT; Walter and Ise Gropius, telegram to Mies, received 13 September 1968, container 42, Mies Papers, for his praise of the New National Gallery.
42. Gavi Dolff-Bonekämper, "Das Berliner Kulturforum: Architektur als Medium politischer Konflikte," in *Bauten und Orte als Träger von Erinnerung,* ed. Hans-Rudolf Meier and Marion Wohlleben (Zurich: v/d/f: Hochschulverlag AG an der ETH, 2000), 133–43.
43. Hermann G. Pundt, *Schinkel's Berlin: A Study in Environmental Planning* (Cambridge, Mass.: Harvard University Press, 1972); and Barry Bergdoll, *Karl Friedrich Schinkel: An Architecture for Prussia* (New York: Rizzoli, 1994).
44. Robert Frank, *Platz und Monument: Die Kontroverse um das Kulturform Berlin 1980–1992* (Berlin: Reimer, 1992).
45. Siegward Lönnendonker, *Freie Universität Berlin: Gründung einer politischen Universität* (Berlin: FUB, 1987).
46. Jaskot, *Architecture of Oppression,* 87–92.

47. gk, "Das ist die Berliner Luft, Luft, Luft...," *Bauwelt* 56 (1965): 1083.
48. "Art Museum Designed by Mies Is Opened in Berlin," *New York Times,* 16 September 1968, 56; Joachim Jäger, *Neue Nationalgalerie: Mies van der Rohe* (Ostfildern: Hatje Cantz Verlag, 2011), 40–43; and Jean Louis Cohen, *Ludwig Mies van der Rohe* (Basel: Birkhäuser, 2007), 160, the last of whom points to the importance of a proposed museum for Georg Schäfter in Schweinfurt.
49. Mies to Kurt Duebbers, 16 August 1966, container 5, Mies Papers.
50. gk, "Projekt für die Galerie des XX. Jahrhunderts in Berlin," *Bauwelt* 54 (1963): 690.
51. See also Mies to Berlin Senator für Bau- und Wohnungswesen [Schwedler], 7 April 1961, container 19, Mies Papers, and the text located in the folder "Voice of America 1962," container 59, Mies Papers.
52. Steven Moyano, "Schinkel's Art Museum and Prussian Arts Policy," *Art Bulletin* 72 (1990): 585–608.
53. Gerrit Engel, *Berlin Photographs: 234 Berlin Buildings in Chronological Order from 1230 to 2008* (Munich: Schirmer/Mosel, 2009), 189, for the limitations of the space designed for changing exhibitions.
54. Johnson, *Mies van der Rohe,* 49–52.
55. Werner Blaser, *Mies van der Rohe: Crown Hall, Illinois Institute of Technology* (Basel: Birkhäuser, 2001).
56. Jäger, *Neue Nationalgalerie,* 95.
57. "Gehobenes Stahldach," *Bauwelt* 58 (1967): 338.
58. Eckstein, "Zur Würdigung und Kritik des Gedächtniskirchen-Wettbewerbs."
59. "A Latter Day Temple in Berlin," *Architectural Design* 39 (February 1969): 87. For an example of the continuity argument see Günter Kühne, "Pure Form," on 89–90 of the same issue.
60. Mies to Douglas V. Freret, 8 February 1960, container 5, Mies Papers.
61. J. M. Richards, "Mies in Berlin: Criticism," *Architectural Review* 145 (December 1968): 410.
62. Rudolf Fischer, *Licht und Transparenz: Der Fabrikbau und das Neue Bauen in den Architekturzeitschrift der Moderne* (Berlin: Gebr. Mann Verlag: 2012), 173–83.
63. After the war, Schwippert hoped to lure Mies back to Germany with a professorship at a new academy of design under consideration in North Rhine-Westphalia. See Schwippert to Mies, 17 June 1947, container 53, Mies Papers. The two collaborated on an unrealized project for a Krupp administration building in Essen. See the folder "Krupp/Industriebau/1961–64," container 6, Mies Papers.
64. Barnstone, *The Transparent State,* esp. 106–37.
65. Mark Jarzombek, "Mies van der Rohe's New National Gallery and the Problem of Context," *Assemblage* 2 (1987): 32–43.
66. Richards, "Mies in Berlin," 410; and Adrian von Buttler, "New Urban Spaces in West Berlin: Breitscheidplatz and Kulturforum," in *Radically Modern: Urban Planning and Architecture in 1960s Berlin,* ed. Thomas Köhler and Ursula Müller (Tübingen: Wasmuth, 2015), 67.
67. A point made by gk, "Das ist die Berliner Luft," 1083.
68. Ulrich Conrads, "Das andere Mies," *Bauwelt* 59 (1968): 1210–11.

Notes to Chapter 3

69. Although Bideau, *Architektur und symbolische Kapital*, focuses on Frankfurt and Berlin, it remains the best discussion of the phenomenon. Thorsten Rodiek, *James Stirling: Die Neue Staatsgalerie Stuttgart* (Stuttgart: Verlag Gerd Hatje, 1984), 9–10, conveys a sense of the anxiety of keeping up to date.
70. "Die Stadt braucht Monumente," *Stuttgarter Zeitung*, 5 March 1984.
71. "James Stirling: Sa conception du musée," *Techniques et Architecture* 369 (November 1986): 147; and "Die Stadt braucht Monumente."
72. Charles Jencks dated modernism's death to 15 July 1972. See his *The Language of Postmodern Architecture* (New York: Rizzoli, 1977).
73. "James Stirling, The New State Gallery, Stuttgart," *Transactions of the Royal Institute of British Architects* 4, no. 7 (1985): 5. As early as 1953 he had written that "the greatest architect of them all, including the above, would be the one who could combine these tendencies which are splitting the modern movement." "The Black Notebook," in *James Stirling: Early Unpublished Writings on Architecture*, ed. Mark Crinson (London: Routledge, 2010), 34.
74. I thank architect John Tuomey, personal conversation, December 2011, for information regarding Stirling's interest in the Alte Pinakothek.
75. Alan Colquhoun, "Democratic Monument," *Architectural Review* 176 (December 1984): 22; William Curtis, "Virtuosity around a Void," *Architectural Review* 176 (December 1984): 42; and Charles Jencks, "The Casual, the Shocking and the Well Ordered Acropolis," *Architectural Design* 54 (1984): 49.
76. Eva Ruthenfranz, "Ein Kunst-Museum als Wahrzeichen der Stadt," *Art—Das Kunstmagazin* 3 (1984): 6; and Rodiek, *James Stirling*, 28–29. For Düsseldorf see Amanda Reeser Lawrence, *James Stirling: Revisionary Modernist* (New Haven, Conn.: Yale University Press, 2013), 154–85.
77. The account of the competition entries appeared as "Stirling in Germany," *Architectural Review* 160 (1976): 289–95, before being republished in *Lotus International* 15 (1977): 58–79, and as "The Monumental Tradition," *Perspecta* 16 (1980): 32–49. John Tuomey, personal conversation, March 2013, described the Düsseldorf entry as the main point of departure for the Stuttgart design.
78. Bideau, *Architektur und symbolisches Kapital*, 82–85, 125–68; for Stirling on Ungers see "Die Stadt braucht Monumente." See also Florian Hertweck and Sebastian Marot, eds., *The City in the City: Berlin; A Green Archipelago* (Zurich: Lars Müller, 2013); and *O. M. Ungers 1951–1984: Bauten und Projekte* (Braunschweig/Wiesbaden: Fried. Vieweg & Sohn, 1985), 136–55, 186–89. Ungers had been a professor at the technical university in Berlin and was at the demonstration in 1967 at which the police killed Benno Ohnesorg. Hartmut Frank, "Crisis or Sea Change? Architecture Debates in West Berlin 1967/68," in Köhler and Müller, *Radically Modern*, 171–72, argues that Ungers left for Cornell because he had little work.
79. Rob Krier, *Stadtraum in Theorie und Praxis* (Stuttgart: Karl Krämer, 1975). The English translation was published in 1979 by Academy Editions, London, but Stirling would have already seen, or at least heard about, the exhibition of this work at the Art Net Gallery in London in 1975.
80. Mark Crinson, *Stirling and Gowan: Architecture from Austerity to Affluence* (New Haven,

Conn.: Yale University Press, 2012), 181–83, for the relationship between Stirling and the Smithsons.
81. Colquhoun, "Democratic Monument," 19–27; Curtis, "Virtuosity around a Void," 41–47; Jencks, "The Casual, the Shocking and the Well Ordered Acropolis," 49–55; Reyner Banham, "Celebration of the City," *Architectural Review* 176 (December 1984): 33; Peter Cook, "Stirling 3: Stuttgart," *Architectural Review* 173 (March 1984): 31–41; Martin Filler, "Cultural Centering: Neue Staatsgalerie and Chamber Theater," *Architectural Record* 172 (September 1984): 140–49; and Peter Blundell Jones, "Man or Superman," *Architect's Journal* 181 (February 1985): 44–55. This is also true of some later accounts. In a much later narrative Anthony Vidler, *Histories of the Immediate Present: Inventing Architectural Modernism* (Cambridge, Mass.: MIT Press, 2008), 103, adds Colin Rowe and Fred Koetter, *Collage City* (Cambridge, Mass.: MIT Press, 1978), to the largely British lens through which he views the building. For a German perspective see "Erweiterung Staatsgalerie Stuttgart," *Bauen + Wohnen* 33 (1978): 85–88.
82. Cook, "Stirling 3," 34, and Filler, "Cultural Centering," 142.
83. Falk Jaeger, "'Big Jim's' Fanal—ein Kuckucksei?," *Sindelfinger Zeitung*, 29 September 1983.
84. For a German account of the building as postmodern see Vittorio Magnani Lampugnani, "Ergriffenheit, Spott und Jubel: Anmerkung zur Architektur von James Stirling," in *Neue Staatsgalerie und Kammertheater Stuttgart* (Stuttgart: Staatliches Hochbauamt, 1984), 47–64.
85. Manfred Sack, "Das Zitatenmuseum," *Die Zeit*, 9 March 1984.
86. Rosenfeld, "The Architects' Debate," 189–225.
87. Leon Krier, ed., *Albert Speer: Architecture 1932–1942* (Brussels: Archives d'Architecture Moderne, 1985).
88. Eduard Beauchamp, "Konstruktiver Pop," *Frankfurter Allgemeine Zeitung*, 10 March 1984. See also Christian Marquart, "Ende des Burgfriedens," *Stuttgarter Zeitung*, 27 February 1984; Karl-Heinz Krüger, "Mein Gott, es ist Metro-Goldwyn-Mayer," *Der Spiegel*, 5 March 1984; Wolfgang Rainer, "Museum im Disput mit sich selbst," *Stuttgarter Zeitung*, 9 March 1984; and Paul Fecker, "Leserbriefe," *Der Architekt* 11 (1984): 483–84. Not everyone was so positive. Gerd Heene's letter to *Der Architekt* 11 (1984): 483–84, states that details of Stuttgart remind him of the work of Albert Speer and Arno Becker.
89. For the relationship between these events and German art see Alex Denchev, "The Artist and the Terrorist; or, The Paintable and the Unpaintable: Gerhard Richter and the Baader-Meinhof Group," *Alternatives: Global, Local, Political* 35 (2010): 93–112.
90. Ellen Lentz, "High German Aide, an Ex-Nazi, Resigns," *New York Times*, 8 August 1978.
91. Frei Otto, "Brutalismus in Stuttgart," *Stuttgarter Zeitung*, 23 September 1977.
92. For other characterizations of the design as Brutalist see Gisela Linden, "Absage an den kühlen Funktionalismus," *Schwäbische Zeitung*, 29 September 1977, and Walter Scheu, "Seltsamer Entwurf Staatsgalerie," *Stuttgarter Zeitung*, 13 October 1977. The first German use of the term *postmodern* in relation to the building that I have located is Jaeger, "'Big Jim's' Fanal—ein Kuckucksei."

Notes to Chapter 3

93. Günter Behnisch, "Streit um Stirlings Preis," *Frankfurter Allgemeine Zeitung*, 29 December 1977.
94. "Baukunst: 'Ein halbes Jahrhundert annulliert,'" *Der Spiegel*, 7 July 1980, 189; and Eckhardt Leipprand to *Bauwelt* 69 (1978): 501.
95. Anthony Vidler, *James Frazer Stirling: Notes from the Archive* (New Haven, Conn.: Yale University Press, 2010), 202–9, and http://www.cca.qc.ca/en/collection, consulted 29 November 2012.
96. "Die Stadt braucht Monument."
97. James Stirling, "The Monumentality Informal," in *Neue Staatsgalerie und Kammertheater Stuttgart*, 9.
98. "Ich bin kein postmoderner Architekt," *Stuttgarter Nachrichten*, 26 August 1989.
99. The relief is palpable in Matthias Schreibe, "Ein nützliches Kunstwerk," *Frankfurter Allgemeine Zeitung*, 23 December 1983; and Jürgen Joedicke, "Eigentlich hart und streng," *Stuttgarter Zeitung*, 15 March 1984; for dissenting voices see Karl Diemer, "Der Falstaff mit dem grünen Proviantköfferlein," *Sindelfinger Zeitung*, 17 August 1984, and Hans Krehl, "Des Kaisers neue Kleider," *Stuttgarter Zeitung*, 23 March 1984.
100. Sack, "Das Zitatenmuseum."
101. Karl Diener, "Sehr wuchtig und gelungen," *Stuttgarter Nachrichten*, 12 February 1982.
102. Ulrich Wanner, "Museum Gral Panoptikum," *Esslinger Zeitung*, 10 March 1984.
103. John Tuomey, personal conversation, March 2013.
104. "Die Stadt braucht Monument."
105. For examples, see Diane Ghirardo, *Architecture after Modernism* (London: Thames and Hudson, 1996).
106. Jencks, "The Casual, the Shocking and the Well Ordered Acropolis," 50.
107. Sack, "Das Zitatenmuseum." Weinbrenner's design for a memorial tomb for Frederick the Great was, according to Tuomey, Stirling's favorite plate from *Dortmunder Architekturausstellung 1977: Fünf Architekten des Klassizismus in Deutschland* (Dortmund: Abt. Bauwesen der Universität Dortmund, 1977), 169, plate 37.
108. Wolfgang Voigt and Roland May, eds., *Paul Bonatz 1977–1956* (Tübingen: Wasmuth, 2010), 228–30. Tuomey remembers that Stirling admired Bonatz's Main Train Station. See also Rodiek, *James Stirling*, 16.
109. Vidler, *James Frazer Stirling*, 39.
110. Alan Berman, ed., *Jim Stirling and the Red Trilogy: Three Radical Buildings* (London: Frances Lincoln, 2010); and Crinson, *Stirling and Gowan*, 271. It was Gowan, however, who designed the faceted skylights at Leicester. Stirling's friend Reyner Banham's enthusiasm for Paul Scheerbart may have played a role here. See Nigel Whiteley, *Reyner Banham: Historian of the Immediate Future* (Cambridge, Mass.: MIT Press, 2002).
111. Geoffrey H. Baker, *The Architecture of James Stirling and His Partners* (London: Ashgate, 2011), 249–302; Lawrence, *James Stirling*; and Vidler, *Histories of the Immediate Present*, 103. Mark Crinson and Claire Zimmerman, eds., *Neo-avant-garde and Postmodern: Postwar Architecture in Britain and Beyond* (New Haven, Conn.: Yale University Press, 2010), also contains a number of thoughtful analyses of Stirling's position.
112. This phase of his career is chronicled in Peter Arnell and Ted Bickford, *Frank Gehry:*

Building and Projects (New York: Rizzoli, 1985), and Mildred Friedman, ed., *The Architecture of Frank Gehry* (New York: Rizzoli, 1986).

113. Philip Johnson and Mark Wigley, *Deconstructivist Architecture* (New York: Museum of Modern Art, 1988). The term was coined by Joseph Giovannini, "Breaking All the Rules," *New York Times,* 12 June 1988.

114. Friedman, *The Architecture of Frank Gehry,* 92–95.

115. Quoted in Arnal Perez, "Frank Gehry: A to Z (collection of texts)," *Quaderns* 185 (April 1990): 18, and Arnell and Bickford, *Frank Gehry,* 13.

116. The Winton Guest House (1987) in Orono, Minnesota, was actually the first such commission.

117. Barbara Isenberg, *Conversations with Frank Gehry* (New York: Knopf, 2009), 74–76.

118. "Museo de Mobiliario y Complejo Industrial," *El Croquis,* November 1990, 65–65, and "Vitra International Furniture Manufacturing Facility and Design Museum," *Quaderns,* April 1990, 32–39, were two of the few journal articles to include both buildings.

119. Mildred Friedman, "Architecture in Motion," in *Frank Gehry, Architect,* ed. J. Fiona Ragheb (New York: Guggenheim Museum, 2001), 293–94.

120. "Un ordre polyphonique: Musée Vitra, Weil-am-Rhein," *Techniques et Architecture* 387 (January 1990): 139.

121. For the connection to Scharoun see Friedman, "Architecture in Motion," 294; Kurt W. Foster, "Their 'Master's Voice': Notes on the Architecture of Hans Scharoun's and Frank Gehry's Concert Halls," in *Architecture between Spectacle and Use,* ed. Anthony Vidler (Williamstown, Mass.: Sterling and Francine Clark Art Institute, 2005), 25–40; Pilar Vidas, "Cranked, Curled, and Cantilevered," *Progressive Architecture* 71 (May 1990): 96–97; and Klaus-Dieter Weiss, "Kunst als Bau," *Werk, Bauen + Wohnen* 3 (March 1990): 9.

122. This account is based upon "Between the Lines: Extension to the Berlin Museum, with the Jewish Museum," *Assemblage* 12 (1990): 18–57; and *Jewish Museum Berlin: Architect Daniel Libeskind* (Berlin: G + B Arts International, 1999). See also Peter Chametzky, "Rebuilding the Nation: Norman Foster's Reichstag Renovation and Daniel Libeskind's Jewish Museum Berlin," *Centropa* 1 (2001): 245–64; Andreas Huyssen, *Present Pasts: Urban Palimpsests and the Politics of Memory* (Stanford, Calif.: Stanford University Press, 2003), 66–71; Rosenfeld, *Building after Auschwitz,* 179–93; Karen E. Till, *The New Berlin: Memory, Politics, Place* (Minneapolis: University of Minnesota Press, 2005), 193–225; and Young, *At Memory's Edge,* 152–83. For the context of Libeskind's contribution to Berlin, Werner Sewing, "Daniel Libeskind in Berlin," *ZWEI: Magazin des Jüdischen Museums Berlin* (2003): 4–7.

123. Jaskot, *The Nazi Perpetrator,* 127–65.

124. Wallis Miller, "IBA's 'Models for a City': Housing the Image of Cold-War Berlin," *Journal of Architectural Education* (1993): 202–16; Emily Pugh, *Architecture, Politics, and Identity in Divided Berlin* (Pittsburgh: University of Pittsburgh Press, 2014), 200–282; and Harald Bodenschatz and Vittorio Magnago Lampugnani, *25 Jahre Internationale Bauausstellung Berlin 1987: Ein Wendepunkt des europäischen Städtebaus* (Zurich: Niggli, 2012). For the international context of such developments see Christopher Klemek, *The Transatlantic Collapse of Urban Renewal: Postwar Urbanism from New York to Berlin* (Chicago: University of Chicago Press, 2012).

125. Florian Urban, *Neo-historical East Berlin* (London: Ashgate, 2009), 143–81.
126. This point was first made to me by Chiara Rodriguez. See also Carsten Ruhl, *Magisches Denken-Monumentale Form: Aldo Rossi und die Architektur des Bildes* (Tübingen: Wasmuth, 2013), 46–51; and Warnke, *Stein gegen Stein*, 345.
127. Ursula Kleefisch-Jobst and Ingeborg Flagge, eds., *Rob Krier: Ein romantischer Rationalist; Architekt und Stadtplaner / Rob Krier: A Romantic Rationalist; Architect and Urban Planner* (Vienna and New York: Springer, 2005).
128. *Five Architects: Eisenman, Graves, Gwathmey, Hejduk, Meier* (New York: Oxford University Press, 1975). For the background of this position see Alexander Cargonne, *The Texas Rangers: Notes from an Architectural Underground* (Cambridge, Mass.: MIT Press, 1995).
129. Peter Eisenman, *Giuseppe Terragni: Transformations, Decompositions, Critiques* (New York: Monacelli, 2003).
130. Peter Eisenman, *House X* (New York: Rizzoli, 1982).
131. Jeffrey Kipnis and Thomas Leeser, eds., *Chora L Works: Jacques Derrida and Peter Eisenman* (New York: Monacelli, 1997).
132. Particularly interesting in the context of his later Memorial to the Murdered Jews of Europe is the memory invoked at the Wexner of the Armory that had once stood on the site, as well as Eisenman's repetition of Stirling's strategy of encouraging pedestrians who have no intention of entering the institution to nonetheless walk through its center.
133. "IBA: Social Housing Berlin, 1981–1985," in *Tracing Eisenman*, ed. Cynthia Davidson (London: Thames and Hudson, 2006), 80.
134. Stanley Allen, "Libeskind's Practice of Laughter," *Assemblage* 12 (1990): 18–24; and, in the same issue, "'I Made It on the Verge': A Letter from David Farrell Krell," 52–58, for a deconstructivist interpretation of it.
135. "Between the Lines," 48; 26–34 for the original diagrams of the geometrical derivation of the design.
136. In two conversations with the author, the most recent of them in June 1997 in Berlin, Libeskind acknowledged the importance of this precedent, which is also mentioned in "Daniel Libeskind Talks with Doris Erbacher and Peter Paul Kubitz," in Bernard Schneider, *Daniel Libeskind: Jewish Museum Berlin* (Amsterdam: G + B Arts International, 1999), unpaginated.
137. Harriet F. Senie, *The Tilted Arc Controversy* (Minneapolis: University of Minnesota Press, 2002), 10.
138. Andrew Shanken, "The Memory of Industry and Its Discontents: The Death and Life of a Keyword," in *Spatial Recall: Memory in Architecture and Landscape*, ed. Marc Treib (New York: Routledge, 2009), 232. See also Daniel Abramson, "Maya Lin and the 1960s: Monuments, Time Lines, and Minimalism," *Critical Inquiry* 22 (1996): 679–709; John Bodner, *Remaking America: Public Memory, Commemoration, and Patriotism in the Twentieth Century* (Princeton, N.J.: Princeton University Press, 1993), 3–12; Marita Sturken, "The Wall, the Screen, and the Image: The Vietnam Veterans Memorial," *Representations* 35 (1991): 118–42; Anne Wagner, *A House Divided: American Art since 1950* (Berkeley: University of California Press, 2012), 67–88; and Robin Wagner-Pacifici and Barry Schwartz, "The Vietnam Veterans Memorial: Commemorating a Difficult Past," *American Journal of Sociology* 97 (1991): 376–420.

139. Kirk Savage, *Monument Wars: Washington D.C., the National Mall, and the Transformation of the Memorial Landscape* (Berkeley: University of California Press, 2011); and Erica Doss, *Memorial Mania: Public Feeling in America* (Chicago: University of Chicago Press, 2010).
140. Kathleen James, "Memory and the Cityscape: The German Architectural Debate about Postmodernism," *German Politics and Society* 17, no. 3 (1999): 71–75; Andrew Shanken, "Planning Memory: The Rise of Living Memorials in the United States during World War II," *Art Bulletin* 84 (March 2002): 13–47; and James E. Young, *The Texture of Memory: Holocaust Memorials and Meaning* (New Haven, Conn.: Yale University Press, 1994), 290.
141. Abraham Duiker to Louis Kahn, 1 February 1972, LIK box 36, Louis I. Kahn Collection, University of Pennsylvania and Pennsylvania Historical and Museum Collections, Philadelphia.
142. Mark Godfrey, *Abstraction and the Holocaust*, 113–39, and Kathleen James-Chakraborty, "Louis Kahn's Monumentality: Theory and Practice," in *Mythos Monument: Urban Strategien in Architektur und Kunst seit 1945*, ed. Carsten Ruhl (Bielefeld: Transcript, 2011), 77–98.
143. Young, *The Texture of Memory*; and John Gillis, *Commemorations: The Politics of National Identity* (Princeton, N.J.: Princeton University Press, 1994), 16–17.
144. Doss, *Memorial Mania*, 127; and Michael Kimmelman, "Out of Minimalism, Monuments to Memory," *New York Times*, 13 January 2002.
145. In the time between when the building was completed and the new Jewish Museum had progressed far enough to install the displays, it became one of the city's most visited attractions. Eduard Beaucamp, "Konstructiver Pop," *Frankfurter Allgemeine Zeitung*, 19 March 1984, details that Stirling would also have liked his building to open without any art installed within it.
146. *Daniel Libeskind: Jewish Museum Berlin*, 10.
147. Ibid., 75.
148. Michael Kimmelman, "Shattered Shapes: Architect's Rhetoric of Suffering," Critic's Notebook, *New York Times*, 14 April 2004.
149. Philip Nobel, "The Height of the Art: Can Daniel Libeskind's 1,776-Foot Tower Reclaim the Symbols of Democracy?," *Metropolis* 22 (June 2003): 102–4.
150. For an exception see James-Chakraborty, *German Architecture for a Mass Audience*, 117–20.
151. For the view that it is an extension see Foster, *The Art-Architecture Complex*; for it as an alternative, Jean-Louis Cohen, *The Future of Architecture since 1889* (London: Phaidon, 2012).
152. Lothar Spaeth, "Ein kulturelles Jahrhundertwerk," *Rhein-Neckar-Zeitung*, 10 March 1984.

4. Critical Reconstruction or Neomodernist Shards?

1. "Streit um Nofretete-Büste: Kairo startet neuen Rückgabe-Vorstoß," *Spiegel Online*, 12 February 2009, http://www.spiegel.de/wissenschaft/mensch/streit-um-nofretete

Notes to Chapter 4

-bueste-kairo-startet-neuen-rueckgabe-vorstoss-a-607232.html, consulted 3 June 2013, for whether or not the bust was legally exported from Egypt following its excavation in 1912.

2. West Berlin's Egyptian Museum was open from 1967 to 2005 in yet another Stüler building; see http://www.egyptian-museum-berlin.com/c01.php, consulted 17 March 2013.

3. *The New Museum Berlin: Conserving, Restoring, Rebuilding within the World Heritage* (Leipzig: Seemann Henschel, 2009); and David Chipperfield Architects in collaboration with Julian Harrap, *Neues Museum Berlin* (Cologne: Walther Koenig, 2009). See also Owen Hatherley, *Landscapes of Communism: A History through Buildings* (New York: New Press, 2016), 361–63.

4. Michael Kimmelman, "For Berlin Museum, a Modern Makeover That Doesn't Deny the Wounds of War," *New York Times*, 11 March 2009.

5. Kimmelman, ibid., reported that more than thirty-five thousand waited in line over three days to tour the building in March.

6. Rik Nys, *David Chipperfield: Form Matters* (Cologne: Walther König, 2009).

7. The transition can be charted in Jörn Düwel and Michael Mönninger, *Von der Soziallutopie zum städtischen Haus: Texte und Interviews von Hans Stimmann* (Berlin: Dom Publishers, 2011). See also Hans Stimmann, ed., *Berliner Altstadt: Von der DDR-Staatsmitte zur Stadtmitte* (Berlin: Dom, 2009); and Hans Stimmann and Martin Kieren, eds., *Die Architektur des neuen Berlin* (Berlin: Nicolai, 2005).

8. Harald Bodenschatz and Thomas Flierl, eds., *Berlin plant: Plädoyer für ein Planwerk Innenstadt Berlin 2.0* (Berlin: Theater der Zeit, 2010); Claire Colomb, *Staging the New Berlin: Place Marketing and the Politics of Urban Reinvention Post-1989* (London: Routledge, 2011); Jane Richter, ed., *Tourist City Berlin: Tourism & Architecture* (Karlsruhe: Braun, 2010); and Werner Sewing, *No More Learning from Las Vegas: Stadt, Wohnen oder Themenpark?*, ed. Florian Dreher and Christine Hannemann (Leipzig: Spector Books, 2016).

9. William Curtis, "Modern Architecture and the Excavation of the Past," in *Louis I. Kahn: The Power of Architecture*, ed. Mateo Kries, Jochen Eisenbrand, and Stanislaus von Moos (Weil-am-Rhein: Vitra Design Museum, 2012), 235–52.

10. Crinson and Zimmerman, *Neo-avant-garde and Postmodernism*, examine this phenomenon, although not in Germany.

11. Fuchs, *After the Dresden Bombing*.

12. Urban, *Neo-historical East Berlin*, 99–142; Lutz Koepnick, "Forget Berlin," *German Quarterly* 74 (2001): 347; and Pugh, *Architecture, Politics, and Identity in Divided Berlin*, 155–99.

13. Nathaniel T. Kenney and Volkmar Wentzel, "Life in Walled-off West Berlin," *National Geographic* 120 (1961): 739, 745. See also Elizabeth A. Strom, *Building the New Berlin: The Politics of Development in Germany's Capital City* (Lanham, Md.: Lexington Books, 2001), 52.

14. Colomb, *Staging the New Berlin*; Sewing, *No More Learning from Las Vegas*; and Koepnick, "Forget Berlin."

15. http://press.visitberlin.de/sites/default/files/berlin_beherbergungsstatistik_dezember

_2015_engl_0.pdf. For the Topography of Terror figures see Julia Emmrich, "Geschichte gucken," *Westdeutsche Allgemeine Zeitung,* 10 July 2012; Sewing, *No More Learning from Las Vegas,* 59–71.

16. Robert Darnton, *Berlin Journal, 1989–1990* (New York: Norton, 1991), 77–78; and Janet Ward, *Post-Wall Berlin: Borders, Space and Identity* (Basingstoke: Palgrave Macmillan, 2010), 95–117.
17. Strom, *Building the New Berlin,* 52.
18. Urban, *Neo-historical East Berlin,* 181–214.
19. *O. M. Ungers: Bauten und Projekte 1991–98* (Stuttgart: Deutsche Verlags-Anstalt, 1998), 252–59.
20. Urban, *Neo-historical East Berlin,* 1–180. See also *O. M. Ungers 1951–1984.*
21. Hans Stimmann, "Neue Berliner Büro- und Geschäftshäuser," in Düwel and Mönninger, *Von der Sozialutopie zum städtischen Haus,* 135.
22. Hans Stimmann, "Learning from the IBA," in Düwel and Mönninger, *Von der Sozialutopie zum städtischen Haus,* 102.
23. Strom, *Building the New Berlin,* 97–114, for the locus of planning within the Berlin city government.
24. Stimmann, "Learning from the IBA," in Düwel and Mönninger, *Von der Sozialutopie zum städtischen Haus,* 101.
25. Hans Stimmann, "Das Gedächtnis der europäischen Stadt," in Düwel and Mönninger, *Von der Sozialutopie zum städtischen Haus,* 167.
26. *Aldo Rossi: Architect* (London: Academy Editions, 1994), a translation of the catalog for the exhibition held at the Martin Gropius Bau in 1993.
27. Düwel and Mönninger, *Von der Sozialutopie zum städtischen Haus,* esp. Hans Stimmann, "Heimatkunde für Neuteutonia," 118.
28. Ibid., 112; see also 135, 186.
29. Jean Nouvel and Philip Jodidio, *Jean Nouvel: The Complete Works 1970–1992* (Cologne: Taschen, 2008), 322–33, 425–26.
30. James, *Erich Mendelsohn and the Architecture of German Modernism,* 126–39.
31. Ibid., 111–15.
32. Dietrich Neumann, *Architecture of the Night: The Illuminated Building* (Munich: Prestel, 2002), 130; and Janet Ward, *Weimar Surfaces: Urban Visual Culture in 1920s Germany* (Berkeley: University of California Press, 2001).
33. Hüter, *Architektur in Berlin,* 25–26.
34. Düwel and Mönninger, *Von der Sozialutopie zum städtischen Haus,* 105–13.
35. Matthias Sauerbruch, "A Sober Look at a City's Flights of Fancy," in Engel, *Berlin Photographs,* 7.
36. Herbert Muschamp, "The New Berlin—Building on the Rubble of History: Once Again, a City Rewards the Walker," *New York Times,* 11 April 1999.
37. Nouvel and Jodidio, *Jean Nouvel,* 425.
38. Ghirardo, *Architecture after Modernism,* 43–106.
39. As quoted in Alan Riding, "The New Berlin—Building on the Rubble of History: A Capital Reinstated and Remodeled," *New York Times,* 11 April 1999.

Notes to Chapter 4

40. Werner Durth and Günter Behnisch, *Pariser Platz: Neubau der Akademie der Künste* (Berlin: Jovis, 2006), 15–53.
41. Matthais Pabsch, *Pariser Platz—Architektur und Technik: Vom manuellen zum digitaler Zeitalter* (Berlin: Reimer, 2002); Ralf Pröve, *Pariser Platz 3: Die Geschichte einer Adresse in Deutschland* (Berlin: Nicolai, 2002); and Cullen, *Reichstag*.
42. Cullen, *Reichstag*, 65–182.
43. Thomas Nipperdey, *Deutsche Geschichte 1866–1918*, vol. 2, *Machtstaat vor der Demokratie* (Munich: C. H. Beck Verlag, 1990), 741–56.
44. Detlev J. K. Peukert, *The Weimar Republic* (New York: Hill and Wang, 1993).
45. Evans, *The Third Reich in Power*, 11–12, 67–68.
46. Cullen, *Reichstag*, 253–79.
47. Voigt, *Gottfried Böhm*, 22–26.
48. Barnstone, *Transparent State*, 138–74; Jenkins, *Norman Foster: Works 4*, 248–302; and Michael Z. Wise, *Capital Dilemma: Germany's Search for a New Architecture of Democracy* (New York: Princeton Architectural Press, 1998), 121–34.
49. Barnstone, *Transparent State*, 175–208.
50. Christo and Jeanne-Claude, *Wrapped Reichstag Berlin, 1971–1995* (Berlin: Taschen, 2002).
51. Huyssen, *Present Pasts*, 31–38.
52. Roger Cohen, "Berlin Journal: The Reichstag Burns, This Time with Hope," *New York Times*, 6 March 1999.
53. Roger Cohen, "Berlin in Search of Itself," *New York Times*, 21 November 1999.
54. Jenkins, *Norman Foster: Works 4*, 248–351; and Chametzky, "Rebuilding the Nation."
55. Durth and Behnisch, *Pariser Platz*; Frank O. Gehry, Liminita Sabau, and Waltraud Krase, *Pariser Platz 3* (Hildesheim: Quensen and Qurdas, 2001); Thomas M. Krüger, *Akademie der Künste Pariser Platz Berlin* (Berlin: Stadtwandel, 2005); Moore Ruble Yudell, *The Berlin Embassy* (Berlin: Aedes, 2008); and *Pariser Platz 5: Die Französische Botschaft in Berlin* (Berlin: Nicolai, 2004).
56. Thomas Michael Krüger and Florian Bolk, *Britische Botschaft Berlin* (Berlin: Stadtwandel, 2002).
57. Hedda Adlon, *Hotel Adlon: The Life and Death of a Great Hotel* (London: Barrie Books, 1958); and Durth and Behnisch, *Pariser Platz*, 53.
58. Kenney and Wentzel, "Life in Walled-off West Berlin," 756.
59. Engel, *Berlin Photographs*, 236.
60. Werner Sewing, *Bildregie: Architektur zwischen Retrodesign und Eventkultur* (Basel: Birkhäuser, 2003), 121. For his attack on the Adlon see 197.
61. Adrian von Buttlar, "Auf der Suche nach der Differenz: Minima Moralia reproduktiver Erinnerungsarchitektur," in Adrian von Buttlar et al., *Denkmalpflege statt Attrappenkult: Gegen die Rekonstruktion von Baudenkmälern—eine Anthologie* (Gütersloh: Bauverlag, 2010), 183.
62. http://www.berlinloveparade.com, consulted 1 August 2016.
63. Columb, *Staging the New Berlin*, and Sewing, *No More Learning from Las Vegas*.
64. Mary McLeod, "Architecture and Politics in the Reagan Era: From Postmodernism to

Deconstructivism," *Assemblage* 8 (1989): 22–59; and Fredric Jameson, *Postmodernism; or, The Cultural Logic of Late Capitalism* (New York: Verso, 1990).

65. Barnstone, *Transparent State*, 138–208; Wise, *Capital Dilemma*, 135–41; and Ulrike Kretzschmar, ed., *The Exhibition Hall of the German Historical Museum* (Munich: Prestel, 2003).

66. Sewing, *Architektur zwischen Retrodesign und Eventkultur*; Huyssen, *Present Pasts*, 62.

67. Jennifer A. Jordan, *Structures of Memory: Understanding Urban Change in Berlin and Beyond* (Stanford, Calif.: Stanford University Press, 2006).

68. Jürg Steiner, "Mein Vorbild war das Farnsworth House von Mies van der Rohe," *Bauwelt* 101 (2010): 31.

69. Andreas Nachama, ed., *Topography of Terror: Gestapo, SS and Reich Security Main Office on Wilhelm and Prinz-Albrecht-Straße* (Berlin: Stiftung Topographie des Terrors, 2010); Till, *The New Berlin*, 63–123; Simon Ward, "Material, Image, Sign: On the Value of Memory in Traces in Public Life," in *Memory Traces: 1989 and the Question of German Cultural Identity*, ed. Silke Arnold-de Simine (Oxford: Peter Lang, 2005), 290–97; and https://www.topographie.de, consulted 2 April 2012.

70. Dieter Hoffmann-Axthelm and Andreas Nachama, "Ein Treffen im 'Sprechzimmer der Geschichte,'" *Bauwelt* 101 (2010): 13.

71. Robert Frank, "Prinz-Albrecht-Straße," *Bauwelt* 81 (1990): 1522–23.

72. oh, "Topographie des Terrors," *Bauwelt* 84 (1993): 916–17, and "Topographie des Terrors," *Daidalos* 49 (1993): 150–53.

73. Steven Spier, "Place, Authorship and the Concrete: Three Conversations with Peter Zumthor," *ARQ* 5 (2001): 30–31.

74. Peter Zumthor, *Three Concepts* (Basel: Birkhäuser: 1997): 52–53, for these comments and 49–67 for the design.

75. Dieter Hoffmann-Axthelm, "Die Topographie sind am Ziel, der Ort geht unter," *Bauwelt* 97 (2006): 14.

76. Nils Ballhausen, "Dokumentationszemtrum der Stiftung Topographie des Terrors," *Bauwelt* 101 (2010): 27.

77. Brian Ladd, *Ghosts of Berlin: Confronting German History in the Urban Landscape* (Chicago: University of Chicago Press, 1997), 145–47. Many aspects of the building's modern infrastructure were probably inspired by Mendelsohn's Columbushaus, whose construction Sagebiel supervised.

78. Hendrik Gerth, *Materials on the Memorial to the Murdered Jews of Europe* (Berlin: Nicolai, 2005); Hanno Rauterberg, *Holocaust Memorial Berlin: Eisenman Architects* (Zürich: Lars Müller, 2005); Mark Godfrey, *Abstraction and the Holocaust* (New Haven, Conn.: Yale University Press, 2007), 239–65; Huyssen, *Present Pasts*, 72–84; Eran Neuman, *Shoah Presence: Architectural Representations of the Holocaust* (Abington, UK: Ashgate, 2014), 149–79; and Till, *The New Berlin*, 160–88, for the Monument to the Murdered Jews of Europe and 197–207 for the emergence of a memorial district including the Jewish Museum.

79. http://www.stiftung-denkmal.de, consulted 3 April 2012.

80. Young, *At Memory's Edge*, 233.

81. Clara Weyergraf-Serra and Martha Buskirk, eds., *The Destruction of Tilted Arc: Documents* (Cambridge, Mass.: MIT Press, 1990).
82. Rosenfeld, *Building after Auschwitz,* 164.
83. Ballhausen, "Dokumentationszentrum," 27.
84. Riding, "The New Berlin"; and Sewing, *Bildregie,* 150–80, for attacks on these buildings, whose virtues are trumpeted, however, in Annegret Berg, *Downtown Berlin: Building the Metropolitan Mix* (Berlin: Bauwelt, 1995); Kieren Martin, ed., *New Architecture Berlin: 1990–2000* (Berlin: Jovis, 1998); and Ulf Meyer, *Berlin: Bundeshauptstadt = Capital City* (Berlin: Jovis, 1999).
85. The argument for the construction of a replica is set forth in Hartmut Elrich, *Der Berliner Schloss: Geschichte und Wiederaufbau* (Petersberg: Imhof, 2008); and Rainer Haubrich, *Das neue Berliner Schloss: Von der Hohenzollern Residenz zum Humboldtforum* (Berlin: Nicolai, 2011). Opposing voices include Dieter Hildebrandt, *Das Berliner Schloss: Deutschlands leere Mitte* (Munich: Carl Hanser Verlag, 2011); and Bruno Flierl, *Berlin—die neue Mitte: Texte zur Stadtentwicklung seit 1990* (Berlin: Theater der Zeit, 2010). See also John Maciuika, "Whose Schlossplatz? Architecture and the 'Materialization' of German Identities in Berlin's Historic Center, 1945–2009," *Bulletin of the German Historical Institute Supplement* 7 (2011): 15; http://www.pdr.kultur-netz.de, consulted 5 March 2013; and Uta Staiger, "Cities, Citizenships, Contested Cultures: Berlin's Palace of the Republic and the Politics of the Public Sphere," *Cultural Geographies* 16 (2009): 309–27.
86. Heinz Graffunder, *Der Palast der Republik* (Leipzig: VEB E. A. Seemann Verlag, 1977).
87. Derek Scally, "Prussian Palace in Berlin Rises from the Ashes," *Irish Times,* 13 June 2013, reported that the cost had risen to 620 million euros, and that only 20 of the expected 80 million in private donations had been received. For the final cost see http://www.rbb-online.de/kultur/thema/stadtschloss-berlin/beitraege/berliner-stadtschloss-richtfest.html.
88. *Schloss Berlin/Humboldt Forum: Realisierungswettbewerb* (Berlin: Bundesministerium für Verkehr, Bau und Stadtentwicklung, 2008).
89. As, for instance, in the emphasis placed on the use of iron in the Neues Museum in Werner Lorenz, "'Core Form and Artistic Form'—the Art of Construction in Prussia under the Influence of Industrialization," in *The New Museum Berlin*, 42–43.
90. Compare Hela Zettler and Horst Mauter, eds., *Das Berliner Schloss: Eine Fotodokumentation der verlorenen Stadtmitte* (Berlin: Argon, 1991), and Goerd Peschken and Hans-Werner Klünner, *Das Berliner Schloss* (Berlin: Propyläen, 1998), with Edwin Redslob, *Barock und Rokoko in den Schlössern von Berlin und Potsdam* (Berlin: Rembrandt-Verlag, 1954).
91. http://berliner-schloss.de/das-historische-schloss/das-schloss-lag-nicht-in-berlin-berlin-war-das-schloss, consulted 1 August 2016.
92. Douglas Klahr, "Wilhelm II's Weisser Saal and Its Doppelthron," *German History* 27 (2009): 490–513; and Arbeitsgruppe Berlin-Wettbewerbe, ed., *Capital Berlin, Central District Spreeinsel, Competition for Urban Design Ideas* (Berlin: Birkhäuser, 1994), 48–51.

93. Peter-Klaus Schuster, "Berlin's Museum Island—a German Educational Landscape," and Elke Blauert, "Neues Museum," in *Museum Island Berlin*, ed. Michael Eissenhauer, Astrid Bähr, and Elisabeth Rochau-Shalem (Berlin: Hirmer, 2012), 129–73. The *Neues Museum Berlin*, targeted more at architects and architectural historians and less at tourists, is more modest in its claims.

94. The *Neues Musem Berlin* gives a full accounting of the conservation work and of what it revealed about the original structure.

95. This is occasionally mentioned in passing in Eissenhauer, Bähr, and Rochau-Shalem, *Museum Island Berlin*. See especially Adrian von Buttlar, "The Museum Island—an Architectural Historical Overview," 94–97, and 101–6; Peter-Klaus Schuster, "Berlin's Museum Island—a German Educational Landscape," 129–34; and Elke Blauert, "Neues Museum," 156–73. See also Sheehan, *Museums in the German Art World*; and Peter Aronsson and Gabriella Elgenius, eds., *National Museums and Nation-Building in Europe 1750–2010: Mobilization and Legitimacy, Continuity and Change* (Basingstoke: Routledge, 2014).

96. http://berliner-schloss.de/en, consulted 1 August 2016.

97. "Berlin's Museum Island," 123–24; and Andrea Wulf, *The Invention of Nature: The Adventures of Alexander von Humboldt, the Lost Hero of Science* (London: John Murray, 2015).

98. Can Bilsel, *Antiquity on Display: Regimes of the Authentic in Berlin's Pergamon Museum* (Oxford: Oxford University Press, 2012), can be compared here with Manfred Rettig, "The Berliner Schloss Turned into the Humboldt-Forum—the Perspective of the Client," in Eissenhauer, Bähr, and Rochau-Shalem, *Museum Island Berlin*, 404–11; or Klaus-Dieter Lehmann, "Weltort für Kunst und Kultur—das Humboldt Forum"; and Hermann Parzinger, "Die Präsentation außereuropäischer Sammlungen im Humboldt Forum," in *Schloss Berlin/Humboldt Forum*, 17–20.

99. Hans-Rudolf Meier, "Vom Siegszeichen zum Lüftungschacht: Spolien als Erinnerungsträger in der Architektur," in Meier and Wohlleben, *Bauten und Orte als Träger von Erinnerungen*, 94.

100. David Chipperfield, "The Neues Museum Architectural Concept," in *Neues Museum Berlin*, 56.

101. Chipperfield, *Neues Museum Berlin*, 11.

102. Huyssen, *Present Pasts*, 54, reinforced in Mary Dellenbaugh, "The Sanitization of Berlin-Mitte's Socialist Past after German Reunification and Implications for Symbolic Dominance in 'Everyday' Space and the Crisis of 'Belonging' in a New Imposed Cultural Context" (paper presented at Belonging: Cultural Topographies of Identity conference, University College Dublin, June 2012).

103. For a defense of reconstructions see Nerdinger, *Geschichte der Rekonstruktion*. For the potential reconstruction of the Bauakademie see http://www.foerderverein-bauakademie.de/ziele.html, consulted 19 July 2017. For a more critical view see Dario Gamboni, *The Destruction of Art: Iconoclasm and Vandalism since the French Revolution* (London: Reaktion Books, 2007).

104. This was far from the only grounds for its demolition, despite what Rettig, "The Ber-

liner Schloss," claims; see Ladd, *Ghosts of Berlin,* 63, and Ward, "Material, Image, Sign," 297–303.
105. One of the most vocal critics of the demolition of the palace and the reconstruction of its predecessor was Bruno Flierl. See his *Berlin—die neue Mitte.* For the efforts to rebuild Mies's Memorial see gk, "Ohne Hackenkreuz," *Bauwelt* 59 (1968): 1244.
106. Sauerbruch, "A Sober Look," 9.
107. Thomas Loy, "Palast der Republik lebt weiter—in Einzelteilen," *Der Tagesspiegel,* 18 November 2012.
108. Ladd, *Ghosts of Berlin,* 60.
109. These observations are based on my own memory of the event, and the many discussions of it in which I participated in Berlin that summer.
110. Arbeitsgruppe Berlin-Wettbewerbe, *Capital Berlin,* 48–51.
111. Lucy M. Maulsby, "Reichsbank Project," in *Mies in Berlin,* ed. Barry Bergdoll and Terrance Reilly (New York: Museum of Modern Art, 2001), 276–79; Erich Mendelsohn to Luise Mendelsohn, 11 February 1933, in *Erich Mendelsohn: Briefe eines Architekten* (Basel: Birkhäuser, 1991), 88; and Mary Fulbrook, "Historical Tourism: Reading Berlin's Doubly Dictatorial Past," in *Memory Culture and the Contemporary City: Building Sites,* ed. Uta Steiger, Henriette Steiner, and Andrew Webber (Basingstoke: Palgrave Macmillan, 2009), 130.
112. Maciuika, "Whose Schlossplatz?," 15.
113. "Nur noch kurz 104,5 Millionen Euro sammeln," *Westdeutsche Allgemeine Zeitung,* 4 July 2012, for the fund-raising problems at that stage, and http://berliner-schloss.de/en/donation-facts, consulted 1 August 2016, for the situation as of May 2016.
114. Andreas Kilb, "Zwei Wahrheiten über Franco Stella," *Frankfurter Allgemeine Zeitung,* 24 July 2011.
115. Michael Kimmelman, "Rebuilding a Palace May Become a Grand Blunder," *New York Times,* 31 December 2008.
116. *Schloss Berlin/Humboldt Forum,* 235. In fact, this was the policy eventually adopted, with private donations paying for the reconstruction of the historical facades, while the national government is constructing the rest. http://berliner-schloss.de/spenden-system/warum-es-auf-ihre-spende-ankommt, consulted 1 August 2016.
117. Personal communication with Manfred Rettig, 18 January 2013, Dublin, Ireland. See also Anja Lösel, "Das Monster am Schlossplatz," 30 June 2011, http://www.stern.de/kultur/kunst/humboldt-box-in-berlin-das-monster-am-schlossplatz-3055460.html.
118. http://www.humboldt-box.com, consulted 27 May 2013.
119. Aleida Assmann, "Rekonstruktion—die zweite Chance; oder, Architektur aus dem Archiv," in Nerdinger, *Geschichte der Rekonstruktion,* 16.
120. Stefanie Bürkle, *Szenographie einer Großstadt: Berlin als städtebauliche Bühne* (Berlin: Parthas, 2013), 111–12.
121. This point was made in the wall text and reinforced by a tour guide when I visited the New Museum in March 2010.
122. James Cuno, *Who Owns Antiquity? Museums and the Battle over Our Ancient Heritage* (Princeton, N.J.: Princeton University Press, 2008).

5. Manufacturing Memory in the Ruhr Region

1. "Zollverein—bedeutend wie die Pyramiden," *Westdeutsche Allgemeine Zeitung*, 15 December 2001. See also Stiftung Zollverein, ed., *The Zollverein World Heritage Site: The Past and Present History of the Zollverein Mining Complex and Coking Plant* (Essen: Klartext, 2008).
2. Roland Günter, *Im Tal der Könige: Ein Handbuch für Reisen zu Emscher, Rhein und Ruhr* (Essen: Klartext, 2000), and Roy Kift, *Tour the Ruhr: The English Language Guide* (Essen: Klartext, 2003). It is also part of the logo of the local Social Democrats. See http://www.spd-schönebeck-bedingrade.de, consulted 7 August 2016.
3. For IBA-generated publicity for the building see "Route: Industriekultur: Endeckerpass 2003," published by the Kommunalverband Ruhrgebiet, which states, "The site was designed in the Bauhaus style and was regarded not only as the most modern but also the most beautiful colliery in the world," and *Internationale Bauausstellung Emscher Park, Katalog der Projekte* (Gelsenkirchen: Rehrmann, 1999), 333–38, in which it is described as the "Kölner Dom der Industriegeschichte." For the IBA itself, see Bettina Günter, ed., *Alte und Neue Industriekultur im Ruhrgebiet* (Essen: Klartext, 2010).
4. Ilse Brusis, Vorwort (anonymously authored editorial), *Internationale Bauausstellung Emscher Park*, 8–14; and Günter, *Im Tal der Könige*, 397–516.
5. http://archiv.ruhr2010.de, consulted 7 August 2016 for the range of activities that occurred that year across the region.
6. An even more massive deindustrialization occurred in Berlin and across East Germany, but it was not for the most part accompanied by the same degree of faith in the ability of design to prompt economic regeneration. For an exception see Kathleen James-Chakraborty, "Beyond Cold War Interpretations: Shaping a New Bauhaus Heritage," *New German Critique* 116 (Summer 2012): 11–24.
7. This is not unique to the Ruhr region. See Paul Tyrer and Mark Crinson, "Totemic Park: Symbolic Representations in Post-industrial Space," in *Urban Memory: History and Amnesia in the Modern City*, ed. Mark Crinson (London: Routledge, 2005), 99–117.
8. Assmann, "Collective Memory and Cultural Identity."
9. Thomas Urban, *Visionen für das Ruhrgebiet: IBA Emscher Park: Konzepte, Projekte, Dokumentation* (Essen: Klartext, 2008), 17. For a romantic view of Bochum's enthusiasm for Richard Serra, see Douglas Crimp, "Serra's Public Sculpture: Redefining Site Specificity," in Rosalind Krauss, *Richard Serra: Sculpture* (New York: Museum of Modern Art, 1986), 49–52, with which the many Bochumers with whom I have discussed the subject all vehemently disagree.
10. The Ruhr Museum inserted in 2010 into the Zeche Zollverein's coal-washing plant drew a quarter of a million visitors in 2015, the same year Berlin's New Museum attracted 726,000. The Landschaftspark welcomed just over a million people in 2011, 2013, and 2014, many of them repeat visitors from the immediate environs. In 2014 the ever more popular Topography of Terror attracted about a third more than this. See http://www.touristiker-nrw.de/ruhr-museum-uebertrifft-eigene-erwartungen-deutlich and http://de.statista.com/statistik/daten/studie/368827/umfrage/anzahl-der-besucher-der-staatlichen-museen-in-berlin; the figures for the Neues Museum are increasing again

Notes to Chapter 5

after a dramatic falloff in 2012–14. See also http://www.duisburg365.de/duisburg/artikel/?tx_ttnews%5Btt_news%5D=8153 and https://www.berlin.de/sen/kultur/aktuelles/pressemitteilungen/2013/pressemitteilung.94192.php. All consulted 5 August 2016.

11. Ulrich Borsdorf and Heinrich Theodor Grütter, eds., *Ruhr Museum: Natur. Kultur. Geschichte* (Essen: Ruhr Museum and Klartext, 2010).

12. Thomas Sieverts, *Cities without Cities: An Interpretation of the Zwischenstadt*, trans. Daniel de Lough (London: Spon Press, 2003).

13. For a pre-IBA perspective see Werner Rutz, "Das Ruhrgebiet als Problemraum," *Baumeister* 69 (1971): 1233–40.

14. Ulrich Borsdorf, *Essen: Geschichte einer Stadt* (Essen: POMP, 2002), 568–78.

15. Stefan Muthesius, *The Postwar University: Utopianist Campus and College* (New Haven, Conn.: Yale University Press, 2000), 224–31.

16. Henry Beierlorzer, Joachim Boll, and Karl Ganser, eds., *Siedlungskultur: Neue und alte Gartenstädte im Ruhrgebiet* (Braunschweig: Vieweg, 1999).

17. Wilhelm Busch, *Bauten der 20er Jahre an Rhein und Ruhr: Architektur als Ausdrucksmittel* (Cologne: J. P. Bachem, 1993). A brick version of expressionism, highly indebted to the architecture of the neighboring Netherlands as well as medieval precedent, was also popular. See Christoph Rauhut and Niels Lehmann, *Fragments of Metropolis: Rhein & Ruhr* (Munich: Hirmer Verlag, 2016).

18. For what was built see ALLBAU [Allgeminer Bauverein Essen AG], ed., *Wohnen und Markt: Gemeinnützigkeit wieder modern* (Essen: Nobel Verlag, 1994). For worker resistance to modernism see Marion Gondau, "Vom guten und schlechten Geschmack: Arbeiter- und Intellektuellenästhetik am Beispiel Wohnen," in *Arbeiterwohnen: Ideal und Wirklichkeit; Zur Geschichte der Möblierung von Arbeiterwohnungen 1850–1950*, ed. Barbara Scheffran (Dortmund: Museum für Kunst und Kulturgeschichte der Stadt Dortmund, 1980), 87–102.

19. Andrea Höber and Karl Ganser, eds., *IndustrieKultur: Mythos und Moderne im Ruhrgebiet; Im Rahmen der IBA Emscher Park* (Essen: Klartext, 1999); "Wandel in Schönheit: Karl Ganser über Nachhaltigkeit, Schönheit und Wandel ohne Wachstum," *Deutsche Bauzeitung* 133 (1999): 101–3; and http://www.iba.nrw.de/main.htm, consulted 5 March 2013.

20. Christoph Gunßer, "Wandel oder Wachstum: Strukturwandel durch Gestaltung?—eine Bilanz," *Deutsche Bauzeitung* 133 (July 1999): 66–71; Sabine Hense-Ferch, "Ein Biotop in der Großstadt," *Süddeutsche Zeitung*, 26 August 2000; Heinrich Lee, "Zukunftswerkstatt Park—IBA Emscher Park," *Deutsche Bauzeitung* 133 (August 1999): 104–6; Arthur Lubow, "The Anti-Olmsted," *New York Times Magazine*, 16 May 2004; Matt Steinglass, "The Machine in the Garden," *Metropolis* 20 (2000): 126–31, 166–67; Udo Weilacher, *Syntax of Landscape: The Landscape Architecture of Peter Latz and Partners* (Basel: Birkhäuser, 2007), 102–33; as well as special editions of *Garten + Landschaft* 10 (1991) and *Topos* 26 (1999). See also Kathleen James-Chakraborty, "Recycling Landscape: Wasteland into Culture," in *Trash Culture: Objects and Obsolescence in Cultural Perspective,* ed. Gillian Pye (Oxford: Peter Lang, 2010), 77–94.

21. Herzog and de Meuron's renovation of the Küppersmühle in Duisburg's inner harbor

into a museum of modern art opened in 1999; a disco has been operating in Bochum's former Prinz Regent Zeche since 1981; Bochum's Bahnhof Langendreer is now a cultural center best known for its art house cinema.

22. http://www.latzanundpartner.de, consulted 16 September 2008, and Weilacher, *Syntax of Landscape*, 82–101.

23. "Bundesgartenschau Dortmund," *Baumeister* 56 (1959): 565; and William S. Saunders, ed., *Richard Haag: Bloedel Reserve and Gas Works Park* (New York: Princeton Architectural Press, 1998).

24. Michael Schwarze-Rodrian et al., *Masterplan Emscher Landschaftspark 2010* (Essen: Klartext, 2005); and Ellen Braea, *Beauty Redeemed* (Basel: Birkhäuser, 2015).

25. The park has won the EDRA Places Award (2005), the 2004 Play and Leisure Award, the 2001 Grand Medaille d'Urbanisme de l'Académie d'Architecture Paris, and in 2000 the First European Prize for Landscape Architecture Rosa Barba, Barcelona.

26. Peter S. Reed, *Groundswell: Constructing the Contemporary Landscape* (New York: Museum of Modern Art, 2000).

27. As explored, for instance, in the Shrinking Cities project. See http://www.shrinkingcities.com/index.php?L=1, consulted 18 June 2011.

28. Thomas Parent, *Das Ruhrgebiet: Kultur und Geschichte im Review zwischen Rhein und Lippe* (Cologne: DuMont, 1984); Günter Streich and Corneel Voigt, *Zechen: Dominanten im Revier; Geschichte, Gegenwart, Zukunft* (Essen: Nobel, 1998); Andreas Rossmann, "Rumpeldipumpel," *Frankfurter Allgemeine Zeitung*, 22 August 2000.

29. David Blackbourn, *The Conquest of Nature: Water, Landscape, and the Making of Modern Germany* (New York: Norton, 2007), demonstrates the paradoxical relationship between this view of nature and the increasingly pragmatic approach taken to waterways.

30. Lubow, "The Anti-Olmsted."

31. Ingo Kowarik and Stefan Körner, *Wild Urban Woodlands: New Perspectives for Urban Forestry* (Vienna: Springer, 2004).

32. See http://www.landschaftspark.de/de/eventlocations/index.html, consulted 16 September 2008.

33. Sieverts, *Cities without Cities*, 115.

34. See Susanne Lange, *Bernd and Hille Becher* (Cambridge, Mass.: MIT Press, 2007), and Heinz Liesbrock, *Bernd & Hilla Becher: Bergwerk und Hütten* (Munich: Schirmer/Mosel, 2010), 5–11, 90–93, for their photographs of the installation that became the Landscape Park.

35. A forceful statement of this equation was the exhibition held in Stuttgart in 1968 to celebrate the fiftieth anniversary of the founding of the Bauhaus.

36. Gary Garrels, *Photography in Contemporary German Art: 1960 to the Present* (Minneapolis: Walker Art Center, 1992).

37. Max Imdahl, *Gesammelte Schriften* (Frankfurt am Main: Suhrkamp, 1996).

38. Crimp, "Serra's Public Sculpture," 49–52.

39. Kynaston McShine and Lynne Cooke, *Richard Serra: Sculpture, Forty Years* (New York: Museum of Modern Art, 2007), 26.

40. http://www.ruhr-guide.de/rg.php?left=menu&mid=artikel&id=11851&kat_id=1&parent_i, consulted 5 March 2013.

41. http://www.robertsmithson.com/essays/interviews.htm, consulted 5 March 2013;

and Robert Smithson, "A Tour of the Monuments of Passaic, New Jersey," in Robert Smithson, *The Collected Writings*, ed. Jack Flam (Berkeley: University of California Press, 1996), 248–56.

42. http://www.latzundpartner.de/projects/detail/18, consulted 16 September 2008.
43. The High Line was designed by a team that included the architecture firm of Diller Scofidio + Renfro. Early in her career, Elizabeth Diller took a study tour through the Ruhr region.
44. Michael Meng, *Shattered Spaces: Encountering Jewish Ruins in Germany and Poland* (Cambridge, Mass.: Harvard University Press, 2011), 113–29, 242–49, for the history of the conversion of the synagogue in Essen first into a design museum and then, with the involvement of the historian Detlev Peukert, into one that commemorated the city's Jewish community.
45. http://www.kulturhauptstadt-europas.de/start.php, consulted 22 December 2005, for the degree to which this building was key to that effort. On the building itself see Walter Buschmann, ed., *Zechen und Kokereien im rheinischen Steinkohlenbergbau: Aachener Revier und westliches Ruhrgebiet* (Berlin: Gebr. Mann, 1998), 414–85; Stiftung Zollverein, *The Zollverein World Heritage Site*; and Rolf Tiggemann, *Zollverein Schacht XII: Von der größten Zeche der Welt zum Weltkulturerbe* (Essen: Klartext, 2007); and Kathleen James-Chakraborty, "Inventing Industrial Culture in Essen," in Paul Jaskot and Gavriel Rosenfeld, eds., *Beyond Berlin: German Cities Confront the Nazi Past* (Ann Arbor: University of Michigan Press, 2007) 116–39.
46. Examples include Kift, *Tour the Ruhr*, 93; almost any citation of the building in the *Westdeutsche Allgemeine Zeitung*; http:://www.unesco.de/unesco-heute/202/zollverein.htm, whose text, written by Birgitta Ringbeck, includes a heading "Vom Bauhaus beeinflusste Industriearchitektur"; http:/www.essen.de/module/meldungen/m_detail.asp?MNR=1281; and http://www.bkkvorort.de/magazin/wellness-und-frezeit/zeche-zollverein-in/essen. These websites were consulted 7 June 2005. All of this changed in 2006 after I circulated an early version of this research. Such references were cut from the website of the bid for the cultural capital status and from the Zeche Zollverein website http://www.zollverein.de/index.php?f_categoryId=85&f_menu3=85, consulted 26 October 2006. That site then included the following, quoted from the English language version: "In view of the extremely reduced buildings, one could come to the conclusion that the design of the architects [was] influenced by the modern revolutionary spirit of the 1920s. Yet it is unknown how much Schupp and Kremmer were interested in the modern movement. Indeed, claims that Zollverein's architecture, like the Bauhaus-school, is to be classed among Nazi-architecture, are clearly incorrect: pure, rational aesthetics arising out of maximum reduction is what classifies Shaft XII, not pure functionality or bombastic ornament. Indeed, the style of construction is based on the classic principles and the desire to be monumental: after all, Zollverein, as the coal mine of the world's second biggest 'megatrust' of the 'Vereinigte Stahlwerke AG,' was a symbol of economic power and a whole generation's absolute belief in progress." Traces of the once ubiquitous rhetoric survived longer in less official places. See, for instance, http://de.wikipedia.org/wiki/Zeche_Zollverein, as well as the unaltered UNESCO description, http://www.unesco.de/318.html, both consulted 18 June 2011.
47. Udo Mainzer, "Die große Geschichte," in *Die Zollverein-Zeche in Essen/Schacht XII/*

Eine Denkmal-Landschaft von Weltrang im Herzen Europas/Eine Denkschrift zur Begründung des Antrags zur Aufnahme in die UNESCO-Liste des Welt-Kulturerbes (Entwurf, Stand: April 1997), 6, in Akten 223, IBA Emscher Park Archiv, Stiftung Bibliothek des Ruhrgebiets, Bochum, Germany.

48. Ibid. For a rare attack on this position see Detlef Hoffmann, "Authentische Erinnerungsorte; oder, Von der Sehnsucht nach Echtheit und Erlebnis," in Meier and Wohlleben, *Bauten und Orte als Träger von Erinnerung,* 39.
49. Ibid., 8.
50. "Die Forderungen der christlichen Bergarbeiter," *Allgemeine Wattenscheide Zeitung,* 2 February 1932.
51. Dirk Hautkapp, "Wenn dem Buxloch 'was nicht gefiel,'" *NRZ Essen,* 1 February 1992. Also ignored is the degree to which the postwar colliery, one of the youngest buildings to be designated a contributing part of a World Heritage Site, was in 1961 denounced by neighbors for its toxic emissions. See Borsdorf, *Essen,* 514. More recently Stiftung Zollverein, *The Zollverein World Heritage Site,* has been far more open about these aspects of its subject's past and of the work built during the Third Reich by its architects. See also the admission in Thomas Parent, "Vom Anfang und Ende der Industriekultur," in Günter, *Alte und Neue Industriekultur,* 45, that Auschwitz's ovens were manufactured in the region.
52. It also fell neatly between the two camps of modern German architecture identified in Manfredo Tafuri, *Architecture and Utopia* (Cambridge, Mass.: MIT Press, 1976), 110.
53. Jeffrey Herf, *Reactionary Modernism: Technology, Culture, and Politics in Weimar and the Third Reich* (Cambridge: Cambridge University Press, 1984); Michael Prinz and Rainer Zitelmann, *Nationalsozialismus und Modernisierung* (Darmstadt: Wissenschaftliche Buchgesellschaft, 1991); Geoff Eley, *Reshaping the German Right: Radical Nationalism and Political Change after Bismarck* (New Haven, Conn.: Yale University Press, 1980); and Geoff Eley, ed., *Society, Culture, and the State in Germany, 1870–1930* (Ann Arbor: University of Michigan Press, 1996). Examples that focus on art and architecture include Lane, *Architecture and Politics in Germany, 1918–1945*; Werner Durth, *Deutsche Architekten: Biographische Verflechtungen 1900–1970* (Braunschweig: Krämer, 1987); Nerdinger, *Bauhaus-Moderne im Natinoalsozialismus*; and Betts, *The Authority of Everyday Objects.*
54. James-Chakraborty, *German Architecture for a Mass Audience*; and Richard Etlin, ed., *Art, Culture, and Media under the Third Reich* (Chicago: University of Chicago Press, 2002). For the implications of this position for place marketing see Claire Colomb, *Staging the New Berlin: Place Marketing and the Politics of Urban Reinvention* (London: Routledge, 2012).
55. Funding for the project came from the city of Essen, the state of North Rhine-Westphalia, and the European Union.
56. Betts, *Authority of Everyday Objects,* for the relationship between class and taste. For Essen election results see Borsdorf, *Essen,* 568–78. See also Paul Tyrer and Mark Crinson, "Totemic Park: Symbolic Representations in Post-industrial Space," in *Urban Memory: History and Amnesia in the Modern City,* ed. Mark Crinson (London: Routledge, 2005), 103.

Notes to Chapter 5

57. The importance of the preservation of working-class experiences is highlighted in Helmut Lackner, "Industriekultur-Kritische Anmerkungen nach drei Jahrzehnten," 31–39, and Thomas Schleper, "Thesen zur 'Versonntäglichung' der Industriekultur," 82, both in Günter, *Alte und Neue Industriekultur*.
58. For an early assessment of the site's history that consistently links the history of heavy industry in the region to the emergence of political democracy in Germany and economic unification in Europe see the *Abschlussbericht der Projektgruppe Zollverein, Aufsichtsrat/ Zollverein/19*. Sitzung/3.9.92, IBA Akten 47, 14–19. The association with the Bauhaus also figures prominently here.
59. http://www.zollverein.de/englisch/start.php, consulted 8 June 2005.
60. Frederic J. Schwarz, *The German Werkbund: Design Theory and Mass Culture before the First World War* (New Haven, Conn.: Yale University Press, 1996).
61. This was particularly true of Walter Gropius and Bruno Taut. See Marcel Franciscono, *Walter Gropius and the Creation of the Bauhaus in Weimar: The Ideals and Artistic Training of Its Founding Years* (Urbana: University of Illinois Press, 1971); Whyte, *Bruno Taut and the Architecture of Activism*; and Pehnt, *Die Architektur des Expressionismus*.
62. Lane, *Architecture and Politics, 1918–1945*.
63. Wilhelm Busch and Thorsten Scheer, eds., *Symmetrie und Symbol: Die Industriearchitektur von Fritz Schupp und Martin Kremmer* (Cologne: Walther König, 2002), especially Ulrike Laufer, "Die Architekten: Fritz Schupp und Martin Kremmer," 15–30.
64. Voigt and Frank, *Paul Schmitthenner 1884–1972*.
65. "Industriebauten der Architekten Schupp & Kremmer, Berlin-Essen," *Baukunst* 4 (1930): 104.
66. Ibid., 107.
67. Manfred Rasch, "Über Albert Vögler und sein Verhältnis zur Politik," *Mitteilungsblatt des Instituts für soziale Bewegung: Forschungen und Forschungsberichte* 28 (2003): 127–56; S. Jonathan Wiesen, *West German Industry and the Challenge of the Nazi Past, 1945–1955* (Chapel Hill: University of North Carolina Press, 2000), 151–55; and Gerald Feldman, *Hugo Stinnes: Biographie eines Industriellen 1870–1924*, trans. Karl Heinz Siber (Munich: C. H. Beck, 1998).
68. Rasch, "Über Albert Vögler und sein Verhältnis zur Politik."
69. Buschmann, *Zechen und Kokereien*, 450. The lettering was removed in the mid-1960s. I thank Hans Hanke for reminding me of its political dimension. See also Claus Steins, "Shaft 12—a Creation of Fritz Schupp and Martin Kremmer," in Stiftung Zollverein, *The Zollverein World Heritage Site*, 76.
70. There were, however, certainly slave laborers at the Zeche Zollverein. See Klaus Tenfelde and Hans-Christoph Seidel, eds., *Zwangsarbeit im Bergwerk: Der Arbeitseinsatz im Kohlenbergbau des Deutschen Reiches und der besetzten Gebiete im Ersten und Zweiten Weltkrieg* (Essen: Klartext, 2005), 624. In 2012 the museum hosted the exhibition *Forced Labor: The Germans, the Forced Laborers, and the War*. http://www.ausstellung-zwangsarbeit.org/index.php?id=273&L=1, consulted 5 March 2013.
71. Gerdy Troost, *Das Bauen im neuen Reich* (Bayreuth: Gauverlag Bayerische Ostmark, 1938), 73.

72. Anson Rabinbach, "The Aesthetics of Production in the Third Reich," *Journal of Contemporary History* 11 (1976): 43–76.
73. Troost, *Das Bauen im neuen Reich*; Durth, *Deutsche Architekten*, 139; and Nerdinger, *Bauhaus-Moderne*, 173.
74. Troost, *Das Bauen im neuen Reich*, 73.
75. Durth, *Deutsche Architekten*, 139, and Nerdinger, *Bauhaus-Moderne*, 173. The photograph published by Troost that reappears in these two later works was originally published in Fritz Bauer, "Zeche 'Zollverein' in Essen-Karternberg," *Zentralblatt der Bauverwaltung vereinigt mit Zeitschrift für Bauwesen* 54 (1934): 101, where no date was given for Pithead XII's construction.
76. "Die Forderungen der christlichen Bergarbeiter," *Allgemeine Wattenscheide Zeitung*, 2 February 1932. The adjective *brotlos* appeared as well in the caption of a photograph of the building published on the same day in the *General Anzeiger für Dortmund und das gesamte rheinisch-westfälische Industriegebiet*, which gave the number of people thrown out of work as one thousand.
77. "Weitere Zunahme der Arbeitslosigkeit," *General Anzeiger für Dortmund und das gesamte rheinisch-westfälische Industriegebiet*, 9 February 1932.
78. Hautkapp, "Wenn dem Buxloch 'was nicht gefiel.'"
79. For the entire bibliography see Buschmann, *Zechen und Kokereien*, 414–15.
80. Betts, *The Authority of Everyday Objects*, 37.
81. Ibid., 39.
82. Walter Buschmann, "Zeche Zollverein in Essen," *Rheinische Kunststätten* 219 (1987): 9, as consulted in Zollverein/im Spiegel der Presse/Teil III/Januar 1992–April 1992, IBA Akten 222. His conclusions are repeatedly echoed in the IBA files. For an early example see Ammerkungen zur Zecheanlage Zollverein Schacht XII, 3, Zollverein XII/AR, 1. Sitzung/12. Febr. 1990, IBA Akten 46. See also Rudolf Fischer, *Licht und Transparenz: Der Fabrikbau und das Neue Bauen in den Architekturzeitschriften der Moderne* (Berlin: Gebr. Mann Verlag, 2012), 77–82. See also Wilhelm Busch, *F. Schupp, M. Kremmer: Bergbauarchitektur 1919–1974*, Landeskonservator Rheinland, Arbeitshefte 13 (Cologne, 1980); and Fritz Schupp, "Schachtanlage in Ruhrgebiet," *Bauen + Wohnen* 12 (1957): 154–56.
83. Mies's conservatism is highlighted in Fritz Neumeyer, *The Artless Word: Mies van der Rohe on the Building Art*, trans. Mark Jarzombek (Cambridge, Mass.: MIT Press, 1991). For Neumeyer this tied Mies to neoclassicism, but Mies's support for Rudolf Schwarz suggests a broader sympathy for less radical modernism.
84. In addition to Busch's dissertation on Schupp and Kremmer, they had access to a series of reports written from a more critical perspective than the publicity that was generated from them. See "Abschlussbericht der Projektgruppe Zollverein," 19, Aufsichtsrat/Zollverein/19. Sitzung/3.9.92, IBA Akten 47. and *Einige Überlegungen zur Umnutzung stillgelegter Schachtanlagen der Zeche Zollverein im Nordosten Essens: Eine Studie der Planergruppe Oberhausen GmbH* (undated, probably 1988), 12, IBA Akten 222.
85. Mko, "FDP will mehr Geld für Kultur," *Westdeutsche allgemeine Zeitung Essen*, 28 February 1992, Zollverein/im Spiegel der Presse/Teil III/Januar 1992–April 1992, IBA

Notes to Chapter 5

Akten 222, reports on the plan to move the museum. A clipping from the Unicum Essen, headlined "Folkwang-Designhochschule Essen," in 37/Sitzung [7 February 1995], IBA Akten 111, includes comments that the Folkwang's music school should not move for this reason.

86. Borsdorf, *Essen,* 533, which notes that this part of northern Essen had the city's highest concentration of Turks.
87. Buschmann, *Zechen und Kokereien,* 447, for photographs from 1932 and 1995 showing the powerhouse flanked by the machine workshop and the electric workshop before and after the demolition of the smokestack.
88. Quoted in *Office Design* 03–97, 60. The clipping can be found in 55. Sitzung [7 November 1997], IBA Akten 113.
89. As observed in site visits made in the summers of 2002 and 2003.
90. http://www.zollverein-school.de, consulted 26 October 2005. The building has since the beginning of 2010 housed the Folkwang University of the Arts. See http://www.folkwang-uni.de/home/hochschule/ueber-folkwang, consulted 5 March 2013.
91. Borsdorf and Grütter, *Ruhr Museum,* for the catalog to the museum's original permanent exhibition, which doubles as an excellent example of the approach local institutions have taken to the region's history since the onset of the IBA.
92. Gerhard Mack, *Herzog & de Meuron 1992–1996* (Basel: Birkhäuser, 2000), 90–113, 212–21.
93. Lowenthal, *The Heritage Crusade and the Spoils of History* and *The Past Is a Foreign Country,* adopted without attribution in Arjun Appadurai, *Modernity at Large: Cultural Dimensions of Globalization* (Minneapolis: University of Minnesota Press, 1996), 31.
94. Local discussions have moved on to the possible demolition of century-old housing no longer needed by a shrinking population. See Gregor Boldt, "Stadtplanung mit der Abrissbirne," *Westdeutsche Allgemeine Zeitung,* 7 July 2012.
95. The closure of the A-40 was the highlight of Essen's year as a cultural capital. See http://www.ruhr2010.still-leben-ruhrschnellweg.de, consulted 7 August 2016.
96. See http://www.landschaftspark.de/de/lage/anfahrtsweg/index.html, consulted 16 September 2008.
97. See http://www.landschaftspark.de/de/home/index.php, consulted 16 September 2009. The Love Parade debacle in Duisburg in 2010 highlighted the manipulation of attendance figures.
98. Matthias Korfmann, "Das Ruhrgebiet schrumpft langsamer," and Christopher Onkelbach, "Bewerbung bei UNESCO: Ruhr-Industrie als Welterbe: Die Region will ihre Markenzeichen schützen. Eine Anerkennung hätte aber auch Nachteile," both *Westdeutsche Allgemeine Zeitung,* 28 October 2011; and "Unternehmer: Industrie ist kein Fall fürs Museum," *Westdeutsche Allgemeine Zeitung,* 29 October 2011.
99. Gudrun Norbisrath, "New York feiert Bochum," *Westdeutsche Allgemeine Zeitung,* 7 July 2008.
100. While toeing the official line, parts of Schwarze-Rodrian et al., *Masterplan Emscher Landschaftspark 2010,* begin to acknowledge its limitations.
101. Scheffran, *Arbeiterwohnen.* See also Sewing, *No More Learning from Las Vegas,* 338–44, for neomodernism as a form of elite culture that breaks with modernism's purported

empowerment of the working class, while Tafuri, *Architecture and Utopia,* remains as relevant as ever.
102. Marc Treib, "Remembering Ruins, Ruins Remembering," in Treib, *Spatial Recall,* 210.
103. For the environmental damage caused by the Zeche Zollverein, see Dietmar Bleidick, "Living with Zollverein: Mining and Urban Growth in the North of Essen," in Stiftung Zollverein, *The Zollverein World Heritage Site,* 89–92.

6. Assimilating Modern Memory

1. "Starker Auftritt der Kölner gegen Rechts," *Kölner Stadt-Anzeiger,* 5 March 2006; http://www.ksta.de/koeln-uebersicht/starker-auftritt-der-koelner-gegen-rechts,16341264,13705300.html, consulted 3 May 2013.
2. Ralph Giordano, "Nicht die Moschee, der Islam ist das Problem," in *Der Moschee-Streit: Eine exemplarische Debatte über Einwanderung und Integration,* ed. Franz Sommerfeld (Cologne: Kiepenheuer & Witsch, 2008), 39.
3. Mark Landler, "Germans Split over Mosque and the Role of Islam," *New York Times,* 5 July 2007, and Tom Hundley, "Will Minarets Rise from Skyline?," *Chicago Tribune,* 12 August 2007.
4. Nicholas Cumming-Bruce and Steven Erlanger, "Swiss Ban Building of Minarets on Mosques," *New York Times,* 29 November 2009; and Volker M. Heins, *Der Skandal der Vielfalt: Geschichte und Konzepte des Multikulturalismus* (Cologne: Campus, 2013). For the more recent influx see http://syrianrefugees.eu, consulted 12 September 2016; and Peter Cachola Schmal, Oliver Elser, and Anna Scheuermann, eds., *Making Heimat: Germany, Arrival Country* (Ostfildern: Hatje Cantz, 2016).
5. An important exception is Ernst-Wolfgang Böckenförde, "Säkularer Staat und Religion," in Sommerfeld, *Der Moschee-Streit,* 130–46.
6. "Wir wollten niemand provozieren," *Köln Stadt-Anzeiger,* 28 June 2006, and "Tiefensees Lob für Moscheebau," *Köln Stadt-Anzeiger,* 30 August 2007. See also Thomas Schmitt, "Mosque Debates in Space-Related, Intercultural, and Religious Conflict," in *Religion and Migration: Christian Transatlantic Missions, Islamic Migration in Germany,* ed. Barbara Becker-Cantarino (Amsterdam: Editions Rodopi B. V, 2012), 207–17, for Merkez as a model mosque.
7. For the mosque design as Ottoman, see "CDU gegen 'Großmoschee,'" *Koln Stadt-Anzeiger,* 21 April 2006.
8. Kai Kappel, *Memento 1945?,* 150–51, 158–59, 265–67.
9. Bernd Nicolai, *Moderne und Exil: Deutschsprachige Architekten in der Türkei* (Berlin: Verlag für Bauwesen, 1998); Burcu Dogramaci, *Kulturtransfer und nationale Identität: Deutschsprachige Architekten, Stadtplaner und Bildhauer in der Türkei nach 1927* (Berlin: Gebr. Mann Verlag, 2008); Sibel Bozdogan, *Modernism and Nation Building: Turkish Architectural Culture in the Early Republic* (Seattle: University of Washington Press, 2001); and Sibel Bozdogan and Esra Akcan, *Turkey* (London: Reaktion, 2012).
10. These observations are based on my conversations with Germans in December 2015. See also Emma Graham-Harrison et al., "Cheering German Crowds Greet Refugees after Long Trek from Budapest to Munich," *Guardian,* 5 September 2015.

Notes to Chapter 6

11. Kamaal Haque, "Iranian, Afghan, and Pakistani Migrants in Germany: Muslim Populations Beyond Turks and Arabs," in Becker-Cantarino, *Religion and Migration*, 193–206.
12. Rita Chin, *The Guest Worker Question in Postwar Germany* (Cambridge: Cambridge University Press, 2007), esp. 158–71; Ruth Mandel, *Cosmopolitan Anxieties: Turkish Challenges to Citizenship and Belonging in Germany* (Durham, N.C.: Duke University Press, 2008), esp. 294–310; and Rebekka Habermas, "Islam Debates around 1900: Colonies in Africa, Muslims in Berlin, and the Role of Missionaries and Orientalists," in Becker-Cantarino, *Migration and Religion*, 123–54.
13. Deniz Göktürk, David Gramling, and Anton Kaes, eds., *Germany in Transit: Nation and Migration, 1955–2005* (Berkeley: University of California Press, 2007); David Deißner, Thomas Ellerbeck, and Benno Stieber, eds., *Wir: 19 Leben in einem neuen Deutschland* (Munich: Piper, 2011); and Fatima El-Tayeb, *European Others: Queering Ethnicity in Postnational Europe* (Minneapolis: University of Minnesota Press, 2011).
14. Christopher Caldwell, "Where Every Generation Is First Generation," *New York Times Magazine*, 27 May 2007.
15. https://www.destatis.de/EN/FactsFigures/SocietyState/Population/Migration Integration/MigrationIntegration.htm, consulted 3 May 2013. For Europe as having long included Muslims see Gerard Delanty, *Formations of European Modernity: A Historical and Political Sociology of Europe* (Basingstoke, UK: Palgrave Macmillan, 2013).
16. Dieter Bleidick, "Living with Zollverein: Mining and Urban Growth in the North of Essen," in Stiftung Zollverein, *The Zollverein World Heritage Site*, 104–6.
17. An early example of the focus on housing is "Wohnsituation der Gastarbeiter," *Bauwelt* 61 (1970): 1821–26, which highlighted the importance to Turkish immigrants of having a mosque in the neighborhood. Gottfried Böhm designed Chorweiler, a largely Turkish district of Cologne, as an alternative to the tenements in which many Turks lived. See Urban, *Neo-historical East Berlin*, 75–77.
18. Sabine Kraft, *Islamische Sakralarchitektur in Deutschland: Eine Untersuchung ausgewählter Moschee-Neubauten* (Munster: LIT Verlag, 2002); Ursula Baus, ed., *Mosques in Germany* (Tübingen: Wasmuth, 2009); Ergün Erkoçu and Cihan Buğdacı, *The Mosque: Political, Architectural and Social Transformations* (Rotterdam: NAi, 2009); Institut für Auslandsbeziehungen, ed., *Kubus oder Kuppel: Moscheen—Perspectiven einer Bauaufgabe* (Tübingen: Wasmuth, 2012); and Holger Kleine, *New Mosques: Design and Vision* (Berlin: Jovis, 2014).
19. http://www.bundespraesident.de/SharedDocs/Reden/DE/Christian-Wulff/Reden /2010/10/20101003_Rede.html, consulted 12 September 2016, and "Merkel—Deutsche werde mehr Moscheen sehen," *Die Welt*, 18 September 2010.
20. "Synagogen im Überblick: Über hundert nach 1945 errichtete Synagogen und Betsäle sind ab 9. November 2008 online," http://www.zentralratdjuden.de/de/article/2065.html, consulted 12 September 2016; and Ulrich Knufinke, "Architektur und Erinnerung: Synagogenbau in Deutschland nach der Shoa . . . ," in Kai Kappel and Matthias Müller, *Geschichtsbilder und Erinnerungskultur in der Architektur des 20. und 21. Jahrhunderts* (Regensburg: Schnell & Steiner, 2014), 93–108.

21. http://www.koelnarchitektur.de/pages/de/home/aktuell/1440.htm, consulted 17 August 2007.
22. "Moderner Kuppelbau mit zwei Minaretten, *Köln Stadt-Anzeiger,* 21 September 2006.
23. http://www.ditib.de, consulted 3 May 2013, and for the population figures "Giordano: Ich bekomme Morddrohungen," *Köln Stadt-Anzeiger,* 25 May 2007.
24. Jonathan Laurence, "(Re)constructing Community in Berlin: Turks, Jews, and German Responsibility," *German Politics and Society* 19, no. 2 (2001): 22–61. For the current situation see Elliot Ackerman, "Atatürk versus Erdogan: Turkey's Long Struggle," *New Yorker,* 16 July 2016, http://www.newyorker.com/news/news-desk/ataturk-versus-erdogan-turkeys-long-struggle, consulted 13 September 2016.
25. Jörg Lau, "Wer ein Haus baut will bleiben—zum Kölner Moscheestreit," http://blog.zeit.de/joerglau/2007/05/31, consulted 24 March 2009. Petra Kuppinger, "Notes on Space, Culture and Islam: Notes on Urban Transformations in Stuttgart, Germany," in *Defining Space,* ed. Hugh Campbell, Douglas Smith and Brian Ward (Dublin: University College Dublin, 2007), 107–8, for the abstract of a conference paper on mosques in Stuttgart.
26. Baus, *Mosques in Germany,* and Peter Eichhorn und Thomas Götz, *Berlin: Sakrale Orte* (Berlin: Grebennikov, 2010), 78–85. See also http://www.dwworld.de/dw/article/0,2144,2570710,00.html, consulted 24 March 2009.
27. "Zweieinhalb Jahre Streit um Zentralmoschee," *Köln Stadt-Anzeiger,* 29 August 2008.
28. Johannes Nitschmann, "Moschee wird gebaut," *Süddeutsche Zeitung,* 28 August 2008.
29. Ibid.
30. Frank Überall, "Neuer Streit um Kölner Moschee: Bauherr feuert den Architekten und Kirchenbaumeister Paul Böhm—aus Strategie? Terminchaos und Kosteneinsteigerung," *Westdeutsche Allgemeine Zeitung,* 31 October 2011; "Kultur," 1; "DITIB bleibt Millionen-Zahlung," *Die Welt,* 8 March 2013; and Andreas Rossmann, "Neubauruine," *Frankfurter Allgemeine Zeitung,* 24 August 2014.
31. Tim Röhn, "Wie Ankara in Köln Weltpolitik," *Welt N24,* 10 May 2016, https://www.welt.de/politik/deutschland/article154711275/Wie-Ankara-in-Koeln-Weltpolitik-betreibt.html, consulted 13 September 2016. On the opening of the new mosque see Tim Attenberger, "Mit fünf Jahren Verspätung: Erstes Freitagsgebet in Ehrenfelder Moschee," *Köln Stadt-Anzeiger,* 9 June 2017; this article includes good photographs of the completed interior.
32. Lawrence Wright, *The Looming Tower: Al-Qaeda and the Road to 9/11* (New York: Vintage, 2007), 345–50.
33. Kishwar Rizvi, *The Transnational Mosque: Architecture and Historical Memory in the Contemporary Middle East* (Chapel Hill: University of North Carolina Press, 2015); and Renate Holod and Hassan Udin Khan, *The Contemporary Mosque: Architects, Clients, and Designs since the 1950s* (New York: Rizzoli, 1997).
34. David Gramling, "'You Pray Like We Have Fun': Towards a Phenomenology of Secular Islam," in Becker-Cantarino, *Migration and Religion,* 175–91. German converts to Islam often do not see themselves as belonging to any foreign tradition. See Esra Özyürek, *Being German, Becoming Muslim: Race, Religion and Conversion in the New Europe* (Princeton, N.J.: Princeton University Press, 2014).

Notes to Chapter 6

35. Mehmet Yildirim, "Die Kölner Ditib-Moschee—eine offene Moschee als Integrationsbeitrag," in Sommerfeld, *Der Moschee-Streit*, 67.
36. Andreas Damm, "Schramma will über Höhen reden," *Kölner Stadt Anzeiger*, 23 August 2007, http://www.ksta.de/koeln-uebersicht/schramma-will-ueber-hoehen-reden,16341264,13378314.html, consulted 3 May 2013. See also http://www.boehmarchitektur.de/deutsch/hochbau/hochbau_zentralmoschee.html, consulted 17 August 2007, for the architects' presentation of their design.
37. Holod and Khan, *The Contemporary Mosque*, 13.
38. An exception is the Omar Ibn al-Khattab Mosque in the heavily Turkish Berlin district of Kreuzberg.
39. "Moderne Kuppelbau mit zwei Minaretten."
40. Michael Lewis, *The Politics of the German Gothic Revival: August Reichensperger* (New York: Architectural History Foundation, 1993), 25–56.
41. For the Steel Church and its relationship to the Glashaus, see Kathleen James-Chakraborty, *German Architecture for a Mass Audience*, 57–63.
42. http://www.boehmarchitektur.de/deutsch/hochbau/hochbau_zentralmoschee.html, consulted 17 August 2007.
43. Manfred Speidel, "Gottfried Böhm's Churches: A Typological Study," in Voigt, *Gottfried Böhm*, 115–18.
44. http://bauwatch.koelnarchitektur.de/pages/de/architekturfuehrer/45.katholische_kirche_sttheodor.htm, consulted 3 May 2013.
45. "Bedingungen für Moscheebauten," *Köln Stadt-Anzeiger*, 5 June 2007.
46. "CDU gegen 'Großmoschee.'"
47. Sabine Kraft, "Moscheearchitektur zwischen Nostalgie und Moderne," in Sommerfeld, *Der Moschee-Streit*, 175–76. See also "Konkurrenz der Religionen," 13 July 2007, *Köln Stadt-Anzeiger*; and Kraft, *Islamische Sakralarchitektur in Deutschland*.
48. http://www.pro-koeln-online.de/artikel2/ditib-moschee.htm, dated 7 March 2006 and consulted 24 March 2009, and Hundley, "Will Minarets Rise from Skyline?"
49. This is addressed in Kathleen James-Chakraborty, "The Debate over the Mosque in Cologne: An Architectural Historian's Response," in *Crossing Borders: Space Beyond Disciplines*, ed. Kathleen James-Chakraborty and Sabine Strümper-Krobb (Oxford: Peter Lang, 2011), 189–203.
50. Sommerfeld, *Der Moschee-Streit*, for the ubiquity of these positions.
51. Joachim Cardinal Meisner, "Keine Angst—aber ein ungutes Gefühl," in Sommerfeld, *Der Moschee-Streit*, 180.
52. Tatjana Kimmel, "Bistum Essen muß Kirchen verkaufen und abreißen," *Die Zeit*, 12 January 2006, 11.
53. Peter Berger, "Zwischen Damla und Scholzen," in Sommerfeld, *Der Moschee-Streit*, 102.
54. Esra Akcan, "Apology and Triumph: Memory Transference, Erasure, and a Rereading of the Berlin Jewish Museum," *New German Critique* 37 (2010): 153–79.
55. Stefan Laurin, "Alltag unter Polizeischutz," *Welt N24*, 10 August 2014, consulted 13 September 2016, and "Radikales Netzwerk plante Sikh-Anschlag in Essen," 28 June 2016, *Westdeutsche Allgemeine Zeitung*.

56. "The Merkez Mosque as a Symbol of New Acceptance," http://www.arabia.pl/english/content/view/197/16, posted 17 September 2006, consulted 13 July 2007.
57. Christoph Schurian, "Kulturen," in Borsdorf and Grütter, *Ruhr Museum,* 143. More recently it has attracted attention as a more conservative faction appeared to gain control. See "Sorge um Muster-Moschee in Duisburg-Marxloh," *Westdeutsche Allgemeine Zeitung,* 12 December 2009.
58. Peter Burger, "Das Problem Köln," *Die Zeit Online,* 21 June 2017, http://www.zeit.de/2017/26/ditib-moschee-koeln-tuerkei, consulted 27 July 2017.
59. Maciuika, *Before the Bauhaus*; and Regina Bittner and Kathrin Rhomberg, eds., *The Bauhaus in Calcutta: An Encounter of the Cosmopolitan Avant-Garde* (Ostfildern: Hatje Cantz Verlag, 2013). For German Orientalism see Mario Alexander Zadow, *Schinkels Blick nach Indien* (Fellbach: Edition Axel Menges, 2013).
60. William S. W. Lim and Jiat-Hwee Chang, eds., *Non-West Modernist Past: On Architecture and Modernities* (Singapore: World Scientific Publishing, 2012); Duanfang Lu, ed., *Third World Modernism: Architecture, Development and Identity* (London: Routledge, 2010); and Joe Nasr and Mercedes Volait, eds., *Urbanism: Imported or Exported?* (Chichester, UK: John Wiley, 2003).
61. Adrian Forty, *Concrete and Culture: A Material History* (London: Reaktion, 2012), highlights this ubiquity while disagreeing that it is necessarily a product of either modernity or modernism.
62. Kathleen James-Chakraborty, "Beyond Postcolonialism: New Directions in the History of Nonwestern Architecture," *Frontiers of Architectural Research* 3, no. (2014): 1–9.
63. Cinar Kiper, "Sultan Erdogan: Turkey's Rebranding into the New, Old Ottoman Empire," *Atlantic,* 5 April 2013.
64. For an expanded counterargument in the case of the United States see Kathleen James-Chakraborty, "From Isolationism to Internationalism: American Acceptance of the Bauhaus," in James-Chakraborty, *Bauhaus Culture,* 153–70. See also Pamela M. Potter, *Art of Suppression: Confronting the Nazi Past in Histories of the Visual and Performing Arts* (Berkeley: University of California Press, 2016), 48–88.
65. Dipesh Chakrabarty, *Provincializing Europe: Postcolonial Thought and Historical Difference* (Princeton, N.J.: Princeton University Press, 2000), for a critique of this position. See also Kathleen James-Chakraborty, "Architecture of the Cold War: Louis Kahn and Edward Durrell Stone in South Asia," in *Building America: Eine große Erzählung,* vol. 3, ed. Anke Köth, Kai Krauskopf, and Andreas Schwarting (Dresden: Thelem, 2008), 169–82.
66. This included Great Britain and Scandinavia, above all Finland, as well as the Balkans. See Luminita Machedon and Ernie Scoffham, *Romanian Modernism: The Architecture of Bucharest, 1920–1940* (Cambridge, Mass.: MIT Press, 1999).
67. Jeannine Fiedler, *Social Utopias of the Twenties: Bauhaus, Kibbutz and the Dream of the New Man* (Wuppertal: Müller + Busmann, 1995); and Pe'era Goldmane et al., *Tel Aviv: Neues Bauen 1930–1939* (Tübingen: Wasmuth, 1993).
68. Esra Akcan, *Architecture in Translation: Germany, Turkey, and the Modern House* (Durham, N.C.: Duke University Press, 2012), and Paul Bonatz, "Hilton Hotel Istanbul," *Baumeister* 53 (1956): 535–51.

69. Bozdogan, *Modernism and Nation Building.*
70. Magnus T. Bernardsson, "Visions of Iraq: Modernizing the Past in 1950s Baghdad," and Panayiota I. Pyla, "Baghdad's Urban Restructuring, 1958: Aesthetics and the Politics of Nation Building," both in *Modernism and the Middle East: Architecture and Politics in the Twentieth Century,* ed. Sandy Isenstadt and Kishwar Rizvi (Seattle: University of Washington Press, 2008), 81–115; and Joseph M. Siry, "Wright's Baghdad Opera House and Gammage Auditorium: In Search of Regional Modernity," *Art Bulletin* 87 (2005): 265–311.
71. This is particularly evident in the case of Brazil. See Zilah Quezado Deckker, *Brazil Built: The Architecture of the Modern Movement in Brazil* (London: Spon, 2001), Fernando Luiz Lara, *The Rise of Populist Modern Architecture in Brazil* (Gainesville: University Press of Florida, 2008), and Richard J. Williams, *Brazil: Modern Architectures in History* (London: Reaktion, 2009).
72. Kathleen James-Chakraborty, *Architecture since 1400* (Minneapolis: University of Minnesota Press, 2014), 424–38; and James-Chakraborty, "Beyond Postcolonialism."
73. Esra Akcan, "A Building with Many Speakers: Turkish 'Guest Workers' and Alvaro Siza's Bonjour Tristesse Housing for IBA—Berlin," in *The Migrant's Time: Rethinking Art History and Diaspora,* ed. Saloni Mathur (Williamstown, Mass.: Clark Studies in the Visual Arts, 2011), 91–114; and Stefanie Bürkle, ed, *Migrating Spaces: Architecture and Identity in the Context of Turkish Remigration* (Berlin: Vice Versa Verlag, 2016).
74. The resemblance to a mosque is acknowledged in Udo Kittelmann and Joachim Jäger, eds., *Rudolf Stingel: Neue Nationalgalerie Berlin* (Cologne: Walther König, 2010). See also Inge Ruthe, "Neue Nationalgalerie: Der Südtiroler Maler Rudolf Stingel bricht die Bauhaus-Aura der Mies-van-der-Rohe-Halle orientalisch Bleib auf dem Teppich," *Berliner Zeitung,* 11 February 2010; and http://blog.arthistoricum.net/en/beitrag/2010/03/07/rudolf-stingel-live, consulted 13 September 2016.
75. Sommerfeld, *Der Moschee-Streit,* 12.
76. These were reprised in the summer of 2016 in France by the debate over the burkini. See Celestine Bohlen, "The Multifaceted 'Burkini' Debate," *New York Times,* 22 August 2016.
77. James-Chakraborty, "The Debate over the Mosque in Cologne," 196–98.
78. Landler, "Germans Split over Mosque and the Role of Islam."
79. German debates over the headscarf have focused on well-educated adult women, often ethnic Germans, who seek to wear it while holding jobs as teachers. Göktürk, Gramling, and Kaes, *Germany in Transit,* esp. 196–233.
80. Lila Abu-Lughod, *Do Muslim Women Need Saving?* (Cambridge, Mass.: Harvard University Press, 2013); and Chandra Mohanty, *Feminism without Borders: Decolonizing Theory, Practicing Solidarity* (Durham, N.C.: Duke University Press, 2003).
81. Matthew Ponsford and Zahra Jamshed, "How My Childhood Made Me the Designer I Am Today," 24 September 2015, http://www.cnn.com/2015/09/24/architecture/roca-architects-before-after, consulted 13 September 2016.
82. "Mohammed Hadid, 92, an Iraqi Who Long Backed Democracy," *New York Times,* 6 August 1999.
83. *The Complete Works of Zaha Hadid* (London: Thames and Hudson, 2009) includes projects for Aachen Berlin, Cologne, Düsseldorf, Glinzendorf, Hamburg, Munich,

and Nabern, as well as the Phaeno (114–19) and BMW in Leipzig (128–31). See also http://www.zaha-hadid.com/archive, consulted 24 May 2013.
84. Johnson and Wigley, *Deconstructivist Architecture,* 68–79.
85. Yukio Futagawa, ed., *GA Architect 5: Zaha Hadid* (Tokyo: A.D.A Edita, 1986), 66–97.
86. *The Complete Works of Zaha Hadid,* 50–53. See also 90–93 for her exhibition hall for an international gardening show on the grounds of the Vitra campus.
87. Jan Otakar Fischer, "Momento Machinae: Engineering the Past in Wolfsburg," in Rosenfeld and Jaskot, *Beyond Berlin,* 89–115.
88. Wolfsburg Marketing GmbH, *Hochspannung in Wolfsburg* (Wolfsburg: Wolfsburg AG, n.d), 16. See also Nicole Froberg, Ulrich Knufinke, and Susanne Kreykenbohm, *Wolfsburg: Der Architekturführer* (Salenstein: Braun, 2011).
89. Phaeno GmbH, ed., *Phaeno-Science Center Wolfsburg von Zaha Hadid & Mayer Bährle* (Wolfsburg: Phaeno, n.d.), 3.
90. Todd Gannon, *BMW Central Building* (New York: Princeton Architectural Press, 2006).
91. Catherine Slessor, "'Top Gear'—BMW Central Building by Zaha Hadid, Leipzig, Germany," *Architectural Review,* June 2005, https://www.architectural-review.com/buildings/2005-june-top-gear-bmw-central-building-by-zaha-hadid-leipzig-germany/8611830.article, consulted 5 September 2016.
92. https://www.bmw-besuchen.com/en/leipzig/index-leipzig.html, consulted 5 September 2016.
93. David Young Kim, *The Traveling Artist in the Italian Renaissance* (New Haven, Conn.: Yale University Press, 2014).
94. Hans Morganthaler, *The Early Sketches of German Architect Erich Mendelsohn: No Compromise with Reality* (Lewiston, N.Y.: Edwin Mellen Press, 1992); and Kathleen James-Chakraborty, "Architecture in Transit: Three High-Tech Historicist Airports," in *Time in German Literature and Culture, 1900–2105,* ed. Anne Fuchs and J. J. Long (Basingstoke, UK: Palgrave Macmillan, 2015), 45–68.

Conclusion

1. http://www.kolumba.de/?language=ger&cat_select=1&category=32&artikle=488target=_parent, and for the controversy his remarks caused, http://news.bbc.co.uk/2/hi/6996251.stm, both consulted 6 May 2013.
2. Kai Kappel, "Erinnern und Überschreiben: Zur Semantik des Kolumba-Areals in Köln," in Kappel and Müller, *Geschichtsbilder und Erinnerungskultur in der Architektur des 20. und 21. Jahrhunderts,* 77–92.
3. Kappel, *Memento 1945?,* 297–304; and Voigt and Flagge, *Dominikus Böhm: 1880–1955,* 170.
4. http://www.kolumba.de/?language=eng&cat_select=1&category=14&artikle=57, consulted 6 May 2013.
5. http://www.kolumba.de/?language=ger&cat_select=1&category=32&preview=, consulted 6 May 2013, for a collection of mostly positive comments.
6. Johanna Blokker, "St. Kolumba in Cologne, Germany: A Case of the Elaboration or

the Elision of Memory?," in *Proceedings of the 2nd International Conference of the European Architectural History Network*, ed. Hilde Heynen and Janina Gosseye (Brussels: KVAB, 2012), 193–95; and Speidel, "Gottfried Böhm's Churches," in Voigt, *Gottfried Böhm*, 85–88.
7. http://www.docomomo.com/history.php, consulted 6 May 2013.
8. http://www.spiegel.de/spiegel/print/d-75638363.html, consulted 6 May 2013.
9. Enrique Juncosa and Christine Kennedy, eds., *The Moderns: The Arts in Ireland from the 1900s to the 1970s* (Dublin: Irish Museum of Modern Art, 2011), and Seán Kissane and Anne Boddaert, *Analysing Cubism* (Dublin: Irish Museum of Modern Art, 2013).
10. Robert Hariman and John Louis Lucaites, *No Caption Needed: Iconic Photographs, Public Culture, and Liberal Democracy* (Chicago: University of Chicago Press, 2007).

Index

Page numbers in italics refer to figures.

Aalto, Alvar, 27, 41, 95, 232
Academy of the Arts (Berlin), 23, 160
Adenauer, Konrad, 39, 48, 52, 61, 241
Adler, Dankmar, 7
AEG, 142, 201, 207
Akhenaten, 137
Albers, Anni, 29
Alte Pinakothek (Munich), 10, 85, 88–92, *89–90*, 103, 109, 115, 134, 176, 181
Altes Museum (Berlin), 10, 81, 84, 88, 96–99, *97–98*, 103, 106, 109, 111, 134, 137, 182
Andre, Carl, 196
Ankara, 215, 227
Arbeitsrat für Kunst, 23
Architectural Review, 234
Arnold, Jörg, 38
Assmann, Aleida, 6, 11, 181–82
Assmann, Jan, 6, 87, 187
Assyria, 24
Atatürk, Kemal, 227–28
Atta, Mohamed, 217
Augustus the Strong, 142
Austria, 28

Baader Meinhof Gang. *See* Red Army Faction
Babylon, 24
Bach, Johann Sebastian, 84
Baden, 41, 88
Baden-Württemberg, 5, 13, 84, 134
Baghdad, 215, 226, 228, 231

Bangladesh, 141
Banham, Reyner, 27, 106
Bartning, Otto, 9, 36, 40–51, 53, 57, 65, 67, 83, 95, 115, 134, 220, 241
Basel, 87, 118, 232; Art Museum, 112–13, *113*
Batista, Fulgencio, 96
Bauakademie (Berlin), 123, 178
Bauen + Wohnen, 94
Bauhaus, 15–16, 18–19, 23, 27–29, 45, 51, 199–200, 201–5, 207, 209
Bauhaus Debate, 39, 51
Baukunst und Werkform, 51
Baumeister, 51, 62, 88
Baumgarten, Paul, 155
Bauwelt, 61–62, 95
Bavaria, 5, 39, 88–89
Beauvais Cathedral, 16
Becher, Bernd, 194–95, *195,* 210–11
Becher, Hilla, 194–95, *195,* 210–11
Beethoven, Ludwig von, 84
Behne, Adolf, 19
Behnisch, Günter, 106, *107,* 156, 158–60, 162–63, 220
Behrens, Peter, 16, 18, 89, 160, 201, 207
Beirut, 231
Belgium, 28, 48, 194
Benjamin, Walter, 127
Bergisch Gladbach town hall (Bensberg), 73
Berlin, 1–5, 10–11, 14, 33–38, 53–54, 56–57, 60, 63–64, 66–67, 69–71, 79, 83, 87, 93, 95–96, 98, 102, 105, 121, 123, 125–27, 131, 134, 137, 140–46, 148,

153–55, 159–63, 164, 166, 170, 175, 179, 182–87, 200, 202, 211–12, 218, 221, 225, 242; Air Ministry, 165, *165*, 168; cathedral, 71; convention center, 179; embassies in, 160; Foreign Ministry of the German Democratic Republic, 178; Kreuzberg, 121, 123, 125, 166; Kurfürstendamm, 35, 55–56, 64, 102; Leipzigerplatz, 150; Lustgarten, 97; Mitte, 33, 139–40, 170, 178; Nikolaiviertel, 142–43; Quartier Schützenstrasse, 147; Stalinallee (Karl Marx), 64, 95, 123, 142, 145, 178; State Council Building, 176, *176*, 178; Tiergarten, 62, 162; zoo, 63. *See also individual buildings*
Berlin Museum, 87, 121, 124–26, 128
Berlin Wall, 1, 3, 10, 33–34, 57, 61, 70, 92, 96, 101, 121, 123–24, 126, 134, 139, 143–44, 148, 153, 165, 167–69, 179, 183, 212, 215
Beuys, Josef, 195
Beye, Peter, 104
Bielefeld, 83
Bill, Max, 27
Bismarck, Otto von, 39, 54
BMW, 215
BMW Central Building (Leipzig), 232–34, *233*
Bo, Jörgen, 106
Bochum, 5, 83, 187–88, 190, 193, 195; Christ Church, 65–66, *65*, 91; Ruhr University, 188, 195; Westpark, 196
Bock, Albert, 204
Bogatzky, Hans Erich, 176
Böhm, Dominikus, 65–66, 72–74, 134, 214, 220, 222, 241
Böhm, Gottfried, 9, 36, 40, 66, 72–78, 108, 120, 134, 155, 158–59, 162, 218–22, 225, 234, 237–41
Böhm, Paul, 214, 218–20, 222, 225, 234
Bonatz, Paul, 14, 23–25, 27, 30–31, 46, 50, 55, 103, 106, 112–13, 201–2, 227, 241
Bonn, 1, 37, 48, 83, 100, 145. *See also* Bundeshaus
Börsig, 174

Bourgeois, Victor, 30
Brandenburg Gate (Berlin), 153, 159–60, 162
Brandt, Willy, 39, 52, 57, 70, 82
Bratislava, 25
Braunfels, Stephen, 141
Bremen, 5, 143
Brussels, 37, 92, 218; German Pavilion, 59–60, 100
Budapest, 25
Buffalo, 26
Bundeshaus (Bonn), 156, *156*, 158–59, 162, 220
Burj Khalifa (Dubai), 179
Buschmann, Walter, 204–5
Bush, George H. W., 180
Buxloh, Friedrich Wilhelm, 201

C. A. Herpich Furriers (Berlin), 149–50, *150*, 162
Cairo, 24, 218
Canada, 87
Castro, Fidel, 97
Catholic Center Party, 39
Catholic Church of St. Anna (Düren), 6, 9, 36, 46–50, *47–49*, 52, 72, 81
Celan, Paul, 127
Centre Pompidou (Paris), 81, 86, 103, 111–12, *111*
Charlemagne, 52, 55
Charlottenburg Palace (Berlin), 137
Chartres, 69
Checkpoint Charlie apartment block (Berlin), 125–26, *126*
Chicago, 26, 51, 92–93, 99, 216; Auditorium Building, 7; Lakeshore Drive Apartments, 92. *See also* Illinois Institute of Technology
Chipperfield, David, 10, 138, 141, 173–74, 176–78, 182, 206, 234
Chomsky, Noam, 125
Christian Democratic Party, 10, 39, 64, 82, 84, 89, 134, 157, 162, 186, 217–18, 222
Christian Social Union, 39, 89
Christo, 157
churches: Catholic, 16, 37–40, 46–48, 55,

71–73, 78–80, 142, 200, 213, 216, 220, 238; Orthodox, 216; Protestant, 37–41, 43–44, 47, 55–56, 60–61, 63, 71–72, 76, 78–80, 142, 223, 242
Churchill, Winston, 93
Church of the Resurrection (Pforzheim), 9, 36, 41–46, *42–43*, 48, 53, 72, 115
City National Bank and Hotel (Mason City), 18
Cleveland, 106
Cohen, Roger, 158
Cologne, 3, 15, 36, 38, 48, 50, 52, 103–4, 142, 213, 215, 217–19, 223–24, 237, 239, 241; churches in, 66, 72, 74, 74, 214, 220–21, *221, 222*. *See also individual buildings*
Cologne Cathedral, 16, 213, 220, 223, 230
Colquhoun, Alan, 9, 106
Columbushaus (Berlin), 149
Communist Party, 64, 142, 178–79, 188, 199–200
Conrads, Ulrich, 33, 95, 102
Cook, Peter, 106
Cornell University, 125
Corpus Christi Church, 46, 48–50, 100, 241
Coventry Cathedral, 66
Craig, Gordon, 20
Cremer and Wolffenstein, 6–8
Crown Prince's Palace (Berlin), 95–97
Crystal Chain, 23, 26
Cultural Forum, West Berlin's, 85, 92, 95–96, 102
Curtis, William, 106

Darmstadt, 46
de Chirico, Giorgio, 25
Delaunay, Sonia, 29
de Meuron, Pierre, 119, 209
Derrida, Jacques, 125
Detroit, 26
Dibelius, Otto, 33, 61, 68, 241
DITIB, 214, 217–19, 223, 226
DITIB Mosque (Cologne), 11, 213–15, *214*, 217–26, 228, 230–31, 234, 237, 241

Döcker, Richard, 27
Döllgast, Hans, 10, 85, 88–91, 176
Dortmund, 83, 147, 187–88; St. Bonifatius, 66; Westphalia Park, 192
Doss, Erica, 130
Doxiadis, Constantinos, 228
Dresden, 84, 142; Church of our Lady, 142, 180; Gemäldegalerie, 84
Drese, Erwin, 48
Duisburg, 187–88, 196, 209–10; Küppersmühle, 209. *See also* Duisburg Landscape Park; Merkez Mosque
Duisburg Landscape Park, 6, 11, 187–98, *191*, 193, 210–11, 224, 241
Durand, Jean-Nicolas, Louis, 98
Düren, 3, 46, 48, 52–53. *See also* St. Anna Church
Durth, Werner, 204
du Ry, Simon Lous, 84
Düsseldorf, 184, 210; Art Academy, 194–95; Kunstsammlung Nordrhein Westfalen, 103–5, *104*; St. Rochus, 65–66

Eames, Charles, 119
Ebert, Friedrich, 23
Eckstein, Hans, 57, 61, 63
Egypt, 18, 24, 137
Eiermann, Egon, 9, 28, 33–35, 37, 40, 46, 53, 56–57, 59–65, 67–69, 71, 76, 88, 100, 105, 176, 209
Eiffel Tower (Paris), 185, 213
Eisenman, Peter, 10, 124–26, 140, 164–65, 169–71, 234
Eldem, Sedad, 227
Endell, Auguste, 22
Erdogan, Recip, 215, 217–18
Essen, 3, 45, 187–88, 198–99, 201, 209–10, 223–24; Church of the Resurrection, 45. *See also* Folkwang Museum (Essen); Zeche Zollverein
European Union, 80, 182

Fahrenkamp, Emil, 201
Farnsworth, Edith, 93

Fasanen Street Synagogue (Berlin), 66–67, *67*, 71, 87
Fehlbaum, Ralf, 118
Feldmeyer, Gerhard, 85
Ferdinand, Prince Louis, 56
Filbinger, Hans, 84–85, 107
Filler, Martin, 106
Finsterlin, Hermann, 27, 107
Fischer, Theodor, 16
Folkwang Museum (Essen), 206–7
Folkwang Museum (Hagen), 20
Ford, Henry, 17, 26
Foster, Norman, 1–2, 4–5, 9, 140, 152, 155–59, 162–63, 185, 196, 199, 205–7, 228, 234, 241
France, 28, 35, 123, 142, 194
Frank, Charlotte, 141
Frank, Josef, 30
Frankfurt, 52, 102–3, 184; Airport, 113; Decorative Arts Museum, 103
Free Democratic Party, 218
Free University of Berlin, 96, 102
Friedrichstadt Passage (Berlin), 10, 140, 145–46, *146*, 148, 171, 186
Friedrich Wilhelm III, 166
Frings, Josef Cardina, 38–39, 48, 61, 72, 241
Fuller, Buckminster, 202
Fussell, Paul, 6

Galeries Lafayette (Berlin), 6, 10, 140, 143–44, *144*, 146, 148–49, *149*, 151–53, *151*, 156, 158–59, 162–63, 170, 183
Ganser, Karl, 190, 206
Gas Works Park (Seattle), 192
Gause, Carl, 160–61
Gehry, Frank, 10, 87, 101, 116–21, 126, 133–35, 159–60, 231, 234, 241
Gehry House (Santa Monica), 116–17, *117*
Gelsenkirchen, 188; Nordsternpark, 196
Gemäldegalerie (Berlin), 84, 101
Gendarmenmarkt (Berlin), 95, 145–46, *146*, 148
Gerlach, Philipp, 124
German Embassy (Washington, D.C.), 60

Giedion, Sigfried, 4, 27, 95
Gies, Ludwig, 238
Giordano, Ralph, 213, 231
Glashaus (Cologne), 8, 16, 19–23, *21–22*, 40, 68–69, 150, 152, 159, 162, 214, 220
Glyptothek (Munich), 84, 88
Goering, Hermann, 168, 204
Graf Zeppelin Hotel, 31, 112
Grassi, Giorgio, 166
Gray, Eileen, 29
Great Mosque (Córdoba), 231
Green Party, 13, 25, 217–18
Gregor, Neil, 38, 56
Grimshaw, Nicholas, 119
Gropius, Walter, 4, 16–25, 27–29, 31, 37, 51–52, 73, 95, 174, 199–202, 207, 226, 228
Guardini, Romano, 49, 52
Guggenheim Museum (Bilbao), 120–21, 134
Gursky, Andreas, 195
Gustav Adolf Church (Berlin), 45–46

Haag, Richard, 192
Hadid, Zaha, 11, 119, 215, 226, 230–34, 242
Halbwachs, Maurice, 6, 86, 133
Hallmann, Heinz, 10, 140, 164–65, 167
Hamburg, 5, 143; St. Nikolai, 66
Hanover, 92, 218; Historical Museum, 85, 91–92, *91*, 133; St. Martin's, 91
Hansaviertel. *See* Interbau
Häring, Hans, 27, 30–31, 107
Hattingen, 188; Heinrichshütte, 190
Heidegger, Martin, 46
Heinz Graffunder and Associates, 171–72
Heise, Heinrich, 66–67
Hejduk, John, 124
Hemmeter, Karl, 68
Henning, Paul Rudolf, 7–8
Herne, 188
Herzog, Jacques, 119, 209
Hessel, Ehrenfried, 66
Heuss, Theodor, 93–94
Hilberseimer, Ludwig, 27

Index

Hillebrand, Elmar, 78
Hitler, Adolf, 25, 52, 92, 100, 155, 198, 203–4
Hoch, Hannah, 7–8
Höfer, Candida, 195
Hoffmann, E. T. A., 127
Hohenzollern dynasty, 10, 55, 61, 64, 71, 95, 171–72, 179, 182
Holocaust, 6, 10, 85, 123, 129–31, 163, 166, 169–70
Holzmeister, Clemens, 227
Hong Kong, 231; Hong Kong and Shanghai Bank, 228
Horta, Victor, 19
Hotel Adlon (Berlin), 10, 140, 154, 159–63, *160–61*
Hotel Prinz Albrecht (Berlin), 165
Humboldt, Wilhelm von, 175
Humboldt Box, 181
Humboldt Forum. *See* palace (Berlin)
Hungary, 70
Huyssen, Andreas, 2–3, 9, 11, 157

Illinois Institute of Technology, 92, 98, 205, *205*
Imdahl, Max, 195–96
Indian Institute of Management (Ahmedabad), 141
Ingenhoven Architects, 25
Institut du Monde l'Arabe (Paris), 148, 228–29, *229*
Interbau (Berlin), 37, 64, 95
International Building Exhibition (IBA) Berlin, 121, 123, 124–25, 140, 166, 232, 234
International Building Exhibition (IBA) Emscher Park, 187, 90, 192, 196, 199–200, 205–6, 209–11
Iraq, 226, 228, 231
Ireland, 242
Islam and Muslims, 67, 213–14, 216–20, 222, 224–25, 229, 231
Isozaki, Arata, 124
Israel, 130
Istanbul, 210, 215, 226

Italy, 76, 87, 125, 229

Jacobi, Gerhard, 55, 60
Jaeger, Falk, 106
Japan, 87, 185
Jeanne-Claude, 157
Jencks, Charles, 106
Jerusalem, 27
Jewish Museum (Berlin), 3, 10, 87–88, 116, 121–28, *122*, *127*, 130–35, *132*, 139, 163, 166, 169, 183, 211, 224, 228, 242
Jews and Judaism, 55, 63, 87, 96, 103, 121, 124–25, 129–30, 134, 144, 160, 165, 169, 217, 223, 226, 228, 231
Joedicke, Jürgen, 27, 37
Johnson, Philip, 92, 98, 117
Jones, Peter Blundell, 106
Jordy, William, 9

Kahn, Louis, 129–31, *130*, 141, 170
Kaiser Wilhelm Memorial Church (Berlin), 3, 9, 33–36, *34–35*, 40, 52–72, *53*, *58–59*, *69*, 76, 79, 86, 88, 95, 100, 102, 137, 153, 158, 176, 178
Kassel, 84
Kempner, Bernd, 7
Kennedy, John F., 70
Khrushchev, Nikita, 70
Kiener, Hans, 88
Kimmelman, Michael, 130–31, 134, 181
Kissinger, Henry, 180
Kleihues, Josef Paul, 121, 125, 145–47, 160, 166
Kleist, Heinrich, 127
Klotz, Heinrich, 82, 84
Klotz, Reiner Michael, 140
Knoblauch, Dieter, 66–67
Koerfer, Jakob, 201
Kohl, Helmut, 162
Kolb, Peter, 7
Kolhoff, Hans, 147
Kolumba Chapel (Cologne), 238–41, *239–40*
Kolumba Museum (Cologne), 237–39, *238*, 241

Koolhaas, Rem, 105–6, 124, 185, 199, 208
Korn, Roland, 176
Körner, Edmund, 201
Kraft, Sabine, 222
Kreis, Wilhelm, 201
Kremmer, Martin, 186, 199, 202, 204–5
Krier, Leon, 105–6
Krier, Rob, 105–6, 123, 145
Kristallnacht, 66
Krupp family, 188
Kuehn Malvezzi, 181

Latz, Anneliese, 192–93, 196–97
Latz, Peter, 192–93, 196–97, 210
Latz + Partner, 187, 191–93, 210
Lauder, Ronald, 180
Lebanon, 130
Le Corbusier, 9, 20, 73, 81, 103, 107, 109, 112, 114, 119
Leipzig, 234. *See also* BMW Central Building
Libeskind, Daniel, 3, 10, 87, 101, 121–23, 125–28, 131–35, 139, 148, 166, 169, 231, 234, 241–42
Lieberman, Max, 160
Liebknecht, Karl, 176, 179
Lin, Maya, 123, 128–31
Loire, Gabriel, 69
London, 37, 105, 139; Architectural Association, 231; Economist Building, 105; St. Dunstan-in-the-East, 66; Tate Modern, 209
Los Angeles, 116–18; Disney Concert Hall, 120
Lowenthal, David, 209
Lübeck, 146
Ludwig I of Bavaria, 88–89
Luxemburg, Rosa, 179

Mackintosh, Margaret Macdonald, 78
Mainzer, Udo, 199
Mannheim, 95
March, Werner, 57–58, 61–62
Marie-Elisabeth-Lüders Haus (Berlin), 141

Matthew Church (Berlin), 100, 102, 109, 133
Mecca, 217
Meier, Richard, 103
Meisner, Joachim Cardinal, 223, 237
Melnikov, Konstantin, 115
Memorial to the Murdered Jews of Europe (Berlin), 10, 140–42, 163–64, *164,* 168–71, 187
Mendelsohn, Erich, 7–8, 19, 24–31, 100, 127–31, 148–51, 168, 174, 180, 201, 234
Merkel, Angela, 215, 217
Merkez Mosque (Duisburg), 214, 224–25, *225*
Mesopotamia, 24
Messel, Alfred, 150
Metal Workers' Union building (Berlin), 127–28, *128,* 131, 135
Meyer, Adolf, 16–18
Mies van der Rohe, Ludwig, 9–10, 23, 27–31, 36, 50–52, 57, 73, 85, 92–101, *94,* 107, 108, 133–35, 140, 149, 156, 168, 174, 179–80, 204–5, 226, 229, 241
Model Factory (Cologne), 8, 16–20, *17–18,* 26, 40
Mondrian, Piet, 102
Montez, Lola, 89
Moore, Charles, 124
Moore Ruble Yudell, 160
Mossehaus (Berlin), 6–9, *7,* 141
Munich, 3, 41, 89, 91, 200; Olympics, 106; St. Bonifaz, 89. *See also* Alte Pinakothek; Glyptothek
Muschamp, Herbert, 150
Museum Island (Berlin), 62, 84, 95–97, 137, 174–75, 182–83
Museum of Modern Art (New York), 31, 92, 117, 126, 192, 231
Mussolini, Benito, 207
Muthesius, Hermann, 16, 22, 24

National Assembly Building (Dhaka), 141
Nefertiti, 137–39, 174–75
Nelles, Roland, 13

Nelson, George, 119
Nerdinger, Winfried, 204
Netherlands, 28, 48, 124, 217
Neumeyer, Fritz, 147
Neutra, Richard, 7–8, 27
Neviges. *See* Pilgrimage Church of Mary
New Museum (Berlin), 10, 116, 137–39, *138,* 141, 171, 173–74, *173,* 176–78, *177,* 182–83
New National Gallery (Berlin), 10, 85, 87, 92–93, *93,* 95–102, *101,* 108–9, 115, 133–34, 140, 156–57, 168, 215, 229–30, *230,* 241
New State Gallery (Stuttgart), 6, 10, 81–87, *82,* 103–13, *110, 112,* 115–16, 123, 133–34, 221
New York, 25, 129–30, 170; Empire State Building, 232; Federal Plaza, 169; Freedom Tower, 131, 133; High Line, 196; Institute for Architecture and Urban Studies, 125; Times Square, 151–52; World Trade Center, 131, 218. *See also* Museum of Modern Art
Nice, 218
Niebuhr, Bernd, 180
Niemeyer, Oscar, 95
Nishizawa, Ryue, 207
Nora, Pierre, 87
North Rhine-Westphalia, 188, 207, 210
Notre Dame (Raincy), 69–70, *70*
Notre Dame (Ronchamp), 20, 119
Nouvel, Jean, 10, 140, 143–49, 151–53, 158–59, 163, 205, 228–29
Nuremberg, 38, 200; Nazi Party Parade Grounds, 60

Oberhausen, 188–90; Eisenheim housing estate, 189; gasometer, 190
Obrist, Hans, 22
Oesterlen, Dieter, 65, 85, 91–92, 133
Office of Metropolitan Architecture, 124, 185, 199, 208
Oldenburg, 55
Old National Gallery (Berlin), 97
Old State Gallery (Stuttgart), 84, 109–10, *110,* 134
Oranienburg Street Synagogue (Berlin), 66
Otto, Frei, 93, 106–7
Oud, J. J. P., 27–28
Ouroussoff, Nicholas, 25
Özdemer, Cem, 13

palace (Berlin), 10, 64, 71, 141–42, 171–76, *172–73,* 178, 180–81, 183
Palace of the Republic (Berlin), 171–72, *172,* 178–81, 183
Palatine Chapel, 52, 55
Palestine, British Mandate of, 227
Pantheon (Rome), 111, 137
Parc de la Villette (Paris), 190, 196–97, *197*
Paris, 20, 25, 29, 69, 218. *See also individual buildings*
Pariser Platz (Berlin), 153–54, 159–60, *160,* 162–63, 169, 186
Park, Jonathan, 197
Patterson, 196
Patzschke, Rüdiger, 140
Paul, Bruno, 16
Pécs, 210
Pehnt, Wolfgang, 9, 78
Pei, I. M., 109, 162
Pei Cobb and Fried, 145
Pelli, Cesar, 109
Pergamon Museum (Berlin), 96, 175
Perret, Auguste, 20, 68–70
Perriand, Charlotte, 29
Pevsner, Nikolaus, 4, 16, 18
Pforzheim, 3, 36, 46. *See also* Church of the Resurrection; St. Matthew's Church
Phaeno Science Center (Wolfsburg), 232–34, *233*
Philharmonie (Berlin), 96, 120, *120*
Piano, Renzo, 81, 111
Pilgrimage Church of Mary (Velbert), 9, 36, 72–78, *73, 75, 77,* 81, 108, 220, 224, 239
Pink Floyd, 197
Pittsburgh, 26
Platz, Gustav Adolf, 61

Poelzig, Hans, 18, 57
Pohl, Günter, 35, 60
Poland, 87, 142, 169, 216
Portzamparc, Christian de, 159–60
Potsdam, 96; Einstein Tower, 26; Palace, 64; Sans Souci, 174
Potsdamer Platz (Berlin), 143–45, 162–63, 165, 170, 181
Poznan (Posen), 54
Prince Albrecht Palais (Berlin), 165–66
Prussia, 39, 88, 171, 175, 180, 182
Putin, Vladimir, 13

Quadah, Badri, 228

Rading, Adolf, 30
Raèv, Svetlozar, 77
Reagan, Ronald, 162
Red Army Faction (Baader Meinhof Gang), 107
Refrath, 73
Reich, Lilly, 29–30, 98, 174
Reichsbank (Berlin), 92, 180
Reichstag (Berlin), 1–2, *2*, 4, 6, 9–10, 40, 62, 116, 140, 143, 152–63, *154–55, 157, 159,* 170, 178, 183, 186, 197, 228, 241
Rhineland, 5, 39, 48, 65, 76, 199, 220
Richards, J. M., 100
Richardson, Henry Hobson, 54
Riemenschneider, Tilmann, 202
River Port Island (Saarbrücken), 192
Rogers, Richard, 81, 111
Rosh, Lea, 169, 187
Rossi, Aldo, 3, 86–87, 105–6, 112, 116, 121, 123–24, 134, 147, 180, 183, 205
Rostock, 47
Rouse, James, 116
Rowe, Colin, 105, 125
Ruf, Sep, 37, 100
Ruff, Thomas, 195
Ruhr region, 5, 11, 48, 65, 76, 185–90, 193–96, 201, 205–6, 209–11, 228, 241
Rusakov Worker's Club (Moscow), 115
Russia, 13, 182

Saarinen, Eero, 27
Sack, Manfred, 44, 108
Sagebiel, Ernst, 168
Sahin, Cavit, 225
SANAA, 185, 199, 207
San Francisco, 27
Santiago de Cuba, 96
Saudi Arabia, 218
Sauerbruch, Matthias, 179
Saxony, 88
Schanken, Andrew, 129
Schaper, Hermann, 55
Scharoun, Hans, 27, 46, 73, 87, 96, 107, 120, 232
Schauspielhaus (Berlin), 140, 145, 148
Scheerbart, Paul, 21
Schindler, Rudolph, 118
Schinkel, Karl Friedrich, 10, 81, 84, 88, 96–99, 101–2, 111, 137, 140, 144–45, 148, 160, 165
Schleiermacher, Friedrich, 127
Schloss. *See* palace (Berlin)
Schlüter, Andreas, 174, 180
Schmitthenner, Paul, 27, 202
Schneck, Adolf Gustav, 30
Schneider, Dieter, 7
Schneider and Schumacher, 181
Schneider-Esleben, Paul, 65
Schocken, Salmann, 27
Schocken store (Stuttgart), 8, 24–28, *26,* 30–31, 37, 40, 106
Scholer, Friedrich Eugen, 14, 23, 106
Schönberg, Arnold, 127
School of Industrial Arts and Crafts (Berlin), 165
Schramma, Fritz, 218
Schultes, Axel, 141
Schupp, Fritz, 186, 199, 201–2, 204–5
Schwarz, Maria, 48
Schwarz, Rudolf, 9, 36, 39–40, 46–53, 57, 67, 74, 100, 104, 133–34, 241
Schwechten, Franz, 34, 54, 64–65
Schwippert, Hans, 37, 46, 48–49, 100, 220
Scott, George Gilbert, 66

Index

Scott Brown, Denise, 112–13, 116, 125, 147
Sedan, 54
Sehring, Bruno, 149
Sejima Kazuyo, 207
Semper, Gottfried, 84
Serra, Richard, 128, 140, 165, 169–70, 190, 195–96, 198, 211
Sewing, Werner, 160
Siedler, Wolf Jobst, 173
Siegen, 83
Siemens, 142
Sieverts, Thomas, 194
Sinsheim, 109
Slessor, Catherine, 234
Smith, G. E. Kidder, 33, 50
Smithson, Alison, 105
Smithson, Peter, 105
Smithson, Robert, 195–96, 198, 211
Social Democratic Party, 10–11, 23, 39, 82, 84, 147, 154, 162, 180, 186, 188–89, 200, 210, 217–18
Soviet Union, 35, 64, 70–71, 96, 156, 160–61, 178, 181–82, 202
Späth, Lothar, 84
Speer, Albert, 59, 92, 100, 106, 203–4
Spence, Basil, 66
Spengler, Oswald, 203
Steel Church (Cologne), 45, *45*, 220
Steffann, Emil, 51, 65–66
Steiff, Margaret, 100
Steiff factory (Giengen an der Brenz), 100
Steiner, Rudolf, 119
Stella, Franco, 171, 173, 180–81
Stimmann, Hans, 10, 145–48, 183, 221
Stingel, Rudolf, 215, 226, 229–30
Stirling, James, 10, 81–82, 85–86, 101, 103–12, 114–16, *114,* 120–21, 123, 133–35, 160, 221, 234, 241
St. Matthew's Church (Pforzheim), 57, 59–60, *60,* 68
Stölzl, Gunta, 29
Stralsund, 47
Stresemann, Gustav, 202–3

Stresemannstrasse apartment building (Berlin), 232, 234
Struth, Thomas, 195
Stüler, Friedrich August, 100, 102, 137–38, 173–74
Stuttgart, 3, 8, 13, 15, 23–25, 27, 31, 36, 81, 83–84, 105–8, 141–42, 147, 202; Crown Prince's Palace, 83; Schlossgarten, 13, 25; Staatsgalerie, 84; Technische Hochschule, 27. *See also individual buildings*
Stuttgart train station, 8, 13–14, *14,* 23–25, 28, 30, 40–41, 49, 81, 106, 201, 241
Sullivan, Louis, 7, 199
Switzerland, 27, 44, 213, 217, 231
Sydney Opera House, 232
Syria, 213

Taut, Bruno, 16, 19–23, 26, 28, 36, 40, 51, 68–69, 72, 74, 114, 150, 152, 158–59, 174, 201, 214–15, 220, 227
Taut, Max, 36
Thatcher, Margaret, 162
Thyssen family, 188
Thyssen Hünnebeck, 179
Thyssen Steel, 190
Tischmann Speyer, 145
Tönnies, Ferdinand, 16
Topography of Terror (Berlin), 6, 10, 140, 143, 163–71, *164–65, 167,* 183, 211
Treib, Marc, 211
Troost, Gerdy, 203–4
Tschumi, Bernard, 196–97
Tugendhat House (Brno), 92
Turkey, 11, 121, 182, 206, 215–17, 222–23, 226–29, 231

Ulbricht, Walter, 179
Ulm, 25
UNESCO, 175 182, 185, 199
Ungers, Oswald Mathais, 10, 105–6, 116, 121, 140, 145–48, 153, 171, 205
United Kingdom, 35, 50, 66, 87, 115, 123, 142, 182, 194, 231

United States, 18, 23–25, 27, 35, 37, 44, 50, 52, 70, 72, 87, 92, 94, 117, 121, 123–24, 129–30, 142, 160, 180, 217, 228, 242
United Steelworks (Vereinigte Stahlwerke AG), 200–202
University of Cambridge, history faculty of, 114–15, *115*
Unter den Linden (Berlin), 62, 148, 153, 160, 174

van Acken, Johannes, 74
van de Velde, Henry, 16, 18–23, 27, 31, 51, 174, 241
Vandreicke, Bertram, 181
Varnhagen, Rahel, 127
Vatican II (Second Vatican Council), 39, 72, 74, 78–79
Venturi, Robert, 112–13, 116, 125, 147
Vereinigte Stahlwerke AG. *See* United Steelworks
Vienna, 54, 84, 88
Vietnam War Memorial (Washington, D.C.), 123, 128–30, *129*
Villa Savoye (Poissy), 9
Vitra Design Museum (Weil-am-Rhein), 10, 87, 118–21, *118–19*, 133–35
Vitra Fire Station (Weil-am-Rhein), 232, *232*, 234
Vögler, Albert, 200, 202–3
von Barth, Gottlob Georg, 84, 110
von Klenze, Leo, 84, 88

Wallot, Paul, 1, 154
Wallraf-Richartz Museum (Cologne), 103–5
Wanner, Ulrich, 108
Waters, Roger, 197
Weimar, 18, 20, 45; Grand Ducal School of Arts and Crafts, 22
Weinbrenner, Friedrich, 111
Weissenhof Estate (Stuttgart), 8, 15, 24, 27–31, *28, 30*, 40–41, 49, 81, 87, 103, 106–7, 112, 120, 189

Wenders, Wim, 35
Werkbund, German, 15–16, 22, 24, 28, 37, 94, 201–2, 204, 207–8. *See also* Werkbund Exhibition
Werkbund Exhibition (Cologne), 8, 15–16, 19, 22–23, 31, 36, 51, 141, 215, 237, 241
Werkbund Theater (Cologne), 8, 16, 18–20, *19*, 22–23, 26, 40
Wertheim store (Berlin), 150
Wexner Center for the Arts (Columbus), 125
Wigley, Mark, 117
Wilford, Michael, 82, 103–4, 160
Wilhelm I, 54, 61
Wilhelm II, 54–56, 61, 67, 174, 180
Wilhelmstrasse housing (Berlin), 124, *124*
Williams, William Carlos, 196
Wilms, Ursula, 10, 140, 164–65, 167, 170
Wings of Desire (film), 35
Wirges, Josef, 218
Witten, 188
Wohlert, Vilhelm, 106
Wolff, Heinrich, 180
World Council of Churches, 61
Wright, Frank Lloyd, 17–18, 100, 228
Wulff, Christian, 217
Württemberg, 88, 106
Würzburg Residence, 174

Yale University, 128
Young, James A., 169
Yudell, Buzz, 160

Zec, Peter, 207
Zeche Zollverein (Essen), 11, 185–89, *186*, 195–96, 198–209, *206–8*, 215–17, 241
Zechlin, Hans Josef, 61
Zionism, 27
Zumthor, Peter, 140, 166–68, 237–39, 241
Zurich, 41

Kathleen James-Chakraborty is professor of art history at University College Dublin. Her previous books include *Architecture since 1400* (Minnesota, 2013) and *German Architecture for a Mass Audience* and the edited collections *India in Art in Ireland* and *Bauhaus Culture: From Weimar to the Cold War* (Minnesota, 2006).